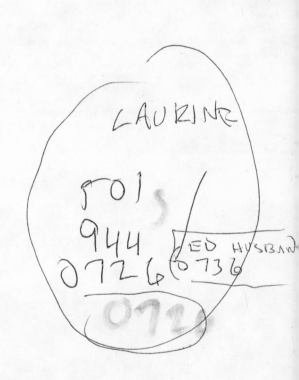

LAURINE

501,
944
0726 (0736

ED HUSBAN

072

English
Romanticism

English Romanticism

Romanticism

The Human Context

MARILYN GAULL

W · W · NORTON & COMPANY
New York   London

Copyright © 1988 by W. W. Norton & Company, Inc.
All rights reserved.

Published simultaneously in Canada by Penguin Books Canada Ltd.,
2801 John Street, Markham, Ontario L3R 1B4.
Printed in the United States of America.

The text of this book is composed in Bembo,
with display type set in Bembo.
Composition by the Maple-Vail Book Manufacturing Group
Manufacturing by the Maple-Vail Book Manufacturing Group
Book design by Jacques Chazaud

First Edition

Library of Congress Cataloging-in-Publication Data
Gaull, Marilyn.
English romanticism : the human context / Marilyn Gaull.
p. cm.
1. English poetry—19th century—History and criticism.
2. Romanticism—Great Britain.   3. Literature and society—Great
Britain—History—19th century.   4. Great Britain—
Civilization—19th century.   I. Title.
PR590.G38   1988
821'.7'09145—dc19   88-1445
CIP

ISBN 0-393-02541-1
ISBN 0-393-95547-8 (pbk.)

W. W. Norton & Company, Inc., 500 Fifth Avenue,
New York, N. Y. 10110
W. W. Norton & Company Ltd., 37 Great Russell Street,
London WC1B 3NU

1 2 3 4 5 6 7 8 9 0

To

Rachael Rebecca

"Child of Joy"

Preface

English Romanticism: The Human Context is designed for several audiences: undergraduate and graduate students of English Romantic poetry who would enjoy knowing about the historical, social, cultural, political, economic, intellectual, philosophical, artistic, and scientific backgrounds of the literature they are studying; and for casual readers who would be interested in seeing the state of the professions, of knowledge, technology, art, social and political arrangements during a period in which many of our own contemporary attitudes, conventions, and institutions originated. For students, I have tried to provide some of the conventional materials they need to understand the language and motives of the Romantic writers, the special tone, atmosphere, and spirit of the period. And I have offered what may appear to students of literature to be peripheral materials, for I believe that it is on such peripheries, on the edges of great events, that most people live and where most literature begins. It is there, in what we now call the environment or the context, that the most significant associations occur, those coincidences that stimulate creativity. Consequently, by juxtaposing Bentham and Keats, Erasmus Darwin and Wordsworth, children's literature and the theater, among others, I tried to demonstrate the complexity of the world that inspired the art, the coherence that authors found in their own times and in their own lives. The age itself recognized the importance of environment, ranging from Wordsworth's belief that language is influenced by landscape to Bentham's belief that the redemption of criminals depends upon the architecture of prisons. And because themes, ideas, and styles, because literature, architecture, art, and philosophy are the expression of individuals interacting with their environment, I have used the biographies of the major figures usually associated with Romanticism to help illustrate the preoccupations of the period.

In the process, I became fascinated with the way individuals accept and become comfortable with alien ideas and imperfect information, the different levels of knowledge a person can tolerate, what leads someone to pursue some ideas, to master and contribute to them, while overlooking others. In this respect, students of literature are very much like the authors they study; they carry around an unusual and often superficial array of information about the stock market, baseball, the internal combustion engine, television and film stars. Much of this information merely helps them relate to their community; it has no special survival or economic value. Similarly, authors, painters, and philosophers during the Romantic period had a store of information about fashions, meteorology, boxing, and making soap, information that may never have entered the literature but conditioned and reflected the mind that created it, bits of experience that contributed to an author's individuality, even his identity. Exploring what authors could and did know as well as what they wrote is particularly illuminating in finding that special quality of mind that distinguishes a Scott, or a Blake, or a Keats, as well as the mind of the audience that responded or failed to respond to him.

Conventionally, the English Romantic period is defined by two kings, George III (1760–1821) and George IV (1821–1830); two wars, the American War of Independence (1775–1783) and the war against France (1793–1815); a political revolution in France (1789–1793), the Industrial Revolution in England (1780–1830), and so many cultural and scientific innovations that one observer, Lord Byron, called it "the age of oddities" (*Don Juan*, I, 1021). My primary concern is the literature, the collective expression of writers such as William Blake, Samuel Taylor Coleridge, William Wordsworth, Sir Walter Scott, Robert Southey, William Hazlitt, Thomas De Quincey, Charles Lamb, Lord Byron, Percy Shelley, John Keats, Jane Austen, Thomas Carlyle, as well as lesser known contemporaries such as George Crabbe, William Godwin, Leigh Hunt, and John Clare. Mostly poets and essayists, they formed no school, developed no dogma, and, more often than not, rejected one another's works and values. Contemporary reviewers and literary critics identified groups of them by geography, personality, or mannerisms as the Lake School, the Satanic School, the Cockney or Regency poets. And yet they did form a kind of community for they reflected as well as influenced the age we call Romantic, an age characterized by transition, transition expressed radically, as in the French Revolution, or subtly, in manners and fashions as a strange combination of the frivolous and the austere. To some, this transition was a sign that civilization was declining while others, especially poets, saw in it the possibility of a new order, new social, economic, and political systems in which they felt deeply implicated. While some were crippled by a sense of personal insufficiency, of futility, others responded with energy, self-confidence, with visions of a redeemed humanity. "The great writers of our own age are," Shelley wrote, "the companions and forerunners of some unimagined change in our social condition or of the opinions that cement it" (Preface, *Prometheus Unbound*).[1]

The opposition between Classicism and Romanticism[2] is persistent and misleading, for the Romantic imagination was assimilative: exploring the past, the Romantics recovered more than they rejected, expanding their heritage through a revival of native themes and subjects that had been dismissed as too vulgar, common, or undignified for the tastes of Augustan gentlemen. Like all writers, as T. S. Eliot explained in "Tradition and the Individual Talent," they had to master their traditions before they could contribute to and ultimately redefine them. And the tradition from which they learned their craft was neoclassical. They adopted classical forms and images, Renaissance subjects and styles, emulated Shakespeare, Spenser, Milton, and lesser though more nearly contemporary and neoclassical writers such as James Thomson (1700–1748), Oliver Goldsmith (1730–1774), William Cowper (1731–1800), William Collins (1721–1759), Edward Young (1683–1765), and Thomas Gray (1716–1771). The differences between the Romantic poets and the neoclassical ones are less matters of style than of values, specifically the dislocation of values that arose with the altered relationship between man and his universe, his society, and himself. But in the popular poetry, the poetry of magazines and annuals, the values as well as style of neoclassicism survived undisturbed through the Victorian period.

Many of the characteristics we associate with Romantic literature are native to the English literary tradition and the culture, although the impulse as well as some ideas and subjects can be traced to European sources. For example, the ballad acquired supernatural machinery while traveling through Germany, and the sentimental belief in the *noble savage* found its most persuasive spokesman in a Swiss named Rousseau. But literary dependencies, like emotional ones, if they work and if they last, arise out of an initial sense of affinity, familiarity, complementing what was already there. I shall focus on the English sources of English Romanticism, including English neoclassicism, reflecting that increased sense of national identity in manners, customs, language, and politics—the provincialism enforced by the twenty-two year war against France. The writers themselves were probably more learned in their national history and more concerned with the entire range of activities in their contemporary society than any previous generation of writers had been and possibly would be.

Admittedly, however preoccupied such a poet as Wordsworth was with native traditions and language, others such as Byron were attracted to the foreign and to the exotic. However committed a poet such as Shelley was to contemporary political issues, others, such as Keats, disengaged themselves from the claims of society. Interest in art competed with enthusiasm for nature; utopian futures coexisted with revivals of the medieval past; poems of joy were as popular as those of melancholy. Partly the writers are exhibiting the national "spirit of contradiction" that fascinated Robert Southey in *Letters from England* (p. 93). But partly they are reflecting that tolerance for diversity that had characterized the eighteenth century in England and that would disappear with the pressures of an emerging collective society. In order to capture this diversity, we shall move through many areas of experience, bringing information from the world in which the literature was conceived and in which it would be read.

Clearly I am not interested in defining Romanticism and believe that the pursuit of such a definition that consumed scholars thirty years ago is well lost. In part, I accept the proposition that Romanticism is a complex set of ideas and expressions, largely philosophical, that reflect a sudden acceleration in the secularizing of man, nature, and society starting in the eighteenth century and brilliantly described by M. H. Abrams in *Natural Supernaturalism: Tradition and Revolution in Romantic Literature* (1971), to which I am, like all contemporary scholars, deeply indebted. But, however appealing the idea that Romanticism is the expression of a great shift from a religious to a secular view of experience—a shift, as Northrop Frye calls it in *A Study of English Romanticism* (1968), from an up-down universe with God in heaven, man in the middle, and everything else down below, to a horizontal one, inhabited by man and the gods he created—however appealing, that idea may be partly an expression of our own increasing secularism. Other students of the period remain devoted to the transcendental dimensions of the literature, exploring the holy purposes it may have served. My study reflects the ambivalence of its time. By seeing art as an expression of human experience and events, I am giving it the same secular status as a building or a law: yet I know that the most moving poetry, music, and art, the most significant thinkers and concepts remain mysteries to me with the status of revelation. This study then, like all inquiries written with affection and admiration, has its inevitable biases, its own human context.

I am fortunate in having been able to work in a major urban area with rich library resources and stimulating colleagues. Among the libraries to which I am most indebted: Temple University, University of Pennsylvania, Free Library of Philadelphia (especially the drama and children's collections), the American Philosophical Society, the Athenaeum, and the British Museum. For special assistance and cheer, I am grateful to the following colleagues: Jacob Gruber, Peter Tasch, Terry Parssinen, Philip Stevick, and Laura Dabundo; and to Roy Goodman, Ronald Gottesman, Kenneth Johnston, John Benedict, and the late Russell Noyes. For stimulating discussions and ideas, I am grateful to my students, to my colleagues at the annual Wordsworth Summer Conference in Grasmere, England, and to the advisers and contributors to *The Wordsworth Circle*. For her expertise and patience preparing the manuscript, I am indebted to Nadia Kravchenko. And for "the fountain light of all our day," to my parents, Edith and Maurie Gaull, my gratitude.

Contents

PART I

The Human Context

CHAPTER I

People during
the Romantic Age

MOST PEOPLE IN England during the opening decades of the nineteenth century showed very little interest in the literature that we now consider important. Those who were literate and able to purchase literary works were primarily concerned with business, politics, war, trade, industry, fashion, sex, status, domestic comfort, horses, servants, marriage, and boxing matches. They discussed their kings: George III's eccentricities, his health, his unruly children, his moralistic attitudes, and his poor taste in political friends; George IV's extravagance, his mistresses, costumes, architectural achievements, and political incompetence. In spite of the loss of the American colonies in the War of Independence, they were cheered by the prospects of a new empire developing through exploration such as Captain Cook's discovery of Australia (1769), through trade and colonization in India, Canada, and South Africa. During the long war against France, they applauded the naval victories of Nelson in Egypt (1798), the continental campaigns of Wellington in Copenhagen (1810), Spain, the Netherlands, and the ultimate victory at Waterloo (1815), which they had financed through the first income tax (1798). In domestic politics their energies were absorbed in debates and shifts of power; the Prime Minister, William Pitt, his cabinet, and an elected Parliament emerged as the true governing body and began an agonizing series of reforms that culminated in the Reform Bill of 1832, enfranchising people of property (£10 householders) while avoiding the trauma of a revolution such as had occurred in France.[1] To writers, intellectuals, the working classes, and religious dissenters, however, the French Revolution was far more important than any domestic political maneuvering. To them it represented the fulfillment of a prophecy; the storming of the Bastille in 1789 and beheading a king signified the renovation of the entire world, the beginning of a reign of peace and prosperity. The collapse of the French Revolution in 1793 initiated a moral and intellectual crisis from which many never recovered, one that irrevocably altered the political ideals of English radicalism. In spite of this heightened political consciousness, many people, particularly country people, remained untouched by and often indifferent to political life, concerned primarily with illness, weather, and crops, the price of bread, and the fear of debt.

No one, on the other hand, escaped the Industrial Revolution, which had been accelerating for some time and began a major transformation of English life in the 1780s. Except for mankind's shift from nomadic to agricultural life, the Industrial Revolution was unquestionably the most important event, if one may call it an event, in the history of Western civilization. Machines, particularly steam-powered engines, were the obvious symbols of the age and increased productivity its goal. Machines depended on sources of energy such as coal and water, which meant that the people who worked them had to be moved to the new industrial centers in Sheffield, Manchester, Birmingham, and Liverpool. With the population dispersed, new means of transportation were required to connect people and products with markets. Engineers built thousands of miles of navigable canals and bridges; they replaced the rutted roads with public highways surfaced by Thomas Telford and John MacAdam. After 1784, coaches carrying mail and passengers at a speedy ten miles an hour created in previously isolated areas an avid interest in news, in current public events. And the great inns built for the exchange of horses, the rest and feeding of passengers, became centers of information. From 1820 to 1845, the stagecoach replaced the mail coach with carriages designed for people and captured the public imagination with their colorful drivers and dramatic titles: the Shrewsbury *Wonder,* the *Nimrod,* the Brighton *Age,* the *Defiance,* and the *Tally-Ho.* The first steam coach appeared in 1801, and by 1833 was making a noisy but popular run from London to Brighton, stopped finally by the 1864 act which limited road speeds to four mph.

The first steamboat appeared in 1813, and the first railway in 1825, connecting Stockton and Darlington with a locomotive invented a decade earlier by George Stephenson. And after the first flight in 1783, it was even possible to travel by balloon. Travel became an industry; maps and guides were published describing roads, inns, views, and monuments that were an indispensable part of every traveler's baggage. In one generation this mania for transportation and for the communication which it made possible overcame social, geographic, and economic barriers, while altering traditional concepts of space, time, and community. As more of England became accessible, more people spent time traveling in small informal groups gathered together around a common timetable and destination, breaking down, as many commentators observed, traditional social distinctions.

But those who worked the mines, built the roads, canals, bridges, factories, and homes of the middle class, who fed the machines and carried the products to market, were excluded from most of the benefits of this growing and profitable system.[2] Crowded together in new urban centers, deprived of even minimal social services, overworked, underpaid, and physically wretched, a new class emerged with the ironic claim to being, as E. P. Thompson says in *The Making of the English Working Class* (1968), "laboring poor." With the example of the French Revolution and the help of many agitators, they developed a consciousness and political influence which for fifty years could be measured by the extreme acts Parliament took to keep them under control. Forbidden by the Combination Acts (1799–1800) to organize, they indulged in a national tradition—rioting. There were the Gordon Riots (1780) against Catholic toleration, the Loyalist riots in Birmingham and Manchester (1791) against French sympathizers, periodic food riots, and even riots against the theaters for raising prices (1815), culminating in the Peterloo Massacre (1819) when the army fired upon thousands of defenseless weavers who had gathered to protest against the laws forbidding them to break the machines that were enslaving them. The Six Acts in 1819, and the founding of a civilian police force (1819) cooled the rioting temper but left little means for the lower classes to express their grievances, and there were many. Indeed, the history of the lower classes during the Romantic period is a chronicle of misery and degradation. Although there was more than enough work available, laborers had no protection against employers who hired and dismissed them at will, treating them as an exploitable commodity. The paupers were the most vulnerable of all; workhouse officials lent them to local industries and their children were given or even sold to textile mills where they worked in exchange for potatoes and salt.

The middle classes began taking their responsibility for the poor with increased though misplaced ardor while resisting the real relief to be purchased through increased taxes or Poor Rates. Some agitated for prison reforms begun by John Howard (1783); others engaged in campaigns to abolish the slave trade (1807); and others founded the largely ineffectual Society for Bettering the Condition of the Poor (1796), and, armed with three volumes of Sir Frederick Morton Eden's *The State of the Poor* (1797), discussed the economics of poverty. While they did not support poor relief, improved social services, or more humane working conditions, they did design a system of education that would, if not reconcile the working classes to their bleak existence, at least subdue them.[3] The lower classes needed food, comfort, and entertainment; they were given Sunday schools, Bibles, tracts, and an austere morality of prudence, restraint, industry, self-discipline, regularity, and cleanliness. When, during the few free hours they salvaged on Sundays, they chose to sing, dance, play, and even travel, they encountered the Sabbatarians, whose opposition to any activity other than prayer converted the day of rest into a day of mourning and contributed ultimately to the besotting of the lower classes who, having nowhere else to go, gathered in the taverns and gin shops.

Because the entire philanthropic and educational program was associated with a religious revival, the rewards for the poor, however intangible, were beyond reproach. An astute government, more concerned with controlling then relieving the poor, helped to orchestrate the religious revival and the charitable activities carried on in its name: in 1818, at the peak of postwar unrest, the government subsidized the building of new churches, although most of the existing ones had only token congregations, and ignored the maimed veterans, starving widows, and orphans. From a social or political point of view, then, the philanthropic activities of the religious sects were misguided. Politically, however, they upheld the power of the landed aristocracy while creating a class of abject laborers who resigned themselves to hardship and deprivation on the basis that it was spiritually good for such naturally corrupt creatures to do so. The poor were led to believe that they had been providentially placed in the care of the middle classes. Enlightened observers, deriding the hypocrisy of contemporary life, longed for either the idealized paternalistic society of the past or a utopian brotherhood of the future.[4]

Whatever their goal, the characteristic method for reaching it among the lower as well as middle classes was to form a committee or club, applying the organizational talents required for running factories to running society. There were philosophical societies and scientific societies, such as the Royal Institution where fashionable people gathered to hear Humphrey Davy lecture on laughing gas. The Royal Lancastrian Society encouraged schools, while the Society for the Suppression of Vice discouraged brothels, pornography, and Sunday games. Societies emerged for protecting the animals and for converting the heathens. The artisans and working classes, prevented from forming unions, formed political organizations such as the Hampden Clubs, the Corresponding Societies, and the "friendly" societies which provided insurance against sickness and funeral costs through subscription. The individualism that flowered during the later decades of the nineteenth century actually arose from an excess of collective activity during the Romantic period that Coleridge, among others, viewed with derision and alarm:

> All individual dignity and power
> Engulfed in Courts, Committees, Institutions,
> Associations and Societies,
> A vain, speech-mouthing, speech-reporting Guild,
> One Benefit-Club for mutual flattery.
> ("Fears in Solitude," ll. 54–58)

And in 1827, William Hazlitt attributed the organizing instinct to a personality disorder of national dimensions: "Why are the English so fond of clubs, corporate bodies, joint stock companies and large associations of all kinds? Because they are the most unsociable set of people in the world" (Howe, 20: 149).

The clubs and societies were merely an overt expression of the regulation, ceremony, and exclusivism that dominated social relations in the upper-middle classes. Questions of status, decorum, propriety were minute and required close observation: what to wear, what to eat, what kind of carriage to use, what form of address, on whom one could call, how long to stay, and what could be discussed. Certainly courtship and marriage rituals were more carefully regulated than trade and currency, with which they were frequently confused. In Susan Ferrier's *Marriage: A Novel* (1818), for example, Lord Courtland defies fashionable sentiment and insists that his daughter, Lady Juliana, accept the conventional marriage dictated by property: "There's no talking to a young woman now about marriage, but she is all in a blaze about hearts and darts, and—and—But hark ye, child, I'll suffer no daughter of mine to play the fool with her heart, indeed! She shall marry for the purpose for which matrimony was ordained amongst people of birth—that is, for the aggrandisement of her family, the extending of their political influence—for becoming, in short, the depository of their mutual interest" (Vol. I, ch. 1). Such a marriage, however calculating and reasonable, could be as Jane Austen illustrates, felicitous. "The wedding was very much like other weddings," she writes at the conclusion to *Emma,* "the wishes, the hopes, the confidence, the predictions of the small band of true friends who witnessed the ceremony, were fully answered in the perfect happiness of the union."

But the rich were different, exempt from external pressure and free to pursue their own inclinations during one of the most repressed periods in English history.[5] In spite of the democratic revolutions that threatened inherited privilege all over the Western world, the English aristocracy, centered in London, enjoyed an unparalleled degree of personal freedom. Hannah More, among others, reproached them in such tracts as *Thoughts upon the Importance of Manners of the Great* (1789) for failing to set an example, but they remained insulated by convention, remote from war and social unrest, morally as well as politically unassailable. After 1811, when George IV became Regent, the decorum and sobriety of "Farmer" George III gave way to the profligacy and exhibitionism of his son, "The First Gentleman of Europe," as he liked to be called. They were urban people, carrying their urban tastes and pleasures back to their country estates where, except for hunting foxes in a regulated and ceremonial fashion, they had little interest in rural life. Charles Lamb expressed the feelings of many Regency gentlemen when he claimed, "A garden was the primitive prison till man with promethean felicity and boldness luckily sinn'd himself out of it" (Lucas, III, 242). And London was "the most wonderful spot on this habitable earth," as Southey called it in *Letters from England,* the London depicted by Thackeray in *Vanity Fair,* a city transformed by John Nashe into a stucco-coated paradise for those few whose major distinctions were titles, land, style, and wealth, immense wealth, spent largely on display: on building country estates or town houses; on carriages, horses, and liveried servants; on dinners, parties, and balls where they met to flirt, to gossip, and to waltz; on resorts such as Brighton and Bath; and on clothes. It was a society that literally lived on what was to become a hilarious metaphor in Carlyle's *Sartor Resartus:* the philosophy of clothes. Tailors, haberdashers, bootmakers, hairdressers, and personal valets were major assets in a society that set its standards by Beau Brummell, the *beau ideal,* the dandy—an impeccably dressed, rude, cynical, humorless, anti-intellectual snob who delighted in gambling, practical jokes, ridicule, cultivated vice, being seen, and being quoted, quoted all over London by his followers in high stiff collars that raised their chins in the unhealthy position we now recognize as snobbery, a position that replaced laughter with an expressive sneer.

Their fashions bespoke the mannered simplicity, the affected ease of their social rituals. Less elaborate and far more revealing than earlier fashions, clothes displayed an interesting combination of puritan austerity and pagan freedom. For example, women exchanged their bird-cage headdresses for ringlets and bonnets, their petticoats and corsets for underpants and grecian or empire-style dampened muslin gowns that clung to their bodies. Men exchanged their powdered wigs for stove-pipe hats, their fitted breeches for trousers and coats in earthy colors; but they also started wearing corsets and starched collars. They liked games, speed, and violence, boxing matches, cockfights, horses, dogs, and duels. They were publicly emotional: the prince wept at tea parties; M.P.'s wept in Parliament; and the women wept over novels, lovers, and small domestic animals. And they cultivated personal comfort with ingenuity and craft, their desires calling forth such refinements as armchairs, reading lamps, cheese toasters, water closets, bathing machines, umbrellas, suspenders, and gas lamps.[6] They were, according to Southey in *Letters from England,* "a people made wanton by prosperity": "Saints and philosophers teach us that they who have the fewest wants are the wisest and the happiest; but neither philosophers nor saints are in fashion in England. . . . this nation offers a perpetual reward to those who will discover new wants for them" (p. 94). The rich did, of course, have their clubs, but they were largely for gambling and drinking at Whites and Watier's for the men, or, for dancing, flirting, and gossiping at Almack's, dominated by the ladies. Marriages were especially open, having often been made for convenience; or, as in the case of the Duke of Clarence and Dorothy Jordan (an alliance that produced ten illegitimate children), marriages were often avoided for convenience.[7] Illegitimacy was high among the aristocracy and among the working classes, but aristocrats were expected to be discrete and provide for their offspring. The most famous hostesses of the age such as Lady Melbourne, adored by Byron, often produced the most genetically interesting progeny along with their assemblies and memoirs. While the upper classes found political advantages in sharing their wives, the lower classes occasionally sold them. One carpenter received ten shillings for his wife; a laborer, a gallon of beer; and, in 1832, a farmer accepted twenty shillings and a Newfoundland dog for a wife whom he described as "a domestic curse": "She can read novels and milk cows; she can laugh and weep . . . make butter and scold the maid . . . sing Moore's Melodies and plait her frills and caps."

However elegant the aristocratic taste in costumes, furniture, architecture, and people, its taste in literature was limited and superficial. It was characterized, according to R. J. White, by a "preference for the concrete and the tangible," a "perennial distrust of ideas."[8] Wordsworth, among others, dismissed fashionable London society: "merely think," he wrote to Lady Beaumont on May 21, 1807, "of the pure absolute honest ignorance, in which all worldlings of every rank and situation must be enveloped, with respect to the thoughts, feelings, and images, on which the life of my poems depends. . . . what have they to do with routs, dinners, morning calls, hurry from door to door, from street to street, on foot or in Carriage?" Curiously, Wordsworth is berating the very class, the urban aristocracy, which had traditionally been the allies of writers, particularly poets, their primary means of support and their major inspiration. They had been the patrons, the ones who had always paid for and therefore valued the prestige of a dedication or the delight of having one's lifestyle commemorated in words or print. But these aristocrats were not educated and their failure to identify with their own tradition of arts and letters contributed to a major change in literature during the Romantic period, for while the governing classes failed to assume a cultural obligation, the lower and middle classes became educated, and technology enabled them to develop, with amazing speed, their own literature and tastes. They became "the reading public," an anonymous and dispersed body of people whose purchasing power gave them enormous and unprecedented influence over what could be written and published, and whose tastes were often inscrutable. Authors approached them with a mixture

of wonder, fear, and contempt. This reading public, how-
ever, and the publishing industry it made possible, con-
tributed as much to the shape of literary expression and the
attitude of the authors as did the literary tradition itself.

CHAPTER II

The
Literary
Marketplace

Publishers

EXCEPT FOR PERIODICAL literature, moral tracts, and popular romances, England did not, as Wordsworth said, offer either an inspiring or receptive environment for its authors in the opening decades of the nineteenth century. Many of the conditions were appropriate for a great literary revival: increased wealth and leisure among the rich, the social and educational aspirations of the middle classes, the spread of literacy among the poor, larger and more diverse audiences in new overseas markets and a native population that grew from seven to over seventeen million during Wordsworth's lifetime alone (1770–1850). But, since the publishing industry was one of the last to be mechanized, books were too expensive to be available to everyone: a novel by Jane Austen would have cost $100 a volume, for example, and up to $500 for a four-volume set by Sir Walter Scott.[1] An iron press introduced in 1798 reduced labor but did not speed production; and the steam press, first used in 1814 to print the London *Times,* did not come into general use until the 1840s. Most typesetting continued to be done by hand by highly paid craftsmen on taxed paper that had nearly doubled in price during the last decade of the eighteenth century. Although circulating libraries in provincial centers made books available at a nominal fee, they helped keep the retail prices above the level that ordinary readers could afford. And while cheap reprint houses such as John Bell's and James Lackington's published English classics of poetry and drama for a few pennies each, they competed with contemporary authors for the less affluent readers. Consequently, the new interest in reading and the proliferation of printed matter that accompanied it focused on newspapers, magazines, reviews, and pamphlets—the useful, the instructive, and the fugitive. The literature we have come to value, the great poetic statements of English Romanticism, with perhaps the exception of Byron and Scott, were insignificant in English society; and many writers, particularly poets, felt like aliens, displaced persons, refugees in a world that was evolving on principles antithetical to art, the principles of a marketplace governed by the laws of competition, of supply and demand, laws to which even literature had become subject. Authors were embittered: Keats and Wordsworth vowed to write for posterity rather than deal with the reading public, and in January, 1829, Charles Lamb concluded, "Damn the age! I will write for antiquity!" (Lucas, III, 203). Nearly every author had something derogatory to say about the reading public.

Whatever its flaws, and however much authors complained about it, the literary marketplace was one of the most important institutions to develop during the Romantic period. It offered more creative freedom, opportunity, fame, and financial reward than the patronage system, which it was gradually replacing. As Vapid, the author in Frederic Reynolds's play "The Dramatist" (1789) comments: "Get into print!—pshaw! everybody get into print now.—Kings and quacks—peers and poets—bishops and boxers, tailors and trading justices—can't go lower, you know—all get into print!"

There were still some private patrons during the Romantic period such as Thomas and Josiah Wedgwood, who provided Coleridge with an annuity of £150, relieving him from having to earn his living as a minister. The Literary Fund, a kind of collective patron, distributed small sums of money to deserving authors who in turn composed poems for presentation at lavish anniversary dinners. Motivated more by utilitarian than aesthetic instincts, however, the Literary Fund was ineffectual, devoting most of its energies, according to David Williams in *Claims of Literature* (1802), to long debates on the function of literature, the danger of encouraging young talent that might better be left to "the discretion and patronage of the government, nobility, and opulent gentry."[2] Politics provided the most visible and controversial forms of patronage; the poet laureateship, for example, had fallen into such disrepute after the political appointment of Henry James

Pye (1799–1813) that Scott declined the post, Southey accepted it with misgivings, and Wordsworth agreed to serve so long as he wasn't expected to write anything. The government also offered indirect patronage through appointments such as Wordsworth's as Distributor of Stamps (for which he was berated by such liberal members of the poetic community as Robert Browning, who depicted him in 1843 as the "Lost Leader" betraying his principles for a "handful of silver") or Tom Moore's absentee post as Registrar of the Bermudas.

However unreliable and often unfair, these various forms of patronage were preferable to the booksellers who were the new patrons, the most powerful figures in the marketplace. They purchased manuscripts, printed them, sold them, and sometimes owned the periodicals in which they were reviewed. While most authors felt exploited by them and complained bitterly, most booksellers were generous and conscientious. Some, like Joseph Johnson, the radical bookseller who went to jail for publishing a seditious pamphlet, held weekly salons that included William Blake, Tom Paine, Mary Wollstone-craft, and William Godwin. John Murray, who published Coleridge, Lord Byron, George Crabbe, Jane Austen, and Washington Irving, gave literary dinners surrounded by por-traits of his most successful authors, and enjoyed the title "Prince of Booksellers" in recognition of his generosity and taste. John Taylor and James Hessey, men of letters rather than of business, invested in the profitless publication of poetry, defended their authors against reviewers, lent money, and raised the funds to send the ailing John Keats to Italy. And when Longmans explained to Tom Moore that his delay in delivering *Lalla Rookh,* for which they had advanced £3,000, made them impatient because of their interest in the work rather than any distrust of the author, they were exhibiting a sensitivity to the artistic temperament which was becoming commonplace. Even a provincial bookseller like Joseph Cot-tle of Bristol could befriend and provide limited patronage to two obscure authors, Wordsworth and Coleridge, whose anonymous work, the *Lyrical Ballads,* he published in 1798.[3]

However scrupulous and sensitive many of the booksellers were, they were still tradesmen, tradesmen whose commod-ity happened to be literature. They purchased works as investments, for profit, favoring those that would sell, those that would appeal to the largest possible audience. Authors who were inspired by transcendant values, who measured their success historically, and who were motivated by aesthetics, viewed booksellers as aliens, with suspicion if not contempt.

The copyright laws, originally designed to protect authors, actually helped to translate art into commodity, depriving an author of his natural ownership and treating a literary work as if it were any manufactured item produced for trade. The Act for the Encouragement of Learning (1709) had guaranteed that unless an author sold his work outright, he owned it for fourteen years after publication or for the length of his life, after which it entered the public domain—except for posthumously published works, which were guaranteed to an author's heirs for twenty-eight years. Although in 1814, the initial term was extended to twenty-eight years, and to forty-two in 1842, the laws still favored only those works which had immediate and popular appeal. Because a poet's reputation grew slowly, so Wordsworth argued, by the time the income from a volume exceeded the costs of production, the author was dead and the bookseller rather than the poet's heirs reaped the benefits. Consequently, Wordsworth withheld *The Prelude* for posthumous publication, for, as he explained in 1839, if he had published it when it was first completed in 1805, before he had any reputation, "neither my heirs nor I would have got a farthing from it" (*LY,* ii, 1291).

For this first generation of authors living with a literary marketplace, there were no precedents, no predictable lifestyles. Some starved, or wasted away, or went insane; others prospered, joined an aesthetic elite, or the country gentry. Authorship proved to be as various an occupation as one could find, and authors shared, if they shared anything, a suspicion, even contempt of the reading public, and a terrible insecurity about their futures. Most authors found other sources of income, such as journalism, reviewing, civil posts, and advised other aspiring young authors to avoid writing for a living. In December 1812, for example, Sir Walter Scott, who was to make and lose more than any writer of his age through publication, advised the young Charles Robert Maturin, "For literature, though an excellent staff, has always proved a wretched crutch to those who relied upon it entirely for support" (Scott's letters). Keats, for example, claimed that he would prefer "to avoid publishing. . . . I would like to compose things honourable to Man—but not fingerable over by Men" (*Letters,* I, 415). Others, authors who at earlier periods would have been too remote from the wealthy and powerful patrons who represented the only available audience, succeeded in the marketplace. Their versatility, energy, and skill were rewarded by a publishing industry that was absorbing masses of written material and producing new forms of publication to satisfy the new audiences. While few of these writers prospered as poets or became memorable as authors, out of a vast and anonymous audience that read their reviews, magazines, newspapers, religious and didactic publications, children's books, and popular novels, they not only shaped the audience for poetry and the higher forms of literature but also aroused the latent talents of a whole generation of authors.

The Reviews

To most authors, the reviewing press, such influential periodicals as the *Edinburgh Review,* the *Quarterly Review,* the *Monthly Review,* and the *Critical Review,* appeared menacing, obstructive, and unfair.[4] Poets especially resented the reviews, believing, for example, that Keats, the young consumptive author of *Endymion,* had indeed been killed by a review in the *Quarterly.* Actually, the reviews provided a steady source of income for many writers, especially Southey, Coleridge, Scott, and Hazlitt, to name a few, who believed that however reprehensible other reviewers were, they performed a useful function. Protected by anonymity, the reviewers, mostly clergymen, lawyers, scholars, and civil servants, assumed the self-appointed task of creating public taste, supporting and directing the development of the arts, preserving the literary traditions through a period of cultural change, and protecting national morality by guiding and even to some degree censoring literary production. However noble their ideals, most reviewers in practice were petty and snide, as Peacock observed in his "Essay on Fashionable Literature": they habitually complained that authors were unintelligible or insane, that whatever work they reviewed had hit a new low of bathos or had put the reviewer to sleep. Still, the reviewers were formidable creatures, many of them educated in the wide-ranging and liberal educational system that prevailed in Scotland, their interests extending beyond literature. Consequently, reviews of literary works appeared alongside books on science, theology, biography, history, travel, philosophy, economics, politics, and cookery.

Following the example of the *Monthly Review,* founded in 1749 by Ralph Griffiths, the reviews compiled and assessed what had been published, recorded and represented the intellectual life of the times, and introduced the reading public to what was useful and new. That there was a need for such activity was proven by the longevity of the *Monthly,* from 1749 to 1845, mostly under the editorship of the Griffiths family. The formula they discovered was basic to the future of periodical publication: people buy journals that reflect their interests or articulate beliefs they already have. According to this formula, the reading public does not value originality. The *Monthly,* then, held its audience by expanding rather than changing, becoming encyclopedic in scope, offering records of events, statistics, opinions, notices of every book published in London (of particular interest to the modern literary scholar), articles on law, medicine, and commerce which served the same functions as a trade journal for the professions and the industrial and mercantile classes. Since most reviewers were paid by the printer's sheet (sixteen pages), they often used long extracts to fill the space, giving generous samples of the original work but little genuine criticism. The *Monthly* acquired an international range through the contributions of William Taylor of Norwich, who helped educate the reading public in continental literature. The *Monthly* also published some original essays and thereby provided income for such writers as Oliver Goldsmith, who could not depend on aristocratic or government patronage, and who were not sufficiently productive or popular to get by on the patronage of booksellers. Dominated by a Griffiths' point of view and by the corporate editorial policy on which he insisted, the *Monthly,* in the years following Waterloo, lost its most talented contributors to the more political *Edinburgh Review* and the irreverent *London Magazine.* But during the tense period from 1793 to 1815, when editors were being jailed for the opinions of their contributors, Griffiths, an editor by blood as well as by trade, took seriously his responsibility to publish and insisted that nothing appear which would offend the government, inflame public reaction, or alienate his audience.

In 1802, periodical criticism entered a new era with the founding of the *Edinburgh Review*.[5] Among its distinctions, the *Edinburgh* was published in Scotland, a country that had achieved the highest literacy rate in the world, a country where literature was considered as serious an occupation as politics, a country that, between 1770 and 1830, was at the peak of intellectual activity.[6] Financed by Archibald Constable, the bookseller, the *Edinburgh* offered generous fees to contributors as well as freedom to write at length on the subject of the book under review, attracting the most ambitious if not talented writers. It quickly acquired intellectual authority, attributable to a policy of reviewing only the most significant books, to an avowed freedom from bookseller's influence, and to its founders and editors: Francis Jeffrey, who served as editor for twenty-six years and later became a judge and a lord;[7] Henry Brougham, who led the movement for the abolition of the slave trade, spent fifty-four years in Parliament, and in 1830 became Lord Chancellor; and Sidney Smith, the Anglican minister who first proposed the review and ended his career as canon of St. Paul's. Although they were not literary men themselves, collectively they set out to purge literature of what they considered to be dangerous tendencies: the corruption of language and of common sense and the violation of social norms and of moral and religious principles. However sober such ideals appear, the *Edinburgh* was never dull, for the reviewers were abrasive, cultivating the splenetic personality associated with those earlier guardians of eighteenth century literary values and public morality, Alexander Pope and Samuel Johnson. But they were less talented than these predecessors, less talented even than the authors they attacked, as Lord Byron charged in "English Bards and Scotch Reviewers," his satirical answer to the *Edinburgh's* review of *Hours of Idleness* (1807). While they claimed to improve public taste, to amend the faults of contemporary authors, and to uphold literary standards, their reviews amounted to little more than ineffectual commentary focusing on the author and his various infirmities, stylistic as well as moral, rather than on the work. Protected by anonymity, the reviewer was himself a fiction, an artifice designed to arouse an audience as much as to educate it, as we learn from Southey's comments on Jeffrey: "Bating the very immoral trade which he set up, publicly speaking ill of books which he makes no scruple to commend in private, a good-natured man who only writes malignantly because it gratifies his vanity and sells his review" (*NL,* I, 407–8).

Philosophically, the *Edinburgh* defended that cheerful eighteenth-century optimism which had long been betrayed by experience, the belief, all evidence to the contrary, that this world was indeed the best possible for the best of all possible people, that all evils were merely temporary or at least necessary to a larger good. This faith isolated them from the major impulse of the literary community, that impulse toward reform, the revolutionary fervor that inspired the best and most original writing. Still, by comparison with the other reviews it was so liberal, so intellectually audacious and politically uncommitted that, following a review in October, 1808, that appeared opposing the war against France, the Tories, led by Sir Walter Scott, defected to start the London based *Quarterly Review.*

Although the *Quarterly* was designed to serve as a corrective to the *Edinburgh,* it closely resembled its rival, offering, among other things, an equally glittering staff.[8] William Gifford, the editor from 1809 to 1824, was a classicist, an editor of Elizabethan drama and the politically conservative weekly *Anti-Jacobin* (1797–1798), and the author of *The Baviad* (1791) and *The Maviad* (1795), poetic satires ridiculing the excesses of contemporary literature. The *Quarterly*'s political credentials were established by John Wilson Croker, First Secretary of the Admiralty, a poet, historian, and editor of Boswell's *Life of Johnson;* and by George Canning, who in 1827 became Prime Minister. Robert Southey, the future poet laureate, and Sir Walter Scott wrote reviews and helped to formulate policy. Although financed by the liberal and affluent John Murray, the *Quarterly* asserted its independence by attacking Lord Byron, his most profitable author. But then, like the *Edinburgh,* it attacked nearly everybody—though with less taste and less accuracy, and with the arrogance that comes from a clear alliance with the political party in power. It was, as Hazlitt wrote in his essay on Gifford in *The Spirit of the Age,* "a depository for every species of political sophistry and personal calumny." Like Jeffrey, Gifford distrusted innovation, originality, and therefore almost everything that the contemporary literary community most valued. But Gifford lacked Jeffrey's intelligence and tone; he lacked Jeffrey's capacity for the magisterial reproach such as his opening remark in his review of Wordsworth's *Excursion:* "This will never do." Instead Gifford, and Croker as well, tended toward petty sniping and personal abuse. It was Croker who wrote the supposedly fatal attack on Keats's *Endymion* and though the review did not, in fact, destroy Keats, it did provoke his incisive remarks on the status of reviews in general and their effects on society: "the Reviews have enervated and made indolent men's minds—few think for themselves—These Reviews too are getting more and more powerful and especially the Quarterly—They are like a superstition which the more it prostrates the Crowd and the longer it continues the more powerful it becomes just in proportion to their increasing weakness" (*Letters,* II, 65).

William Hazlitt

However unhappy Keats was with the reviews, he considered one reviewer's "depth of taste" among the "three things to rejoice at in this Age" (*Letters,* I, 203). He was referring to William Hazlitt, a prolific reviewer, whose range of talents and energies, whose combative nature and sense of rectitude found an ideal expression in the reviews and periodical press.[9] Critic, reviewer, cultural commentator, fifty years earlier Hazlitt would probably have been that clergyman his father had expected him to be, and a hundred years later, along with Coleridge, Southey, Carlyle, and De Quincey, a university professor. Hazlitt's characteristics became qualifications for later critics: an inquisitive mind, a classical education, practical experience in arts and letters, fluency and power as both a writer and a speaker, a sense of history and of the present and their relative claims, a coherent system of values, a capacity to comprehend, analyze, appreciate, and judge diverse forms of artistic expression, a sensitivity to one's own response, an urge to define, disseminate, and enlarge the cultural tradition, to educate the public while guiding artists and authors. Defining his critical function, then, as guardian, teacher, and architect of culture, he took as his subject arts and letters, the theater, the art galleries and collections, political and religious sects and behavior, the manners, attitudes, values, diversions of those mostly urban men and women who bought the periodicals for which he wrote. His discursive and sometimes elliptical style, his use of detail, definition, and example, his formal manner, his conversational tone, even the topics he considered—wit and humor, "On the Pleasure of Hating," "On Going on a Journey"—still influence the way students learn to write expository prose. And the way students and their instructors comment on literature in lectures, term papers, published articles—in fact, what they call the literary tradition—is attributable to Hazlitt's influence on his own and subsequent generations.[10]

Hazlitt's preparation for this task was long, indirect, arduous, as it would always be for someone who was born with few advantages, one who had to create the occupation suited to his skills. Born in 1778, the youngest of three surviving children, Hazlitt was the son of a minister, an ardent supporter of the American Revolution, who, in 1783, moved to America, participated in the development of American Unitarians, and, returning to England in 1787, accepted an undistinguished post at Wem, Shrewsbury, that would enable him to support his family. William attended the local schools and, after two years at the Unitarian College at Hackney, concluded his formal education, observing: "Everyone brought up in colleges and drugged with Latin and Greek for a number of years firmly believes *that there have been about five people in the world, and that they are dead"* (Howe, 20:296). While his education prepared him for a life of independent thought, he was to regret his lack of polite arts and social skills, as he reveals in a letter to his son in which he claims that dancing "is of the greatest consequence to . . . success in life": "Perhaps you will find at the year's end, or towards the close of life, that the daily insults, coldness, or contempt, to which you have been exposed by neglect of such superficial recommendations, are hardly atoned for by the few proofs of esteem or admiration which your integrity or talents have been able to extort in the course of it."[11] The letter reveals a man who, having spent his life identifying the good things in art and civilization, knew himself to be deficient in accomplishments that would have made all his talents meaningful, knew himself to be as Coleridge described him in 1803, "a thinking, observant, original man" whose "manners are 99 in 100 singularly repulsive; brow-hanging, shoe-contemplative, strange . . . kindly nature, . . . fond of, attentive to, and patient with children," but "jealous, gloomy, and of an irritable pride" (*CL,* II, 990).

Coleridge wrote that evaluation when he was feeling fond of Hazlitt, having met him a few years earlier, in 1798, when he went to preach at the elder Hazlitt's church. At the time, Hazlitt, brooding over his future, had been reading independently, mostly in literature and modern philosophy, while trying to finish *An Essay on the Principles of Human Action,* published in 1806. In this work, contradicting the belief that human beings are motivated by self-interest, he proposed the sympathetic imagination as the faculty that allows people to identify with their own future selves and therefore with other people, an idea that was to become central to his and subsequently Keats's aesthetics. An exhibit of Titians and Raphaels in London revived his ambition to become, like his older brother, a painter. After studying at the Louvre, Paris, and London, he visited the Lake District in 1803, doing portraits of Coleridge and Wordsworth, portraits that made Coleridge, according to Southey, look like a guilty horse thief on trial, and Wordsworth as if he were about to be hanged. Hazlitt left in haste, pursued by an angry mob of Keswick citizens who claimed that he had assaulted a country girl who had resisted his advances. Both Wordsworth and Coleridge gave him refuge, but neither forgave him for the embarrassment the incident caused.

Fortunately, he returned to the loyal friendship of Charles and Mary Lamb, who appreciated his eccentricities and tolerated his tactlessness, his short temper, his suspicious nature, his sullen fits and peevish disposition, often defending him to less generous contemporaries: "I wish he would not quarrell with the world at the rate he does," Lamb wrote to Southey in 1823, but "I think W. H. to be, in his natural and healthy state, one of the wisest and finest spirits breathing. . . . I think I shall go to my grave without finding . . . such another companion" (Lucas, I, 234). The Lambs introduced him to Sarah Stoddart, a difficult and opinionated spinster, who, by contemporary standards, was unmarriageable because she was over thirty. He married her in 1808, and, in her cottage at Winterslow, tried to earn money by assorted writing assignments such as *A New and Improved Grammar of English,* published as a textbook by William Godwin.

In 1812, he gave a series of lectures on British philosophy at the Russell Institution, an activity that had become lucrative as the middle classes acquired the time, money, and inclination to improve themselves. From the abstraction of philosophy, he moved to the particularity of journalism, accepting a position as parliamentary reporter on the *Morning Chronicle,* then as drama critic, for the *Times.* With the prospect of a regular income, and a new son on whom he doted, Hazlitt rented a cottage with odd and provocative associations: it adjoined the garden of Jeremy Bentham who also owned it, and it had been inhabited once by John Milton and more recently by James Mill, father of John Stuart Mill, who considered it uncomfortable and unhealthy. The Hazlitt household was disorderly and young William undisciplined, but Hazlitt worked well here and acquired a reputation as a forceful critic. For several years he wrote for the liberal *Champion,* the equally liberal *Examiner* published by John and Leigh Hunt, reviewing drama, art, literature, and attracting the attention of Francis Jeffrey, who invited him to review for the *Edinburgh.* He was outspoken, dogmatic, irritating, anonymously attacking Wordsworth, Coleridge, and Southey as political apostates for having once supported the French Revolution but, after the war broke out with France, supporting the monarchy, the corrupt aristocracy, the Establishment. His support of Napoleon, even in defeat in 1815, led to the end of his journalistic career, but he had another voice developed through contributions to the "Round Table," a series of informal essays mostly on aesthetics by Leigh Hunt and Hazlitt appearing in Hunt's *Examiner*. Like many of his contemporaries, Hazlitt feared the power in the new popular audience to create artistic reputations without any understanding of artistic values, the tendency to equate mere popularity, contemporaneity, or novelty with artistic excellence. But he also feared that the artists and writers would be lured into satisfying these criteria. The publication of the collected essays in 1817 had an enormous influence on John Keats, who concluded: "I know he thinks himself not estimated by ten People in the world—I wishe he knew he is" (*Letters,* I, 116).

Hazlitt began to identify what he considered to be the major literary tradition and its virtues with *Characters of Shakespeare's Plays* (1817), dedicated to Charles Lamb, designed to rescue Shakespeare from the irrelevant principles of classical rhetoric and form, and to provide insight into his genuine strength, the delineation of character. In *A View of the English Stage* (1818), a collection of his theatrical reviews, and *Lectures on the English Poets* (1818), he placed contemporary theater and poetry in historical perspective, contributing a comprehensive definition of poetry based on intent and response rather than form, on passion and imagination rather than meter or rhyme: "All that is worth remembering in life is the poetry of it" (Howe, 5:2). In *Lectures on the English Comic Writers* (1819), and, again, in the less successful *Lectures on the Dramatic Literature of the Age of Elizabeth* (1820), he attempted to redefine the literary tradition itself, offering some of the first commentary on Henry Fielding, Samuel Richardson, Laurence Sterne, and such otherwise neglected or underrated authors as John Lyly, John Marston, Thomas Heywood, Thomas Middleton, George Chapman, Thomas Dekker, and Phillip Massinger, finding their value in how well they reflected their age, responded to it, and influenced it. This emphasis on environment was emerging, as we shall see, in all disciplines—biology, philosophy, political science, economics—and became a common theme in literary theory, ranging from Wordsworth's complaint in the Preface to *Lyrical Ballads* that urban crime and war were creating a taste for sensationalistic literature to Shelley's claim in *A Defense of Poetry* that the greatness of drama is attributable to the political system in which it is produced.

In 1820, at age forty-two, Hazlitt changed his own environment, taking a room in the house of a tailor with whose daughter, Sally Walker—ignorant, plain, flirtatious—he fell

obsessively, absurdly, and unaccountably in love, rhapso-
dizing over her beauty, virtue, and divine origins: "Oh, thou,
who, the first time I ever beheld thee, didst draw my soul
into the circle of the heavenly looks, and weave enchantment
round me . . . in that gentle form . . . I saw all that I ever
loved of female grace, modesty, and sweetness!" (Howe,
8:310–11). After a year and a half of such one-sided rapture,
fearing that he was losing her, Hazlitt convinced his wife to
join him in Edinburgh for the three-month residence required
for a divorce,[12] after which he returned to London to dis-
cover that his divine Sally had become involved with some-
one else. Partly as therapy and partly as self-punishment,
Hazlitt described the entire humiliating affair in *Liber Amoris*
(1923), one of the few literary works published during the
Romantic period dealing with love.

However distracting and unsatisfactory his emotional life,
Hazlitt was prospering as a writer, largely from his associa-
tion with the *London Magazine,* a bright, urban magazine
receptive to the personal commentary at which Hazlitt excelled,
and the pointed and informed theatrical reviews. Under the
general title of "Table Talk"—a title that conveyed his infor-
mal, conversational manner, his associative form, and his
choice of topics suited to after-dinner discussion—Hazlitt began
with an essay "On the Qualifications Necessary to Success in
Life," and continued with essays on national traits, character
types, diversions, politics, literature, and manners, in essays
such as "On the Pleasures of Painting," "On the Pleasures of
Hating," "On the Conversation of Authors," "On Coffee-
House Politicians," and "On the Ignorance of the Learned"
in which he expressed his habitual dislike of his own profes-
sion: "It is better to be able neither to read nor write than to
be able to do nothing else." In his idiosyncratic fashion he
pursues this opposition between the active and contemplative
life in "The Indian Jugglers," beginning with a description of
a performance of Indian juggling and comparing it with his
writing, ashamed to admit that he can do nothing so well as
the juggler manipulates four little brass balls: "The utmost I
can pretend to is to write a description of what this fellow
can do. I can write a book: so can many others who have not
even learned to spell. What abortions are these Essays! What
errors, what ill-spaced transitions, what crooked reasons, what
lame conclusions! How little is made out, and that little how
ill! Yet they are the best I can do." The world of action appealed
to him, especially in "The Fight," describing the famous
prizefight between Tom Hickman, "The Gas Man," and Bill

Neate on December 11, 1821. With no rounds, no time limit, and no rigid rules, prize-fighting, illegal and conducted in secrecy, was especially gruesome, but Hazlitt saw in it the "high and heroic state of man," a metaphor for his life as a reviewer.

After publishing his *Sketches of the Principal Picture-Galleries in England*, a celebration of great English artistic resources and of the patrons that assembled them, he began his own picture gallery, a series of verbal portraits of personally significant contemporaries, some appearing in the *New Monthly Magazine*, the *London Magazine*, and the *Examiner*, but most published first in the *The Spirit of the Age* (1825). From his experience as journalist, reviewer, and philosopher with particular concern for human motivation, Hazlitt saw the age expressed in eleven authors (Coleridge, Scott, Byron, Southey, Wordsworth, Campbell, Crabbe, Tom Moore, Leigh Hunt, Charles Lamb, and Washington Irving), seven political figures (Horne Tooke, James Macintosh, Lord Brougham, Sir Francis Burdett, Lord Eldon, William Wilberforce, and either George Canning or William Cobbett—depending on the edition), two editors (William Gifford and Frances Jeffrey), a Calvinist preacher (Mr. Irving), and three philosophers (Jeremy Bentham, William Godwin, and Thomas Malthus). The purpose of the work was both public and personal, as implied in the epigraph from *Hamlet*: "To know another well were to know one's self." On a personal level, then, Hazlitt was assembling those figures who had most influenced his sense of the age and of himself, and on a public one, he was offering the urban, review-reading public a survey of figures they would recognize as sources and reflections of the intellectual, artistic, and political atmosphere. Adapting the descriptive procedure, the balanced judgments of the literary review, he overcame the contentious posture that had alienated his contemporaries and found virtue even among those with whom he remained at war. Only Gifford, "by a happy combination of defects" editor of the *Quarterly*, remained beyond redemption.

His choice of figures is subjective and puzzling: they were people he knew, who had engaged his interest, on whom he reported as a journalist, or whose work he reviewed, mostly people of some talent who missed greatness because of a flaw in character, or because they were born at the wrong time, or devoted themselves to trivial tasks or ideas, or lacked focus, or became allied with the wrong political party. To Hazlitt the spirit of the age consisted of such oppositions, such unfulfilled promise.[13] Notably absent are popular and characteristic authors such as Keats, Shelley, Blake, and Jane Austen; actors such as Edmund Kean, John Kemble, and Mrs. Siddons; painters such as Thomas Lawrence, Joseph Turner, and John Constable; military leaders such as Admiral Nelson and General Wellington; architects such as John Nashe and Humphry Repton; scientists such as Joseph Priestley and Sir Humphry Davy; men of fashion such as George "Beau" Brummell or the Prince Regent; or even cranks such as Joanna Southcott. In fact, there are no women at all. But if the contents do not identify a central, obvious, and prevailing characteristic of the first quarter of the nineteenth century, the attempt to identify such characteristics, to do so in such an allusive and eccentric manner is very much in the spirit of the age, as John Stuart Mill pointed out in his essay, "The Spirit of the Age" in *The Examiner* (1831). While other authors called the age variously one of revolution, reform, reaction, expansion, concentration, fragmentation, industrialization, an age of conquest, of inquiry, of tranquility, or anxiety, Mill claimed it was an age of transition. All agreed that the present in England especially was identifiable and unique, and the attempt to define it symptomatic of a new self-consciousness. For Hazlitt, the spirit was impalpable, emanating from individuals and influencing them as well, a set of unspoken possibilities and restrictions. Locating it in the manners, attitudes, and achievement of people rather than in the style of architecture, in forms, as many Victorians would do, or in technology such as the twentieth-century space age, Hazlitt offered an incarnation of ideas, abstractions, and events.

Even before *The Spirit of the Age,* much of which he confesses to writing in a state of extreme depression, he became more generous toward his contemporaries, more critical of himself, as he concludes in his essay "On the Pleasures of Hating": "Seeing meanness, spite, cowardice, want of feeling, and want of understanding, of indifference towards others and ignorance of ourselves, seeing custom prevail over all excellence, itself giving way to infamy . . . always disappointed where I placed most reliance; the dupe of friendship, and the fool of love; have I not reason to hate and despise myself? Indeed I do; and chiefly for not having hated and despised the world enough" (Howe, 12:136). He had found a formidable opponent in himself. Keats called him "your only good damner and if ever I am damned (damn me if) I shouldn't like him to damn me. . . ." (*Letters,* I, 252). He was fortunate in 1824 to meet and marry the mysterious Mrs.

Isabella Bridgewater, the young widow of a barrister with a small income, who supposedly fell in love with him for his writing, travelled with him to France and Italy, entertained his friends admirably in London when the occasion required, and ultimately left him in 1827, antagonized by his adolescent son, who made life uncomfortable for her.

Like a figure from *The Spirit of the Age,* Hazlitt devoted his best and final years to a project that was unsuited to him, ill-timed, and perhaps trivial, a four-volume *Life of Napoleon Buonaparte* defending him against Sir Walter Scott's popular nine-volume biography. The first two volumes were hardly noticed; the publisher went bankrupt; and Hazlitt, responsible for some of the debts, went to debtor's prison. Nine months later, at age fifty-two, he died impoverished, attended by his son, by Charles Lamb and two other friends.

However seriously the reviewers saw themselves, to the majority of their readers they were, in fact, popular diversions, attracting a large audience because they seemed to offer useful opinions and instant knowledge. The *Edinburgh* reached a circulation of 13,000 in 1814, and the *Quarterly* a circulation of 14,000 in 1818 (but each copy was read by five to fifteen readers). Their influence on public taste and literary reputations was incalculable, for even negative reviews, as Coleridge concedes in Chapter III of the *Biographia,* provided visibility: "To anonymous critics in reviews, magazines and news-journals of various name and rank, and to satirists with or without a name, in verse or prose, or in verse-text aided by prose-comment, I do seriously believe and profess that I owe full two-thirds of whatever reputation and publicity I happen to possess."

Magazines

The character of the magazine was defined by one of the first, *The Gentleman's Magazine* (1731–1907), the function of which was to summarize and condense, according to the editor Edmund Cave, "All the Pieces of Wit, Humour, or Intelligence, daily offer'd to the Publick in the News-Papers (which of late are so multiply'd as to render it impossible, unless a Man makes it a Business, to consult them all)." A peculiar anarchy, of interest to students of communications as well as of literature, created the need for a publication that selected from the events and opinions of the day those that belonged in a semi-permanent record, a living history, that would reveal not only what happened but also how people felt about it, and what interested them. Designed especially for diversion, entertainment, and to some degree, education, the magazines published original essays, anecdotes, stories, poems, riddles, and illustrations of what seemed to be the entire range of human knowledge, including book reviews. "A happy mixture of indolence and study," Hazlitt called it, "of order and disorder": "Who, with the *Gentleman's Magazine* held carelessly in hand, has not passed minutes, hours, days, in *lackadaisical* triumph over ennui!" The *Gentleman's Magazine* inspired a host of imitations, adapting even specialized topics such as travel, science, humor, and fashion to the miscellany format.

The literary magazine originated tentatively with the *Midwife or Old Woman's Magazine* (1750–1753), edited by Christopher Smart and John Newbery, followed by the *British Magazine* (1760–1767) with its even more luminous editors, Tobias Smollett and Oliver Goldsmith, and led to the *Monthly Magazine and British Register* (1796–1843), that listed among its contributors William Godwin, William Taylor of Norwich, "Peter Pindar," William Hazlitt, William Wordsworth, and even Thomas Malthus. Although the editor avoided political issues, he ultimately appeared to be sympathetic with France, for it had been the source of most civilized virtues for over a hundred years, even though after 1793 it was technically the enemy.

However subtle and incidental its politics, the *Monthly's* popularity provoked the Tory ministry to sponsor the influential and volatile weekly, *The Anti-Jacobin* (1797–1798), which, according to George Kitchin in *Survey of Burlesque and Parody* (1931), initiated the "golden age of parody." It opposed any kind of literary fashion or innovation ranging from the preciousness of Robert Merry and the Della Cruscans to Erasmus Darwin's versified botanical sermons in *Loves of Plants,* parodied as *Loves of Triangles*. It objected not only to the rarified emotionalism and supernaturalism of contemporary novels and drama but also to the pedestrian manners that were beginning to replace them, the colloquial diction and concern for the poor that appeared, for example, in Southey's early ballads, parodied in "The Friends of Humanity and the Knife-Grinder":

> 'Needy Knife-grinder! wither are you going?
> Rough is the road, your Wheel is out of order,
> Bleak blows the Blast;—your Hat has got a hole in't,
>   So have your Breeches!'

And it found philosophical verse an irresistible target, illus-
trated in the following parody of Pope's *Essay on Man,* an
antiquated appeal to the natural order:

> First—to each living thing, what e'er its kind,
> Some lot, some part, some station is assigned.
> The feathered race with pinions skim the air
> Not so the mackerel, and still less the bear. . . .
> Ah! who has seen the maild lobster rise,
> Clap her broad wings, and soaring claim the skies.

Parody was particularly appropriate for the new forms of
publication in magazines, reviews, and newspapers, and it
appealed to the middle-class reading audience to which these
publications were directed. More obvious than satire, more
subtle than burlesque, parody excelled at simplification,
focusing on contemporary manners, or on art in perfor-
mance, protecting convention, the familiar, from anything
that could be considered deviant, eccentric, or foreign. In the
period of increased patriotism that accompanied the war against
France (1793–1815), of increased class and regional self-con-
sciousness, parody enhanced a developing sense of group
identity and the values of conformity. Ackermann's *Poetical
Magazine* survived from 1809 to 1811 on one extended par-
ody of literature and manners called *The Schoolmaster's Tour,*
later published as *The Tour of Dr. Syntax in search of the Pic-
turesque* (1812), written in verse by William Combe and illus-
trated by Thomas Rowlandson. Visual parody—the cartoon—
flourished, having acquired range and popularity during the
eighteenth century from improved methods of engraving and
the talents of Hogarth, Rowlandson, Gillray, and later,
Cruikshank.[14]

By 1815, the magazine had become the dominant form of
periodical publication. More flexible in form with less ideo-
logical commitment than reviews, the magazine reflected the
rising spirits of the middle-class reading public, its increasing
demands for entertainment, information, and the kind of sta-
tus that owning and reading these magazines could convey.
For example, in the *Morning Post,* January 13, 1817, William
Jerden announced that he was about to publish a weekly
magazine "expressly designed for the Polite Circle," one
through which "Authors may address themselves exclusively
and at once to Men of Letters." For the next forty-five years
middle-class Englishmen could become Men of Letters by
purchasing *The Literary Gazette and Journal of Belle Lettres,*

Politics . . . Comprising Original Essays on Polite Literature; The Arts and Sciences; A Review of New Publications; Poetry; Criticism on the Fine Arts; The Drama, etc.; Memoirs and Correspondence of Distinguished Persons; Anecdotes, Jeux D'esprit, etc.; Sketches on Society and Manners; Proceedings of Public and Literary Societies; Summary of Politics and News; Literary Intelligence, etc., etc. The elaborate title suggests the sense of self-importance and patriotism that it fostered. Similarly, Rudolph Ackermann's lavish *Repository of Arts, Literature, Commerce, Manufacturers, Fashion, and Politics* (1809–28) offers an interesting and typical example of what three thousand "Nobility and Gentry" could purchase at four shillings per month. Along with the elaborate color plates, often hand-tinted, of ladies' costumes (including swatches of fabric pasted to the illustrations), sketches of furniture (the *chaise lounge* and the window seat), London shops and carriages, they read recent papers from the Royal Society on heart muscles and galvanic batteries, or from the Wernerian Natural History Society on the minerology of East Lothian, the causes of a fatal chicken disease, and the origins of a sea-snake cast ashore at Orkney. They learned how to treat Merino sheep in Spain, how to breed canaries, how to heal trees, how to prepare medicinal coffee (according to the German method), how to manage the insane, and how to calculate interest at 5 percent. They read the history of British birds, of British seashells, of Ireland, Chili, and Turkey, and of the "Useful and Polite Arts"— a serial which began "At the commencement of the new year," footnoted: "The computation of the beginning of the year has been varied at different periods of our history," a footnote that continues for two pages. They found notices of all the prices at all the markets and fairs, of weather, marriages, deaths, recent and forthcoming publications, plays, musical events, legal proceedings, political prospects, bankruptcies, dividends, and anecdotes of familiar nobility depicted invariably as pious, industrious, and charitable. The section devoted to literature included memoirs, sermons, anecdotes, short stories, translations from the Greek, observations on old age, letters from Italy and Montreal, poems by the poet laureate, H. J. Pye, anonymous elegies, ballads, tributes to various ladies and to the fashionable virtues of hope, cheer, and sensibility. Clearly, Ackermann provided his readers with an impressive array of topics to discuss over tea and during the long country-house weekends with which they occupied themselves.

Leigh Hunt

Leigh Hunt, believing that a magazine should reflect as well as shape its age, believing that, as he wrote in *The Reflector*, it should be a "Chronicle for posterity," not a collection of trivia, began at least a dozen periodicals.[15] With an enviable verbal skill, a genial manner, and talented friends as his primary resources, he became the most prolific editor of the age as he repeatedly tried to find the perfect accommodation between his own voice and the inarticulate spirit of his audience. This ambition was extraordinary for someone who was by nature and by disposition an alien among his fellow creatures. Born in 1784, the eighth and last child of a Quaker-American mother and a West Indian father driven from America for his loyalist politics, Hunt was the only member of his own family born in England. He was educated at Christ's Hospital, a contemporary of Charles Lamb, Coleridge, and a host of other writers. With his father's enthusiastic approval, Hunt began his career as a poet, offering, first, the usual *Juvenilia* (1801); then, after a long silence, the often revised satire of contemporary poets, *The Feast of the Poets* (1814); *The Story of Rimini* (1816); the collection of *Foliage* (1818); *Hero and Leander;* and *Bacchus and Ariadne* (1819). Although his style was influential—the luxurious surface, the sensual and soporiphic atmosphere, the predilection for the "sweet" and delicate—he actually wrote very little memorable verse, except for such trivia as "Jenny Kissed Me," addressed to Mrs. Carlyle. His importance as a poet was inflated by his critics, specifically in a series of derisive articles published in *Blackwood's Edinburgh Magazine* (1817) in which he was attacked as the leader of the "Cockney School of Poetry," that included John Keats. The thrust of the attack was personal: this exemplary husband whose library was a treasure-house of English and Italian literary works and whose company was sought by the most eminent writers of his generation was accused of "ignorance and vulgarity," of "extreme moral depravity," and of a "want of respect for all that numerous class of plain upright men, and unpretending women in which the real worth and excellence of human society consists."

Primarily a journalist himself, Hunt was accustomed to the acrimonious and often brutal assaults of the reviewing press. In 1808, with his brother John, he founded the first weekly, *The Examiner: A New Sunday Paper upon Politics, Domestic Economy, and Theatricals*. Within two years it was the most influential literary paper in London, read by politicians and men of letters alike for the theater reviews, the trenchant observations on contemporary political life, and contributions by Lamb, Hazlitt, Shelley, Byron, even Wordsworth.

Although Hunt confessed to being liberal merely by sentiment and to having only a passing concern with reform, he enjoyed baiting authority. In 1812, the Hunts were both convicted of libel, fined £500, and imprisoned for two years for writing an article attacking the Prince Regent and the Establishment press which had protected him. The *Examiner* flourished; 10,000 copies were sold the day the verdict was announced, and Hunt's prison became one of the most agreeable places in London. His cell, which opened onto a small garden, was papered with rose trellises and the ceiling painted with a blue sky and white clouds. It was amply furnished with everything necessary to edit the *Examiner,* educate his children (one of whom he delivered himself), and entertain such luminaries as Byron, who brought him pheasants, Charles Lamb, Hazlitt, and Jeremy Bentham.

After his release, he settled in the Vale of Health, Hampstead, a model of domesticity, a political martyr, who was to originate an extraordinary number of journals: *The Reflector* (1810–1812); *The Indicator* (1819–1821), the literary weekly in which Keats's "La Belle Dame Sans Merci" first appeared; and *The Liberal: Verse and Prose from the South* (1822–1823), on which he was supposed to have collaborated with Byron and Shelley in Italy but Shelley drowned a week after his arrival and Byron lost interest after contributing *The Vision of Judgment,* an irreverent parody of Southey's elegy on the death of King George III. The later journals, which he mostly wrote himself, displayed his interest in Italian literature, his pleasure in London, the theater, and the commonplace, their tone and range suggested in the titles: *The Companion* (1828), the *Chat of the Week* (1830), *The Tatler, A Daily Journal of Literature and the Stage* (1830–1832), *Leigh Hunt's London Journal* (1834–1835), and *Leigh Hunt's Journal: A Miscellany for the Cultivation of the Memorable, The Progressive, and the Beautiful* (1850–1851). He edited the *Monthly Repository* (1838), contributed to Dickens's *Household Words* (and appeared as Harold Skimpole in Dickens's *Bleak House*), wrote vast quantities of trivial prose including popular aesthetics, translations, and memoirs, and cultivated such eccentricities as collecting locks of hair (including Milton's, on which Keats wrote a sonnet) and a philosophy of cheerfulness—eccentric because it was so remote from the doleful mood of his contemporaries.

Such personal idiosyncrasies distorted his perceptions and

prevented him from becoming what he so ardently desired: the chronicler of the age. At best he was representative of that legion of eccentrics who populated the Romantic period even as the profession of editing was moving away from idiosyncrasy toward the impersonal, corporate, and anonymous voice with which we are now familiar. At one extreme was the *New Monthly* (1814–1836), a magazine without any editor at all between 1818 and 1821, attracting the most talented writers who were delighted to send their contributions directly to the printer. And at the other extreme was *Blackwood's Edinburgh* (1817), whose collective originality is credited with starting the modern era of magazines.

The style of "Maga," as *Blackwood's* was called, was abrasive and its editorial position mercurial. The goal was lively copy and the staff, sheltered by anonymity, rose to it: John Gibson Lockhart, a young lawyer who was to become editor of the *Quarterly* and Scott's son-in-law and biographer; John Wilson, "Christopher North," who was to hold the prestigious Chair of Moral Philosophy at Edinburgh; James Hogg, "the Ettrick Shepherd" and author of the gothic curiosity *The Private Memoirs and Confessions of a Justified Sinner* (1824); and, later, William Maginn, the nineteenth-century humorist who founded *Fraser's Magazine*. They began publication with the "Chaldee Manuscript," a libelous allegorical parody, using Biblical language to ridicule a number of public figures. A few lawsuits by indignant victims helped raise the circulation to an astronomical 100,000 during the first year. However scandalous or banal, *Blackwood's* contributed a good deal of vitality to a languishing periodicals market, a modern format, and the inspiration for *London Magazine* (1820)[16] John Scott, the first editor, created through the *London* a literary fraternity as well as a journal. Offering community, a collective identity, the *London* attracted the most versatile and creative minds of the age: Lamb, De Quincey, Hazlitt, Landor, Darley, Keats, Clare, Stendahl, even Carlyle, lending prestige and permanence with *Essays of Elia, Table Talk,* and *Confessions of an English Opium-Eater*. The common center of interest was London itself, its literary life (challenged by Edinburgh) and its social character (threatened by an accumulating, alien, and transient population). John Scott's bias was geographical, urban, and cultural, rather than political. He set out to demonstrate that London, particularly the glittering new Regency London, was as interesting a subject for literature as it was a center for commercial activity.

However attractive such a notion sounds, however much

talent and prestige were associated with it, the *London* was not a financial success. To raise some interest along with circulation, Scott, on behalf of Hazlitt, Keats, and the rest of the London literati, launched a series of virulent attacks on *Blackwood's,* accusing the anonymous editors of fraud, cowardice, slander, and an assortment of dishonorable practices. Lockhart eventually challenged John Scott, and, after an unsuccessful attempt to mediate the quarrel, in February, 1821, John Christie, Lockhart's second, killed Scott in a duel that some say took place by mistake. The notoriety of the duel attracted many new readers to the *London,* raising the circulation to a peak of 1,600. But the power and appeal of primarily literary magazines was waning. Utilitarian publications such as Jeremy Bentham's *Westminister Review,* founded in 1824, boldly attacked the value of imaginative literature. Cheap serial publications such as Knight's *Penny Magazine* or Chambers' *Edinburgh Journal* and weekly newspapers competed for the magazine audience. And recurrent publishing depressions starting in 1825 forced even the most altruistic publishers, such as Taylor and Hessey, who assumed direction of the *London,* to reconsider their priorities.

Thomas De Quincey

Six months after John Scott's death in 1821, Thomas De Quincey, age thirty-six, destitute and unknown as a writer, published an essay in the *London Magazine* on the unusual topic of opium addiction and dreams, entitled *Confessions of an English Opium-Eater.*[17] Unlike Leigh Hunt, who spent a journalistic lifetime trying to become the chronicler of his age, to reflect his time, De Quincey, a cerebral and introspective man with philosophical ambitions, wanted to be a leader, to shape an intellectual revolution using the only means available to him—the pages of a magazine. Unfortunately, magazines were not suited for revolutions of any sort; their publishers and readers preferred instruction, philosophical commonplaces, intellectual simplifications, and sensationalism respectably disguised in analytical discussions of murder, for example, or opium addiction. Moreover, leading intellectual revolutions and writing for magazines as well were difficult occupations for a man like De Quincey, a disorganized, restless, solitary, and procrastinating man who explored the countryside as tirelessly as he explored his own dreams. They were nearly impossible occupations for a writer who was most productive when he was dosed with opium, besieged by creditors, menaced with impending deadlines, immersed in urban life, and separated from the family, library, and hearth that he identified with happiness. And yet, from his first publication to his death thirty-eight years later, at age seventy-four, he wrote almost three hundred articles, a translation from a German novel, a gothic romance, and a book on political economy. Unfortunately, given the rate magazines paid per page, unless De Quincey wrote an entire issue himself or wrote for several magazines at once (neither of which would any editor allow),[18] on his earnings as a journalist De Quincey could not have supported his wife, his eight children, an opium habit, and his many, often simultaneous residences.

Long before Freud, De Quincey, like his friend and contemporary William Wordsworth, recognized the importance of childhood experiences and of early family relationships in shaping the adult, and from his own childhood he created the myth of the opium-eater. Born in 1785, he was the fourth child of a prosperous Manchester linen-merchant, who was often away from home, and an emotionally austere mother with social aspirations. De Quincey was educated erratically, moving among tutors and grammar schools at Bath and Manchester, usually proving himself superior to his teachers, especially in the classics. The death of two sisters and his father before De Quincey was ten years old left him preoccupied with suffering and death, and, from his otherwise comfortless environment, he escaped into reveries. At age seventeen, he ran away from school because he claimed the headmaster deprived him of the exercise he needed to restore his health, and, after tramping through Wales, he turned to London where he hoped to borrow money against his inheritance. During the winter of 1803, he struggled to survive the cold and hunger, mingling by day among the prostitutes of Oxford Street and finding refuge at night in the abandoned building where his lawyer kept his offices. His companion was a half-starved girl, possibly the illegitimate daughter of the lawyer; together they would huddle through the night amid rags and legal papers, protecting each other from the cold, the rats, and the ghosts with which the young girl was haunted.

In the spring, reconciled to his family, he attended Oxford but, after finishing the first half of his final exam with distinction, inexplicably ran away without taking a degree. His only other attempt at a formal education was to register as a law student at the Middle Temple, London, although he never actually attended. Mostly, he educated himself, collecting a library so massive that at one time he had to rent a cottage to contain it. It was through his voracious reading of contemporary literature that he had encountered in 1799 what he called the greatest event in his intellectual life: the *Lyrical Ballads,* published anonymously the year before by William Wordsworth and Samuel Taylor Coleridge. It took nine years to gather the courage to introduce himself to Coleridge (to whom in characteristic generosity he later gave an anonymous gift of £300) and then to Wordsworth, whose house, Dove Cottage, he leased to make Grasmere and the nearby countryside his home. Here, between frequent and often extended trips to London, surrounded by his books and such congenial friends as John Wilson, who later became editor of *Blackwood's Edinburgh Magazine,* he cultivated what he called the "science of happiness" at the very center of which was a decanter of opium, which he began taking in 1804 to relieve the pain of a toothache.

The Wordsworths were the most pervasive influence in De Quincey's life.[19] In 1809, while Dorothy decorated the cottage, De Quincey was in London supervising the publication of Wordsworth's rousing political pamphlet, *The Convention of Cintra,* defending the principle of national determination. In an age of increasing nationalism, the pamphlet might have been influential if De Quincey's fastidious editing and his disregard of deadlines had not delayed its publication. Frustrated with De Quincey's work habits, Wordsworth nonetheless continued to share his observations and work including *The Prelude* with him. This autobiographical epic, published after his death in 1850, acquired a kind of preexistence in the theories of memory and growth De Quincey expressed in his own autobiographical writings. De Quincey also participated in Wordsworth's family life, becoming so devoted to his young daughter, Catherine, that when she died in 1812, at age four, he was inconsolable. His display of grief, which included sleeping on her grave, exceeded even Wordsworth's, to whom it was a cause of great concern. But De Quincey, who habitually universalized his own emotions, considered his grief a chapter in the "psychological history of mankind," and Catherine's tombstone its monument.

The same subtle differences in character and disposition that separated De Quincey from many of his contemporaries led to his alienation from the Wordsworths. Although he lived in the Lake District among enthusiasts of nature, he was more interested in books than in landscapes and preferred making his excursions at night when the scenery was barely visible.

Unlike Wordsworth and his contemporaries, who had been actively concerned with such social and political issues as the French Revolution, the war against France, poverty, and homelessness, De Quincey was a political conservative, an advocate of rank and privilege (although he befriended prostitutes and married a peasant girl to whose family he was fiercely loyal), and a theorist who proposed writing his own "Prolegomena to all Future Systems of Political Thought" because modern economics, with the exception of David Ricardo, he thought, represented "the very dregs and rinsings of the human intellect." But the grandiose schemes, the failure of will, the sloth, torpor, and financial irresponsibility alienated Wordsworth, for they were associated with the opium addiction that had wasted Coleridge's talents and were clearly wasting De Quincey's.

In 1818, following De Quincey's marriage to an illiterate farmer's daughter several months after their son was born, Wordsworth, however much he disapproved of the marriage, helped De Quincey acquire his first paying position at age thirty-three, as editor of *The Westmorland Gazette*. For one year, in spite of opium addiction, mounting debts, and attacks from a rival paper, De Quincey met the relentless weekly deadlines. But he was not attuned to the interests of his rural audience: along with pieces on local dialects and rituals, he published essays on German philosophy, lurid reports of murder trials and sexual abuse, a galvanic experiment on a corpse, and other exotica that he had lifted and occasionally rewrote from the London newspapers. Asked to resign, De Quincey was free to accept John Wilson's invitation to assist him in preparing lectures for his new position as Professor of Moral Philosophy at the University of Edinburgh and to write for *Blackwood's Magazine*. After many promises, and delays, he produced only a trivial essay and an insulting letter to Mr. Blackwood, the owner, describing a recent issue, to which he was supposed to have contributed, as a "dreary collection of dulness and royal stupidity."[20] Although in the quarrel with the *London Magazine* that led to Scott's death, De Quincey had supported *Blackwood's* and encouraged Wilson and Lockhart to retaliate, six months after the infamous duel, De Quincey offered his essay on opium to the new owners of the *London Magazine,* John Taylor and James Hessey, benevolent publishers of the late John Keats.

Pursued by creditors who threatened to imprison him for debt, De Quincey wrote the essay on opium as a fugitive, moving frequently and hiding in the busy coffee-rooms of coach inns around London, so debilitated by opium that he was unable to keep track of his own papers. *The Confessions of an English Opium-Eater,* published in two parts, in September and October of 1821, was immediately successful, reviewed, imitated, and published the following year as a separate volume.[21] The title was appealing and ambiguous, implying both the penitential attitude of religious confession and the lurid exhibitionism of criminal or erotic adventures. This ambiguity permeates the book itself: De Quincey claims both that he is the hero of the book (for having taken more opium than anyone in history and survived to conquer it— an impression he attempted to correct in an appendix to the 1822 edition), and that opium is the "true hero," its "marvelous agency . . . for pleasure or for pain."[22] Such ambiguity reflects the inconsistencies of the addict, which is the real subject of the book: the vacillation, insecurity, and bravado; the self-doubt and arrogance; the ambition and inertia; the defiance and defensiveness; the need to reveal and the fear of exposure; the self-concern and the total absence of self-knowledge; the desire to please and the complete indifference to others. In a piece of personal journalism, one of the first, De Quincey, explicitly but anonymously, reveals the contradictions, self-delusions, and compromises of the addictive personality. The subject was the opium-eater, not the opium; the dreamer, not the dreams.

To modern readers, De Quincey's description of the hallucinogenic experience is familiar: the sense of religious ecstasy, the "apocalypse of the world within," the distortion of time and space, the extreme exhilaration and despair, and the increased sense of creativity, which he overvalues. From one of the few dreams De Quincey does recount, it is difficult to imagine choosing to endure such an experience for he depicts himself as a terrified prisoner in a world populated by everything he feared or found contemptible:

> I was stared at, hooted at, grinned at, chattered at by monkeys, by parrakeets, by cockatoos. I ran into pagodas and was fixed for centuries at the summit or in secret rooms; I was the idol; I was the priest; I was worshiped; I was sacrificed. I fled from the wrath of Brahma through all the forests of Asia; Vishnu hated me; Siva laid wait for me. I came suddenly upon Isis and Osiris; I had done a deed, they said which the ibis and the crocodile trembled at. I was buried for a thousand years, in stone coffins, with mummies and sphinxes, in narrow chambers at the heart of eternal pyramids. I was kissed with cancerous kisses, by croco-

diles and laid, confounded with all unutterable slimy things amongst reeds and Nilotic mud.

But some were "charmed by its terrors": at least six young men were led to kill themselves with overdoses after reading the *Confessions*. Others, such as Thomas Carlyle, were dissuaded from ever taking opium, however common an anodyne for pain.

The success of the *Confessions,* as journalism and as popular literature, indeed the success of De Quincey's most eccentric essays, lay not in their eccentricity but in the core of common experience they represented, the affirmation they gave to aberrations within the private, inward experiences of the most common readers. On a fictional level, the terrors he recounts and his response to them were familiar, part of the commercialization of terror that had been prospering for at least half a century in the popular literature and entertainments on the stage, in novels, magazines, and street literature. Forbidden knowledge, passionate extremes, social alienation, corrupt appetites, unrepentant guilt, and exotic detail drawn from a world of fallen nature were commonplaces on the stage and in such gothic romances as William Beckford's *Vathek* (1786) or Mrs. Ann Radcliffe's *Mysteries of Udolpho* (1794). By 1821, however, when De Quincey published the *Confessions,* the style had been played out, parodied by Thomas Love Peacock in *Nightmare Abbey* (1818) and Jane Austen in *Northanger Abbey* (written 1789, published 1818). De Quincey shifted the interest from the content of the gothic to the nature of the mind that generated it and to which it appealed, its origins in dreams, their origins in personal history and commonplace reality.[23] Wandering the streets of London, or dozing by his fire in Grasmere, De Quincey showed the proximity in the human mind, and in experience as well, between the innocent and the macabre, the normal and the deranged, separated by a moment, by a mere knock on the door as he illustrated throughout his long career, in his essay "On the Knocking on the Gate in *Macbeth*" (1823) and in the Postscript to "On Murder Considered as One of the Fine Arts" (1854).

"On Murder Considered as One of the Fine Arts" was published in the respectable *Blackwood's Magazine* in two parts, the first appearing in 1827, shortly after De Quincey moved to Edinburgh, and the same year as the first murder mystery, *Richmond: Scenes in the Life of a Bow Street Runner.*[24] It parodies the popular fascination with the criminal mind, on which

Dickens was to build a career; the intellectualization of evil, which had preoccupied philosophers, poets, and dramatists throughout the Romantic period; and, on a formal level, the excesses of the public lecture. In a fictional address before the monthly meeting of the Society for the Encouragement of Murder, the detached but informed speaker analyzes the aesthetics, history, and protocol of murder. Treating murder as if it were a painting or poem, De Quincey illustrates how the savage forces of contemporary life can appropriate and destroy the civilized ones. The major target is the speaker, a parody of the urban mentality Wordsworth had predicted as early as 1802 in the Preface to *Lyrical Ballads* where he claimed that the crowding, the conformity, and the sensationalism of the city had served to "blunt the discriminating powers of the mind." Excessive exposure to crime had so desensitized the speaker, so disordered his moral priorities that he objects to murder on the grounds that it leads to worse crimes: robbery, drinking, Sabbath-breaking, and from that to incivility and procrastination, De Quincey's own besetting sin. In his Postscript (1854), De Quincey emphasizes the psychology of crime, describing in chilling detail the thought processes of the victims, the killers, and the spectators to murder.

Similar emphases on personal aberration account for the success of the biographical sketches and recollections he wrote between 1834 and 1840, for *Tait's* magazine in Edinburgh, while taking refuge from his many creditors in the debtor's sanctuary of Holyrood, from which he was allowed to emerge only on Sundays. Over his lifetime, whatever the mayhem within, De Quincey's gentle demeanor, his soft-spoken courtesy, and rather pitiful appearance had given him easy access to a broad range of people including, in his youth, some landed gentry, George III, Hannah More, Mrs. Siddons, Charles Lamb, William Godwin, Sir Humphry Davy, Robert Southey, Coleridge, Wordsworth, and the Carlyles.[25] In his reminiscences, however, he was often brutal, "one of the greatest scoundrels living," according to the genial Robert Southey after reading the four-part reminiscence of the recently deceased Coleridge in which De Quincey identified his plagiarisms and berated him for failings that De Quincey himself shared. In other reminiscences, his early idealization of Wordsworth had declined into accusations of pride, narrow-mindedness, self-involvement, excessive attention to business and insufficient attention to books. Dorothy Wordsworth, of whom he had been very fond, is depicted as awkward and deficient in female accomplishments. He extended this technique even to the formidable Immanuel Kant, whom he described as crude, insensitive to art, and incapable of perspiring—an attribute, De Quincey explained in a characteristically pedantic footnote, he shared with the English poet William Cowper and his own cousin, who supposedly shot himself out of boredom. In the decline of his own fortunes, reputation, even his dignity, De Quincey comforted himself by writing reminiscences and biographical sketches that demonstrated the common flaws of even the most distinguished people, deflating myths and perpetuating personal gossip. He found a receptive audience in the Scottish magazine-reading public whose democratic spirit fostered an irreverance for public figures, especially English and European ones to whom this highly civilized but politically impotent nation had been forced to defer. It was this same public that accepted his simplifications of European philosophy, derivative essays that showed very little understanding of what he read, although De Quincey had prided himself on being a philosopher. And his literary criticism was similarly derivative, mostly from Wordsworth, and had little impact except for his essays on Wordsworth's poetry itself, which he understood and could illustrate with great swatches from the unpublished *Prelude* to which Wordsworth had in better days given him access.[26]

In 1845, a year after the publication of his long-delayed and disappointing *Logic of Political Economy,* paralyzed by depression, struggling with the pains of opium-withdrawal, De Quincey began a series of dream-visions, prose-poems called *Suspiria de Profundis,* "Sighs from the Depths." Intended as a sequel to the *Confessions,* it included his theory of mind as a "palimpsest," an ancient manuscript from which nothing is ever lost, and his myth of suffering in which all the poor, mournful, and dead female figures who had haunted his life are canonized as "Our Ladies of Sorrow." The work was so long, elaborate, mysterious, obscure, and demanding that *Blackwood's* could not publish it as he wished, and De Quincey abandoned it after four installments. Fortunately, he reserved a section called *The English Mail-Coach,* which he published separately in 1849, one of his most original, ranging, and complete works. It starts with the common stuff of magazine essays, an anecdotal memoir of his travels on mail coaches, especially one memorable journey in which a coach bringing news of a victory in the Napoleonic Wars, long past, nearly collided with a small gig containing a young couple: "the turn of the road carried the scene out of my eyes in an

instant and into my dreams forever." Here the journalist
became the dreamer, illustrating in what he called a dream-
fugue, how dreams are an extension, a fulfillment of experi-
ence.[27]

In his final years, De Quincey kept to his room for months
at a time in a chaos of papers while he tried to assemble the
collected edition of his works, published first, starting in 1851,
in America in twenty-one volumes and in England under the
title *Selections Grave and Gay* starting in 1853. In 1856, he
expanded the *Confessions* to fill a volume, still justifying and
dramatizing himself, amplifying the trivial and accidental into
the material of dreams, which never fulfilled their promise.
At age seventy-four, a sickly, lonely, disheveled old man who
had survived his friends, his enemies, his debts, his wife, even
some of his children, De Quincey died in 1859, attended by
two of his daughters, to whom he apologized, and the ghost
of his sister: "Death we can face," he had written in *Suspiria
de Profundis,* "but knowing, as some of us do, what is human
life, which of us is it that without shuddering could (if con-
sciously we were summoned) face the hour of birth?"[28]

Newspapers

During the Romantic period newspapers developed from
a harmless source of information about commerce and trade
for the urban middle class into a powerful weapon for polit-
ical reform identified with the laboring classes.[29] Offering an
easy source of income and immediate access to the largest,
most diverse audience, newspaper journalism attracted force-
ful and talented writers: in the eighteenth century, Swift,
Fielding, Addison, Steele, Defoe, Samuel Johnson, Edmund
Burke, and Oliver Goldsmith had all enhanced their reputa-
tions and their incomes writing for the press. Later, Cole-
ridge, Wordsworth, Southey, and Lamb all contributed to
the *Morning Post,* ably edited between 1795 and 1803 by Dan-
iel Stuart. Wordsworth wrote patriotic sonnets; Coleridge
offered advice, many essays, and early versions of some of
his best verse, including *Dejection: An Ode;* and Lamb wrote
six jokes a day between 5:30 A.M. and breakfast for six pence
each, an experience he describes wryly in "Newspapers Thirty-
Five Years Ago." Fascinated by the potential power of the
press, Coleridge started two newspapers of his own: *The
Watchman* (1796) and *The Friend: A Literary, Moral, and Polit-
ical Paper* (1809–1810) designed to counteract frivolous and
partisan journalism.

Unfortunately, the very power of the press provoked legal restrictions that ultimately inhibited its development. To control the distribution of news, in 1713 the government imposed a stamp tax on paper and another on advertisements, keeping the price of newspapers up, the size and circulation down. A hundred years later, in 1815, during the post-war unrest, the tax went as high as four pence on every publication appearing more frequently than twenty-six days, printed on two sheets (four pages), and offering news of a political nature. Consequently, an average daily newspaper such as the *Times* cost a forbidding seven and a half pence. Newspapers were shared, borrowed, rented, then sold in the provinces several weeks or even months later at a discount.

The government also tried to restrict the sources of information: reporters were excluded from Parliament until 1771, prevented from taking notes until 1783, and thereafter periodically excluded from the gallery. Finally, after 1792, a series of acts against "criminal and seditious" writings turned journalism into a hazardous occupation. All editors and printers were required to register and identify themselves, and any criticism of the King or government was considered treason, punishable by imprisonment or, on second offense, up to seven years transportation. While many were arrested, few were convicted, and political dialogue moved from newspapers to pamphlets, for which responsibility was difficult to assign. Nonetheless, newspaper circulation soared: the *Times* alone had a daily circulation of 5,000 and the evening *Courier,* edited by Stuart, ran from 10,000 to 16,000 as the public awaited news of the war. In fact, during the war years from 1793 to 1815, the public became addicted to news; to overcome the government's monopoly on information, editors became increasingly resourceful in providing it. In 1802, the *Times* appointed its first foreign correspondent, Henry Crabb Robinson, who later became the unofficial diarist of his generation. Eventually, as these reporters became more adept, the government began to depend on the press for information and intercepted packets sent by journalists from the battlefields. "The Newspapers must be a powerful political engine," Southey observed in *Letters from England,*

> The ministry have always the greatest number under their direction, in which all their measures are defended, their successes exaggerated, their disasters concealed or palliated, and the most flattering prospects constantly held out to the people. . . . The English have a marvellous faculty of believing what they wish, and nothing else. . . . A staunch ministerialist believes every-

thing which his newspaper tells him, and takes his information and his opinions with the utmost confidence from a paragraph-writer, who is paid for falsifying the one and misleading the other. (p. 343)

While there were some corrupt editors who were willing to repress news in exchange for money or favors, on the whole newspapers were increasingly independent and developing professional standards of journalism. In spite of the legal harassment, freedom of the press was becoming a reality rather than verbal ideal. Under Thomas Barnes, appointed editor in 1817, the *Times* developed that anonymous and authoritative voice on which statesmen came to depend. The press created a community, a community based on information and opinion as well as class and economic status. Such a community was essential to a representative government, for it engaged the entire literate population in political life.

In appearance, most daily papers tended to reflect their origins in such eighteenth-century publications as "The Public Ledger, a Daily Register of Commerce and Intelligence" (1760), consisting largely of gossip, scandal, advertisements, and letters from correspondents in place of paid journalists. At the turn of the century an average newspaper such as the *Morning Chronicle* or the *Times* offered a page of foreign news and one of domestic, advertisements for books, concerts, theater programs, patent medicines, real estate, domestic help, horses, dressmakers, schools, a variety of merchandise, shipping news and stock reports, marriage, birth, and death notices. However the advertisements appeared to trivialize newspapers, they revealed contemporary interests, knowledge, and productivity. As Southey astutely observed, "the miscellaneous contents are truly characteristic of the freedom and the follies of this extraordinary people" (p. 343).

The weekly radical press, surviving on sales alone, exhibited an astonishing growth during this period and an enviable rapport with its readers.[30] The talented and industrious editors of the radical or "pauper" press such as James Montgomery, the popular poet who edited the *Sheffield Iris,* Thomas Wooler of the *Black Dwarf,* William Hone of the *Register,* and William Cobbett shared most of the practical and political problems of their audiences, wrote most if not all of the material themselves, and, audaciously tested the libel laws, willingly going to jail after colorful trials in which their offenses were read into the record, thereby finding their way into the legitimate press where they were then sanctioned by law. Here was a new breed of writer, self-made and opinionated, best represented by William Cobbett.[31]

William Cobbett

Cobbett was certainly the most visible if not the most talented journalist of the age, "unquestionably," Hazlitt wrote in *Spirit of the Age,* "the most powerful political writer of the present day . . . one of the best writers in the language." Politically, he was a member of the permanent opposition, at war with systems, institutions, "The Thing," as he called them collectively—organized religion, public education, poor laws, libel actions, taxes, and paper money—systems that originated in response to some kind of social need, provided a public service, acquired a life of their own, grew remote from the people they were designed to serve, and finally exploited and enslaved them. He lost the first of many battles with the "Thing" when he exposed the dishonesty of his superior officers in the army, in which he served from 1784 to 1791. His life endangered, he fled, first, to France with his new bride, Ann Reid, then, in 1793, to America, where for the next seven years as teacher, bookseller, pamphleteer, and journalist writing under the name of "Peter Porcupine" he advanced his unlikely position as a British loyalist in favor of slavery and against the French Revolution. After losing a libel suit to the distinguished Dr. Benjamin Rush, whom he had accused of fraud, he returned to England in 1802, and founded *Cobbett's Weekly Political Register* which he edited through eighty-eight volumes until his death in 1835.

In England, Cobbett's position was an anachronism. In spite of impressive evidence to the contrary, he passionately believed in the rural paradise he recollected from his childhood as a ploughboy: "In the whole world there was not so happy a country as England was. In the reading of our books and in the hearing of verbal descriptions of cottages in England; of the industry, the neatness, the order and the regularity of those dwellings of our labourers, the people of other countries think they are listeners to romances. . . . The labourers were happy. Each had his little home. He had things about him worth possessing and worth preserving . . ." (*PR,* July 26, 1817). By merely standing still, Cobbett turned from a patriot and constitutionalist to a radical, a fugitive, and a representative of reform, tenaciously clinging to the principles from which even the government itself had defected.

After serving a term in Newgate for writing against flogging in the army, a term in a comfortable cell from which he continued to publish the *Political Register* and entertain political sympathizers, he started the *2d Register,* in which he tried to educate the working classes to seek redress through petition rather than their customary rioting, a service that some say helped avert the violent revolution that Englishmen feared.[32] Supporting such popular causes as freedom of the press, universal suffrage, and Parliamentary reform, he was again threatened with imprisonment. He chose instead to exile himself again to America, where he wrote what some consider his most important work, the *Grammar of the English Language,* designed to help the poor teach themselves to read. Returning to England in 1819, with the bones of Tom Paine (an atheist in political exile, he had been buried in unconsecrated ground), Cobbett spent the next ten years trying repeatedly to be elected to Parliament while writing some of his best works, notably the series of essays *Rural Rides* (begun in 1821 and collected in 1830) depicting his journeys on horseback about the English countryside, a fond and careful record of the landscape and the people, the customs and rituals of a moribund agrarian world. As a counselor to these country people, he published *The Farmer's Friend* (1822), *Cottage Economy* (1821–1822), *The Poor Man's Friend* (1826), *Advice to Young Men and (incidentally) to Young Women, in the Middle and Higher Ranks of Life* (1829), partly political but mostly practical guides to such diverse activities as growing herbs, healing sick animals, brewing ale, keeping a budget, and choosing a mate. His *History of the Protestant Reformation in England and Ireland* (1826–27) analyzes on a high intellectual level what he considered to have been the beginning of England's decline.

Elected to the first reform Parliament in 1832, he served until his death in 1835, agitating with little success for reforms that in effect would have reversed the order of history and restored the idealized England of his youth. Although his political career seems mercurial, Cobbett was in fact consistently dedicated to a few simple propositions: that laborers were "the superior race," that they should be made happy, that they could be made happy if they had "a full belly," and that they would be made happy if they had the practical knowledge and self-esteem that he claimed it was his greatest delight as a writer to impart. Through a rare reconciliation of roles as farmer, politician, journalist, teacher, businessman, and father, he created a model of a new man of letters, offering his audience a symbol of their best selves. His achievement is better understood when set against those who challenged his claims to the reading public, a reading public he had himself created, the challenge of those "stupid," "malignant," and "roguish" Religious Tracts which in Cobbett's eyes subverted everything in which he believed: the "millions of 'Tracts, Moral and Religious' for the purpose of keeping the poor from cutting the throats of the rich. . . . Now we had a busy creature or two in every village, dancing about with 'Tracts' for the benefit of the souls of the labourers and their families."[33]

Religious Tracts: Hannah More

However little literary or intellectual merit the religious tracts exhibited, they were the single most influential form of publication in England at the opening of the nineteenth century.[34] The combined circulation was astronomical: from over 300,000 in 1804 to over 10,000,000 in 1824, each copy shared by several people. The impetus was political: when the second part of Tom Paine's *The Rights of Man* appeared in a six-penny version in 1793, capturing the volatile lower-class reading public, the government responded with a series of censorship laws against seditious or inflammatory writings, the laws under which Cobbett and Hunt were tried, and subsidized the publication of propaganda by such distinguished figures as the agriculturalist Arthur Young and the theologian William Paley. They attacked the idea of political equality as contrary to nature and commended the pleasures to be found in poverty. Using dialogue and the logic peculiar to this reactionary movement, Mrs. Hannah More, the "Bishop in Petticoats," as Cobbett called her, wrote a popular and lively pamphlet: "Village Politics, Addressed to all Mechanics, Journeymen, and Labourers in Great Britain. By Will Chip, a Country Carpenter," written "to counteract the pernicious doctrines which, owing to the French revolution, were then seriously alarming to the friends of religion and government in every part of Europe." Mrs. More's religious affiliation was Evangelical, an energetic sect within the Anglican church dedicated to social action, moral reform, religious revival, and political stability. However admirable their intentions, the Evangelicals, especially Mrs. More, had been accused of making the lower classes susceptible to the influence of such infidels as Paine by teaching them to read in Sunday schools. Believing, however, that the poor were susceptible not because they could read (since they actually didn't read very well anyway and never learned to write) but because they lacked appropriate reading matter, the Evangelicals encouraged Mrs. More to publish material that would counteract the seditious writings of the political radicals as well as the penny chapbooks and ballads to which they attributed the loose habits and assorted vices they saw among the poor.

In many ways Hannah More (1745–1823) was an ideal figure to direct this project. The youngest of five daughters of a provincial schoolmaster, she was educated to be an accomplished middle-class lady. At age twenty-nine, equipped with a small annuity from a suitor who was reluctant to marry, she moved to London where her charm, wit, and intelligence qualified her as a Blue Stocking, a term describing a group of literary ladies renowned for their stimulating conversation. In the company of Samuel Johnson, Horace Walpole, Sir Joshua Reynolds, and David Garrick, actor and manager of the Drury Lane Theater, Mrs. More blossomed. She was inspired to write several plays, successful ones centering on the conflict between duty and passion, some fashionable poetry, and, later, a moralistic novel, *Coelebs in Search of a Wife* (1808). At age forty-four, having become an ardent philanthropist, she retired to Cowslip Green near Bristol to organize along with her sister, who had been managing a fashionable girls' boarding school, a series of schools and, in exchange for assistance, agreed to write the Cheap Repository Tracts, her most successful venture and perhaps the most successful publishing venture of all time.

Enthusiastic promotion by ministers, schoolmasters, neighborhood volunteers, booksellers, and pedlars accounted for the 2,000,000 copies of monthly installments sold by the second year of publication. They were sold at fairs and on London street corners by barrow-men along with hot tea and rental newspapers, and donated to jails, hospitals, and churches. Along with aggressive marketing, Mrs. More's shrewd sense of audience, her recognition that the devices of popular literature, the ballads, sentimental narratives, and parables offered by simple characters in simple language with which readers identified were more engaging and therefore more effective than sermons and homilies, accounts for the success of the tracts. *Betty Brown, the St. Giles Orange Girl; Tom White, the Post-Boy; A Cure for Melancholy: Shewing the Way to Do Much Good with Little Money,* among others, provided manuals of conduct, exemplary tales on how to live virtuously in an age in which traditional roles, the duties and manners associated with them, had begun to disintegrate without new models to replace them. Not only did Mrs. More promote the usual virtues of industry, thrift, piety, humility, patience, and cheer, but she also instructed the poor on how to get by in a world that dispensed its rewards with an unequal, often arbitrary hand, how to resist temptation, and how to avoid being cheated. While helping to create a reading public among the lower classes, she offered a moving presentation of life among the poor, teaching the middle classes, as Wordsworth was to say, that "men who do not wear fine cloaths can feel deeply" (*EY*, p. 263).[35]

Hannah More stopped writing the Cheap Repository Tracts in 1798, and the Religious Tracts Society, founded in 1799, attempted to continue her role as provider of cheap but safe reading matter for the lower classes. They produced conventional tales about repentant sinners, urging their readers to abandon sloth, prostitution, and drink, and to observe the Sabbath. Every town or village, as Cobbet complained, had a society to distribute tracts from door to door along with sententious comments on life among the poor. Aided by the British and Foreign Bible Society, founded in 1804, they managed by the end of the century to place a Bible in every British home and to distribute them all over the world in 152 languages and dialects.

Whatever social good they may have achieved, the religious tracts had an unfortunate influence upon the preferences of readers and writers alike during the Romantic period. Primarily, they created an artificial distinction between piety and intellect, between religious belief and the literary imagination. These distinctions contributed to a curious displacement of imaginative literature at the very time when the economic and technical means had become available for supporting a creative revival. Children's literature, another successful publishing industry to develop during this period, reveals the influence of the religious tracts, particularly the dichotomy between the moral and imaginative life, and anticipates certain preferences of the adult middle-class reading public for whom children's literature had served the same function that the tracts served for the working classes.

CHAPTER III

Children's Literature
and Education

The Didactic Background

As early as 1693, in *Some Thoughts Concerning Education,* John Locke claimed that children required different reading materials from adults, that young minds needed something more agreeable than the macabre tales of suffering from John Foxe's *Book of Martyrs* (1563), the austerities of *Pilgrim's Progress* (1676), the cautionary tales in *Aesop's Fables* (first published in England by Caxton, 1485), and the dismal *Exact Account of the Conversion . . . and Joyful Deaths of Several Young Children* from the expanded title of James Janeway's otherwise innocuous sounding *Token for Children* (1671). But Locke's concept of pleasant reading specifically excluded what we normally consider to be the very essence of children's literature: fairy tales, adventures, romances, tales of magic, and nursery rhymes, all of which he considered diversions from the main object of juvenile reading: to accommodate to the world of experience, to learn to deal with the concrete problems that it presented.[1] Consequently, such otherwise adult books as Defoe's *Robinson Crusoe* (1719), and Swift's *Gulliver's Travels* (1726), enjoyed a curious double life in adaptations for children while the tales of Mother Goose, translated in 1719 from the *Contes de ma Mère L'Oye* (1696) by Charles Perrault, were considered decadent and circulated surreptitiously as chapbooks.[2] Given their sources in the aristocratic nurseries and ladies' salons at the bawdy court of Louis XIV, "Sleeping Beauty," "Little Red Riding Hood," "Blue

Beard," "Puss-in-Boots," and "Cinderella" may well have sexual implications that would have been alarming to the English middle classes and their norms of juvenile decorum. But, they were more threatened by that other great body of imported French fantasy, *The Arabian Nights,* translated in 1708 from the Oriental tales of Antoine Galland, for here such social misfits as Sinbad the Sailor and Aladdin acquired worldly success by luck or a magic lamp rather than the industry, self-discipline, piety, and breeding which the English preferred their children to value. It was not, however, the social models or economic goals that attracted children to these tales. Rather, in the exotic atmosphere of the *Arabian Nights* and even in such native adventures as "Jack the Giant Killer," "Tom Thumb," and "Guy of Warwick," children found the supernatural dimension which was otherwise disappearing from their experience. In penny chapbooks sold by pedlars or "running stationers," the tales provided examples of the unpredictable, the inexplicable things on which young imaginations feed and grow. However disreputable this literature, hardly a writer of the Romantic period failed to acknowledge his debt to the romances and tales. It was just these tales, for example, that fascinated the young Coleridge and haunted him. Recalling that his father had burned his copy of *Arabian Nights,* Coleridge claimed it had helped him become "habituated *to the Vast"* and that he knew of "no other way of giving the mind a love of 'the Great' & the Whole" (*CL,* I, 347).

Conventionally, English children's literature in the eighteenth century was not imaginative, but useful, exemplary, and moralistic. The trend was set by amiable John Newbery, who, trading under the sign of the Bible and Sun in St. Paul's churchyard, offered along with Dr. James's powders and other patent medicines the first publication designed specifically for children: embossed and gilded volumes at six pence each containing an assortment of things invariably described as pretty or useful, such as "pretty rhymes" of "Nurse Truelove," histories of places, natural history, mathematics, science, and that first piece of English juvenile fiction, *The History of Little Goody Two-Shoes* (1766), its blatantly commercial morality condensed in the subtitle: "otherwise called Mrs. Margery Two-Shoes, with the Means by which she acquired her learning and Wisdom, and in consequence thereof her Estate. . . ." Newbery was immensely successful, proving that publishing children's literature was an important and profitable activity. A generous and kindly man, Newbery's influence was incalculable: many writers, such as Robert Southey, attribute the awakening of their interest in literature to reading Newbery books as children.

In the latter half of the eighteenth century, children's literature was dominated by a group of pious and industrious women who collectively set out to raise a generation of docile, self-disciplined, moralistic, and informed children. The most successful of these were Mrs. Barbauld (1743–1825) and Mrs. Sarah Trimmer (1741–1810), about whom Lamb complained to his friend Coleridge: "Mrs. Barbauld['s] stuff has banished all the old classics of the nursery. . . . Mrs. B's and Mrs. Trimmer's nonsense lay in piles about.—Is there no possibility of averting this sore evil? Think what you would have been now, if instead of being fed with Tales and old wives' fables in childhood you have been crammed with Geography and Natural History? *Damn them.* I mean the cursed Barbauld Crew, those *Blights and Blasts* of all that is *Human* in man and child.—" (*Letters,* II, 81–82). An elegant and fashionable lady, Mrs. Barbauld collaborated with her brother John Aiken, editor of the *Monthly Review,* in publishing verse and prose designed originally to educate her adopted son, Charles.[3] The *Easy Lessons for Children* (1760), *Hymns in Prose for Children* (1781), and *Evening at Home* (1792) were informative and good-natured conversational pieces offering, through a dialogue between a mother and child, basic information about the world of commonplace things.

Mrs. Trimmer, on the other hand, was a tireless woman with a number of causes: twelve children whose education she chose to supervise; a religious dedication that inspired her through six ponderous volumes of *Sacred History for Children* (1782–1784); and a commitment to charitable education, particularly the Sunday school movement. Recognizing the value of the developing periodical press, she founded the first children's magazines and magazines for domestic reading. She is best remembered for her own *Fabulous Histories Designed for the Instruction of Children Respecting their Treatment of Animals* (1786), later issued as *The History of the Robins,* featuring those talky and endearing feathered lecturers on natural history and moral virtue, Robin Jr., Dicksy, Flopsy, and Pecksy, who, Mrs. Trimmer assures her readers in the preface, were animated merely for the sake of the tale: "consider them, not as . . . the real conversation of birds (for that is impossible we should ever understand), but as a series of Fables intended to convey moral instruction applicable to themselves, at the same time that they excite compassion and tenderness for those interesting and delightful creatures, on which such wanton cruelties are frequently inflicted, and recommend *universal benevolence.*" Through the *Guardian of Education,* a family magazine she began publishing in 1803, she convinced a considerable audience of middle-class families and their servants to avoid the literature of fantasy, for it was personally corrupting and undermined public authority. She assailed works ranging from "Cinderella" to the otherwise respectable *Robinson Crusoe* as pernicious, misrepresenting the grim uncertainties of "real life" to which young people should become reconciled before reading fiction.[4]

A number of other women worked in this narrow and largely unimaginative genre of domestic instruction. For profit, Joseph Johnson urged Mary Wollstonecraft to write *Original Stories from Real Life with Conversations Calculated to Regulate the Affections and Form the Mind to Truth and Goodness* first published in 1788, and illustrated by William Blake in the second edition of 1791. According to a modern critic, Geoffrey Summerfield, it has "a strong claim to be the most sinister, ugly, overbearing book for children ever published" (p. 229), as "grim, humourless, tyrannical" as its heroine, Mrs. Mason, whose task it is to "regulate the appetites" of her two charges, to control any impulsive and irrational behavior in favor of reason and the denial of feeling. Mary Butt Sherwood (1775–1851) wrote *The Fairchild Family,* which appeared in installments from 1818 to 1847, to console herself after the death of her two children in India, where her husband had been stationed with the army. Like the others, her conversational tales were designed for domestic discussion focusing on problems of family authority and social relationships. But her preoccupation with crime, punishment, death, and damnation, and the macabre incidents she used to illustrate them— a visit to a neighborhood garden, for example, where the owner's corpse was still hanging in the place where he had murdered his brother—placed her in what retrospectively appears to be a juvenile gothic tradition, although at the time the motivation was intensely religious.

Rousseau and His Influence

This aversion to fantasy, this anti–intellectualism shared by the community of factual and moralistic English female writers, acquired a philosophical dimension in the writings of Jean Jacques Rousseau (1712–78). Rousseau, who lost his mother at birth and was abandoned by his father, spent most of his life as an emotional and intellectual orphan as well, forced by circumstances to invent himself or, better, to invent a world in which someone like himself could be happy and esteemed, an invention he accomplished through a series of books including *La Nouvelle Héloise* (1761), a novel representing the ideal society; *Émile* (1762), a novel representing the ideal education; *The Social Contract* (1762), a treatise explaining the philosophical basis of democracy; and the *Confessions* (1765–1770), an autobiography of his psychological development. All these works share a vision of the unique individual, born free of sin, free from all social and material commitments, developing in harmony with nature, and cultivating his feelings as a guide to virtue. In *Émile,* specifically (trans. 1763), he presents a child raised in a secluded, culturally antiseptic but natural environment, where, with the aid of a non-directive tutor, he discovers everything he had to know by merely following his native reason and instincts. After age twelve, he is permitted to read one book—*Robinson Crusoe.*

For those who believed in egalitarianism, in the values of resourcefulness, curiosity, spontaneity, instinct, common sense, and who could somehow evade the pressures of conventional domestic life, Rousseau's *Émile* offered an immensely attractive model, one that some resourceful English parents attempted to apply with mixed consequences. On the one hand, there was Thomas Malthus, who overcame his Rousseauistic education sufficiently to articulate one of the most powerful and rigorous social theories of the nineteenth century; on the other hand, there was Richard Lovell Edgeworth, who raised his son according to a mechanical version of Rousseau's theories, then, after observing young Richard in conversation with Rousseau himself during a trip to Paris, complained that he was a charming but boorish and provincial lout.[5] Richard's education was completed by a series of conventional tutors, but the damage was irremediable: he had failed to acquire the basic information about the world he lived in—history, philosophy, language, aesthetics, the human achievements of Western civilization—and the social skills necessary to function in it. He died at age thirty-two in America, where he had been trying to become a farmer.

Edgeworth's friend, Thomas Day (1748–1789), had no better luck in his experiments, but, aside from his £1,000 annuity and classical education, he wasn't well favored in anything. Repeatedly rejected as a suitor, this humorless, slovenly, eccentric, ill-mannered, and solitary man selected two foundlings to educate as what he thought would be ideal wives, following a modified and austere version of Rousseau.

His goal had been to combine in a woman both "purity" and "fortitude," to raise a woman who had no regard for fashion or manners and no interest whatsoever in such trivial pleasures as dancing or clothes. He renamed his foundlings Sabrina and Lucretia and took them to France where, isolated from society, he could have complete control over them. They quarrelled constantly and contracted smallpox. After the first year, Lucretia was sent to London, to be apprenticed to a milliner, and Sabrina became the sole object of his attention. Failing to develop her tolerance for pain and discomfort by dropping hot sealing wax on her arm or firing off pistols by her ear, he turned her over to the care of Anna Seward, a poetess known as the "Swan of Litchfield." Having rejected both his wards, he married an heiress, and died after being thrown from a horse which he had been trying to train according to a contemporary theory of equine benevolence. He did, however, write *Sandford and Merton* (1783–1789), a book adapting Rousseau's theory to a rural English community. Harry Sandford, a courageous, industrious, and benevolent farmer's son, serves as a model for Tommy Merton, the rich, foolish son of a retired Jamaican planter, the transference of virtue mediated by their tutor, the inevitable clergyman, Mr. Barlow. In spite of the social paradigm of downward mobility, in spite of such unlikely scenes as the cheeky Sandford's lecturing his host, Merton's father, on the extravagance of the dinner they have just eaten (recommending that they emulate the animals by living on herbs and water), in spite of the deflating moral that it is better to be "useful than rich or fine," "more amiable to be good than great"— according to Sandford at any rate—most middle-class readers enjoyed it and kept it popular well into the nineteenth century. Charles Dickens complained about that "hypocritical young prig," Sandford, and the rest of the baggage that was supposed to be a substitute for the dangers of fantasy: "What right had [Mr. Barlow] to bore his way into my Arabian Nights? Yet he did. He was always hinting doubts of the veracity of Sinbad the Sailor. If he could have got hold of the Wonder Lamp, I know he would have trimmed it and lighted it, and delivered a lecture over it on the qualities of sperm oil, with a glance at the whale fisheries."[6]

Maria Edgeworth

The most talented author of children's literature, Maria Edgeworth (1767–1849), Richard Lovell Edgeworth's second eldest child, inherited her father's predilection for the rational and experimental, his self-confidence, and his verbal skill, escaping the effects of most of the zany educational theories that had destroyed her brother—although, as a child, she was hanged from ropes and pulleys in the misguided belief that such a ritual would make her taller.[7] At age fifteen, she joined her father on his estate in Ireland, Edgeworthtown, where she spent the rest of her life assisting him with his finances, his schemes for improving the land, and the education of his twenty other children (by four wives).

In 1798, she collaborated with her father in writing *Practical Education,* the most important work on educating children since Locke's over a century earlier. Basically utilitarians, they argued that pleasure rather than fear is the best motive for learning, that an environment contrived to stimulate curiosity and reduce frustration is more important than overt teaching and discipline, that the ideal goal is a cheerful and receptive child, an industrious, dutiful, and above all, useful adult. To amplify the theory, Miss Edgeworth published a series of tales: *The Parent's Assistant* in three volumes in 1798, and six in 1800; *Moral Tales,* and ten volumes of *Early Lessons* in 1801. While she shared the preoccupation with social order, moral rectitude, and factual information that characterized the juvenile fiction of her contemporaries, Miss Edgeworth's work is distinguished by the authentic and lively, though not necessarily likable, children who populated her tales, children fashioned after her many siblings, for whom the tales were written. In stories such as "The Purple Jar," "Lazy Lawrence," and "Simple Susan," children learned that life is a series of transactions for which prudence, honesty, self-discipline, and foresight are the major requisites; they learned that virtue is its own reward, that most mischief is attributable to poor judgment rather than original sin, and that foolish decisions lead to humiliating consequences.

The Edgeworth system, with its emphasis on using the world as a source of useful information, totally altered the character of teaching within a generation and made enormous demands on teachers, with whom Charles Lamb commiserates in his essay, "The Old and the New Schoolmaster":

> The modern schoolmaster is expected to know a little of everything, because his pupil is required not to be entirely ignorant of anything. He must be superficially, if I may so say, omniscient. He is to know something of pneumatics; of chemistry; of whatever is curious, or proper to excite the attention of the youthful mind; an insight into mechanics is desirable, with a touch of sta-

tistics; the quality of soils, etc., botany, the constitution of his country, *cum multis aliis.* . . .

All these things—these, or the desire of them—he is expected to instil, not by set lessons from professors, which he may charge in the bill, but at school-intervals, as he walks the streets, or saunters through green fields (those natural instructors), with his pupils. The least part of what is expected from him, is to be done in school-hours. . . . He must seize every occasion—the season of the year—the time of the day—a passing cloud—a rainbow—a waggon of hay—a regiment of soldiers going by—to inculcate something useful. He can receive no pleasure from a casual glimpse of Nature, but must catch at it as the object of instruction.

Although they were the models and heroes of this generation, Maria Edgeworth's Harry, and Lucy, and Rosamond, and Frank, and the rest of them were not the source of her literary reputation as "one of the Wonders of our age," as Sir Walter Scott called her, acknowledging his debt in the Waverly novels. Rather, in *Castle Rackrent* (1800) she had originated the family saga, the regional novel recording the decline of a family over several generations narrated by the "faithful" steward, Thady Quirk, whose son had acquired all the master's property. Her concern with the commonplace, with the authentic voice, with the terrestial life that had limited her juvenile writing, became the strength of her adult fiction. But more than local color, she offered a modern notion of character as limited by time, place, experience, and family origins or genetic accident. The gods, fates, and other assorted supernatural agencies whose special function it had been to control individual destiny became for Maria Edgeworth, as it did for the entire generation of Romantic writers, embodied in circumstances and environment. Miss Edgeworth is clearly a part of the same social and philosophical revolution as Bentham, whose work she admired, and as Darwin, Marx, and Freud, all of whom envisioned human beings surviving more or less well if they could arrive at a productive truce with the laws of history or nature. Even her novels, then, demonstrate the value of knowledge and work, specifically knowledge of the legitimate expectations one could have of oneself or the world, carefully avoiding, as she wrote in the Preface to *Parent's Assistant,* "inflaming the imagination, or exciting restless spirit of adventure, by exhibiting false views of life, and creating hopes, which, in the ordinary course of things, cannot be realized." While Maria Edgeworth wrote many novels of importance to her contemporaries—*Belinda* (1801), *Tales from Fashionable Life* (1809, 1812), *Harrington* and

Ormond (1817), and *Patronage* (1814), included in the ten volumes of her collected works—novels that may have departed from the landscape and society that she knew best, she never stepped beyond those parameters of possibility that define the Edgeworth character. And while she may have made intelligence and literacy respectable in children's literature, she left it as barren of imaginative life and fantasy as she found it, perhaps in fact, because of her preference for the useful over the moral, even more barren.

There is little indication even among the Edgeworths that the system worked. While Coleridge recommended that his children learn to read from *Practical Education,* he admits hearing that the Edgeworths were "most miserable when children." Like Julie and Maria Bertram in Chapter II of Jane Austen's *Mansfield Park,* children educated according to this system could be identified by their accumulation of unrelated factual knowledge, their peculiar insensitivity to themselves and others. Although the Bertram's cousin Fanny could "read, work, and write," the girls found her "prodigiously stupid" and complained that she could not "put the map of Europe together," or "tell the principal rivers in Russia," or "the difference between water-colours and crayons!" They, on the other hand, could repeat "the chronological order of the kings of England," "the Roman emperors . . . a great deal of the Heathen Mythology and all the Metals, semi-Metals, Planets, and distinguished philosophers."

Educational Systems

Some domestic academies had better resources than others, such as the one Southey supervised for his and Coleridge's children at Greta Hall, where the teaching was conducted by Mrs. Coleridge, her sister, Mrs. Southey, and two doting aunties. Using Southey's rich library, they managed to teach not only arithmetic and writing, but also English, Latin, Greek, Italian, French, and Spanish, while finding time for long daily walks through the countryside. Local dame schools (informal classes run by women) supplemented such teaching, or local tutors, often clergymen, who prepared boys for a grammar or public school, leading, if they chose, to the university. Wordsworth, for example, initially taught to read by his father, whose library included Spenser, Shakespeare, Milton, Fielding, and a volume of the *Arabian Nights* (which he preferred to *Sandford and Merton*), attended a dame school in Penrith, then Hawkshead Grammar School, an endowed school founded in 1585, one that was so successful in preparing the children in classics and mathematics for a university education that they came from all over Great Britain, even Edinburgh, to attend. Not all were so fortunate. For example, although his schoolmates were amiable and corporeal punishment abandoned, De Quincey reports in *The Confessions of an English Opium-Eater* that he ran away from the Manchester Grammar School because the headmaster allowed no exercise, which he believed would improve his health. At Christ's Hospital, an endowed charity school, attended at various times by Charles Lamb, Coleridge, and Leigh Hunt, the children were threatened by savage discipline, according to Lamb in his essay "Christ's Hospital Five and Thirty Years Ago," including public whipping, dungeons, fetters, flogging, and deprivation. They studied scripture, math, Latin, penmanship, and composition, the latter directed by Reverend James Bowyer, a sadistic tyrant of a man who, according to Coleridge in the *Biographia Literaria,* "showed no mercy to phrase, metaphor, or image unsupported by a sound sense," and often tore up a whole week of compositions before the boys' eyes (pp. 3–4). Shelley, like most gentry, suffered more from his classmates than his teachers; he was tormented at Syon House Academy for his effeminate manners, and again at Eton for preferring reading and science over athletics. The Dissenting academies and others based on enlightened and liberal philosophies such as Enfield, attended by John Keats and his brothers, attracted students who, disqualified by religion from attending universities, enjoyed an innovative curriculum. Keats, for example, learned to read French fluently, studied science, math, and Latin, and cultivated a garden plot that John Clarke, the humane headmaster, allocated to the boys for their hobbies. But most schools were run as a source of income and taught by people who could do nothing else. Charles Dickens's mother, for example, set up a school in 1822 to educate the children of English soldiers and civil servants stationed in India. Aside from having taught her own children how to read, she had nothing to offer but an acceptable address. Many children, then, learned to read, but not necessarily to understand or to write.

With no regulations for certifying teachers, for accrediting schools, for establishing curricula, or for measuring achievements, the education of children was chaotic and wasteful, available to the wealthy and to paupers on Sundays, but to very few other children at any other time.[8] For over a hundred years before the passage of the 1870 National Education Acts, social reformers debated the advantages of education, opinion being divided not only on how to educate children but on whether it was a good thing to do at all. In 1776, Adam Smith had appealed in *The Wealth of Nations* for state supported education to help protect the working classes from superstition and the torpor of factory work, while Robert Raikes started the Sunday school movement in 1780, believing that ignorance was the major cause of crime, and Tom Paine, a radical and atheist, advocated schooling in 1794 in the *Rights of Man* to secure political equality. In *An Enquiry Concerning Political Justice* (1793), William Godwin advocated an education that would help bring all people to their full potential for happiness, virtue, and freedom, but insisted that it be kept out of government control, while his adversary, Thomas Malthus, in his *Essay on Population* (1798), argued that the government should educate the people, especially the poor people, to make them self-supporting and reduce their dependence on religious and public charity. In *Chrestomathia* (1815) Bentham similarly proposed a national and secular education confined to useful learning, the goal being happier, more productive, and useful citizens. But government officials, who would be in charge of such a system, feared that literacy would make people unhappy with their lives and contribute to civil unrest. And Wordsworth thought "a Government which for twenty years resisted the abolition of the Slave Trade; and annually debauches the morals of the people" with such devices as "distilleries and Lotteries" (*MY*, p. 251) especially unfit to conduct education.

Moreover, many, like Wordsworth, recognized that the population was too diverse for a single educational system. A diversity Wordsworth implicitly preferred: "Heaven and Hell" he wrote, "are scarcely more different from each other than Sheffield and Manchester, etc. differ from the plains and Vallies of Surrey, Essex, Cumberland, or Westmoreland. We have mighty Cities and Towns of all sizes, with Villages and Cottages scattered everywhere. We are Mariners, Miners, Manufacturers in tens of thousands: Traders, Husbandmen, everything. What form of discipline, what Books or Doctrines, I will not say would equally suit all these; but which, if happily fitted for one, would not perhaps be an absolute nuisance in another" (*MY*, p. 250). Nonetheless, by 1815, in a footnote to a passage in *The Excursion* on the necessity of a national education (IX, 293–302), Wordsworth endorsed the system devised by Dr. Andrew Bell (1753–1832) while he was teaching Indian orphans and the children abandoned by

British fathers at the Military Male Asylum in Madras. In 1797, two years after returning to England, Bell had published *An Experiment in Education,* describing the advantages of using students as teachers or monitors to improve the learning process, and thus create inexpensively a large number of literate and self-reliant people. He improved the teaching of writing by introducing a syllabic method still used and overcame the shortage and expense of paper by teaching children to write on a slate covered with dry sand. While he allowed the children to impose their own discipline, he emphasized rewards over punishments, believing that happy children learned more readily.

Bell's system, "the Steam Engine of the Moral World," as he called it, appealed to an industrializing country, for it adapted to the classroom the model for mass production, cooperation, and division of labor that had accounted for the success of manufacturing. It was, perhaps, the only system possible for educating an entire population without enough teachers to do it. Mrs. Trimmer wrote a pamphlet in defense of Bell, and the hierarchy of the Church, recognizing a means of competing with the Dissenters' Sunday school movement, encouraged him as well. Southey liked the individualism and the humanity of the system. He explained it in *The Origin and Nature and Object of the New System of Education* and brought Dr. Bell to Grasmere to meet Wordsworth. Bell visited the school where Wordsworth's sons were enrolled, and hired the schoolmaster for one of his own schools, leaving Wordsworth, his sister Dorothy, and wife Mary to teach the children. Nonetheless, Dorothy befriended him and helped him revise his pamphlets for publication.[9]

But Bell was not the only one to develop a cooperative system. It had been used in a number of grammar schools, in Robert Raikes's Sunday schools, in prison schools, and by an odd but talented Quaker, Joseph Lancaster (1778–1838). A splendid teacher, he attracted more students than he could instruct, and, lacking funds to hire an assistant, he instituted the system that he described, genuinely believing it original, as *Improvements in Education* (1803). According to his system, instead of merely revising teaching methods in existing schools, he would found whole new schools accommodating about 1,000 students each. They were to be staffed by one hundred monitors supervising squads of ten students at the cost of five shillings per head per year. With so many children being supervised by inexperienced tutors, an especially strict code of behavior was required; transgressions were punished in public to amuse the spectators and humiliate the delinquent. Boys were put in cages and hoisted up to the roof, or they were required to walk backwards all day while wearing a yoke, or they were slapped and washed by girls if they were slovenly, or called derisive names. Lancaster's system was successful. He attracted the patronage of George III, acquired two schools, a training college, a printing press, and a slate factory. With such expansive and extravagant tendencies, however, he was chronically in debt until his friends formed the Royal Lancastrian Society (1808) and gave him a salary and a teaching position. In 1814, after a dispute, he quit; in 1818, he emigrated to America; and in 1838 he died in poverty in New York.

James Mill believed that an intensive study of Greek and Latin, history, philosophy, and mathematics starting at an early age and maintained at a level just beyond what a student could be expected to do would produce the kind of rational and analytical mind required by the demands of contemporary life. Using his son John Stuart as a model, Mill began by teaching him Greek when he was three and completed his education at age fourteen with a commentary on the contemporary political economist, David Ricardo. At age twenty, John Stuart Mill suffered a nervous collapse which in his posthumously published autobiography he attributed to an education that neglected his imaginative and emotional development, a flaw he overcame by a belated but appreciative reading of poetry, especially Wordsworth and Coleridge.

But other young people were less fortunate, for Bentham's and Mill's utilitarian philosophy ultimately dominated most educational systems. In 1815, Bentham's theoretical *Chrestomathia* described a secular education for the middle and upper classes based on utilitarian ideals. Intending to start such a school in his own garden, according to William Hazlitt, his neighbor and tenant, Bentham proposed cutting down the cottonwood trees and removing a stone in the wall inscribed to Milton, who had originally lived in the house. This disregard of tradition and nature, Hazlitt writes in *The Spirit of the Age,* demonstrates "how little the refinements of taste or fancy enter into our author's system." Bentham's school never materialized, but his theories had immense influence.

The industrialist Robert Owen sponsored the first Infant School to educate the children of employees in his industrial utopian community of New Lanark, adapting Bentham's principles on environment to children as young as one year, and Bentham became a patron. Henry Brougham, Bentham's most important ally, presented the first education bill to Parliament in 1820, proposing a national system of education based on the Lancastrian system, the value of which he demonstrated through the first statistical analysis of education in Great Britain. In 1824, adapting a model designed in 1801 by Dr. George Birkbeck in Glasgow, Brougham helped develop the London Mechanic's Institute, which offered libraries, evening classes, and lectures to the workingmen, emphasizing the development of technical and scientific skills to help them participate in the unfolding industrial age. Within twenty-five years, there were over seven hundred such institutes all over the country with over 100,000 participants. In 1825, Brougham participated in the founding of University College, London, a secular Benthamite institution of higher learning admitting students regardless of religious faith, and emphasizing science and medicine among other useful arts. And in 1827, he founded the Society for the Diffusion of Useful Knowledge, parodied by Thomas Peacock in *Crotchet Castle* as the "Steam Intellect Society," that published pamphlets on such useful subjects as math, mechanics, inventions, calculations, and animal husbandry. The closely printed thirty-two page pamphlets, often written by the faculty at the University College and distributed by local committees, sold up to 28,000 copies each, with many more readers.[10]

Such systems could educate large masses of people with diverse backgrounds and expectations, but they required a conformity, a standardization, a concept of children as trainable animals or machines. Modern education began and remained committed to the narrow principles represented succinctly in Charles Dickens's *Hard Times* by Thomas Gradgrind's advice to his schoolmaster: "Teach these boys and girls nothing but Facts. Facts alone are wanted in life. Plant nothing else, and root out everything else. You can only form the minds of reasoning animals upon Facts; nothing else will ever be of any service to them." Creativity and the entire imaginative dimension of life were banished along with the fantasy, the fairies, goblins, and improbable events on which young minds grow. Increased literacy, as writers such as Wordsworth realized, offered little advantage to literature, for while education stimulated publication, the material published was manipulative, unimaginative, encouraging an unhealthy self-involvement, offering the children repeated projections of themselves, their best and worst manners, attitudes, social skills:

Oh! give us once again the wishing cap
Of Fortunatus, and the invisible coat
Of Jack the Giant-Killer, Robin Hood,
And Sabra in the forest with St. George!
The child, whose love is here, at least, doth reap
One precious gain, that he forgets himself.

(*The Prelude* V, 341–46)

William Godwin

It may seem odd that William Godwin, radical and philo-
sophical anarchist, would enter the business of publishing
textbooks, the most effective and subtle instrument for
standardizing thought, for insuring conformist attitudes and
behavior, but he was able to use this publishing activity to
introduce a level of fantasy into readings that would other-
wise be unacceptable, for he knew the law of this market-
place. "It is children that read children's books (when they
are read); but it is parents that choose them," he wrote to
Charles Lamb, reproving him for what he considered a lapse
of taste in Lamb's version of *The Adventures of Ulysses* that
Godwin intended to publish in 1808 (*Letters,* II, 278). And
the parents, the contemporaries of Mrs. Barbauld, Trimmer,
More, and Miss Edgeworth, the "cursed . . . Crew," as Lamb
called them, "those *Blights and blasts* of all that is *Human* in
man and child," chose books designed to adapt children to
the rapidly changing world, to provide the information nec-
essary for them to function, the manners and deportment
necessary for success. As an alternative, Godwin chose to
revive the classics for children. To an audience denied fairy
tales and romance, Shakespeare and Homer offered far more
magical, supernatural, and fantastic material than anything to
be found in the eighteenth-century chapbooks. Because they
were either native or ancient, they were acceptable in a way
that Perrault was not.

In adopting the role of publisher and mirror of public taste,
Godwin gave up the rebellious role that had won him the
acclaim of nearly every young writer in England less than a
decade earlier.[11] Primarily a political thinker, he had acquired
his reputation from *An Enquiry Concerning Political Justice* (1793)
in which he had argued, among other things, that if people
were allowed to follow their own rational impulses there
would be no need for any government at all, attributing great
importance to the early education that would cultivate these
impulses. In 1797, in *The Enquirer: Reflections on Education,*

Manners and Literature, he explained: "The first object should be to train a man to be happy; the second to train him to be useful, that is, to be virtuous." Godwin began to create a literature for children that might help him fulfill these goals when, after the death of his first wife, Mary Wollstonecraft, he married Mary Jane Clairmont, who suggested they publish children's literature to help them support their children: Fanny Imlay, Godwin's stepdaughter by Mary; his own daughter Mary Godwin, who was to marry Shelley; and his new stepdaughter Claire Clairmont, who was to bear a child by Byron. Mrs. Godwin brought with her a keen business sense and experience in editing and translating short stories, dramas, and fables for children.[12]

Like most of the creative and original people of his generation, Godwin objected to the emphasis on information and the neglect of the imaginative faculty in contemporary writing for children: "I hold that a man is not an atom less a man, if he lives and dies without the knowledge they are so desirous of accumulating in the heads of children. Add to which, these things may be learned at any age, while the imagination, the faculty for which I declare, if cultivated at all, must be begun with in youth. Without imagination there can be no genuine ardour in any pursuit, or for any acquisition, and without imagination there can be no genuine morality, no profound feeling of other men's sorrow, no ardent and persevering anxiety for their interests" (*Political Justice,* II, 119). Among the books recommended "to excite the imagination" and "quicken the apprehension of little children," he considered Mother Goose the "best," followed by such otherwise suspicious selections as "Beauty and the Beast," "Fortunatus," *Robinson Crusoe* ("if weeded of its methodism"), and the *Arabian Nights.* Like Wordsworth, indeed, like Blake and Lamb, he was very much opposed to the developing body of literature written especially for children, readings that were too boring, superficial, or simple for adult tastes.

In 1805, he opened the Juvenile Library, offering textbooks, stationery, writing materials, histories of England, Greece, Rome, and Aesop's fables by "Edward Baldwin," the name he assumed to avoid contaminating the business with his radical political reputation. Among the more than twenty volumes Godwin was to publish in the Juvenile Library, including a grammar by William Hazlitt, his most significant achievement was to engage the talents of Charles (1775–1831) and Mary Lamb (1764–1847).

Charles and Mary Lamb

Aside from Lamb's aversion to contemporary children's literature and his preoccupation with his own childhood, there is no reason why Godwin should have expected him to be able to write children's books. When they met, Charles was a bachelor employed as a clerk in East India House living with his unmarried sister, Mary.[13] A genial and sociable pair, they liked to entertain their friends on Wednesday evenings: "We play at whist, eat cold meat, and hot potatoes, and any Gentleman that chuses smokes" (Marrs, III, 5). Their guests included Hazlitt, Coleridge, Leigh Hunt, Wordsworth, Southey, journalists, lawyers, painters, musicians, actors, and other clerks, companions, as Charles said in his self-descriptive preface to *The Last Essays of Elia,* chosen for "some individuality of character," "persons of uncertain fortune," "a ragged regiment . . . floating on the surface of society," among whom he was a "boy-man," someone who "resented the impertinence of manhood." But if Lamb were truly child-like, he could never have endured the responsibilities, the discipline, the griefs that shaped his life. Retrospectively, his childhood represented an ideal state, passed in the ancient and sequestered courts of law at the Inner Temple near the heart of London, where his father was a clerk to lawyer Samuel Salt. Until the age of fifteen, Lamb had a rich and traditional education at Christ's Hospital, where he was a contemporary of Coleridge and studied writing with the rigorous Reverend James Bowyer. He never attended university: a speech impediment limited his potential either to teach or to serve in the church, for which such an education would have prepared him.

Mary, his sister and best friend, eleven years his senior, helped support the family by sewing in the crowded rooms she shared with her crippled mother, her senile father, and her aging Aunt Hetty, who was absorbed in her Catholic prayer books and a major source of discomfort to everyone. Mary was aware of her own mental instability, but it was Charles who suffered the first mental collapse in 1796 after a disappointing love affair, an experience he described to Coleridge with his characteristically defensive humor: "The 6 weeks that finished last year & began this your very humble servant spent very agreeably in a mad house at Hoxton—, I am got somewhat rational now, & don't bite anyone" (Marrs, I, 4). The following year, returning home from a walk, he found Mary holding a kitchen knife with which, in a fit of insanity, she had just assaulted their father and murdered their mother. He paid for Mary's care in a private Quaker asylum at Hoxton to save her the humiliation of a public institution, where the inmates were exhibited for a fee. During her long periods of lucidity, they lived together in what Charles called "double singleness," a relationship now enshrined in the *Essays of Elia* with Mary in the role of Cousin Bridget. Under the idyllic surface of the literary presentation lay the real anguish of Charles Lamb's life, here drawn from one of his few overt statements in a letter to Coleridge, May 12, 1800:

> I dont know why I write except from the propensity misery has to tell her griefs.—Hetty died on Friday night, about 11 o Clock, after 8 days illness. Mary in consequence of fatigue and anxiety is fallen ill again, and I was obliged to remove her yesterday.—I am left alone in a house with nothing but Hetty's dead body to keep me company. . . . Tomorrow I bury her, and then I shall be quite alone, with nothing but a cat, to remind me that the house has been full of living beings like myself.—My heart is quite sunk, and I dont know where to look for relief.—Mary will be better again, but her constantly being liable to such relapse is dreadful,—nor is it the least of our Evils, that her case & all our story is so well known around us. . We are in a manner *marked*.—Excuse my troubling you, but I have nobody by me to speak to me. . . .
> I am completely shipwreck'd.—My head is quite bad. . . . I almost wish that Mary were dead. . . .
>
> (*Letters,* I, 202–3)

But whatever his own sufferings, he had immense toleration for his friends, especially the sensitivities of the creative ones, a strong sense of himself, his tastes, needs, and priorities, enabling him, among other things, to hold out for his own urban preferences, celebrating among a generation of rural sentimentalists the "sweet security of streets":

> Streets, streets, streets, markets, theatres, churches, Covent Gardens, Shops sparkling with pretty faces of industrious milliners, neat sempstresses, Ladies cheapening [bargaining], Gentlemen behind counters lying, Authors in the street with spectacles . . . Lamps lit at night, Pastry cook & Silver smith shops, Beautiful Quakers of Pentonville, noise of coaches, drousy cry of mechanic watchmen at night, with Bucks reeling home drunk if you happen to wake at midnight, cries of fire and stop thief, Inns of court . . . old Books stalls. . . . These are thy Pleasures O London with-the-many-sins—O City abounding in whores.
>
> (*Letters,* I, 248)

In 1819, Fanny Kelly, an actress about whose talents he had rhapsodized in several poems, rejected his proposal of marriage, for, as he possibly realized, the match was impossible. She was an actress whose subtle beauty had driven some admirers to shoot each other, others to follow her around the country attending all her performances, while Charles, however secure financially and surrounded with artistic and interesting friends, was nonetheless a forty-four-year-old clerk living with a spinster sister who suffered from periodic fits of madness. The following year he began publishing essays under the pseudonym of "Elia" in the *London Magazine,* essays that would secure his literary reputation, essays demonstrating the sense of merriment that charmed his friends, the pleasure in the ordinary, the urban, the social rituals that had animated his letters, the firm sense of self that had allowed him to survive a life of anxiety and loss, the realization of boundaries to which most people must become acclimated if they are to survive at all. In 1823, Charles and Mary adopted Emma Isola, a fifteen-year-old orphan, which is as close as they ever came to being parents.

Although childless themselves, and without any personal involvement with education, for six years, between 1806 and 1811, Charles and Mary wrote for children, an audience they gave very little evidence of understanding and to which they had no particular commitment. While Charles idealized childhood in dreams, reveries, and memories, he preferred to keep real children at a distance where he could observe rather than relate to them: "Boys are capital fellows in their own way, among their mates; but they are unwholesome companions for grown people," he wrote in "The Old and New Schoolmaster." For Charles, engaged in a long literary apprenticeship in which he successively approached a whole array of possible forms—poetry, journalism, dramatic criticism, a novel, tragedy, farce—writing for children was merely another literary experiment, this one conducted primarily for money.

At the suggestion of Mrs. Godwin, Mary Lamb agreed to write twenty tales based on the plays of Shakespeare. Charles, inspired by her enthusiasm, undertook six of the tragedies although he found the work onerous, "groaning all the while," according to Mary. The book appeared in 1807 as *Lamb's Tales from Shakespeare, Designed for Young Persons. By Charles Lamb.* Mary was happy enough at the prospect of earning fifty pounds a year, but Charles was offended by the omission of his sister's name. Godwin's explanation that the book would earn more money if it had an exclusively male author was especially ironic since his own first wife, the late Mary Wollstonecraft, had written the stirring appeal for women's equality, *A Vindication of the Rights of Woman,* a book Mary Lamb had read with approval when it came out in 1793. The *Tales* themselves, like other works of the period written for children, were moral, didactic, and exemplary, emphasizing, as Lamb explained in the Preface, social virtues:

> What these Tales have been to you in childhood, that and much more it is my wish that the true Plays of Shakespeare may prove to you in older years—enrichers of the fancy, strengtheners of virtue, a withdrawing from all selfish and mercenary thoughts, a lesson of all sweet and honourable thoughts and actions, to teach you courtesy, benignity, generosity, humanity: for of examples, teaching these virtues, these pages are full.

The plays were compressed, expurgated, and simplified. In *King Lear,* for example, he omits the story of Gloucester and his two sons until the end where Edmund, the bastard son, is introduced as the object of Goneril's and Regan's "guilty love" to illustrate how "false" daughters will also be "false" wives. All actions are explicitly interpreted: when Goneril, imprisoned for killing Regan, commits suicide, Lamb writes, "Thus the justice of Heaven at last overtook these wicked daughters." On the death of Cordelia, "whose good deeds did seem to deserve a more fortunate conclusion," he writes, "it is an awful truth, that innocence and piety are not always successful in this world," a truth that would be especially useful to a generation of children growing up in the competitive world of the nineteenth century.

The next work, recommended by Godwin, was *The Adventures of Ulysses* (1808), translated and adapted for children from the difficult although fashionable translation of the Elizabethan playwright, George Chapman (1559–1634), the translation that Keats commemorated in his sonnet, "On First Looking into Chapman's Homer," which begins "Much have I travell'd in the realms of gold." Godwin objected to Lamb's realistic and detailed presentation of the Cyclop's eating the sailors, of the vomit, and of "the minute and shocking description of the extinguishing the giant's eye," to which Lamb replied: "If you want a book which is not occasionally to *shock,* you should not have thought of a Tale which was so full of Anthropophagi & monsters . . . I assure you I will not alter one more word" (*Letters,* II, 278–79). Since booksellers were held responsible for the indiscretions of their authors, fined, and even jailed, Lamb's position was an especially difficult one for Godwin to accept. Fifteen years later in an essay called "Witches and other Night Fears," Lamb, describing the nightmares that plagued him as a child, explained why he objected to censoring literature designed for children: "It is not book, or picture, or the stories of foolish servants, which create these terrors in children. They can at most but give them a direction." A child raised without superstition, deprived of goblins, ghosts, evil creatures and sad stories will generate his own, "and from his little midnight pillow, this nurse-child of optimism will start at shapes, unborrowed of tradition, in sweats to which the reveries of the cell-damned murderer are tranquility." All the monsters, "Gorgons, and Hydras, and Chimaeras . . . may reproduce themselves in the brain of superstition—but they were there before. They are transcripts, types—the archetypes are in us, and eternal."[14]

After the translations and Shakespearean adaptations, Charles and Mary turned to children's poetry and narratives, conventional forms, though each acquired that degree of human interest with which these two special people endowed the most ordinary things. *Mrs. Leicester's School* (1809) consists of ten tales told by some young ladies who, in order to become acquainted at their new school, relate what they consider the most interesting thing that had ever happened to them. It was a fine performance in itself, enriched by a certain self-referential quality, half-concealed autobiographical ironies and revisions. In the first story, for example, the narrator, Elizabeth Williers, explains that her father taught her the alphabet by reading the letters on her mother's tombstone. In one of the most powerful, "The Father's Wedding Day," written by Mary, a young girl recounts that on the day her father, a widower, was to marry a woman of whom she was not particularly fond, she had dressed in splendid new clothes and, thinking that her mother would have been delighted to see her, rushed to her mother's bedroom door forgetting that she was dead—and that her death had been the occasion for the marriage of her father and therefore the clothes she was wearing. In 1831, twenty-two years after publication, Walter Savage Landor, an author of exquisite classical taste, recommended the story to Henry Crabb Robinson: "A fresh source of the pathetic bursts out before us, and not a bitter one. If your Germans can show us anything comparable to what I have transcribed, I would almost undergo a year's gargle of the language for it" (Lucas, III, 483).

Poetry for Children (1809), Charles confessed, was "taskwork," distinguished by "the number of subjects, all of children, picked out by an old Bachelor and an old Maid" (*Letters*, III, 14). The interesting and varied "subjects," mostly dialogues or anecdotes, focus on young people coping with negative feelings such as envy, anger, discontent, resentment, selfishness, and cruelty, especially to animals, birds, and butterflies. There are poems commemorating rites of passage such as "Going into Breeches" ("Joy to Philip, he this day / Has his long coats cast away"), going to school, writing a letter, and others offering avuncular advice on "The Duty of a Brother," "Cleanliness," and "Moderation in Diet," which begins with the concession that, while "Dear Jim" is too young to be addicted to alcohol, his addiction to sweets is equally reprehensible:

> Go buy a book; a dainty eaten
> Is vanished, and no sweets remain;
> They who their minds with knowledge sweeten,
> The savour long as life retain.

The book never reached a second edition. Charles was, at best, a skillful versifier who considered poetry itself a vanity which he gave up twice: first, early in life because it conflicted with his responsibilities and again, later, shortly before he died, because it was "nonsense."

Charles and Mary Lamb brought to children's literature not so much an understanding of children, as an understanding of how the childlike survives within the adult. Complaining in "Old Benches of the Inner Temple" about the removal of the artificial fountains in the Inner Temple because they are childish, Lamb asks, "Is the world all grown up? Is childhood dead? Or is there not in the bosoms of the wisest and the best some of the child's heart left, to respond to its earliest enchantments?" The survival of the child within the adult was a major preoccupation among the Romantic writers, especially Wordsworth, who found in it the "fountain light of all our day" ("Ode: Intimations of Immortality," l. 153). But Lamb knew, as Wordsworth may not have known, the dark and all too terrestrial motives of children, that what survives may be a curiosity about the sinister, and an inclination for the grotesque.

Poems for Children

Lamb's poetry for children was representative of the verse published for children in the early decades of the nineteenth century, a time when many authors publishing for children believed, along with Mrs. Barbauld,[15] that poetry was too elevated a form to be adapted to the needs of young minds. Consequently, between Isaac Watts's *Divine and Moral Songs for Children* (1715) and *Original Poems for Infant Minds* (1804) by the Taylor family, nursery rhymes were the major body of verse available for children. Like the folk songs they resembled, nursery rhymes are obscure in origin and meaning as well. They seem to arise spontaneously in infant prattle or singing games. They survive in the oral tradition and tend to reflect the geographical location of their origins in diction and allusion. As part of the antiquarian interest in folk literature, nursery rhymes—including mysterious remnants of charms, prayers, lullabies, games, mnemonic devices, work, love, and drinking songs—were first collected and published as *Tommy Thumb's Pretty Song Book for All Little Masters and Misses . . . by Nurse Lovechild* (1744). The "pretty" songs included such harmless counting rhymes as "Baa, Baa, Black Sheep," "Mistress Mary, Quite Contrary," "Little Bo-Peep," "Little Miss Muffet" (referring to the ill-fated Mary, Queen of Scots), "Hickory, Dickory, Dock" (derived from an ancient druidical ritual for choosing who would be "it," the human sacrifice), "Little Sally Waters" (originating in a pagan marriage ritual performed at Bath in Roman Britain), "Sing a Song of Six-Pence" in which twenty-four naughty boys were baked in a pie, and, usually omitted from later editions, the taunting "Piss a bed / Piss a bed."

By 1805, all of the traditional rhymes had appeared in such collections as *Mother Goose's Melody,* Joseph Ritson's *Gammer Gurton's Garland, or the Nursery Parnassus: Choice Collection of Pretty Songs and Verses for the Amusement of all Little Good Children who can Neither Read nor Run* (1784, 1799, 1810, and so on), and *Tom Tit's Song Book: A Collection of Old Songs with which most Young Wits have been Delighted* (1790, etc.). The allusion to music in the titles suggest their close association with the oral tradition and their suitability for performance, but, in spite of the references to pleasure, delight, and amusement, they offered a catalogue of mayhem and crime, of unrewarded virtue, unrequited love, of murder, larceny, gluttony, theft, betrayal, rejection, abandonment, cursing, madness, misery, and brutality. For example, *Tom Tit's Song Book* offered a domestic homily that was primarily designed for learning the days of the week:

I married a wife on Sunday
She began to scold on Monday,

Bad was she on Tuesday,
Meddling was she on Wednesday,
Worse she was on Thursday,
Dead was she on Friday;
Glad was I on Saturday night,
To bury my wife on Sunday.

Charles Lamb enjoyed sending it to his friends, translated into Latin.

In transmission, losing touch with their original locale, dialect, and cultural functions, most of the rhymes had lost their significance, and some deeply subversive political statements or erotic initiation rites appeared as harmless nonsense. The old woman who lived in a shoe, for example, who might at best serve as a Malthusian warning against overpopulation or an instance of child abuse, was a covert attack on the King's tyranny over the British Isles, for the King was often represented as an old woman, and the British Isles are shaped like a shoe.[16]

Along with fairy tales, rationalist and moralist writers for children dismissed nursery rhymes as trivial and disreputable, but they adapted the dactylic and anapestic feet, the nonsense rhymes, the lambent humor and animistic fantasy to their own ends in writing a didactic verse usually illustrative of the mischief or foibles of children and the retribution they encountered. Most of this poetry was written by Ann (1782–1866) and Jane (1783–1824) Taylor. They came from a family of prolific writers: Isaac, the father, started his own Sunday school and wrote pamphlets on commerce, biography, geography, and moral improvement; Ann, the mother, bore eleven children (of whom six lived), wrote conduct manuals, advice to mothers, and many editions of *Maternal Solicitude for a Daughter's Best Interests* (1814). Of the many poems published by the daughters, only "Twinkle, twinkle, little star" from the collection of *Original Poems for Infant Minds* (1804–1805) has survived, and that in an abbreviated form. The other poems became either models for Sunday school poetry later in the century or objects of parody by Lewis Carroll and other Victorian humorists who could count on their being recognized by young audiences. Their verse displays a rare talent for the rhythms of nonsense, for the dactylic and anapestic feet, and a shameless appeal to the social and national prejudices of the middle classes. For example, "The English Girl," "The Irish Boy," "The Welsh Lad," and "Contented John," whose "station was humble":

Pass'd thro this sad world without even a grumble
And I wish that some folks, who are greater and richer,
Would copy John Tomkins, the hedger and ditcher.

There were social deviants such as "Greedy Richard," "Dirty Jack," "Meddlesome Matty," and "The Chatterbox." And, in a mode that was becoming increasingly popular, the animal tale, "The last Dying Speech and Confession of Poor Puss":

Oh what have I suffered with beating and banging,
Or starv'd for a fortnight, or threatend with hanging
But kicking and beating, and starving, and that
I've borne with a spirit becoming a cat.

In 1805, John Harris, who had inherited the Newbery business, published *The Comic Adventures of Old Mother Hubbard and Her Dog,* which has never been out of print. The poem was composed by Sarah Catherine Martin (1786–1826), mistress at one time to the Duke of Clarence, later King William IV. Drawing on several different conventions, including the oral tradition, the volume appealed to a larger class of readers than any other contemporary poetry written for children, selling 10,000 copies within the first few months.[17] Aside from the beguiling nonsense of the literal plot, an adult as well as a juvenile working-class audience would have responded to the bleak economic reality of a bare cupboard, the humiliation of an authority figure by a tyrannical dog, and the parody of the fashionable concern for the feelings of animals.

This personification of animals, dignified by the tradition of Aesop, provided a device for acceptable fantasy in original verse written for children. One of the first, *The Butterfly's Ball,* by historian, banker, and botanist William Roscoe, M.P., from Liverpool, began with an invitation to an unlikely festival of insects:

Come take up our Hats and away let us haste
To the Butterfly's Ball and the Grasshopper's Feast.
The trumpeter, Gadfly, has summon'd the crew,
And the Revels are now only waiting for you.

Although intended as a private amusement for his young son, Robert, Roscoe's poem inspired a host of imitations and sequels, including Mrs. Dorset's *The Peacock at Home* (1807, twenty-eighth edition 1817), *The Elephant's Ball, The Lion's Masquerade,* and *The Lobster's Voyage to the Brazils.* Cheerfully illustrated and hand-colored, often by children, they were the first group of books in which the pictures could be considered as important as the text (Darton, p. 214). Their influence was ranging, parodied by Lewis Carroll and acknowledged by some of the most accomplished writers of the nineteenth century. In 1885, for example, in tribute to a beloved tale recollected from childhood, John Ruskin republished (with illustrations by Kate Greenway) *Dame Wiggins of Lee and Her Seven Wonderful Cats,* written "by a lady of ninety."

Robert Southey and "The Three Bears"

While it appeared too late to influence public taste, "The Three Bears" remains the most widely acclaimed contribution to the literature for children published during the Romantic period. Like the nursery rhymes, its origins are obscure in the oral tradition and its variants are many.[18] It first appeared in September, 1831, in a metrical version by Eleanor Mure, written for her nephew's birthday. The part of Goldilocks, a Victorian invention, was played by an old woman, a common figure of both fear and ridicule in the popular literature of England. It concluded with the violence such little old women usually encountered in nursery rhymes:

> On the fire they throw her, but burn her they couldn't
> In the water they put her but drown there she wouldn't;
> They seize her before all the wonderful people
> And chuck her aloft on St. Paul's church-yard steeple. . . .

The version with which we are most familiar appeared in *The Doctor,* an autobiographical fiction with which Robert Southey amused himself during more than thirty years of his literary life, from 1805 to 1837, when the seventh and final volume appeared. The narrative—digressive, anecdotal, full of verbal play and nonsense—follows the childhood, education, and marriage of Dr. Daniel Dove. It began as a family joke: "He *will* write it!" his wife insisted. "He will never be so foolish," his sister-in-law, Mrs. Coleridge, replied. Mrs. Southey: "He is foolish enough for anything." Here we glimpse the domestic personality, the private drollery of an otherwise taciturn public man, reviewer, poet laureate, by reputation the most industrious and methodical literary man in England, but one who by disposition and experience was perhaps the only major writer prepared to write a literature for children. Southey did not merely like children; he believed, for no particular philosophical reason, in the necessity of them:

"It is said to be a saying of Dr. Southey's that 'a house is never perfectly furnished for enjoyment, unless there is a child in it rising three years old, and a kitten rising six week' " (*The Doctor,* III, 328). Greta Hall, the house in Keswick he shared with the Coleridge family and Robert Lovell's widow, was full of children—his own seven, Coleridge's three, and Lovell's one, all of whom he helped to educate—legions of cats with magnificent names, and his own incomparable library, to which everyone had free access.[19]

According to his own recollection, Southey's childhood had lacked the whimsical dimension he brought to the children at Great Hall. Between the ages of two and six, he lived with his rich, beautiful, eccentric, and tyrannical aunt, Elizabeth Tyler, who took him to parties and to the theater but made him lie perfectly still in her bed while she slept in the mornings. "I had many indulgences, but more privations, and those of an injurious kind, want of playmates, want of exercise, never being allowed to do anything in which by possibility I might dirt myself . . ."[20] His formal education was irregular but he compensated for it by writing epics, translations, and plays, many inspired by twenty Newbery books he received as a gift and to which he attributed the origins of his literary career. While preparing for the clergy at Balliol College, Oxford, Southey met Coleridge, with whom he shared that radical sympathy for the ideals of the French Revolution that characterized so many young intellectuals of the time. Along with Robert Lovell and Tom Poole, they planned to emigrate to America and create a Pantisocracy, a utopian community based on equality, simplicity, shared labor, and common property. With that ideal community in mind, they were married to three sisters, Southey to Edith Fricker, Lovell to Mary, and Coleridge to Sarah. After a year in Portugal with his uncle, Herbert Hill, Southey abandoned the idea of emigrating to America, and began to study law in London while writing for the periodical press.

In 1803, he settled permanently at Greta Hall, Keswick, and became an author by profession, professional writing being what Isaac D'Israeli called in *Calamities of Authors* (1812) the major calamity of all. But Southey found it otherwise, for he read with pleasure, wrote habitually, and had the capacity for heroic self-discipline: "although literature in almost all cases is the worst trade to which a man can possible betake himself, it is the best and wisest of all pursuits for those whose provision is already made, and of all amusements for those who have the leisure to amuse themselves," Southey wrote in 1812, contemplating a review of the *Calamities*. The following year he was appointed Poet Laureate. Coleridge, for whose wife and children he had provided a home, would have rather been a "Shoemaker" than a professional writer: "I am forced to write for bread . . . my happiest moments for composition are broken in on by the reflection of—I *must* make haste—I am too late. . . . O way-ward and desultory Spirit of Genius!" (*CL,* I, 185–86). But, then, Southey had little pretension about the "Spirit of Genius"; he wrote histories of Brazil, of the Church, of the Peninsular War; biographies of Nelson and Wesley, translations, editions, observations, essays on current events, reviews, occasional and fashionable verse, and epic poems in exotic settings such as *Thalaba the Destroyer* (1801), *Madoc* (1805), *The Curse of Kehama* (1810), and *Roderick, The Last of the Goths* (1814). Best known for his poetry, he gave it up as unprofitable (*NL,* I, 471).

Although some tried to embarrass him for his youthful radicalism by publishing an early work called *Wat Tyler* in 1817, and Byron ridiculed his loyalty to the throne in *The Vision of Judgment,* Southey enjoyed an impeccable reputation. Recalling their first meeting in 1807, De Quincey wrote in *Tait's Edinburgh Magazine* (July 1839), "A man of more serene and even temper could not be imagined; nor more uniformly cheerful in his tone of spirit; nor more unaffectedly polite and courteous. . . . I believe Southey to be as exemplary a man as can ever have lived."[21] And in an otherwise unflattering portrait in *The Spirit of the Age,* Hazlitt, that implacable radical, calls Southey's character: "prophetic of good; . . . He cannot bear to give up the thought of happiness, his confidence in his fellow man, when all else despair."

However sheltered and cheerful, Southey suffered several personal tragedies: the death of his ten-year-old son, Herbert, and of his fourteen-year-old daughter, Isabel, and the subsequent emotional collapse of Mrs. Southey and her death in 1837. In 1839, he married Caroline Bowles and, after a long period of mental deterioration that some attributed to overwork, died in 1843. Like most writers, the major drama in Southey's life took place behind his eyes, for that was his field of action. Opportunities arose for him to participate in public life as more than the ornamental Poet Laureate—editing the powerful London *Times,* or holding a seat in Parliament, or even a baronetcy—but he preferred to remain an observer, to pass his "days among the dead," as he wrote in his most famous lyric, among the thousands of books that comprised his almost legendary library.

"The Three Bears," a story Southey first heard from his Uncle William, is unquestionably grim. In the version published in *The Doctor,* Southey follows the popular convention of using, in the role of Goldilocks, an "Impudent, bad old Woman" who vandalizes the house of the "good Bears, who did nobody any harm," and whose "ugly dirty head" defiles the bed of the "good and tidy" Little Small Wee Bear before she is chased out a second story window: "whether she broke her neck in the fall; or ran into the wood and was lost there; or found her way out of the wood, and was taken up by the constable and sent to the House of Correction for a vagrant as she was, I cannot tell."

The pleasure in the story is clearly in the performance rather than in the conclusion that society takes better care of its bears than of its senior citizens, that their safety takes priority over hungry old women with no place to live. To emphasize the oral significance of the tale, Southey printed it in different sizes of type, the Great, Huge Bear in Gothic, and urged "little children" to have their relatives read it aloud to them. As a professional author, Southey's livelihood had been created by the sudden expansion of print and literacy, but his allegiance, particularly in *The Doctor,* was to the oral tradition, its intimacy and vitality, that relationship between storytelling adults and children which was being impoverished by the otherwise admirable goal of universal literacy. Published anonymously and poorly revised, nonetheless, *The Doctor* is a more characteristic monument to Southey's talent than the epics and histories and biographies by which he earned a living: "No where else can one find," Edward Dowden wrote in *Southey* (1879), "so much of his varied erudition, his genial spirits, his meditative wisdom. . . . To know that he had added a classic to the nursery would have been the pride of Southey's heart."[22]

The Hog in the Garden
The Birth of Fantasy

Before *The Doctor,* there had been other attempts to revive the oral and imaginative tradition in children's literature. In 1818, Sir Richard Phillips collected *Popular Fairy Tales; or a Lilliputian Library* containing all of Perrault, "Beauty and the Beast," Aladdin and his magic lamp, all regularized to make the tales acceptable for middle-class nurseries. Almost single-handedly, John Harris, the Newbery heir, had nursed a strain of whimsy, of fantasy, of juvenile grotesquerie in Mother

Hubbard, Mother Bunch, *The History of Sixteen Wonderful Old Women* (the earliest book of limericks), and finally, the lavish *Court of Oberon; or, The Temple of Fairies* (1823), which included conventional favorites as well as the *Arabian Nights.* The following year Edgar Taylor began publishing *Popular German Stories* (1824–26), translated from the fairy tales collected by the Brothers Grimm, a project motivated by scholarly and patriotic interest in their own native folklore. Taylor used the collection to challenge the moralistic influence of Mrs. Trimmer and Mrs. Barbauld and the utilitarian one of Maria Edgeworth, particularly their aversion to fanciful and idle reading: "The popular tales of England" he wrote in the introduction, "have been too much neglected. They are nearly discarded from the libraries of childhood. Philosophy is made the companion of the nursery: we have lisping chemists and leading-string mathematicians; this is the age of reason not of imagination, and the loveliest dreams of fairy innocence are considered as vain and frivolous." While Taylor contributed to the diversity of literature available for children, supplemented in 1846 by Mary Howitt's translation of Hans Christian Andersen's fairy tales, his was a minority voice; in England, the "charm'd magic casements," to paraphrase Keats, still opened on "faery lands forlorn" ("Ode to a Nightingale," ll.69–70). In 1853, George Cruikshank, who had illustrated Taylor's translation of Grimm, published the *Fairy Library,* revising traditional tales into tracts mostly against drinking—Cinderella, for example, after much negotiation, has a dry wedding and the Giant at the end of "Jack and the Beanstalk," deprived of his liquor, stops beating his wife, acquires a useful occupation quarrying stones for the royal roads, and even "they lived happily for many years."

Whatever else Cruikshank did, he aroused Charles Dickens's indignation: "We have lately observed, with pain, the intrusion of a Whole Hog of unwieldy dimensions into the fairy flower garden," he wrote in "Frauds on the Fairies," which appeared in *Household Words* (October 1853).[23] The essay began with a defense of fairy tales and some belated cautionary advice: "In an utilitarian age, of all other times, it is a matter of grave importance that Fairy tales should be respected. . . . every one who has considered the subject knows full well that a nation without fancy, without some romance, never did, never can, never will hold a great place under the sun." From Dickens's historical perspective it appeared that the theater was responsible for destroying "these admirable fictions—and having in a most exemplary manner destroyed itself, its artists, and its audiences, in that perversion of its duty." While Dickens may not have been in a position to see the complexity of such causal relations, he did recognize that the same ethical and utilitarian biases that displaced the fairy tales in children's literature were clearly at work in the theater. A generation of children educated in that tradition—didactic, practical, pious, moralistic—to which Godwin, Lamb, and Taylor, among others, had objected, became the audience for melodrama and for spectacle, the two most popular forms of theatrical entertainment during the Romantic period. While religious, political, economic, even architectural factors contributed to the development and success of these forms, they were also a clear and immediate expression of popular taste, the melodrama appealing to the unsophisticated moral sensibilities of the audience and the spectacle compensating for its unawakened imaginative life.[24]

CHAPTER IV

The Theater

ACCORDING TO MOST writers, critics, and commentators, the theater during the Romantic period was a wasteland, ruined by legal restrictions, by architecture, by unruly audiences, by reviewers, and by the actors themselves.[1] Since Coleridge's *Remorse* was the only play by a distinguished author to appear on the stage, most *literary* histories perpetuate the impression that from 1789 to 1830, indeed from 1737 to 1843, the period covered by the Licensing Act, the English theater was insignificant. But to the vast contemporary audiences of all ages, classes, and intellectual achievement, the theater was immensely interesting, interesting enough to justify 160 newspapers, magazines, and journals devoted exclusively to the theater between 1800 and 1830; and in 1825, nineteen daily theatrical periodicals;[2] interesting enough to lure thousands of spectators into poorly ventilated and uncomfortable theaters to watch plays that perpetuated the values and problems of an irrelevant aristocracy, plays that were rendered nearly incomprehensible by poor lighting, poor acoustics, and the rowdy behavior of the spectators themselves.

Licensed Theaters

Believing that religious, political, and sexual excess would corrupt the lower classes and lead to civil unrest, the govern-

ment had passed the Licensing Acts in 1737, laws which, until
1843, confined the London productions of spoken drama to
a few easily supervised theaters called "patent" theaters: Covent
Garden and Drury Lane from September through June, and
the Haymarket theater in the summer. The other theaters were
supposedly rendered harmless by the regulation that all pro-
ductions be performed to music. Holding the monopoly on
spoken drama, the managers of the patent theaters enlarged
and decorated them to attract large audiences. By the open-
ing of the nineteenth century, up to 3,000 people a night could
be crowded into tiers, pits, and galleries for performances
that lasted often over six hours at, for example, Covent Gar-
den.

In 1807, Southey, in the persona of a Spanish visitor in
Letters from England, described a visit to Drury Lane: "I had
heard much of this theatre, and was prepared for wonder;
still the size, the height, the beauty, the splendour, astonished
me. Imagine a pit capable of holding a thousand persons, four
tiers of boxes supported by pillars scarcely thicker than a man's
arm, and two galleries in front, the higher one at such a dis-
tance they they who are in it must be content to see the show,
without hoping to hear the dialogue; the colours blue and
silver, and the whole illuminated with chandeliers of cut glass,
not partially nor parsimoniously; every part as distinctly seen
as if in the noon sunshine" (p. 98). In spite of a fire curtain
and a reservoir on the roof, after a performance on the night
of February 24, 1809, Drury Lane burned down, only a year
after Covent Garden had met the same fate. Rebuilt in 1812,
it was redecorated in 1817, in a Chinese motif reflecting the
influence of the Prince Regent's Pavilion at Brighton. Covent
Garden had been rebuilt in a Grecian style, resembling the
Temple of Minerva on the Acropolis. In 1817, gas lighting
was introduced at both theaters, in spite of objections to the
ghastly effects of lighting up the actor's faces from below.
Since the entire auditorium was illuminated as well as the
stage, the gas jets dispersed throughout depleted the oxygen,
and many spectators complained of dizziness, drowsiness, and
headaches.[3] In 1828, following an explosion at Covent Gar-
den, gas was replaced by oil lamps and candles.

The audiences in these great theaters had little expectation
of being comfortable. Since waiting in line did not become
customary until late in the century, they formed mobs out-
side the theater, and inside they crowded into pits, boxes,
and galleries ranging up into the rafters at such a steep pitch
that some spectators, called the "gods," could only see the

actors' feet. Given the lighting, acoustics, and ventilation, even those in the best seats had difficulty concentrating. But then audiences had not yet discovered the advantages of sitting quietly and attentively during a performance: they talked, ate fish and oranges, drank, flirted, wandered about shouting insults at the actors or each other, and even threw food on the stage. If they disapproved of the play, as they often did, they responded like animals, "Like a congregation of mad geese," Charles Lamb wrote, describing the reaction of the audience to his farce, *Mr. H.* at Drury Lane in 1806, "with roaring sometimes like bears, mows and mops like apes, sometimes snakes, that hiss'd me into madness" (Lucas, I, 412). So boorish were the London audiences that many authors, such as Sir Walter Scott, refused to write for them. For the fashionable audience, attendance at the patent theaters was dangerous and morally compromising; pickpockets and other petty thieves flourished in and around the theaters, and prostitutes solicited customers, even those accompanied by ladies, during plays that were so rigidly censored that no one on the stage could even allude to any part of the female anatomy.

The audience that so repelled these authors was a curious combination of the unfashionable rich and their servants, the urban middle-class, merchants, apprentices, clerks, and such literary types as Charles Lamb, William Hazlitt, Leigh Hunt, William Godwin, John Keats, and the ubiquitous dandies, a diverse and volatile community, capable, as in 1794 at a command performance at the Drury Lane, of trampling each other to death in the rush to get seats in the pit. In 1809, after the management at Covent Garden had raised the prices and created more private boxes, the audience rioted for sixty-four nights; they arrived in costume at half-time chanting, bearing placards, giving speeches, dancing with rattles, bells, horns, live pigs, pigeons, trumpets, reducing the performance on the stage to mime until the management finally agreed to reduce prices again and enlarge the pits. Through sheer numbers, then, and a proprietary attitude toward the stage, this audience bullied and shouted until the theater, the most restricted of institutions, reverted to its popular origins, democratized well ahead of other institutions that were to respond to popular pressure later in the century.

Ironically, they were assisted by the very laws designed to limit free expression. By confining spoken drama to a few houses and censoring whatever productions were allowed, the Licensing Acts have often been blamed for destroying the dramatic tradition and for inhibiting creativity, and in some ways they did.[4] Certainly, prohibiting the representation of religious and political subjects deprived dramatists of the two topics on which the greatness of ancient Greek and Renaissance drama had depended. While the censors may have thought they were protecting the sacred by keeping it off the stage, objecting to even such harmless celestial allusions as calling one's sweetheart an angel, in fact they contributed to the dislocation of religion in public life, and to the secularization of art. Similarly, the strictures against representing politics, designed a century before to discourage volatile theater audiences from rioting, forced dramatists to focus on the common rather than the exceptional man, the domestic and peripheral concerns of the middle and lower classes, producing a tame and uninspiring domestic drama. Unfortunately, these laws contributed to the political irrelevance of the drama itself, as Edward Bulwer-Lytton observed: "To see our modern plays, you would imagine there were no politicians among us."[5] European, South American, Arabian, and Oriental emperors flooded the stage, while the English aristocracy appeared as comic villains or foundlings, and *King Lear* was retired completely because of the unfortunate parallels between the insane protagonist and George III. By inhibiting the presentation of political and religious subjects, the censors, then, were actually encouraging innovation, experimentation, indeed the very creative freedom that artists themselves now defend with such vigilance against political and religious intervention.

Compensating for the loss of traditionally stirring subjects and the limitations of spoken drama in cavernous and noisy theaters, the managers of the patent houses filled their stages with pageantry, showmanship, and sublime visual effects from both nature and industry introduced at the Drury Lane as early as 1771 by the Alsatian, Philippe de Loutherbourg.[6] Cataracts, volcanoes, storms, historical battle scenes, perspectives, backdrops, costumes, gauzes, transparencies, mechanical motion, and music gave artistic status to legions of carpenters, painters, dressmakers, and musicians, expanding the popular basis of the theater, the involvement of the laboring classes in the production as well as the performance. A productive alliance between theater and painting, between entertainment and technology, gradually shifted the emphasis from verbal to visual effects and to the elevation of documentary as opposed to aesthetic values. From de Loutherbourg's Eidophusikon (1781), a miniature moving stage on which he depicted scenes from history or nature accompanied by sound and lighting effects, developed visual exhibitions of light and sound called diorama and panorama requiring special round halls that by 1815 were as numerous as movie houses are today. Here spectators, often assisted by elaborate narrative programs, either climbed a central platform or sat in a rotating auditorium, to view massive scenes of natural disasters such as the eruption of Pompeii, battles such as Nelson at the Nile, landmarks such as Venice at different times of day, and landscapes such as the Alps at different seasons. In 1824, another Frenchman, P. M. Roget, presented a paper to the Royal Society explaining that the human brain processed isolated images, modifying them into a single movement, composing pictures out of separate fragments. Using a spinning toy to illustrate after-images, he proved that sight was in the brain, not the eye,[7] a physiological fact that was essential for the invention of moving pictures later in the century.

Unlicensed Theater

Access to such technical innovations as well as a monopoly over the spoken word gave the patent theaters little financial advantage. They paid for their Shakespeare and other serious drama by importing popular entertainments from the unlicensed theaters such as Sadler's Wells and Astley's Circus, which had in turn drawn upon the street culture, the taverns, pleasure gardens, fairs, and marketplaces to develop their own special alternatives to the traditional drama—mime, dance, spectacles, animal acts, acrobatics, fencing, jugglers, hippodrama, aquadrama, melodrama, and burletta—a rhymed comedy of singing and recitative accompanied by music.[8] While the theater in general, as Bulwer-Lytton complained, seldom represented great political events, the unlicensed theaters and the patent theaters following them did provide a chronicle of the times, "dramas of living men / And recent things yet warm with life" (*The Prelude*, VII, 310f.) as Wordsworth described the performances he enjoyed at Sadler's. He recognized, as many did not, the similarity between contemporary theater and the ancient theater (*The Prelude*, VII, 310–15), a theater that predated the traditional drama they were prohibited from presenting. One such piece, *Edward and Susan, or, the Beauty of Buttermere* (1803), based on the recent seduction and abandonment of Mary Robinson, an "artless daughter of the hills" whom he knew, by John Hatfield, a bigamist later hanged for forgery, he considered "too holy theme for such a place" (*The Prelude,* VII, 317).[9] But Mary Lamb reported in a letter to Dorothy that the opera enacted at "the lowest and most London-like of all our London amusements," had a happy ending, that Charles "laughed the whole time," and that Southey, who joined the party, "fell asleep" (*Letters,* II, 117).

Along with sentiment and anecdotes, the unlicensed theater used whatever was novel or eccentric in contemporary culture such as Dr. James Graham's Celestial Bed exhibited at the Temple of Health and guaranteeing fertility to those who could afford to spend a night in it, Vincenzo Lunardi's first London ascent in a balloon, and whatever dancing horses, singing ducks, and learned pigs happened to catch the public fancy at the time. In fact, many events which the censors would not allow on the licensed stage appeared at Sadler's. For example, on August 31, 1789, they presented *Gallic Freedom; or, Vive La Liberté,* a pageant depicting the recent fall of the Bastille in exhaustive detail based on interviews and drawings. For the next twenty-five years, during the long war against France, Sadler's specialized in these documentary pageants. Diverting the New River that ran by the theater, in 1804, Charles Dibdin installed a ninety-foot tank on the stage in which he represented such contemporary battles as the seige of Gibraltar using 117 miniature ships made in exact scale of one inch to the foot, workable wind-blown sails, and canons that exploded.[10]

In spite of Dibdin's efforts to adapt *Macbeth,* the adventures of the explorer Mungo Park, and domestic melodrama to his tanks, the popularity of Sadler's declined after the war, and, by 1820, the taste for the accurate depiction of contemporary events, for documentary drama, was being satisfied at the patent theaters, most notably "The Coronation," produced at the Drury Lane in August, 1820. Employing over one hundred tailors, one thousand carpenters, painters, countless scholars and consultants, Robert Elliston, who also played the lead, mounted a ninety-minute replica of the coronation of George IV, including a facsimile of the interior of Westminster Abbey and Hall and a procession of about four hundred authentically costumed actors.[11] The spectacle ran for a record 104 performances, a gorgeous, opulent, patriotic, timely, and convincing representation of the peaceful transfer of power, the survival of ceremony, and the strength of tradition, an affirmation of the right of a remarkably decadent aristocracy to enjoy its privileges untouched by the democratic revolutions that were transforming societies all over the Western world. Ironically, the royally sanctioned theater had appropriated and made to serve its elitist ends an entertainment developed in the popular theater and perfected in *Gallic Freedom,* which was a celebration of popular rights.

But this affirmation of privilege and status would have been irrelevant to the poor and illiterate who constituted an especially ardent group of theater-goers. Unable to afford either the minor or the patent houses, they developed their own theaters, the "penny gaffs" or "blood tubs" where troupes of actors evaded the law and imperiled their freedom by moving frequently and performing clandestinely in old storefronts, warehouses, and even pits dug in the ground.[12] For a few shillings a week, sickly, undernourished, uneducated children; prostitutes; actors who had failed on the stage; itinerants of all sorts, performed up to six shows a day, six days a week to audiences ranging from several hundred to a thousand people. Frequently arrested for speaking on stage, imprisoned as "rogues and vagabonds," they returned inevitably to a new location, another stage, circulating through the alleys and gin shops the news that once again they were offering their lurid representations of local crimes, burlesques of middle-class manners, sentimental pieces, bawdy songs, and twenty-minute versions of Shakespeare.

After 1811, middle-class children, especially boys, enjoyed a domestic entertainment in the juvenile drama or toy theater. Purchasing printed sheets illustrating the main characters from current plays in characteristic attitudes along with scenes, properties, costumes, and abbreviated scripts, they cut, pasted, and colored them, then mounted productions on miniature versions of Drury Lane or Covent Garden stages for a doting circle of relatives and friends. Here was not only a respectable and unique theatrical experience that might otherwise have been unavailable especially to the country gentry but also one of the few records of many Regency productions, for the actual scenery, scripts, and costumes were destroyed in the various fires that afflicted the patent houses.[13]

Finally, there were many private theatricals in the country houses, mounted with considerable care and expense, with scenery, costumes, rehearsals, indeed everything but a large audience, for plays were performed for the amusement of the participants and local gentry. For young people, whose social interactions were so restricted, the plays provided an occasion for at least ceremonial delinquencies while satisfying that "itch for acting" as Mr. Yates described it in Jane Austen's

Mansfield Park, where, in chapters 13–21, the implications of such theatricals are brilliantly exposed.

The "blood tubs" and "penny gaffs," the toy theaters, the private theatricals, the excess and spectacle of the patent theaters, the vulgarity and eccentricity of the unlicensed theaters, were all indirect responses to legal restrictions on the stage. These restrictions were created and perpetuated by the same mentality that had banished magic from the nursery, and turned fairy tales into forbidden literature. But passion, imagination, and fantasy emerged with greater potency in new dramatic and narrative forms. Like fairy tales and the folk tradition, the theater expressed the need to believe in the impossible, in transformations, in the conquest of evil, in the survival of innocence, in virtue rewarded. At its best, the theater in the opening decades of the nineteenth century, like the fairy tale and the religious ceremonies from which it evolved, provided in the enactment of certain essential narratives an adaptive mechanism for living within a mysterious, irrational, or unjust world. The narratives of Greek drama had such a ritual basis; they offered a means of adapting to a world governed by inscrutable, wayward, and powerful gods, gods who were morally and intellectually inferior to the mortals they controlled. Similarly, Elizabethan drama, primarily political, concerned with the relations among men and the distribution of human power, portrays how individuals survive in a society where evil has as much and often more power than virtue, where good men and women must patiently wait until evil finds its own retribution—if at all. Such drama, even if it could be freely performed, was inappropriate to the needs of the audience in the opening decades of the nineteenth century, an audience that was unconsciously participating in an amazing transfer of power from gods to men, from kings to clerks, a complete secularization and democratization of a once sacred and elite art.[14]

The declining status of traditional drama was pointedly symbolized in the description De Quincey offered of the fire that destroyed Drury Lane, especially the "mimic suicide" of Apollo as his statue, visible on the burning roof, "as if by some impulse of despair . . . appeared not to fall, but to throw himself into the fiery deluge" followed by "a sustained uproar of admiration and sympathy" (1854, Postscript to "On Murder Considered as One of the Fine Arts"). Although dramatists and critics complained about the decline of public taste, the enthusiasm for spectacle and pathos, the public was supporting dramatic forms, especially pantomime and melodrama, that overcame the legal restrictions while satisfying the ritual requirements of an audience that from childhood had been emotionally and imaginatively deprived.

Pantomime

Primarily because it satisfied these ritual requirements, the pantomime or harlequinade was perhaps the most popular and significant theatrical experience. The plot is familiar: two young lovers are prevented from marrying by an unsympathetic father, guardian, or similar authority figure who prefers an older, richer, and / or less appealing suitor. The father plans to banish, imprison, or even kill the young lover, who, because of his ardent and virtuous nature acquires the aid of a friendly, often supernatural agent. This agent transforms him into Harlequin, his sweetheart into Columbine, the father into Pantaloon, and the rival lover into Clown or Dandy lover. In performance this transformation was accomplished by removing large pasteboard heads and loose-fitting costumes that covered the traditional comic uniforms, implying that the pantomime characters represent some essential aspect of human nature while the other roles were superficial social conventions. Harlequin, equipped by his friendly agent with a magic bat that can transform cheese into carriages, animals and vegetables into people, escapes with Columbine and begins a quest to prove himself worthy of her, while Pantaloon and Clown pursue them, delayed by their own stupidity and baffled by the transformations. In the pursuit, all the technical achievements of the theater were displayed, twenty or thirty different scenes, diorama, panorama, and various mechanical devices simulating flight, explosions, storms, and the passage of time. In a rather explicit sexual allegory (called the "dark scene" because it takes place in a cave or grotto where Harlequin has come with Columbine to celebrate their successful escape), Harlequin loses his magic bat to Pantaloon and with it control of Columbine. Fortunately, the friendly agent intervenes, reconciles the lovers, and transports them all to a scene of "apotheosis" in a palace or temple, where they are married to live happily ever after.

Introduced to England by touring *commedia dell'arte* companies in 1660, the pantomime acquired a native form before the passage of the Licensing Act.[15] Primarily an adult entertainment, new pantomimes were presented seasonally by both the patent and the minor theaters on December 26 (Boxing Day), Easter Monday, perhaps early in July when the minor theaters were open, and often on November 9 (Lord Mayor's Day). Relying on visual effects, clever scenery and properties, songs and dances, the pantomime was suited both to the legally restricted minor theaters and to the patent houses that could afford more opulent productions. Audiences of fashionable and literary people, family parties, clerks, tradesmen, and laborers crowded all the theaters and sat attentively for one to two hour performances that often included as many as twenty-two scene changes. The titles—*Harlequin and Cinderella, Rudolph the Wolf or Columbine Red Riding-Hood, Harlequin Horner or the Christmas Pie, Harlequin and Mother Goose*— reveal the origins of many pantomimes in popular legends, folk and fairy tales, *The Arabian Nights* (trans. 1708), and *Mother Goose* (trans. 1719). Like the literature itself, composed to amuse the idle French aristocrats in the bawdy court of Louis XIV, pantomime was an adult entertainment; it gave audiences legally sanctioned access to a body of literature of enchantment and erotic allegory which had been denied to them as children.

Because the pantomime was arranged or improvised rather than authored, and because it was performed by characters in disguise, it was difficult to assign legal responsibility for the contents; consequently, contemporary subjects that might normally be forbidden on the stage appeared regularly in the pantomime. Indeed, like the popular documentary theater with which it shared a great deal, contemporaneity was a major characteristic of pantomime: contemporary fashions, values, events, laws, dramatic and literary styles, any kind of excess, pretention, or authority were objects of parody. While Clown was a funny lout, for example, he was also a dandy and therefore represented the profligate aristocracy otherwise protected from criticism, or a squire representing an unfair system of rural justice, or a soldier in an army that had been known at Peterloo to shoot down its own citizens. In fact, the development of the role of Clown from a supporting comic to the Lord of Misrule, a center of mischief and conflict, of the performance itself from a simple diversion to a powerful instrument for social criticism, defines what has been called the golden age of pantomime. Dated as beginning with the Christmas pantomime of 1806, when Joseph Grimaldi appeared as Clown in *Harlequin and Mother Goose* at Covent Garden, it ended with his tearful retirement in 1828, when, as Dickens wrote at the conclusion of his memoirs, "The genuine, the grimacing, filching, irresistable Clown left the stage . . . and though often heard of, has never since been seen."[16]

Grimaldi's Clown, supposedly in pursuit of Colinette but often in escape from everyone else, violated both human and natural law, a saucy, resourceful, mercurial fellow, clever, silly, dancing, weeping, singing, fencing, howling, fiddling, juggling, lusting after women, stealing and then devouring huge quantities of food, throwing furniture, dishes, and small children in the paths of his pursuers. If he mutilated his adversaries, they recovered, and so did he—his nose is glued on, his arms repaired by carpenters. Even the dead revived, for in pantomime evil has no power, nor is there shame, guilt, or repentance. His irreverence, his defiance of authority, decorum, manners, pieties, and social conventions provided a vicarious satisfaction for the unappeased appetites of the lower classes, a vicarious release from the self-imposed restrictions of the middle classes, restrictions that simultaneously beset individuals and guaranteed their survival, a vicarious expression for their hostility, frustration, and anxieties.

Melodrama

Melodrama, the other popular theatrical form to emerge during the Romantic period, also served primarily ritual rather than aesthetic ends. Identified by Rousseau in *Pygmalion* (1775) as nothing more than a scene of heightened emotion, mime, and music, melodrama developed in the feverish emotional climate after the fall of the Bastille into entire dramas expressing the terror, passion, idealism, and inflated rhetoric to which the newly liberated citizens of France were addicted. The melodrama was officially introduced to the English stage by Thomas Holcroft in his 1802 translation of a French production he called *A Tale of Mystery*.[17] Actually, however, many of the characteristics of melodrama were indigenous to the English theater—detailed musical accompaniment had been required by the Licensing Act in the minor theaters and had gradually been adopted by the patent theaters to attract audiences; spectacle, sensationalism, and violence in the service of morality had long characterized popular theatrical taste in England. Although after 1820, the familiar melodrama of either rural or urban domestic life emerged, during the first fifteen years of the century, coinciding with the long war against France, gothic melodrama dominated the stage. Dealing in mystery, with murders, injustices, imprisonments, incest, parricide, infanticide, and suicide, the plots were often built on false identities and supernatural interventions, implying in both forms a perilously narrow margin between illusion and reality, between the spiritual and the material world. Like pantomime, melodrama exploited all the technical possibilities of the stage, especially the sublime visual effects to be found in storms, earthquakes, and volcanoes.

The basic plot was the very same as appeared in most of the tragedies,[18] the comedies, and indeed the pantomimes with which melodrama often shared the program: young lovers or a married couple are separated by authority, accident, politics, or vice; they encounter and overcome dangers, temptations, discomforts of various sorts and are reconciled, purging the community of a pervasive and disruptive evil, embodied in the villain who, like Clown, is motivated by greed, lust, revenge, jealousy, or simply a tyrannical, mischievous disposition. Their relationship to pleasure and power constitutes the difference between Clown in pantomime and the villain in melodrama, a difference to be found in their archetypes, Dionysius and Satan. Clown is allied with pleasure, fertility, joy, and delight, while the villain is permanently at war with them. While Clown can cause temporary confusion, discomfort, embarrassment, or bad temper, pleasure prevails; in the end, all wounds are healed, pain forgotten, decorum restored. The pantomime is an especially suitable expression for a society that philosophically conceives of human beings as creatures who pursue pleasure and avoid pain, as Bentham, among others, claimed. The melodramatic villain, on the other hand, is alien, mysterious, representing pointless and self-isolating evil, especially menacing because he has the power to cause irreparable harm, anguish, even death. He is an anachronism, of sorts, a secular embodiment of the inexplicable evil that had, in more believing ages been embodied in his prototype, Satan.

The dramatists were not only especially sensitive and responsive to the expectations of their audience but also they were able to adapt themselves to the resident companies for, at a time when scripts were poorly written, altered by censors, and ultimately inaudible because of poor acoustics or noisy spectators, actors took priority over scripts, personality over plot. The cast, according to Michael Booth, had to include a hero, a heroine, a villain, several comics in the roles of confidantes, perhaps a child if one were available, an aged parent, and a band of something: gypsies, pirates, soldiers, oriental priests, bandits, whatever used up the rest of the company.[19] The heroine had to appear innocent and fragile, poor but possibly of noble descent, loyal, resourceful, capable of extreme suffering, penitence, defiance, and forgiveness, misunderstood and / or rejected by a lover, abandoned by a husband, cursed by a father, pursued by a villain; forced to hide in a forest, starve in a garret, or get lost in a storm, while her lover-husband and / or father, who hardly deserves her anyway, is unjustly imprisoned in a dungeon, jail, or madhouse, tempted, tortured, threatened with death. The villain, played by the leading man, was older, inevitably richer, either a nobleman, a pirate, a landlord, or a lawyer, costumed in black, an impatient, greedy, jealous, arrogant, peevish, and rather stupid creature usually defeated by his own ineptitude, miscalculating the time, distance, or loyalties of his confidante and the heroine's husband-lover and / or father. The hero-husband-lover is poor, if the heroine is rich, and / or of noble descent, especially if she isn't; either disguised or suffering from mistaken identity, he endures fires, storms, attacks, natural disasters, physical abuse, and overcomes barriers, bandits, and / or his own weaknesses for gambling or alcohol to claim or recover the heroine (who is usually saved by his confidante or by herself, for she is, in fact, stronger and frequently more intelligent than the hero). The hero, heroine, and even the villain have confidantes, usually comic characters, occasionally coming in pairs, who display good sense, loyalty, and the unobtrusive manners one prefers in servants; the confidante helps the hero / heroine or villain, often saving the former and betraying the latter, and, most importantly, providing comic relief, which also saves many of the dramas. The heroine might have a child who is inevitably cold, hungry, and in desperate need of the parent who is not there. She may also have an elderly relative, usually a dependent uncle or father who tends to curse, complain, grieve, worry, and lament for the days gone by.

Like the pantomime, melodrama was derivative, assimilating both contemporary events, especially crimes, and the literary tradition—lurid and sensational Elizabethan dramas such as *The Duchess of Malfi* or *The Spanish Tragedy,* and contemporary novels by Horace Walpole, Mrs. Radcliffe, and Sir Walter Scott. But in such ritualistic forms, originality is less important than the repeated and meticulous working out of the formula. Both pantomime and melodrama were collective rather than private expressions, drawing on common knowledge, reflecting the values of the audience more than any individual author. The writers had a special affinity with the expectations of this audience, with whom they had much in common, for they were craftsmen, overworked and underpaid, rather than artists, poor people who prided them-selves on their speed and resourcefulness, writers who how-ever prolific, are mostly forgotten: William Dimond, Isaac Pocock, Edward Fitzball, Douglas Jerrold, Thomas Morton, James Planché, and William Moncrieff, and the industrious Dibdin brothers, Charles and Tom, who wrote hundreds of plays and pantomimes, thousands of songs, and over sixty melodramas each while directing productions and managing theaters. While Coleridge, Keats, Southey, Wordsworth, and Lamb, indeed most of the major authors, thought there was money to be made from the theater, and were repeatedly foiled by what they thought was an exclusive system, Charles Dib-din, manager and resident dramatist at the Surrey, wrote, at the height of his powers in 1825, twenty-one pieces in twenty-eight weeks, many over a weekend, for about £5 a week.

In 1820, the year George IV acceded to the throne and the ultimate spectacle, "The Coronation" was played at Drury Lane, a gradual shift in public taste began to emerge, illus-trated in the work of William Moncrieff (1794–1857) whose more than two hundred plays display a remarkable sensitiv-ity to dramatic fashion and an equally remarkable facility in adapting to the stage the novels that were serialized in mag-azines, sometimes before the installments were finished. Dickens was so annoyed that he depicted Moncrieff in *Nicho-las Nickleby* as "the literary gentlemen . . . who had drama-tized 247 novels as fast as they had come out—some of them faster than they had come out. . . ."[20] His five melodramas in 1820 included three gothics, an adaptation of Scott's *Ivan-hoe,* and a domestic melodrama called *The Lear of Private Life; or Father and Daughter,* adapted from a novel by Mrs. Amelia Opie. The use of "King Lear" in the title partly signals the return to the stage of a play that, along with all allusions to mad kings, had been banned while George III was alive, and partly signals the domestication of an aristocratic tragedy, that transfer of interest from the nobility to the working classes. The play itself, however, has very little to do with *King Lear:* against her father's wishes, Agnes elopes with Alvanley, who then abandons her and her child because his father will not allow them to marry. Agnes discovers her father wandering in a snowstorm, having escaped from an asylum where he had been committed after going insane over her loss. She guides him home, restores his health, and ultimately marries Alvanley, who returns after his father dies. This play, full of cultural and psychological signals, explored the conflicting loyalties and family obligations, the idealization of rural virtue, the patriotism, and the failure of aristocratic values that characterize domestic melodrama whether set in a cottage, a factory, or city environment, and that were to dominate the Victorian stage.

Whereas gothic melodrama reacted against the practical, sterile, and moralistic ends of an uninspired education designed by Rousseau, Hannah More, and Maria Edgeworth, domestic melodrama was a fulfillment of them, didactic, empirical, and secular in orientation. But for all its lapses of taste and social decorum, gothic melodrama was concerned with such traditionally religious topics as the nature of good and evil, of reward and retribution, of death and afterlife, topics that John Larpent and later George Colman the Younger, as Examiner of Plays, between 1778 and 1836, were particularly wary about allowing on the stage if they contained any religious, especially Christian allusions. Consequently, although the myth of Cain and Abel was especially pertinent to the social and domestic issues of the period, and many writers attempted to dramatize it, including Coleridge, Wordsworth, and Byron, the plays were not produced because the censors considered putting Biblical matter, even familiar quotations, on the stage blasphemous.[21] Such an ardent defense of the church helped to turn the stage into an essentially godless world and to isolate the church from public and cultural life. Deprived of sacred texts, dramatists, especially gothic dramatists, drew on devils, imps, witches, and magicians for supernatural effects, those symbolic and allegorical figures generated by primitive and superstitious minds to account for the evils that plagued them. To the popular mind that made gothic melodrama such a successful form, the play was a means of addressing and placating the psychic gods that unaccountably disrupted their lives, the gods that the established church disregarded. This ritual function accounts for the formal, repetitive, and artificial quality of the action and language, for such stylized and inflated language, according to Robertson Davies, is the "high rhetoric" of universal archetypes on which the ceremonial is based.[22]

Actors

The acting in this period was as stylized and exaggerated as the language, though for different reasons.[23] Moreover, it was codified; an actor was expected to master approximately sixty gestures from a handbook, each depicting a different emotion. This stylized presentation grew out of the miming required in the unlicensed theaters and helped overcome the acoustical problems in the patent theaters. But also it served as an inconography of mental and emotional states. As surrogate priests in these mainly ceremonial dramas, as intermediaries, the actors were expressing the inner world of still undiscovered psychic gods, representing it in the social world, the world of common day. The actors, as Hazlitt, Lamb, and Keats, among others pointed out, were not only reflections of our ideal selves but also of those secret selves whose wayward impulses threaten our very survival.

The dramatic importance of the actors was enhanced by the existence of mass-circulation newspapers and magazines, specialized journals and reviews, and drama critics such as Hazlitt and Leigh Hunt, which all contributed to the first age of publicity, of media personalities such as "Master Betty" (1791–1874). Performing Shakespeare at the age of thirteen, Betty dominated the stage at both Covent Garden and Drury Lane, driving all other actors into temporary retirement while his fans followed him through the streets.[24] A slight boy, merely four feet, ten inches tall and eighty-seven pounds, he had a light, prepubescent voice, a phenomenal memory, an exceptionally attentive drama coach, an ambitious father, and an androgynous beauty that attracted a large, influential, and primarily male aristocratic following, one that especially enjoyed, according to one observer, crowding his dressing room after a performance while "his father was rubbing down his naked body from the perspiration after the exertion in performing his part on the stage." As London audiences became accustomed to the absurdity of a thirteen-year-old boy playing Hamlet, his popularity declined and he retired after an ineffectual Richard III. Nonetheless, Edmund Kean was so humiliated at being replaced by Betty in the provinces that he ran away and lived in the fields off turnips and carrots.

Mrs. Sarah Siddons (1755–1831), whose reputation was created by the same reviewers, is still considered "the greatest actress of the English stage," "tragedy personified," as Hazlitt called her (Howe, 5:189).[25] Born Sarah Kemble, the eldest of twelve children in a theatrical family that could be traced on her mother's side back to Shakespeare's time, she learned her art in her father's strolling company, and spent her career performing the parts of an injured, suffering, and often bereft wife, or an innocent lady victimized by circumstances, or an heroic consort or mother, or the malevolent and strangely helpless Lady Macbeth. In *Isabella,* she believed that Biron, her husband, was dead, and married another to solve her financial difficulties and protect her son from her cruel father-in-law. Biron returns and is killed in a duel after which Isabella kills herself in grief. So moving was this presentation of pathos and grief that Mrs. Siddons often collapsed after her performances, and in Edinburgh, in 1784, Miss Gordon of Gight, Aberdeen, later to be the mother of Lord Byron, became hysterical and had to be carried from the theater screaming "Oh, my Biron! My Biron!", a line from the play. As Mrs. Haller in *The Stranger* (1798), translated from von Kotzebue's German text by Benjamin Thompson, she plays a lady who has become the housekeeper in a castle to repent for her infidelity to her husband. The stranger, her husband, played by her brother John Philip Kemble, moves into a cottage at the castle gate and tries to lure her back. Just as they agree that they will meet again only in "a better world," the children appear, and the play concludes with the following tableau: "They press the children in their arms with speechless affection; then tear themselves away—gaze at each other—spread their arms and rush into an embrace. The children run and cling round their parents." The play offers a fine index of taste in its endless wringing of emotion, its sentimentalism, its lack of moral and intellectual content, its liberal attitude toward adultery, and the public displays of emotion that it evoked in audiences and cast alike, for it was considered a mark of breeding to weep and moan and lament, even in public, and Mrs. Siddons provided many occasions for it.

In appearance, she was large, dignified, and handsome, with a heavy brow and a melancholy expression, largely attributable to her private life, which was often as sad as the parts she played. Like all actresses, in spite of the adulation, her life was difficult. She bore seven children: only five survived infancy but they died before her. She had to learn and retain many parts on insufficient notice and with little rehearsal in plays that might not run more than a night. She had to work for dictatorial managers, mostly her brother, John Philip Kemble, and with actors who were so undisciplined that they were fined for forgetting lines, for being on or off stage at the wrong time, for wearing the wrong costume. For the elegant and royal parts she played, she had to provide her own wardrobe, appropriate not only to her and to her parts but to the enormous theaters in which she worked—a collection of royal robes, jewels, crowns, and yards of lace acquired from the wardrobe of the beheaded Marie Antoinette, all destroyed when Covent Garden burned. And, of course, her audiences not only shrieked, groaned, wept, and collapsed in fits but also made crude and inappropriate comments. "As the truly virtuous love virtue," one German commentator noted, "so must an English actor love his art,—for its own sake alone,—and trouble himself little about his reception for the audiences are so rude, ignorant, and unmannerly."[26] Yet she was, as her friend Mrs. Piozzi reported, "Handsome, celebrated, enriched, adored. Everybody worships that admirable creature except her own family—to them she is no heroine—tho contented to make herself Valet de Chambre." Sir Joshua Reynolds painted her as the Tragic Muse and signed his name on the edge of her dress explaining, "I have resolved to go down to posterity on the hem of your garment."[27]

As a tragic heroine, Mrs. Siddons was expected to maintain an impeccable public image, in spite of her philandering husband, while her comedic counterpart, Mrs. Dorothy Jordan (1761–1816), was allowed to deviate considerably from ordinary standards of morality so long as she appeared on stage as expected.[28] Like Mrs. Siddons, she was burdened by the pedestrian concerns of bearing and providing for children while her public cast her in an ethereal role, as a fertile but androgynous creature descended from the Bacchae. "A childlike spirit," Lamb called her, "who shook off the load of years from her spectators; she seemed one whom care could not come near; a privileged being, sent to teach mankind what it most wants, joyousness" (Lucas, I, 185). Yet most of her life seemed joyless. The illegitimate daughter of a provincial actress, Dorothy was seduced at age nineteen and, to provide for her illegitimate daughter, played comic roles at the Drury Lane, the male impersonations called "breeches" parts with which Shakespeare's comedies abound. After three more illegitimate children, she became the mistress of the Duke of Clarence, third son of George III, who was to become King William IV. Over the next twenty years she bore him ten children, and, by seldom missing a performance in London or the provinces, supported herself, her first daughter, and paid the Duke's gambling debts. The duke, who had spent his youth in the navy, was a handsome, good-natured though salty creature, with nautical manners and a warm heart, doting on his mistress and his children, for whom he provided while living a conventional domestic life. They parted in 1811, he, as possible heir to the throne to find a more suitable mate in a German princess who died childless allowing his niece Victoria to become Queen. After their separation, Mrs. Jordan, weary, heartbroken, and even bored with her profession, worked at a frantic pace to help provide for her family. In 1816, she died, lonely and destitute in Paris.

While Mrs. Siddons and Mrs. Jordan, assisted by the press, represented timeless archetypes of tragedy and comedy, Edmund Kean embodied a contemporary one, a symbol of the flawed grandeur, the contradictions, the misdirected energy, the consuming passion, and the satanic inclinations of a certain kind of personality, literary and historical, generated by the age. A self-invented creature, Kean made it difficult for others to trace his origins.[29] Born in 1787 or 1789, abandoned by both his father, a carpenter, and his mother, an actress, he was introduced to the stage of Drury Lane by his aunt when he was only four years old. After years as a penniless strolling player in the provinces, he arrived in London in 1814, during the longest and worst frost in history. Grieving over the death of his six-year-old son just a month before, he made his way through the freezing rain, his costume and wig in a package under his arm, to play Shylock in *The Merchant of Venice* in a dreary and half-empty theater. There, a reluctant critic, William Hazlitt, sent by the editor of the *Morning Chronicle* to say something positive about the performance, witnessed "one of the greatest debuts in theatrical history" (Howe, 5:174).

Kean's originality, his emotional intensity, his spontaneity, the strength of his passion to possess, destroy, and revenge made his Macbeth, his Shylock, his Richard III, his Iago, inimitable. So convincing was his range of malice, villainy, and even insanity that when he played Sir Giles Overreach in *A New Way to Pay Old Debts,* his fury made actresses faint on the stage, ladies shriek in the audience, and Lord Byron have a convulsion from "the agony of reluctant tears." Byron, one of the few aristocrats Kean could tolerate, befriended him, called him "a wonder," "a triumph of mind over matter for he had nothing but countenance and expression—his figure is very little and even mean" (*L and J,* 6:206; 4:216). Unfortunately, Kean's rage was genuine, a reaction to years of abuse, neglect, poverty, that he blamed on the managers, the playwrights, the audiences who adulated him, and the aristocracy who courted him. He was extravagant, petulant, insulting, riding his horse up and down the stairs at Drury Lane, floating down the Thames in a boat with his pet lion, boxing in dining rooms, carousing with whores—up to three a night in his dressing room while audiences waited for the play to resume. He ruined plays by refusing to rehearse, failing to learn his lines and cues, and even missing performances.

At first, the public tolerated and encouraged him: "Kean! Kean!" Keats wrote of the reprobate actor on his return to the stage following a drunken binge, "have a carefulness of thy health, an in-nursed respect for thy own genius, a pity for us in these cold and unfeeling times! Cheer us a little in the failure of our days! for romance lives but in books. The goblin is driven from the heath, and the rainbow is robbed of its mystery."[30] His public needed to believe that the self-ishness, insensitivity, cruelty he depicted on the stage was an illusion, an expression of contempt for the austerity and restrictions of contemporary life. But Keats, Hazlitt, all of his most ardent admirers were to be victims of such false expectations; they had created a charismatic figure out of a drunk and a profligate. In 1819, hearing that Kean could not play in his tragedy, *Otho the Great,* Keats concluded, "What a set of barren asses are actors" (*Letters,* II, 149). Of course, Kean was very much responsible for the disenchantment of his public and their reaction against him, for by identifying with the malevolent creatures he was supposed to be merely impersonating, he had betrayed them, betrayed his ceremonial role, and betrayed himself as well.

Threatened with paternity suits, bad debts, and weary from drunken orgies and entanglements, he undertook several American tours, which ended in the same riots as his London engagements. In 1833, he played Othello to his son's Iago, collapsed on the stage, and died a few weeks later at age forty-five. His son Charles, educated at Eton, married Ellen Tree, and acquired considerable fame for his accurate Shakespearean productions at the Princess Theater and for developing an understated, restrained style of melodramatic acting, the very opposite of his father.

Edmund Kean's capacity to portray unconscionable evil inspired many dramas, the most controversial and successful being *Bertram; or the Castle of St. Aldobrand* (1816) by Charles Maturin, an Irish parson who delivered popular sermons and paid for his extravagances, his dancing parties, gambling, and odd costumes by writing gruesome gothic tales, preferably in his living room surrounded by his large quarrelsome family.[31]

Although called a tragedy, the popularity of *Bertram* is in part attributable to the melodramatic commonplaces it assimilated: spectacles such as storms, ship wrecks, processions of knights, robbers, monks, interiors of castles, chapels, a cliff, a forest, a cave, helpless women and children, corrupted clergymen, insanity, suicide, adultery, infanticide, jealousy, revenge, and murder. They were all compressed into a rather simple though repulsive plot: the villain, who begins the play with our sympathies, is unjustly driven into exile by Aldobrand, who then marries his sweetheart, Imogine. Years later, Bertram is shipwrecked, washed ashore on his native island, and finds refuge in a monastery where the Prior inflames his desire for revenge. He seduces Imogine and kills Aldobrand, driving Imogine insane and leading her to kill her child (or at least to our suspecting she has killed her child), then herself in front of Bertram as he is being led to his execution, which he evades by committing suicide. The play contained everything theater audiences of 1816 loved. Coleridge considered it "melancholy proof" of the degradation of the public mind (*Biographia,* Shawcross, II, 202).[32] Byron thought it needed "lowering," that it was still too elevated for contemporary audiences (*L and J,* IV, 336).

Poets as Playwrights

To us the play is an index to what was considered presentable or even successful drama, as opposed to the unacted and possibly unactable drama,[33] the rich and diverse array of plays by the major poets of the period, such as Wordsworth's *The Borderers* (1796–1797); Byron's *Manfred* (1817), *Cain* (1821), and *Werner* (1921–1822); Shelley's *Prometheus Unbound* (1819), *The Cenci* (1819), *Hellas* (1821), and *Swellfoot the Tyrant* (1819); Keats's *Otho the Great* (1819) with Charles Brown, and *King Stephen;* and twenty-two plays on the passions published between 1798 and 1812 by Joanna Baillie (1762–1851), "a model of an English Gentlewoman," as Wordsworth called her, "the bold enchantress," as Scott claimed, whose "fearless hand and heart in flame" could "restore the ancient tragic line."[34]

Born into a dour and religious family in Scotland, educated at a girls' boarding school in Glasgow, Joanna Baillie moved to London in 1783 with her mother and sister to keep house for her brother Matthew who, educated at Oxford to be a physician, had inherited their Uncle John Hunter's School of Anatomy. When Matthew married in 1790, she moved to Hampstead where, in 1798, stimulated by her literary contacts, she published anonymously the first volume of plays called *Plays on the Passions. De Montfort,* a tragedy on hate, was performed eight times at the Drury Lane in 1800, with Mrs. Siddons and John Philip Kemble in the leads. In 1821,

Scott convinced Byron, on the committee at the Drury Lane, to revive *De Montfort:* extravagantly mounted with Edmund Kean in the lead and Elliston's "Coronation" spectacle on the same bill, the play ran only five performances.

Although her plays failed on the stage, she continued to publish them while caring for a blind and crippled mother and entertaining such literary luminaries as Wordsworth, Landor, Byron, Southey, Maria Edgeworth and her dear friend, Sir Walter Scott. The mystery of Joanna Baillie is how an uneducated and inexperienced lady, a lady whose library was sparse and who seldom attended the theater, whose sheltered life conformed to the expectations of her sex and age, nonetheless wrote twenty-six plays on passions she could not have experienced and rarely observed.[35]

According to Joanna Baillie's introductions, the plays, all designed for the stage, were supposed to demonstrate the inner struggle of an individual with a dominating passion. However appealing actors may have found the opportunity to present boundless anger, jealousy, pride, revenge, these plays about single passions were too monotonous, subtle, introspective, and philosophical for contemporary taste, too eccentric for the ritual requirements of popular drama. Her interest in motive rather than deed, in what makes people act rather than action, on the psychology of human behavior rather than the choreography of the players, showed how remote she was from the demands of the contemporary stage. She did, however, contribute to the development of a special secular morality suited to a stage from which representations of God, of religion, or of religious texts had been banished. Assuming that human beings are motivated from within, not above, that the forces moving them are internal, not supernatural, irrational, and often unknown to them, Joanna Baillie was helping to translate contemporary theories of human behavior into drama.

Indeed, this exploration of motives and personality, of what makes some people self-defeating and destructive while others are benevolent and virtuous, became the major function of drama during the period. Poets, especially, tried to find a secular explanation of evil; they depicted it not as an alienation from God but an alienation from oneself, a matter of incorrect information, of misapplied talents, of false values, distorted priorities, excess, imbalance, ignorance, even bad taste. "Let us suppose a young man of great intellectual powers," Wordsworth wrote in his preface to *The Borderers,* a play he wrote in 1796, "yet without any solid principles of genuine benevolence. His master passions are pride and the love of distinction. . . . He goes into the world and is betrayed into a great crime" (*Prose,* I, 76). Wordsworth, having supported the French Revolution and watched it turn into the Reign of Terror, having fathered and abandoned a child and her mother because of political and religious circumstances, knew, as Joanna Baillie, perhaps, did not, that good men often do wicked things for which there is no expiation, and that their worst flaw may be a capacity for self-deceit. "The study of human nature suggests this awful truth," Wordsworth wrote in 1842, "that, as in the trials to which life subjects us, sin and crime are apt to start from their very opposite qualities, so there are no limits to the hardening of the heart, and the perversion of the understanding to which they may carry their slaves" (*Prose,* I, 69). Most of the dramatists seemed intent on finding the limits.

Shelley, unlike Wordsworth, wrote for the stage, and his play, *The Cenci,* appeared to offer everything the public could have wanted while exploring the limits of evil in a world where neither divine nor human justice prevails.[36] After holding a banquet to celebrate the murder of his sons, Count Cenci rapes his daughter Beatrice to punish her for publicly accusing him of impiety. Assisted by her stepmother and younger brother, she has him assassinated, an act she justifies by appealing to higher law. Nonetheless, the Pope condemns her to be beheaded along with her stepmother. It is a play which violates all expectations, all natural affections, all human relationships. Count Cenci himself, a role designed for Kean, is the epitome of sin, believing his fiendishness has some divine end. While Shelley and most of his advocates believed that the play was rejected by Covent Garden because it was written by an atheist (although it was submitted anonymously), it is, in fact, the constant invocation of God that made it inappropriate for the stage. Similarly, while Shelley, and his followers as well, believed that the incest theme was too offensive for the stage, it was, in fact, among the repertoire of horrors to which audiences of the period had become acclimated through gothic melodrama and even found especially appealing. If anything, he brought too much talent to the stage, too much concern for aesthetic as opposed to ritualistic values. He aimed at realism in an age that required illusion; he emphasized language, psychology, and feeling, in an age that required action and spectacle. In fact, his sheer imaginative power, the energy and thought he invested in the play, the intensity of the language and the passions it represented, the

authenticity of the characters and their responses to the dis-
eased world in which they were living, made the incidence
of incest and parricide far more repulsive than similar or even
worse indecencies depicted by Maturin, for example, who
used the artificial but conventional language and character of
the ritualistic popular theater with which audiences were
familiar and to which they had in some ways become inured.

Serving on the committee that ran Drury Lane, Byron was
more involved with the theater than the other writers, and,
while he wrote more plays than the others, they were intended
for "mental" rather than popular theater.[37] As a nobleman
who enjoyed more acclaim than any of his contemporaries
other than Sir Walter Scott, Byron could afford to disregard
popularity, even representation, as a motive for writing plays.
In doing so, he showed that the closet drama was not merely
"unactable" drama but a legitimate form for the exploration
of character, for the very modern concept that character may
be known apart from action. The character he most fre-
quently explored was a composite of contemporary person-
alities including himself, Napoleon, "Monk" Lewis, even
Kean, as well as such literary figures as Faust, Cain, and Pro-
metheus. So compelling, representative, and interesting was
this figure that in spite of Byron's intent, his plays found an
audience in the smaller theaters and among the more psycho-
logically oriented spectators who appeared later in the cen-
tury.

As a form, closet drama had been developing its own char-
acteristics and creating a reading audience since the Com-
monwealth (1641–1660), when the theaters had been closed.
The rise of such inexpensive publications as the twenty-one
volume *Bell's British Theater* (1776), *Bell's Shakespeare* (1791),
the twenty-five volume *British Theatre* published by Long-
man with introductions by Mrs. Inchbald, gave middle-class
readers access to Shakespeare and other Elizabethans, as well
as contemporary drama, without having to endure the dis-
comfort of the theaters, the vulgarity of the audiences, or the
criminal element that surrounded the theaters. Like panto-
mime and melodrama, the existence of a closet drama helped
playwrights to overcome the restrictions of the theater, for
in closet drama they could explore religious topics based on
Biblical texts, and political ones. Coleridge, Hazlitt, Hunt,
Lamb, and other critics further enriched the reading experi-
ence with lectures and essays that dealt with text rather than
performance. Indeed, in "On the Tragedies of Shakespeare
Considered with Reference to Their Fitness for Stage Repre-

sentation" (1811), Lamb claimed that Shakespeare was too good for the stage, that *King Lear,* for example, was too powerful to be acted out except in the imagination.[38] Drama, then, far from being in a decline, acquired a double life in the Romantic period, as performance and as publication.

Thomas Lovell Beddoes

Exemplifying all the contradictions and extremes of the period, Thomas Lovell Beddoes (1803–1849), is to me one of the most interesting of the Romantic dramatists. Son of Thomas Beddoes, an energetic, high-spirited, and eccentric physician, poet, and revolutionary, young Thomas grew into an erratic and unpredictable man whose loyalties, like his father's, were divided between science (that for him meant spending most of his life dissecting corpses in Switzerland) and poetry. After his father died, Thomas moved to Edge-worthtown with his mother, one of Richard Edgeworth's twenty-two children, where he joined that extraordinary nursery of Edgeworth children, presided over by his aunt, Maria, who was trying out her practical and moralistic tales before publishing them in *The Parent's Assistant.* Here he encountered that bias against fairy and folk tales that was to influence the character of the entire British population. He was, "to pay bitterly and dearly," Royall Snow, his biographer, wrote, "for a mind trained to be so reasonable, so penetrating, it could not deceive even itself."[39] He studied medicine at Pembroke College, Oxford, befriended the widowed Mary Shelley as a disciple of her late husband, and exiled himself to Europe where he died in 1849, considered by many to be insane. He wrote one doleful poem about a lover who is struck dead by lightning while caressing his sweetheart on the eve of his wedding, and two plays that gave him a reputation as, variously, the last Elizabethan, the one person who understood contemporary drama, and a precursor of the theater of the absurd.[40]

In 1825, in a letter more widely quoted by literary historians than any of his plays, Beddoes explained his goal: "I am convinced the man who is to awaken the drama must be a bold trampling fellow—no creeper into worm-holes—no reviser even—however good. These reanimations are vampire-cold—such ghosts as Marlow—Webster &tc. are better dramatists, better poets, I dare say, than any contemporary of ours—but they are ghosts—the worm is in their pages—& we want to see something that our great-grandsires did not

know. With the greatest reverence for all the antiquities of
the drama I still think, that we had better beget than revive—
attempt to give the literature of this age an idiosyncrasy &
spirit of its own & only raise a ghost to gaze on not to live
with—just now the drama is a haunted ruin."[41]

Death's Jest-Book or The Fool's Tragedy, started in 1825, and
published posthumously in 1850, was intended to represent
such a new and appropriate drama, and in some ways it was.
In a preface composed in 1828, Beddoes stated explicitly that
modern drama would depict human beings as subject to the
consequences of their own actions, responsible for their
behavior rather than victims of destiny, circumstance, envi-
ronment, biology, history, whatever. In spite of this heroic
concept of human action, however, the characters in Bed-
does' play behave just the same as the characters in all the
contemporary plays, helpless before their own passions, will-
ful, destructive, self-defeating, jealous, resigned. In both
substance and tone, the play itself is a "haunted ruin," a pro-
jection of his obsession with death, decay, futility, disease,
corruption, composed at intervals between dissecting corpses
and periods of debauchery. However it may have changed
over the twenty-five years that Beddoes worked on it, the
plot remained essentially the same: Duke Melveric of Mün-
sterberg has killed the father of Isbrand (who seeks revenge)
and of Wolfram (who does not seek revenge but in fact who
saves the Duke's life while they are in Egypt). Fearing that
Wolfram's goodness will win the heart of Sibylla, the Duke's
beloved, he kills Wolfram. Later, in a ceremony in which the
Duke tries to call up the spirit of his late wife, with whom he
is also still in love, he summons Wolfram's spirit by mis-
take—his body has been exchanged by Isbrand for the body
of the late Duchess; Sybilla falls in love with Wolfram's ghost
and kills herself to join him. Later, after surviving an attempt
on his life by Isbrand, who also tries to murder his sons and
is in turn killed by a political fanatic, the Duke is dragged,
still alive, into the world of the dead by Wolfram. The hero
of the play is Death itself, a grinning skull reminiscent of
Clown in pantomime, as is the episodic structure of the play
itself: disregarding virtue, status, defeating every human
aspiration toward love, power, dignity, justice, he renders
human wickedness impotent.

However unlikely it may sound, the play is genuinely funny,
for it is the loss of humor, of imagination, of the ridiculous
that Beddoes laments more than the fact of death itself. Man-
drake, a foppish, superstitious, pseudo-scientist, possibly

representing Beddoes, serves as his spokesman: "O world, world! the gods and fairies left thee, for thou wert too wise; and now, thou Socratic star, thy demon, the great Pan, Folly is parting from thee. 'The oracles still talked in their sleep,' shall our grandchildren say, 'till Master Merriman's kingdom was broken up! Now is everyman his own fool, and the world's cheerless.'" As his own fool, Beddoes created that grotesque humor to which the modern theater of the absurd is so indebted, an interpenetration of beauty and pain, of deformity and laughter, of the irrational and the true. By juxtaposing superstition, fantasy, the occult with realistic detail, in fact scientific imagery drawn from such contemporary paleontologists as Baron Cuvier, by dwelling on the details of the dead with an anatomist's eye then depicting a ceremony that successfully conjures up a spirit, although the wrong spirit, Beddoes demonstrates the limitations of the reasonable and empirical world into which he was educated, that cheerless "Socratic star."

While it may be considered modern, *Death's Jest-Book* also recalls the ironic, realistic, and admonitory tapestries of the medieval period and assimilates the graveyard poetry of the eighteenth century, such as Young's "Night Thoughts" (1742–1744), Blair's "The Grave" (1743), and Gray's "Elegy Written in a Country Churchyard" (1751), expressing those fashionably mournful feelings that were becoming associated with beauty, refinement, and taste. To this macabre, self-indulgent poetry, a poetry that made feeling, religious melancholy especially, an end in itself, Beddoes brought the secular, scientific, and skeptical attitudes that had developed in the intervening years, helping to fulfill his ambition to "give the literature of this age an idiosyncrasy and spirit of its own." But as Hazlitt and John Stuart Mill, among others, observed, by the second decade of the century it was impossible to identify a single dominating spirit by which to characterize the age and therefore its literature, for civilized life had become so complex, diverse, and specialized. Consequently, although Wordsworth's *Prelude* appeared in 1850, the same year as *Death's Jest-Book,* and although it was a poem celebrating life, joy, selfhood, the triumph of mind over nature, of spirit over matter, however different from *Death's Jest-Book,* it had had an equal claim to represent the "idiosyncrasy & spirit" of the age.

Unfortunately, idiosyncrasy was inappropriate for a popular form such as theater, which thrived on the common, anonymous collective expression of the public that supported it. The human psyche, its transcendental yearning, its private terrors or delinquencies, were irrelevant if not dangerous to the public world of the theater. While artists such as Wordsworth and Shelley were learning to negotiate their inner worlds, to communicate with their own buried selves, they were losing the means to communicate with the external world and the collective life that was coming to dominate society in the nineteenth century. The artist's relation to this changing and often contradictory new world of public discourse and what it consisted of are the major concerns of the following chapter on politics and political thought.

CHAPTER V

Poets and a Gallery of "Sophisters, Economists, and Calculators"

Poetry and Power

WHEN HOMER SANG of national wars, or Chaucer performed at court, or Shakespeare dramatized the chronicles of kings, politics and poetry shared the same frame of reference: the activities and interests of the aristocracy, the center of political power.[1] But during the Romantic period, poets became active in political activities that had no poetic precedence, for they lived in an age of democratic revolution, engaged in political dissent, and identified with the people. In his youth, William Blake associated with Joseph Johnson, the radical bookseller jailed for selling Tom Paine's *The Rights of Man,* and later was himself tried for treason. Coleridge and Southey, after supporting the French Revolution, designed what they called a pantisocracy, a cooperative community which they planned to start in America along the banks of the Susquehanna. Wordsworth's political consciousness was awakened by Michel Beaupuy, the Royalist soldier whom he met in France during the Revolution; and later during the war against Napoleon he wrote a pamphlet, "The Convention of Cintra," defending the right to national self-determination. Lord Byron, the only aristocrat among the major poets, addressed the House of Lords in defense of the laboring poor and Catholic emancipation and was preparing to fight in the Greek War of Independence when he died of a fever. And Shelley spent most of his meager fortune and his honeymoon writing pamphlets to the illiterate Irish peasants encouraging them to revolt; barely escaped arrest as a spy when he was discovered setting another of his pamphlets to sea in a wine bottle; and, during his self-imposed exile in Italy, wrote political verse urging the Manchester weavers to continue their resistance against high taxes and government restrictions. Finally, Keats divided a seminal year, 1816, between Old Pan and *Libertas,* between dreams of pastoral retreat and visits to Leigh Hunt, whom he first met while Hunt was in prison for publishing statements deriding the Prince Regent.

Though Blake, Shelley, and Keats composed myths of political revolution, and Byron, Coleridge, and Wordsworth wrote topical verse dealing with political figures and events, the degree of their political concern was disguised in their major poetry, appearing, as Carl Woodring explains in *Politics in English Romantic Poetry* (1970), as a subtle inspirational force: "They found their belief in imagination at odds with the interpretations of man argued or implicit in political, social and economic tracts issued steadily by both liberals and conservatives of their day" (p. 33). The poets' concepts of imagination placed priority on subjective experience, the binding truths to be found in the inner life, the laws of growth, the demands of creativity, the individualism that comes from believing, as Wordsworth did, that all "genuine liberty" is within.[2] But the evolving political theory, the people and events that generated it, were antithetical to such "genuine liberty," for the ideal of more freedom for more people involved systems that would ultimately deprive some people of the freedoms, the private freedoms, they already had.

Politically, the Romantic movement falls within the reign of George III (1760–1820), who ruled a prosperous and politically successful nation for sixty years while the rest of the Western world was in turmoil, some of which was caused by his own insistence on maintaining the status quo. Sir William Blackstone had analyzed the constitution in *Commentaries on the Laws of England* (1765–1769) and decided it was perfect. After the beheading of Charles I in 1649 and the Glorious Revolution in 1688, the government had been simplified, its role defined as protector and preserver of poverty. The limited monarchy, subject to an elected Parliament, could levy only sufficient taxes to maintain a standing army, an investment that helped create new markets through foreign conquest. New religious toleration encouraged the Protestant middle class, who considered prosperity a sign of grace, to do the trading. Accumulating wealth, they purchased land, the source of political power, and in fifty years turned England into what Adam Smith called "a nation of shopkeepers," one that was building "a great empire for the sole purpose of raising up a people of customers."[3]

In George III the middle class had a king in its own image, according to Leigh Hunt, "an extraodinary mixture of domestic virtue with official duplicity; of rustical, mechanical tastes and popular manners, with the most exalted ideas of authority, of a childish and self-betraying cunning, with the most stubborn reserves; of fearlessness with sordidness; good-nature with unforgivingness; and of health and strength of temperance and self-denial, with the last weakness of understanding, and passions that exasperated it out of its reason. The English nation were pleased to see in him a crowning specimen of themselves—John Bull."[4] Like his granddaughter, Victoria, he was thrifty, self-righteous, and intellectually commonplace, devoted to domestic virtues, useful knowledge, trade, and agriculture. He enjoyed being called "Farmer George," a title he earned while riding around the countryside visiting pig farms and breweries, and contributing articles on turnips to Arthur Young's *Annals of Agriculture* under the pseudonym "Ralph Robinson." The year after he assumed the throne at age twenty-two, he married the seventeen-year-old German princess, Charlotte (familiarly known as "Old Snuffy" for her habit of sniffing during conversation), and issued "A Proclamation for the Encouragment of Piety and Virtue, and for the Preventing and Punishing of Vice, Profaneness and Immorality." Although he had been eager to recover the historical authority of the throne, it was as a moralist rather than a political leader that he dominated public life. In 1776, while he was hopelessly trying to retain his American colonies, Adam Smith claimed in *The Wealth of Nations* that it was an empire existing "in imagination only"; and Gibbon published, ominously, the first volume of *The Decline and Fall of the Roman Empire*. In 1788, he suffered the first of his periodic bouts with madness and in 1811, nearly twenty years into a devastating war against France, his son was named Regent.

But no amount of personal charm or intellectual acumen would have improved George III's prestige, for the age of kings was clearly over; and power, instead of descending on the monarch from heaven, ascended through Parliament. The vision of society as a hierarchical structure based on inherited wealth and position, based in other words on status, was evolving into the uncertain but vital one based on contract, the competitive exchange of goods and services. Just as the traditional relationship between man and God, man and nature, had been shifting, so the traditional relationships among men had been opened to question, specifically to discover what the best and necessary relationships were. As soon as individuals, particularly those productive members of society engaged in agriculture, manufacturing, or trade, attributed their livelihood to other men rather than to God or to nature, as soon as the post-feudal system of obligation and dependencies was replaced by one of rights and duties, by what Locke called the Social Contract, the social sciences—economics, political science, and sociology—emerged to help define that contract, the distribution of rights, duties, and rewards.

Adam Smith, Thomas Malthus, Jeremy Bentham, Edmund Burke, Thomas Paine, William Godwin, Mary Wollstonecraft, Robert Owen, and Samuel Taylor Coleridge—some social, economic, and political theorists and activists whom we shall discuss—had no traditional body of knowledge on which to draw in defining their community of interests, if in fact they had a community at all; for they had very little in common aside from a concern for the way people related to one another and a sense of being implicated in a fateful historical moment. "We are touching on a period big with the most important changes," Thomas Malthus wrote in 1798, the year of Wordsworth's *Lyrical Ballads,* "changes that would in some measure be decisive of the future fate of mankind." And, like the poets, whatever tradition they did have was a translation of religious concepts into a secular frame of reference. Concepts of suffering and salvation, fate and revelation, the terror, fear, and even messianic joy of Biblical prophecy appeared in many disguises, lending a sense of inevitability to their designs.[5] Again, like the poets, they saw in the world about them reflections of their personal if not subjective experience, which they universalized. The social models they formulated, then, were inventions rather than discoveries, autobiographical allegories verifying their own experience or ideals just as Shakespeare did in his plays, Wordsworth in his poems, or Dickens in his novels. But most importantly, they were all preoccupied with the same problem we have encountered among the poets: how to reconcile and turn to account the fundamental antagonism between private interest and public obligation, between individual freedom and social responsibility, between the egotistical instinct and the altruistic one. For Alexander Pope writing *An Essay on Man* in 1734, this identity of interest had been axiomatic: "Thus God and Nature linked the general frame, / And bade self-love and social be the same." Within a generation, the complex world of the marketplace raised issues for which neither God nor Nature offered sufficient explanations.

Adam Smith

By showing how a person's capacity for sympathy could overcome his self-interest, Adam Smith (1723–1790) in *The Theory of Moral Sentiments* (1759) offered the first secular explanation for the natural identity of interests, which became the basis for Hazlitt's and ultimately Keats's theory of the sympathetic imagination. As his first published work reveals, then, Smith's primary interest was in human relationships, and he founded his economic theories upon them.[6] From childhood, he had observed that wealth or, more specifically, value lay in labor and human exchange rather than in land or treasure. At age four he had been kidnapped by gypsies and later abandoned as unprofitable baggage when they failed to collect a ransom for him. Although his family was wealthy enough to send him to Oxford, the village of Kirkaldy, Scotland, where he grew up, was so remote from the world of commerce that many of the 1,500 citizens still used nails for money. At Oxford, Smith learned the enervating effects of legal protection from competition; while he educated himself in contemporary philosophy and English history, his tutors read current romances and slept through public debates. By age twenty-eight, he held both the Chair of Logic and of Moral Philosophy at the University of Glasgow, collecting his salary directly from the students who attended his lectures, among them James Boswell. Apparently, the students felt sufficiently rewarded, for they refused his offer to refund half their fees when he left at mid-term in 1764 to enjoy aristocratic patronage as tutor to the young Duke of Buccleuch. During their stay in France, Smith met Dr. François Quesnay, personal physician to Madame Pompadour and founder of an influential school of political economy called Physiocracy. The Physiocrats defined wealth as deriving from the land and circulating like blood through the body, invigorating the entire society so long as it was unrestricted. While Smith agreed with the idea of *laissez-faire*—of the self-realization that individuals and societies were capable of achieving if left to their own devices—he took exception to the agricultural thesis, for he came from what was then the most industrialized country in the world. In 1776, Adam Smith published his own declaration of independence, *The Wealth of Nations,* a panoramic survey of the laws that governed the market-place, many of which he had himself encountered.

Historically tracing the economic forms through which society had developed—from hunting, through herding, farming, and then to commerce—Smith proved to the great delight of the English revolutionaries that the political insti-tutions in England were no longer appropriate because the nation had moved from an agricultural to an industrial econ-omy.[7] His most striking innovation, his theory of value, located wealth in human activity rather than in material objects: "Labour . . . is the real measure of the exchangeable value of all commodities. The real price of everything, what every-thing really costs to the man who wants to acquire it, is the toil and trouble of acquiring it" (p. 133). But the system he proposed was more utilitarian than humanistic; the only legitimate motives for work, he claimed, were self-interest and the desire for material gain. If not more beneficial to soci-ety than moral or religious motives, they were at least more reliable: "It is not from the benevolence of the butcher, the brewer, or the baker, that we expect our dinner, but from their regard to their own self-interest" (p. 119). Competi-tion, "the invisible hand," prevents self-interest from becoming exploitation of the consumer, keeps prices down to the level of wages, wages up to the level of subsistence, and, in turn, subsistence at the level of supply. The system was as clear, rational, just, and self-regulating as the Newtonian universe: the butcher sells a lamb chop, which is as good as it should be, at a price his customer can afford, while paying the shep-herd enough to survive, in order to keep the shepherd and the customer; he is not motivated by any particular respect for lamb-chop-eaters or an aesthetic appreciation of lamb chops.

While competition rules the marketplace, cooperation, through the division of labor, rules production: while one man could perhaps make one pin in a day while growing his food, weaving his clothes, and building his shelter, ten men, dividing the tasks, could produce 48,000 pins in a day and create work for those who would provide his necessities, which he could then afford to purchase. Claiming that the mark of a civilized society was the degree to which tasks were divided and production was cooperative, Smith, like the utilitarian and utopian thinkers who followed him, made sheer productivity a goal, equating it with progress and success—in fact, with happiness.

We can see Smith's economic theory both vindicated and refuted in two industries that so altered the quality of life during the Romantic period that no one escaped their effects. An extraordinary series of inventions for producing and harnessing power appeared during the first decade of George III's reign, culminating in Edmund Cartwright's power loom, which made possible the cheap and efficient production of cotton. While the cotton manufacturers profited from these inventions, so did the toolmakers who made the machinery, in turn stimulating the iron and coal industries, the shipping industry, and the merchants who provided the raw materials or exported the finished product, the cotton farmers in America and the slave traders who supplied them with labor. The poor had work, in fact, too much work: twelve to fourteen hours a day, men, women, and children left the cottages and fields for the mills, the mines, and the factories in Manchester, Lancashire, Sheffield, and the rest of the industrialized Midlands and north country. Even prison inmates were rented out to local manufacturers. Cheap cotton for underwear supposedly improved the health of this new class called, curiously, as E. P. Thompson notes,[8] the laboring poor, and even may have extended their lives, but economically speaking, within a generation these cotton garments became the rags that would be recycled into cheap paper. The production of cheap paper provided more work for the poor, more profit for the industrialists, and inexpensive reading matter which stimulated writers, journalism, and indirectly contributed to the rising literacy among the laborers themselves. The effects were ranging: English shipowners became rich transporting slaves to America to grow cotton, imported to England where it was spun and woven, tailored, sold, worn, and discarded, destined for the ragpickers such as the affluent Golden Dustman in Dickens's *Our Mutual Friend*. The novel-reading public was familiar with the Dustman, but not with how he was profiting from the slavery and exploitation against which their philanthropic societies agitated, nor did they see how the slaves themselves, through the far-reaching effects of free enterprise, had contributed to the novels in their cotton-swathed laps.

Had they been wearing wool, they would have been contributing to another system, one which, unlike the cotton industry, was protected from the competitive marketplace by law, refuting Smith's theory. As early as 1235, it had been evident to landowners that wool was more profitable than grain, and common land, which the peasants had used to raise food, became subject to a series of enclosure acts which turned arable fields into pastures and an independent class of working peasants into paupers and rural vagrants. Between 1331, when John Kennedy introduced the art of wool weaving from Flanders, and 1760, wool nonetheless provided a stable cottage economy; and so long as one worked in the fields he was protected by the Act of Elizabeth (1598), which provided him with sufficient wages to buy bread, a rent-free cottage, and common rights to gather fuel.

But the mechanical advances in weaving that appeared in the middle of the eighteenth century disrupted this rural economy, and the rate of enclosures accelerated until it exceeded that rate at which industries could absorb the dispossessed peasants and redundant agricultural laborers. Entire villages were displaced, forcing some inhabitants, such as Goldsmith described in "The Deserted Village," to emigrate and others to move to the cities where they formed a class of urban poor: the excess of manpower kept wages down while the loss of land under cultivation sent food prices soaring. Parliament, dominated by the landed interests, passed a series of Corn Laws taxing imported wheat and supporting their own prices by protecting them from foreign competition, although they intensified the suffering of the poor. When they rioted, as they did periodically during the years of drought and war in the 1790s, philanthropists like Hannah More advised them to eat potatoes. Potatoes may have been a solution for a pauper but a laborer worked for bread, sometimes three days for one loaf, and potatoes were an affront to his dignity.[9] Rioting, crime, vagrancy created massive social problems for the landed gentry who could not see that it was in their "self-interest" to repeal the Corn Laws, to moderate enclosures. While in Westmorland and Cumberland counties, Wordsworth celebrated the marginal but independent existence of the traditional freeholder—"Man free, man working for himself, with choice / Of time, and place, and object" (*The Prelude,* VIII, 104–5)—the Duchess of Sutherland in the famine years following the Napoleonic wars dispossessed 15,000 tenants from her land, apportioning seven acres to each sheep, and two acres to each family. In 1832, when the Reform Bill enfranchised the industrial and mercantile interests, the Corn Laws were repealed. While Adam Smith's *laissez-faire* economy ultimately prevailed, it was at the expense of that one resource that he had identified as wealth: the laboring classes, labor, "the first price, the original purchase-money that was paid for all things."

Adam Smith was not unaware of the poor, but he objected to any kind of protective legislation that would interfere with the laws of the marketplace: if the rich were permitted to follow their own insatiable desires, they would provide work for the poor and ultimately comfort and prosperity would be available to anyone capable of work. Although Smith had merely exposed certain economic principles in an authoritative manner, *The Wealth of Nations* became a businessman's bible, acquired the aura of a surrogate religion, which as late as 1850, Wordsworth condemned with a particularly apt metaphor: "how dire a thing / Is worshipped in that idol" (*The Prelude*, XIII, 76–77). By locating wealth in labor rather than nature, Smith did, however, revive a basic religious archetype: the fallen Adam earning his bread by the sweat of someone's brow. As Elie Halévy explains, "to maintain that labor is the sole source of wealth and the sole standard of value is to maintain that every pleasure is purchased at the cost of an equivalent or almost equivalent pain, that man is born to plenty, that a parsimonious nature doles out to him in scanty measure the means of subsistence, and that population exercises on its resources an unremitting pressure."[10] It was this flaw that Thomas Malthus recognized in the optimistic philosophies of the eighteenth century and exposed in his *Essay on the Principle of Population*.

Thomas R. Malthus

Thomas Robert Malthus (1766–1834) was an unlikely person to refute the optimism of the Enlightenment and to become the villain of the Romantic generation. Following an idyllic childhood in which, along with his eight brothers and sister, he was educated at home by his father, a disciple of Rousseau, Malthus graduated from Jesus College, Cambridge, with honors in mathematics. To those who knew him, according to the inscription over his tomb, he was "one of the best men and truest philosophers of any age or country . . . he lived a serene and happy life devoted to the pursuit and communication of truth, supported by a calm but firm conviction of the usefulness of his labours, content with the approbation of the wise and good."[11] Some of the "wise and good" disagreed with this estimate: "Parson, I have during my life despised many men, but never anyone so much as you," William

Cobbet wrote in the *Political Register,* May 1819. In *Spirit of the Age,* William Hazlitt accused him of spreading "a gloom over the hopes . . . of man," and of casting "a slur upon the face of nature." Shelley accused Malthus of spreading the "gloom and misanthropy [that] have become the characteristics of the age." Byron, on the other hand, preoccupied with the discrepancies between professed ideals and actual behavior, concluded, "If he be right, war and pestilence are our best friends, to save us from being eaten alive in this best of all possible Worlds."[12]

What this amiable preacher had done in *The Essay on the Principle of Population* (1798) was, first, to contradict the providential interpretation of natural law, and, second, to reject the prevailing concepts about the way populations grow. In spite of his sheltered life and commitment to mathematical abstraction, Malthus's interpretation of the economy of nature was concrete, simple, brutal, obvious: man's sexual appetites, his power of procreation, exceed the power of nature to provide sustenance; population increases at a faster rate than production. Specifically, population increases geometrically (2, 4, 8, 16, 32, . . .), while the production of food increases arithmetically (1, 2, 3, 4, 5, . . .). Consequently, society is constantly engaged in a competition for limited resources and the majority of human beings must forever live in "misery and vice," the natural controls on population: "unwholesome occupations, severe labour and exposure to the seasons, extreme poverty, bad nursing of children, great towns, excesses of all kind, the whole train of common diseases and epidemics, wars, plagues and famine." But it was not until 1801 that his thesis acquired any authority, for, after long resistance to a census that one member of Parliament had described in 1756 as "subversive to the last remaining laws of English liberty," the population was counted, and it was estimated to have nearly doubled within a hundred years from 5½ to 9 million. Because most had assumed that the population was declining, the Poor Laws had made allowances to encourage large families in the form of rates, supplements to wages that were too low to support families. Malthus recognized the motive behind such bills and exposed it along with the disastrous consequences of such uninformed legislation. Any poor relief, he wrote, "under the deceitful garb of benevolence," was an aristocratic device to increase the supply of labor while keeping wages down; instead of relief, government intervention created more misery and vice. Any laborer, he wrote, "who marries without being able to support a family may in some respects be considered as an enemy to all his fellow laborers."

But it was more than the census which verified his thesis: it was the entire dismal drama of supply and demand that he examined with an undeluded eye. War was indeed keeping the population in check, for between 1793 and 1795 alone, 40,000 lives had been lost, mostly from famine and disease during a pointless campaign in the West Indies, and in the twenty-two-year war against Napoleon, 100,000 more were lost. At home, the severe winter and crop failures of 1795 threatened many with starvation. In Deddington, according to F. M. Eden in *The State of the Poor* (1797), the laborers seized a boat of flour on the canal and forced the miller to sell it to them at a fair price. But what was a fair price? Eden estimated that a family, including a wife and three children, spent £16.18 a year on bread out of a total income of £22.15, leaving £5.17 for housing, fuel, clothes, and something to eat with the bread besides water. When 20,000 of the starving citizens of London rioted, carrying small loaves on the ends of pikes, and attacked the King's carriage, the government responded by increasing the supplements paid to the poor.

In 1803, Malthus provided his solution in a revised edition under the heartening title *An Essay on the Principle of Population; Or a View of its Past and Present Effects on Human Happiness; with an Inquiry into our Prospects Respecting the Future Removal or Mitigation of the Evils which it Occasions*. Malthus had concluded that vice and misery were not the only checks on population, that man himself was capable of keeping population at the level of subsistence by "moral restraint," "restraint from marriage which is not followed by irregular gratification," and celibacy within marriage itself. To Shelley, Coleridge, and most of his contemporaries, voluntary celibacy was not a viable alternative to starvation, merely a prelude to abortion, abandonment, or castration. In 1822, Francis Place, a tailor, started one of the quietest revolutions in English social history when he recommended in *Illustrations and Proofs of the Principle of Population* to "married persons to avail themselves of such precautionary means as would, without being injurious to health, or destructive of female delicacy, prevent conception," and within a year handbills advocating birth control were being distributed among the poor. Finally, when Darwin confessed in his autobiography that his theory of natural selection, the gradual evolution of the species through competition for limited resources and the survival of the fittest, had been inspired by the *Essay on Pop-*

ulation, Malthus, at least in the scientific community, was finally vindicated.

Jeremy Bentham

Jeremy Bentham's lifetime (1748–1832) covered a revolution in English society for which he provided the dominant theme in a philosophy called, by his disciple John Stuart Mill, "utilitarianism."[13] A precocious and lonely child of a prosperous London family, Bentham entered Oxford at age twelve, graduated at fifteen, and began preparing himself for the bar, although English law, based on precedent, was totally alien to his iconoclastic nature, his impatience with authority and tradition. Unwilling to accept money for interpreting a legal system in which he did not believe and sufficiently wealthy to support himself without it, Bentham abandoned the law after his first case and spent the rest of his life as a bachelor and free-lance intellectual. In the tradition of Locke, questioning the rational basis for all institutions, customs, ceremonies, rituals, and beliefs, he rejected history and universality as tests of truth in favor of human, verifiable experiences and their consequences. However in tune with contemporary liberal sentiment Bentham may have seemed through this rejection of history, he was too practical and terrestial to be a revolutionary, distrusting those generalities, abstractions, slogans, "sacramental expressions" which the French Revolution and the Declaration of Independence had brought into fashion.[14] While radical thinkers such as Paine and Godwin espoused natural rights, which Bentham considered nonsense, and the natural identity of interests, which he dismissed as a fiction, Bentham elevated security over liberty, and pursued a just and functioning legal system, laws and institutions that would promote virtue by dispensing rewards and punishment through a more cogent and compelling means than any existing political, religious, or moral system.

Such a goal required no less than a redefinition of virtue itself. At age twenty, following Hume, Bentham adopted a morality that identified virtue with pleasure and evil with pain, assuming that people are sufficiently egotistical to pursue pleasure and avoid pain. In 1776, in *A Fragment on the Principles of Government,* and, in 1780, in *An Introduction to the Principles of Morals and Legislation,* Bentham applied these hedonistic principles to the function of government: to promote the greatest happiness for the greatest number by harmonizing the individual pursuit of pleasure with the greater good of society. Acting out of self-interest, seeking pleasure, or more specifically, the sources of pleasure in wealth, power, prestige, sensual gratification, or even such moral activities as benevolence, charity, and duty, an individual, following the principle of utility, behaves virtuously, fulfills himself, and serves society.

Recognizing that people are prone to error, Bentham devoted his most productive years and his entire fortune to the problems of criminal behavior. In *Panopticon: On the Inspection House,* published in 1791 but outlined in a series of letters written from Russia in 1786, Bentham responded to the agitation for prison reform initiated by John Howard's report, *The State of Prisons* (1777), and offered the design of a model prison that in architecture and administration would not only reclaim criminals but prevent crime. Circular in form with private cells around the circumference and an observation tower in the center, the structure, Bentham claimed, would serve equally well for prisons, schools, hospitals, indeed any custodial institution. Although Bentham did not believe in God, Gertrude Himmelfarb writes in her detailed examination of the ill-fated Panopticon, "he did believe in the qualities apotheosized in God. The Panopticon was a realization of the divine ideal, spying out the ways of the transgressor by means of an architectural scheme, turning night into day with artificial lights and reflectors, holding men captive by an intricate system of inspection," in which the inspector becomes, like God, the "invisible eye."[15] Arguing that the management of prisons would best be handled by private contractors whose self-interest would insure the profitable and humane use of the prisoners, Bentham volunteered to be the first inspector, purchased the land, and spent twenty years petitioning the government to enact the necessary legislation for establishing his model prison. In 1811, he abandoned the project and, as Mrs. Himmelfarb concludes, having learned that the greatest happiness for the greatest number depended on the greatest power of the greatest number, spent the rest of his life in the service of political reform.

Bentham's goals were themselves admirable, but he oversimplified human nature. He failed to recognize the unfortunate truth that Dostoevsky was painfully to render in *Notes from Underground:* human beings do not always pursue their best interests, do not always prefer a pleasure with assured consequences; they suffer from competing motives and often choose the less rewarding one simply because it is a choice, an exercise of free will. As Hazlitt explained in his portrait of

Bentham in *The Spirit of the Age,* "Our moral sentiments are made up of sympathies and antipathies, of sense and imagination, of understanding and prejudice. . . . All pleasure is not, therefore (morally speaking) equally good. . . . There are some tastes that are sweet in the mouth and bitter in the belly; and there is a similar contradiction and anomaly in the mind and heart of man" (p. 174). But his primitive psychology was less damaging to the society he ultimately came to influence than his atomistic, mathematical approach to human behavior. Having reacted against the excesses of feeling and instinct that had pervaded the society in which he was reared, Bentham created an analogous reaction among those who during the Romantic period valued emotion, spontaneity, and belief. His moral arithmetic or pleasure calculus, measuring individual pleasures quantitatively, according to their "intensity," "duration," "certainty," "propinquity or remoteness," "fecundity," "purity," and "extent," excluded those softer and ineffable pleasures that poets and artists especially savored. Bentham had, however, rejected more than the literary sensibility, the aesthetic morality that equated truth with beauty; he had rejected all creative literature because it lacked utility, just as he rejected religion and its transcendental morality, its unverifiable system of rewards and punishment, because it did not promote pleasure, quantifiable happiness.[16]

As Bentham matured, his prose style, according to Hazlitt in *The Spirit of the Age,* became increasingly "unpopular, not to say unintelligible," "a barbarous philosophical jargon." If his abstruse language seemed to contradict his ideals of simplicity, clarity, and logic, it reflected his way of coping with the contradictions he encountered both in society and in himself—by evasion, abstraction, and withdrawal. Intellectually devoted to what was useful and productive, he never had to earn his living, never held a public office, never published unless it was absolutely necessary, and spent most of his life in the quixotic pursuit of an ideal prison. Equally devoted to the goals of pleasure and happiness which he conceived of in collective or communal terms, he lived an austere and solitary existence and seems to have known very little pleasure at all, "his natural humour, sense, spirit, and style," to quote Hazlitt again, hidden in "the dust and cobwebs of an obscure solitude." Although he considered both literature and religion at best idle and pointless, he owned, lived in, and at one time rented to Hazlitt "the cradle of Paradise Lost," the house at 19 York Street where Milton had lived. Finally, although according to John Stuart Mill, who attributed his own nervous collapse at age twenty-three to his strictly utilitarian education, Bentham was one of "the two great seminal minds of England" (the other being Coleridge), he was inexperienced, "a boy to the last. Self-consciousness, that demon of the men of genius of our time, from Wordsworth to Byron, from Goethe to Chateaubriand, and to which this age owes so much both of its cheerful and its mournful wisdom, never was awakened in him."[17] He died on the evening before the passage of the Reform Bill in 1832 and failed to see this monument to his work become law. And the man who distrusted symbols, who destroyed icons, became his own icon: his fully clothed skeleton with waxen head and walking stick in hand sits contemplatively in a glass case on one of the busier corridors at the University of London.

Edmund Burke

Edmund Burke (1729–1797), venerating tradition, the aristocratic class in which it is embodied, and the organic means by which it evolved, is the very antithesis of Bentham. And yet Bentham, the founder of modern liberalism, and Burke, the founder of modern conservatism, began with the common assumption that government should provide the structure which both restrains individuals and enables them to find fulfillment. "Government," Burke explains in *Reflections on the Revolution in France,* "is a contrivance of human wisdom to provide for human wants."[18] But Burke believed in the intangibles, especially religion, "the basis of civil society, and the source of all good and all comfort." Born in Dublin of a Protestant father and Roman Catholic mother and initially educated by a Quaker, Burke developed a deep though tolerant piety which was to sustain him through the troubled times ahead. After graduating from Trinity College in 1750, he arrived in London to study law, encountering the disabilities of his obscure and unfashionable origins. By the end of the first year, he abandoned his studies in favor of literary journalism, married, and established his first household, which included his cousin Will, a man of dubious reputation, and his younger brother Richard, a gambler and spendthrift. The success of *A Philosophical Inquiry into the Origins of our Ideas of the Sublime and the Beautiful* (1757) brought literary fame and political connections. In comparing the exalting, terrifying, and isolating experience of the sublime with the orderly, harmonious, and civilizing experience of the beautiful, Burke had identified the extremes of social behavior which he spent his life contemplating, exhilarated by the sublime, seeking the beautiful, and advocating moderation.

After serving briefly as editor of *The Annual Register,* Burke spent twenty-nine years in Parliament, during a period of unparalleled and repeated crises in English political life, of shifting loyalties, of domestic and foreign confrontations, of trial and tension for the parliamentary system which was barely a hundred years old. As he sought to protect what was permanently valuable within the system, to maintain a delicate balance between theory and practice, between power and justice, between the opposing motives within man and society, Burke's eloquent voice was frequently in the minority. Hazlitt, who had little sympathy with Burke's ideas, conceded nonetheless that he was out of place in the House of Commons, "that motley crew of knights, citizens, and burgesses" (Howe, 8: 202); Coleridge, who was considered by many to be Burke's political heir, lamented that his talent was wasted in "a Noah's arc, with a very few men and a great many beasts."[19] His public life was an extension of his private one: his most impressive social credential, Beaconsfield, a vast country estate purchased in 1769, was largely populated by a vast number of impoverished and raucous Irish relatives who profited from his sense of loyalty and enjoyed his hospitality, but failed to recognize the place in English tradition which the possession of land represented to Burke.

Although Coleridge was to perceive that Burke habitually appealed to general principles in formulating his political positions rather than responding to the particularities of immediate events, to many he seemed inconsistent. While he defended the American colonists in their threatened revolt against the Stamp Tax, he was opposed to the French Revolution. Having labored for parliamentary reform, befriending many liberal causes, Burke was antagonized into a conservative position by mob violence and by the theoretical liberties the radicals espoused. When Dr. Richard Price, a dissenting minister and mathematician, preached a sermon and sent a public letter congratulating the French National Assembly for reenacting in France the Glorious Revolution of 1688, for proving once again that the people had the right to choose their own rulers, to hold them responsible for misconduct, and to design their own government, Burke was appalled. Instead of a defense of the abstract rights of man, Burke found in the precedent of 1688 an affirmation of the ancient rights of Englishmen, the rights embodied in the Constitution and the community which they defined: "a partnership between not only those who are living, but between those who are living, those who are dead, and those who are to be born," as he wrote in *Reflections on the Revolution in France* (1790). Burke deplored "all systems built on abstract rights," as Wordsworth explains in *The Prelude,*

> the majesty proclaims
> Of Institutes and Laws, hallowed by time;
> Declares the vital power of social ties
> Endeared by Custom; and with high disdain
> Exploding upstart Theory, insists
> Upon the allegiance to which men are born.
>   (VIII, 512–17)

His commitment to institutions and to tradition may be attributed to his fear of the very individualism which the economists defended as self-interest: "We are afraid to put men to live and trade each on his own private stock of reason because we suspect that the stock in each man is small . . . ," and he dismissed the restless masses in both England and France as "the swinish multitude," a phrase which raised more satirical talent than anger among countless popular writers in such pamphlets as *Hog's Wash, Pig's Meat,* and culminating in Shelley's *Oedipus Tyrannus: or Swellfoot the Tyrant* in which the chorus of pigs, boars, and sows petition the king for the clean straw, thatched sties, and rutabaga which they are guaranteed by law. But Burke, although his origins were nearer the lower classes than the aristocracy, was offended by any irreverence toward what he considered valuable in civilization: "the age of chivalry," "the glory of Europe is extinguished forever. Never, never more shall we behold that generous loyalty to rank and sex, that proud submission, that dignified obedience, that subordination of the heart, which kept alive, even in servitude itself the spirit of exalted freedom." It has been succeeded by an age "of sophisters, economists, and calculators."

It was this allegiance to an idealized past, to its continuous organic development that made Burke's political philosophy ultimately so attractive to writers such as Southey, Wordsworth, and Coleridge, for it was the only available contemporary political philosophy which could be reconciled with their theories of imagination once they had overcome their youthful radicalism. And he was a consummate writer. Even those who condemned Burke's attitude toward the poor and the helpless, granted, for better or worse, his rhetorical skill, his verbal power.

In 1794, just before he was to assume his own post in Parliament and carry on the tradition Burke venerated, Richard, Burke's sole surviving son, died of tuberculosis at age thirty-seven. Burke was devastated, haunted by the fear that his son's death was a divine judgment for his own neglect. He withdrew to Beaconsfield, reluctant to show the world the face of a man marked by the hand of God (VII, 70). To have become a victim of some inscrutable judgment was the insufferable correlative of Burke's philosophy: individual human beings are either unredeemably wicked or subject to the superior forces of history, society, royalty, God. Free will, the right to choose and the ability to shape one's life well were no more available to someone who believed in organicism, in what had grown as opposed to what had been made, than they were to those more obvious mechanistic thinkers, such environmental determinists as Bentham and the other utilitarians.

Thomas Paine

Among the many voices raised by Burke's denunciation of the French Revolution, none was more persuasive than Tom Paine's whose reply, *The Rights of Man,* was so forceful that he was exiled, his bookseller Joseph Johnson was jailed, and the book itself circulated more widely among Burke's "swinish multitude" than anything since *Pilgrim's Progress.* Paine's response contributed simultaneously to the intellectual liberation of the artisan class and to the repressive censorship laws which were to impede the development of literature and the theater for the next twenty-five years. Yet Tom Paine (1737–1809) was an unlikely candidate to have created such a political commotion in the cause of liberty. Born into a humble Quaker family in Norfolk, he left school at age thirteen to serve as apprentice corset-maker to his father, then failed successively as a tax assessor, a teacher, and a tobacconist, before joining the other social misfits and malcontents on the other side of the Atlantic where he found himself in the middle of a revolution, endowed with a verbal ability equal to its challenge. In 1776, Tom Paine, a small and by contemporary standards disheveled person with a pitted and peculiarly orange complexion, a fanatic's eye, and taciturn social manner, began a career of urging his fellow patriots to enlarge their vision; to transcend the provincialism of time, place, and heredity; and to recover the original promise, the essential joy, the natural freedom of life.[20]

His first pamphlet, *Common Sense* (1776), was irresistible in its simplicity, and in *The Crisis* pamphlets, written to be read to the disheartened American troops retreating across New Jersey in the dismal winter of 1776, he sounded such an appealing call to action that it is quoted even now by many who do not even know the source: "These are the times that try men's souls. The summer soldier and the sunshine patriot will, in this crisis, shrink from the service of his country; but he that stands it *now,* deserves the love and thanks of man and woman." In 1787, he returned to England bringing a scale model of an iron bridge, ultimately built over the Wear River, and his favorite though least successful invention, the smokeless candle. Until 1791, he moved freely between Paris and London, trying to reduce the tensions between the two countries and conversing with the leading politicians of the day, including Burke, whose home he visited.

But when Burke published his *Reflections* defending the monarchy, the constitution, the aristocracy, and the established church, Paine was indignant; for these institutions, he argued in *The Rights of Man* (1791), were contrivances justified only by time. Clearly, they had failed to embody the larger principles of freedom to which everyone should have access: "Every age and generation must be as free to act for itself, *in all cases,* as the ages and generations which preceded it. The vanity and presumption of governing beyond the grave, is the most ridiculous and insolent of all tyrannies." Vehemently he objected to Burke's literary rhetoric, to his elevating symbols over principles and the select elite over the many, to his lamenting the loss of chivalry while countless suffered from its tyranny: "He pities the plumage, but forgets the dying bird. Accustomed to kiss the aristocratical hand that hath purloined him from himself, he degenerates into a composition of art. . . ."

The Rights of Man was sufficiently successful, especially among the artisans and religious dissenters, to justify a second part the following year, an explicit call to revolution. The government, unnerved by the insurrection in France, by the radical agitation at home, and by the threat of war, responded with a series of repressive acts extending the concept of treason, intensifying censorship, prohibiting meetings, and finally, in 1795, suspending *Habeas Corpus,* which meant that evidence of criminal behavior was no longer necessary for imprisonment. An unofficial ministry of propaganda associated with the Methodist and Evangelical movements helped to enforce the new censorship laws and provided alternative reading to Paine in broadsides and pamphlets such as Cheap Repository Tracts, that for the lower classes became the major sources of reading matter after the Bible.

Accused of sedition himself, Paine returned to Paris shortly after the September Massacres of 1792, and, like Wordsworth, who arrived at the same time, found the city ominously quiet, "unfit for the repose of night, / Defenseless as a wood where tigers roam" (*The Prelude,* X, 91–93). An outlaw in England, he was elected to the French National Assembly before being jailed in France for suspected treason, since he had opposed on humanitarian grounds the execution of the King that had taken place nearly a year before. Under the shadow of the guillotine, Paine composed *The Age of Reason,* making rational deism, formerly the religion of gentlemen, available to the poor by showing how religious cults, mysteries, priesthood, the Bible, indeed all of institutional religion were personally debasing, politically tyrannous, and deprived people of their natural liberties. Released through the intervention of James Monroe, the American ambassador, Paine ultimately returned to America, and the man who had participated in two revolutions, who had aroused the consciousness of the English working class at the opening of the great reform movements of the nineteenth century, the man whose concept of personal freedom took precedence over religious cults and chauvinistic labels, who proclaimed, "My country is the world, and my religion is to do good," died in 1809, lonely and estranged, considered an infidel without any country at all. Paine's principles, however, evolved under the pressures of events, were contagious, and to the reflective and excitable temperaments of those who shared his fervor provided a source of great joy and creativity.

"Bliss was it in that dawn to be alive!" Wordsworth recalled, "But to be young was very Heaven!" (*The Prelude,* X, 693–94). Such was the mood of the artists and writers whose heady conversations filled the nights over Joseph Johnson's bookshop during the 1790s: such figures as Paine, Joseph Priestley, Henry Fuseli, William Blake, William Godwin, and Mary Wollstonecraft, radicals, republicans, and religious dissenters, sharing an aversion to external authority, to institutional religion, and to inherited power. Their preoccupation with economic inequities translated into political reform envisioned on a universal rather than local level, an extensive program of human liberation addressed chiefly to the masses and founded on the belief that progress was inevitable, that it begins with the reform of each individual heart and mind. For these radicals the perennial problem of reconciling private interest and public good became a problem of reducing public influence to the degree that natural virtue and benevolence could flower. Through such individual redemption, the entire society would be redeemed. Their ideas encouraged the utopian inclinations of the young Southey, Coleridge, and Wordsworth, as well as Blake and Shelley. Unlike their more sober and pedestrian contemporaries, unlike Adam Smith, Malthus, Bentham, and Burke, for example, the pragmatists and utilitarians, they had little influence on the course of political reform.

Mary Wollstonecraft

Described by the painter Henry Fuseli as a "philosophical sloven" for her unkempt appearance and extravagant ideas,[21] Mary Wollstonecraft (1759–1797) was one of the more loquacious members of the Johnson group. The daughter of a weaver, she started in the only career available to a bright girl without prospects: as a companion and teacher in an uninspiring country family. In 1787, she moved to London and, while translating for Joseph Johnson, wrote a novel, *Mary,* and a successful collection of moral parables for children, *Original Stories from Real Life.* Her *A Vindication of the Rights of Woman* (1792), which established her as a thinker and rhetorician, was among the earliest replies to Burke's *Reflections.* While Burke had lamented the passing of the "age of chivalry," Mary railed, "Man preys on man; and you mourn for the idle tapestry that decorated a gothic pile, and the dronish bell that summoned the fat priest to prayer. . . . Hell stalks abroad;—the lash resounds on the slave's naked sides; and the sick wretch . . . steals to a ditch to bid the world a long good night—or, neglected in some ostentatious hospital, breathes its last amidst the laugh of mercenary attendants." She concludes, "Such misery demands more than tears—I pause to recollect myself; and smother the contempt I feel rising for your rhetorical flourishes and infantine sensibility." She stated, reiterated, illustrated, and argued for 452 pages that women were inadequately educated, kept ignorant so they could be easily subjugated. By cultivating the "arbitrary power of beauty," however, women contributed to their own enslavement. Apparently, as Ralph Wardle reminds us, women had so exploited their sexual power that it had become a political threat, for as late as 1770 Parliament passed a bill declaring that "all women of whatever age, rank, profession or degree, whether virgin, maid or widow, that shall . . . impose upon, seduce, and betray into matrimony any of His Majesty's subjects by means of scent, paints, cosmetics, washes, artificial teeth, false hair, Spanish wool, iron stays, hoops, high-heeled shoes, or bolstered hips, shall incur the penalty of the law now in force against witchcraft and like misdemeanours, and that marriage upon conviction shall stand null and void."[22] Disarmed and uneducated, a woman had only her property to offer in exchange for the insecure comforts of marriage, insecure insofar as the property became her husband's anyway.

Among the laboring poor, the women themselves were property, on the same level as children: they worked in coal mines for eighteen hours a day as preferred labor because they ate less, drank less, and took up less space than men unless, of course, they were pregnant—when they were permitted to haul carts. And such wealthy, self-educated, or well-connected women as Lady Mary Wortley Montagu, Madame de Staël, and blue stockings such as Hannah More, author of *Strictures on the Modern System of Female Education,* were on the whole satisfied with their roles, resenting Mary Wollstonecraft's interference. "I am sure," Mrs. More wrote to Horace Walpole in 1792, "I have had as much liberty as I can make use of, now I am an old maid; and when I was a young one, I had, I dare say, more than was good for me." Mary Wollstonecraft was neither the first nor the most influential in the cause of equal education but she was probably the most notorious if not abrasive, inspiring such satires on the rights of minorities as *A Sketch on the Rights of Boys and Girls* and *A Vindication of the Rights of Brutes.*

The rest of Mary Wollstonecraft's life illustrates how much she shared with the generation of radicals whom she met over Johnson's shop, a series of disappointments when her fervent but untried convictions collided with experience. In Paris she fell in love with the improvident American Gilbert Imlay by whom she had a daughter Fanny. After following him for several years, she discovered his affair with a young actress in London and, when he refused to permit her to form a *ménage a trois,* she attempted suicide. Later, she met William Godwin, whom she married when she was several months pregnant, and, although he kept a separate home for himself, this brilliant, eccentric couple seemed supremely well suited to each other. She died in 1798, after giving birth to Mary, the future wife of the poet Shelley. Before the year was out, Godwin published her *Memoirs of the Author of "A Vindication of the Rights of Woman,"* in which he described in detail her love affairs, her suicide attempts, her final painful illness, and her immense influence on him, the emotional and imaginative awakening for which he expresses his gratitude.

William Godwin

Of all political and economic thinkers we have been discussing, none was so versatile, talented, prolific, intellectually significant, and politically harmless as William Godwin (1756–1836), whose eighty years encompassed a massive cultural upheaval that left him almost untouched, certainly ignored, and, by those whom he at one time influenced, repudiated.[23] The course of his religious transformations alone suggests that he had either an exceptionally flexible mind or, as many claimed, an exceptionally superficial one. Son of a dissenting minister, he was educated as a Calvinist, became a Sandemanian (a heretical sect which interpreted the New Testament literally and politically), then an ordained Unitarian minister, an unbeliever, an atheist, a theist, and, finally, wrote for posthumous publication a series of essays called "The Genius of Christianity Unveiled." Politically, he started as a Tory, turned republican, philosophical anarchist, and in 1833 accepted an ornamental government post as Yeoman Usher of the Exchequer. After a brief career in journalism, he developed in *Political Justice* and in *Caleb Williams* a moral doctrine rejecting the emotions and traditional social sentiments then spent most of his subsequent career writing sentimental novels, children's literature, and histories of Greece, England, and "eminent" necromancers. Although the contradictions between his public assertions and his private behavior are endless and fascinating, this bizarre and often feckless individual would have gone unnoticed among the many other eccentrics of his age if his political theory had not been so engaging.

In 1791, at the height of the radicals' response to Burke's *Reflections,* Godwin began *An Enquiry Concerning the Principles of Political Justice, and Its Influence on General Virtue and Happiness,* published in 1793, revised and expanded in 1796 and 1798, at the height of political censorship. Godwin's scheme was as subversive to monarchy as anyone's, but—because it was impractical, because he opposed revolution, because he counseled inaction, because he was essentially a moralist and philosopher rather than a political activist, and because his book, at three guineas a copy, was expensive and

boring to a reading public addicted to gothic romances—
Godwin escaped prosecution. Even intellectually, Godwin's
radicalism was primarily an inevitable working out of basic
and familiar concepts that had informed the most respectable
eighteenth-century thinkers: Reason, Equality, Perfectibility,
and Necessity. In the tradition of Locke and the Enlighten-
ment, Godwin had elevated Reason as the principle faculty
and guide to action, a view of Reason compatible with the
dissenting tradition in which Godwin was trained. The dis-
senters believed in the truth of the inner voice or light over
institutional authority, leaving each individual as responsible
and independent as his intellect, education, and experience
permitted. This combination of the secular Enlightenment
tradition and the religious dissenting one appealed particu-
larly to the young Romantic poets for reasons Wordsworth
best explained in recalling his own conversion to God-
winism:

>   . . . the dream
> Was flattering to the young ingenuous mind,
> Pleased with extremes, and not the least with that
> Which makes the human Reason's naked self
> The object of its fervour. What delight!
> How glorious! in self-knowledge and self-rule,
> To look through all the frailties of the world,
> And, with a resolute mastery shaking off
> The accidents of nature, time, and place,
> That make up the weak being of the past,
> Build social freedom on its only basis,
> The freedom of the individual mind,
> Which, to the blind restraints of general laws
> Superior, magisterially adopts
> One guide, the light of circumstance, flashed
> Upon an independent intellect.
>   (*The Prelude* [1805], X, 815–30)

Godwin rejected some feelings: the self-indulgent sentimen-
tality portrayed in fashionable literature, the hysterical enthu-
siasm aroused and betrayed by the French Revolution, and
the moral sentiments such as guilt, gratitude, or charity that
served the political purpose of subordinating the lower classes.
By 1799, when he wrote *St. Leon,* Godwin had compromised
to include friendship and domestic affections as legitimate
means of social development, reflecting the humanizing
experience of his marriage to Mary Wollstonecraft and the
grief over her death. But he did not associate this capacity for

sentiment with the lower classes. Indeed, his middle-class orientation offended the young radicals who otherwise acclaimed him as an inspiration.

Overtly, Godwin considered himself an egalitarian, and set social equality as his major goal, justice and generosity as the means for achieving it. The political basis for this social equality, however, was based on the social contract according to which Godwin argued, to Paine's consternation, that individual men have no rights. Moreover, appealing to utilitarian principles, he maintained that general good takes priority over individual pleasure: "The change we are contemplating," he wrote, "consists in the disposition of every member of the community voluntarily to resign that, which would be productive of a much higher degree of benefit and pleasure, when possessed by his neighbor, than when occupied by himself" (*P. J.*, II, 474–75). Since private property is a source of greed, of war, of injustice, and since contractual arrangements such as marriage are the source of jealousy, Godwin proposed that they be abandoned, that each individual be granted what he needs and be permitted to trade on his rational and generous impulses, to form his own alliances and relationships without any external coercion or motive other than self-fulfillment and, its Godwinian analogue, selflessness. Then, Godwin wrote, "Labour would become light as rather to assume the appearance of agreeable relaxation and gentle exercise. Every man would have a frugal yet wholesome diet; every man would go forth to that moderate exercise of his corporal functions that would give hilarity to the spirits. None would be made torpid with fatigue, but all would have leisure to cultivate the kindly and philanthropic affections and to let loose his faculties in the search of intellectual improvement. . . ."

Godwin's optimism was an extension of the generally acknowledged belief in perfectibility that had gathered strength from scientific theories of evolution emerging in the latter half of the eighteenth century. But while other optimists believed that evil was a matter of perspective, or a lesser form of good, or an expression of God's generosity, Godwin maintained that society was responsible for evil through the corrupting forms of education and government. Crime, then, was merely an error in judgment requiring reform rather than retribution, a principle illustrated by his hero-criminal-victim Falkland in *Caleb Williams: Or Things as They Are* (1794): "A nobler spirit lived not among the sons of men. But of what use are talents and sentiments in the corrupt wilderness of human society? It is a rank and rotten soil, from which every finer shrub draws poison as it grows."

To eliminate the corrupting influence of society, one need only rely on Reason, on "the light of circumstance, flashed / Upon an independent intellect," as Wordsworth said. Then people would govern themselves and traditional political institutions would ultimately become superfluous, even disappear. These ideas led many to believe that Godwin was an anarchist, and others like Hazlitt, to conclude in *The Spirit of the Age* that he was simply naive, that he "conceived too nobly of his fellows" and "raised the standards of morality above the reach of humanity" (p. 184). Fortunately, Godwin was patient: "Undoubtedly," he wrote, "this state of society is remote from the modes of thinking and acting which at present prevail. A long period of time must probably elapse, before it can be brought entirely into practice" (*P. J.,* II, 475). This same progress toward individual freedom included the physical basis of life itself, for science eventually would conquer disease and man would become immortal. Rationally, then, human reproduction would no longer be necessary. At this point Malthus began to compose his rebuttal in *The Essay on Population,* asserting that human reproduction was not governed by reason and that it would always exceed the resources available for sustaining life.

Malthus, with his rigorous empirical method, had opposed one natural law against another, but Godwin invoked an ancient belief in the law of Necessity, an historical determinism that assisted man in his quest for perfection. Necessity, another term for fate, or Adam Smith's "invisible hand," or the Calvinist doctrine of predestination, carried the authority of myth, and served with equal force in both scientific and religious thought. The doctrine of Necessity was particularly suited to those thinkers and writers who sought large intellectual syntheses such as Joseph Priestley, who explored it in *The Doctrine of Philosophical Necessity Illustrated* (1777), and Shelley, who embodied it in the figure of Demogorgon in *Prometheus Unbound* (1818–1819), the shadowy figure who augers the triumph over tyranny and tradition, the millennium when man becomes, "the king / Over himself." It was the metaphysical sanction of Necessity that made Godwin's otherwise impractical, derivative, and sterile system so powerful. As Hazlitt wrote in *The Spirit of the Age,* "no work in our time gave such a blow to the philosophical mind of the country as the celebrated *Enquiry.* . . . Tom Paine was considered for the time as Tom Fool to him; Paley an old woman;

Edmund Burke a flashy sophist" (p. 183). And Shelley claimed that *Political Justice* had made him "a wiser and better man. I was no longer a votary of Romance; till then I had existed in an ideal world—now I found that in this universe of ours was enough to excite the interests of the heart. . . . I held, in short, that I had duties to perform. . . ." (*Letters*, I, 227–28). One of those duties was to help support Godwin out of his own meager annuity after he married Mary, Godwin's daughter by Mary Wollstonecraft.

Being a theorist rather than an activist, Godwin survived longer and in some ways better than any other member of his generation. But his brilliant and wayward family, indeed that entire band of radicals with whom he associated, suffered enormously for their sensitivity and iconoclasm. They had all believed that man by his unaided reason could arrange a more satisfactory life than any derived from custom or enforced through the institutions by which society perpetuates itself. What they could not account for were those accidents of mortality against which reason could not defend them nor for that human propensity to use reason itself for selfish as well as altruistic ends. Consequently, along with the real and unavoidable sorrows of merely being human, they suffered from the rational behavior of their fellow man in whose potential for goodness they firmly believed. Their ideals predisposed them to being victimized either by history, or by society, or by their environment on which they had projected so much power and which they blamed for their suffering:

> O, why was I born with a different face?
> Why was I not born like this envious Race?
> Why did Heaven adorn me with bountiful hand?
> And then set me down in an envious land?

The poem: "Mary." The poet: Blake. The year: 1803. Johnson in jail, Paine in exile, Godwin married to an unpopular wife and becoming increasingly conservative, Blake himself accused of treason by a drunken soldier. So much intellect and imagination invested in the cause of liberty and so little personal freedom—while the freest but soon to be the most abject figure, Napoleon, was planning his invasion of England.

Robert Owen

Robert Owen (1771–1851), one of the self-made men who dominated the industrial age, responded to the political and economic challenges of his time by acting selectively on the best of the liberal democratic theories we have been discussing.[24] At age nine, he was apprenticed to a linen draper; at eighteen, he was manufacturing textile machinery; at twenty, he was managing a factory; and by twenty-five, he had purchased the mills at New Lanark in Scotland, married the former owner's daughter, and established a model factory which made him not only one of the richest men in England but also earned him the admiration and respect of rulers all over Europe. He presented living evidence that the poor could become productive, that if they were drunken, deceitful, or dishonest, as most middle-class people believed, it was because of their environment and because they had no motive to be otherwise. His model factory vindicated the theories he had been advancing in a series of essays written between 1813 and 1818, published collectively as *A New View of Society*. Many had recognized the dislocations caused by the factory system (initiated in England less than a century before, in 1718, when John Lombe built a five-story silk mill on an island in the Derwent River near Derby): the disruption of family life, of guild and village relationships; the artificial divisions of time from seasonal rhythms to machine rhythms; the demands on individual workers for cooperative activity, for discipline, and for efficiency. But until Owen, no one had addressed himself to how such an activity as manufacturing could be organized for any goal other than profit. No one had asked, as Owen did, "What are the best arrangements under which these men and their families can be suitably and economically lodged, fed, clothed, trained, educated, employed, and governed?" The key to his influence, embodied in the Factory Act of 1819, his appeal to his fellow industrialists and political leaders is the term "economically," for in the tradition of Adam Smith and the utilitarians Owen appealed to self-interest as the motive for philanthropic activity.

To Owen it was only logical that if six-year-old children were set to work from six in the morning until eight at night, if they were confined to cramped and fetid work areas, allowed forty minutes over the entire day to eat a meager meal of salt and potatoes, and then forced to spend fourteen hours on Sunday in borrowed clothes under the same tyrannical regime learning to be humble, grateful, submissive, and neat, they would produce, if they lived to produce, a generation of physical and intellectual dwarfs. Or, worse, they would grow up and rebel like the Luddites of 1812, and break the machines that, having been the source of their livelihood were also the symbol of their wretchedness. In New Lanark, Owen estab-

lished his workers' paradise: a textile mill employing up to
1,600 adults, providing free medical care, cottages, gardens,
evening lectures, and public services such as garbage collec-
tion, a cooperative store, and free education up to the age of
ten. When a Parliamentary committee was investigating the
best way to alleviate the poverty and distress following the
Napoleonic wars in 1817, Owen contributed plans which
would have led to a whole series of New Lanarks called Vil-
lages of Co-operation. Architecturally, they were designed
as a series of self-sustaining, cooperative garden communities
arranged in parallelograms. Functionally, they were com-
munes with eight to twelve hundred self-governing resi-
dents, some engaged in light industry, others working the
fields around the village, and others teaching or caring for
the children. The middle classes rejected the plan as contrary
to a universe that clearly operated on the principle of *laissez-
faire*. The aristocracy resented and ultimately dismissed it as
essentially godless, for Owen had excluded the church. The
more vocal reformers such as Cobbett rejected the villages as
no more than glorified workhouses, prisons, "parallelograms
of pauperism." But the laborers who were to own the land
they worked were very much in favor of Owen's plan.

In 1824, Owen invested his entire fortune in a tract of land
on the banks of the Wabash River in Indiana, and on July 4,
1826, New Harmony, a colony of 800 settlers, was officially
dedicated. The compelling idea for emigrating to America
had been that in the abundance of nature, in this perfectly free
environment, the settlers would be rich and free. To insure
this freedom and to preserve their independence, they out-
lawed private property, organized religion, and marriage.
Equipped with more theories than skills, they settled in,
excluded the deviants, cut down the forests, set up a distil-
lery, polluted the air and water, and ultimately became rich
on the labor of slaves. But Owen was saved from this final
disenchantment, for within two years he had seen that, how-
ever perfect the new environment, adults would import vices—
selfishness, acquisitiveness, dishonesty—from the old. After
selling the land, in 1828, he returned to England where he
began a series of cooperative societies for the production, sale,
and exchange of inexpensive goods and labor. With the
founding of the Grand National Moral Union of the Produc-
tive and Useful Classes, an unsuccessful experiment resem-
bling a national trade union, Owen's economic crusade became
a moral one. Although his practical experiments failed, he
was becoming a true force in society: something of a spiri-

tualist, certainly a visionary, he was considered by Friedrich Engels, among others, the founder of modern socialism. Attracting thousands of followers among the embittered and alienated laboring poor, he showed that through unity and cooperation there was power; through a common purpose they could become a class in themselves, the working class, creating a better life through their own efforts rather than waiting to have it bestowed on them by fiat or through some kind of spiritual apocalypse.

If Owen is the fulfillment of the early liberal philosophies, he also illustrates the contradictions within them, contradictions arising from what may be called a mechanical bias, the architectural or engineering mentality of the industrialists, their excessive faith in the manipulation of external circumstances in order to improve the condition of individual lives and social relationships. By 1829, in "Signs of the Times," Carlyle was protesting that the machine itself had so become the prevailing metaphor of the age that even government was called "the Machine of Society," and he deplored the belief that "mere political arrangements," the "structure of legislation," would assure human happiness. But the political ideology of the liberal reformers, which was coming to dominate society, was derived from Enlightenment philosophy, particularly that of Locke, a philosophy that appealed to the increasingly powerful manufacturers because it was based on a mechanism, a theory of machines. Assuming that, first, man was the product of his environment, and that, second, all men being equal they were also the same, the liberal reformists concluded that individuals would profit from a legislated world which guaranteed their equality by enforcing their "same-ness." Consequently, they began to design a society as deterministic and as stultifying as the rigid class structure of inherited wealth and privilege which the legislative reform itself was supposed to have abolished. They replaced the tyranny of king and church with a tyranny of majorities and of systems. Anticipating the penalties of their success, creative thinkers such as Carlyle insisted, "Man is not the creature and product of mechanism; but in a far truer sense its creator and producer: it is the noble people that makes the noble Government." Similarly, all the Romantic poets rejected the mechanistic assumptions of the liberal political philosophies because they denied freedom for the sake of equality and because they conflicted with the organic assumptions of the poets' creative philosophies. Ultimately, however, as later thinkers such as John Stuart Mill and Matthew Arnold were to argue, the liberal philosophers failed to recognize that the quality of life is not limited to the quality of the environment, of food, clothing, and shelter. Rather, the good life is an expression of mind and of heart. It was this preoccupation with the temporal and material conditions of life, with contemporary institutions, the pursuit, distribution, and even rejection of wealth, to which Coleridge attributed the fragmentation of society and the inevitable failure of all attempts at reform. It was a poet, then, who created a vision of society designed to promote the fulfillment of human life.

Samuel Taylor Coleridge

Although primarily remembered as a poet, aesthetician, and literary critic, to many of his contemporaries Coleridge (1771–1834) was an original though not necessarily effectual political thinker.[25] In 1840, John Stuart Mill concluded that every Englishman was "by implication either a Benthamite or a Coleridgean."[26] Coleridge's political theory was indeed the very antithesis of the empirical, utilitarian, and secular theories associated with Bentham, enacted by Owen, and dominating the reform movement. But Coleridge started with preoccupations different from those of contemporary political thinkers. What interested him were not so much human relationships, the reconciliation of self-interest and social goals, as the relation between individuals and the large, permanent principles of human experience. From his earliest youth he had been haunted by a sense of fragmentation: the "universe itself," he wrote in 1797, seems "but an immense heap of *little* things" while he "ached to behold and know something great—something *one and indivisible*" (*CL,* I, 349). Observing the isolated gestures toward political reform, the self-defeating riots and revolutionary rhetoric, the attempts to devise individual laws for specific offenses and events, Coleridge concluded that such activity only contributed to the fragmentation, delaying rather than resolving crises. Relating contemporary experience to the permanent, the universal values, principles, or laws that had informed with greater or less success all societies in all times, Coleridge, following Burke, sought political wholeness and social coherence. But, unlike Burke, Coleridge chose as his Archimedean point the most encompassing idea of all, God and the political version of the Christian society found in the Bible, a synthesis of religion, politics, and morality. As early as 1794, he advised one young radical: "Talk not of politics, Preach the Gospel."

While the religious bias of Coleridge's mature political thought was predictable, the conservative one was not. Like Godwin he was the son of a dissenting minister and though he preached, wrote sermons, and approached ordination, he never formally entered the church. In 1791, he associated at Jesus College, Cambridge, with a number of young Unitarians and radicals sympathetic to the French Revolution. Yet, in 1793, Coleridge joined the army under the pseudonym "Silas Tomkyn Comberbache," to fight against France. Rescued by his brother, he returned to Cambridge, where, partly reacting to the failure of the French Revolution and partly responding to his reading of *The Rights of Man, Political Justice,* and Plato's *Republic,* Coleridge, along with Robert Southey, began to plan the founding of an ideal cooperative community—a Pantisocracy—along the banks of the Susquehanna River in Pennsylvania. Their concept was simple and resembled most of the contemporary, agrarian utopian schemes: in a pristine environment twelve men and twelve women with a minimum number of needs would each labor in the fields two or three hours a day and spend the rest of their time in discussion, or study, or educating the children. Four of the women were to be from the same family, exceptionally self-sufficient women raised by the widow Fricker. Coleridge married one daughter, Southey another, and Robert Lovell a third. Coleridge was exuberant: "My God! how tumultuous are the movements of my Heart," he wrote, "America! Southey! Miss Fricker. . . . Pantisocracy—O I shall have such a scheme of it! My head, my heart are all alive" (*CL,* I, 103). But the scheme collapsed from insoluble though pedestrian problems: money, transportation, extended bickering over whether women should work in the fields, and so on. But mostly Coleridge had come to realize that such utopian communities merely replaced one narrow ideal with another, that, for example, the otherwise commendable Godwinian ideal of universal benevolence excluded private affections and domestic duties which he felt were basic for any commitment to humanity at large. Moreover, depending as it did on a carefully restricted environment, the pantisocracy deprived its members of many more freedoms than it bestowed, freedom merely to move about and associate with the larger community of man.

Still, Coleridge continued to seek something "one and indivisible," a quest that was to become more urgent as he gained experience in political life by editing his own periodicals such as *The Watchman* (1796) and *The Friend* (1809–1810), reporting for the *Morning Post,* and serving as a public official in Malta (1804–1805). While this political exposure provided more evidence that public life was fragmented, a "heap of *little* things," it also motivated him to look further for the unifying principle that would inform his age, a search that became increasingly philosophical: "In every state, not wholly barbarous," Coleridge wrote in the *Courier,* December 3, 1814, "a philosophy, good or bad, there must be. However slightingly it may be the fashion to talk of speculation and theory, as opposed . . . to practice, it would not be difficult to prove, that such as is the existing spirit of speculation, during any given period, such will be the spirit and tone of the religion, legislation, and morals, nay, even of the fine arts, the manners, and the fashions. Nor is this the less true, because the great majority of men live like bats, but in twilight, and know and feel the philosophy of their age only by its reflections and refractions."[27]

In 1816, Coleridge began a series of works developing those concepts he had come to believe would lend contemporary political life coherence and continuity, that would align political activities with permanent principles and some kind of transcendent authority, that would in brief, identify and encourage the philosophical spirit latent in the age. The very titles are resonant with religion: *The Statesman's Manual or the Bible, the Best Guide to Political Skill and Foresight: A Lay Sermon Addressed to the Higher Classes of Society* (1816) and *A Lay Sermon Addressed to the Higher and Middle Classes on the Existing Distresses and Discontents* (1817). Coleridge addressed the lay sermons to those whose responsibility it was to shape the lives and environment of the poor, to people of influence and of power. Through Biblical precedents and analogies, Coleridge reminded the ruling classes of their patriarchal responsibility to those who were dependent upon them, a particularly effective device since the same scriptural evidence had been used by the church and defenders of the status quo to justify social inequities and the sufferings of the poor as part of a divine plan. But Coleridge's entire orientation was constructive and affirmative. The government he proposed reflected structurally his theory of mind, the psychological nature of the citizens. Rather than creating a legislative structure for mutual protection such as the utilitarians envisioned, Coleridge conceived of a government whose primary goal was to provide the means by which the citizens could fulfill themselves.

In his last published prose work, *On the Constitution of Church and State* (1830), Coleridge revealed the grand scheme toward which he had been moving for at least thirty years, an idea of a state which reconciled all the competing interests into a harmonious whole, embodying both the transcendant first principles which gave it authority and a theory of mind which gave it life. In the fifth chapter Coleridge analyzed the state into three classes or estates defined by their function and forming a natural balance of powers. The two major estates—the landed class representing permanence and law, and the commercial or manufacturing class representing progress and personal freedom—were unified by the crown and shared the responsibility for civilization, by which Coleridge meant the material comforts and achievements of the nation. But antecedent to civilization is culture, "the harmonious development of those qualities and faculties that characterize our humanity," for, Coleridge concludes, "we must be men in order to be citizens." The protection and extension of culture were to be the special responsibility of the clerisy, a third estate associated with a secular body called the National Church and endowed with a portion of the national wealth or Nationality. A few of the clerisy were to "remain at the fountain heads of the humanities," "cultivating and enlarging the knowledge already possessed," "watching over the interests of physical and moral science," and, most importantly, educating the rest of the clerisy who were to live among the people so that even the smallest community would have "a resident guide, guardian, and instructor."

Poets and Politics

Coleridge's ideas contributed to political life only tangentially, at best perhaps to the revival of the church or to state-supported education. He did, however, influence his times on a far more fundamental level through that "spirit of speculation" which he had claimed conditioned "the spirit and tone of religion, legislation, and morals." His vision of a society designed to engage all human faculties for the perfecting of all human beings challenged the utilitarian ideology and its tendency toward mechanistic thinking that was reducing life to a "heap of *little* things." In developing this vision Coleridge relied on the poetical faculty, for he confronted the fragmentation of his times and conceived of a solution as a poet, the one who, as he wrote in *Biographia Literaria,* Chapter XIV, "brings the whole soul of man into activity, with the subordination of its faculties to each other according to their relative worth and dignity," diffusing "a tone and spirit of unity, that blends . . . each into each." His voice, moreover, was not an isolated one, for as early as 1800 in the Preface to *Lyrical Ballads* Wordsworth had assigned a similar political function to the poet: "an upholder and preserver, carrying everywhere with him relationship and love," binding "together by passion and knowledge the vast empire of human society, as it is spread over the whole earth, and over all time."

Even Shelley, that implacable radical, deploring the Lake poets' conservatism, shared their sense of social fragmentation and of the poet's political mission to create harmony and relationship. To the witty utilitarian challenge of Thomas Love Peacock's "The Four Ages of Poetry" (1820), which dismissed poetry as a frivolity, an excess, an inappropriate expression in contemporary rational society, Shelley replied in "A Defense of Poetry" (1821; published, 1840) that poetry, as an expression of the imagination, is the unifying and creative faculty which operates in art, religion, law, and morals, that it is "never more to be desired than at periods when, from an excess of the selfish and calculating principle, the accumulation of the materials of external life exceed the quantity of the power of assimilating them to the internal laws of human nature." Finally, choosing the political metaphor, Shelley concludes that insofar as poets have the power to mediate between the claims of the material world and the needs of human nature they are "the unacknowledged legislators of the world."

That the most extravagant political claims for poetry were made by a comparatively helpless exile in Italy epitomizes the political role of poets during the Romantic period: never was a generation of writers so remote from the centers of power and so critically aware of the political dilemmas which beset their society. The legislative role that Shelley assigned the poets, like the educative and social roles assigned by Coleridge and Wordsworth, was analogous to the religious roles poets filled during ages of belief: to articulate the highest ideals of society, both the transcendent and the terrestrial ones, and to relate individuals to them. But when political life became secularized as it did in the eighteenth century, when the social scientist replaced the priest as an arbiter of human relationships, the architect of social forms, then the poet turned from a religious prophet into a political one. And just as all the economic and political thinkers we have discussed recognized in one way or another the major problem in human relationships to be the reconciliation of self-interest and social goals, so the poets, whatever their political persuasion, believed in the poetical faculty, the imagination, as the instrument for achieving it.[28] That the concept of the sympathetic imagination was partly the invention of Adam Smith indicates how closely politics and art were allied on the most fundamental level during the Romantic period, for both were preoccupied with discovering the secular explanations of human behavior, how and why people relate to one another.

Given this basic affinity, it seems even more difficult to account for the increasing dislocation of poets and artists as well in society, the displacement of those who could cultivate the means to turn society into community. In part, the poets themselves contributed to their own isolation, for many preferred cultivating their private experience to public service, their own personal idiom to public discourse. Even if a poet did choose to address the public, existing poetic conventions were not meaningful, familiar, or appropriate for the new forms of publication, for the new journalism and the audiences it generated. Wordsworth, for example, disheartened with the materialism and vanity of London, proclaimed "Milton! thou shouldst be living at this hour: / England hath need of thee" to "raise" the people, to give them "manners, virtue, freedom, power," and he wrote in the form of Milton's political sonnets. But in 1802, such a form, even such sentiments, were ineffectual, trivial, and of little interest to those who needed them most. Similarly, Shelley wrote a sonnet "England in 1819," but the unemployed laborers he wrote it for were largely illiterate, and reading sonnets would have been irrelevant to the rioting and machine-breaking that characterized their political style. Even the human iconography, the public figures, the heroes upon which poets and artists relied to make conventional forms relevant to contemporary tastes and issues were missing. Contemporary society did not generate symbols of its best self, did not offer any heroes to inspire them.

CHAPTER VI

Heroes
and
Heroism

The Decline of Heroism

IN 1849, CHARLES DICKENS began his autobiographical novel, *David Copperfield,* with the following proposition: "Whether I shall turn out to be the hero of my own life, or whether that station will be held by anyone else, these pages must show." By the middle decades of the nineteenth century to be the hero of one's own life was a modest and perhaps the only possible aspiration, for heroism had virtually disappeared from politics, religion, literature, history, all the public arenas where heroic action traditionally had been found. True, the Romantic period had been an age of heroic experience: the French Revolution, the social and industrial revolutions, religious revivals, technological achievements demonstrating a growing mastery over nature, and twenty-one years of war against Napoleon, the most formidable general since Julius Caesar or Alexander the Great. But, as we shall demonstrate, such events produced cults, not heroes, as Byron complained at the opening of *Don Juan:*

> I want a hero; an uncommon want,
>   When every year and month sends forth a new one,
> Till, after cloying the gazettes with cant,
>   The age discovers he is not the true one.
>   (Canto I, 1–4)

The "true" heroes, the kings, saints, knights, priests, warriors, even plowmen and gods—the traditional subjects of heroic literature, of national and religious epic, romance, and tragedy—had acquired their moral authority and public stature from the institutions they represented, from the church or monarchy in the days when kings ruled by divine right, when gods entered human affairs, and when wars were fought ostensibly for honor and justice. But such models of heroism had been undermined either by the social and political revolutions of the eighteenth century or by the secular ideals of the Enlightenment. In place of these "true" heroes the Romantic writers offered a bewildering array of characters: Wordsworth's poetic "self" in *The Prelude* (1850, published a year after *David Copperfield*) or a philosophic pedlar in *The Excursion* (1815), Coleridge's deranged Ancient Mariner, Keats's moonstruck shepherd Endymion, Shelley's fallen Prometheus, Jane Austen's sensible Elizabeth Bennet, Byron's self-pitying Childe Harold and foolish Don Juan, and De Quincey's opium-eater. Even Carlyle's series of lectures "On Heroes, Hero-Worship, and the Heroic in History" (1840) examined how "Great Men" appeared "in our world's business, how they have shaped themselves in the world's history, what ideas men formed of them, what work they did . . . ," an industrial and commercial ideal. Apparently, these writers still believed in the heroic, still believed, with Keats that "Great spirits now on earth are sojourning," but they lacked models.

Some, like Southey and Scott, turned to the past and produced hybrid figures who fought ancient battles for contemporary reasons. In *Joan of Arc,* for example, Southey turned St. Joan from a patriotic and religious martyr into a country girl defending the nonheroic values of domestic life. Similarly, Scott's Marmion—whatever his offenses against society, whatever his prowess as a fighter or glamour as an outlaw—articulated the values of contemporary middle-class gentry. Wordsworth, on the other hand, openly repudiated the heroic ideals of the past: "Sage, patriot, lover, hero," he wrote, "it seemed / That their best virtues were not free from taint / Of something false and weak . . ." (*The Prelude,* XI, 59–74). He turned the Great Man into the Great Many, universalized the heroic, identified it with the very principle of life itself, the "grandeur in the beatings of the heart" (*The Prelude,* I, 441); for, he concluded, "there's not a man / That lives who hath not had his god-like hours" (*The Prelude,* III, 191–92). Most writers, discerning what was "false and weak" both in the tradition and in contemporary life, persistently questioned the conventional bases of power, of grandeur,

rejected the necessary illusions by which institutions are per-
petuated and from which individuals derive authority, and
invented heroes who were more often than not rebellious,
"Souls," as Bryon wrote in *Cain,* "who dared look the
Omnipotent tyrant in / His everlasting face, and tell him that /
His evil is not good!" (I, 138–40).

To Carlyle, even the literary inventions were inadequate;
having no basis in reality, they inspired no actual heroism,
merely new cults: "No ideal Chivalry," he writes in *Charac-
teristics,* "invites to heroism, prescribes what is heroic: the old
ideal of Manhood has grown obsolete, and the new is still
invisible to us, and we grope after it in darkness, one clutch-
ing this phantom, another that: Wertherism, Byronism, even
Brummelism, each has its day." A brief survey of the mon-
archy, the church, and the military in England, the three
institutions that conventionally generate heroic ideals, may
help explain this loss during the Romantic period.[1]

The Royal Family and Friends

In 1814, while Francis Jeffrey berated Wordsworth in the
Edinburgh Review for having made a "super-annuated pedlar"
the hero of *The Excursion,* King George III, having reigned
for fifty-four years, was confined at Windsor, mad, blind,
deaf, intermittently conversing with the illustrious dead who
had come to seek his advice.[2] Because he was a generous
patron, he had been painted more than any other English
monarch. When he died in 1820, the Poet Laureate, Robert
Southey, waited nearly a year for the inspiration to compose
an appropriate elegy, "The Vision of Judgment." The poem
was so absurd (George is forgiven by such former enemies as
George Washington and welcomed into heaven by the usual
population of angels, saints, and cherubs as well as Chaucer,
Milton, and Shakespeare) that Byron's satire of it, "The Vision
of Judgment," is directed against the poet as well as the King.
George III's family was perhaps his major achievement: fif-
teen children, borne by the patient little Queen Charlotte, of
whom five daughters and seven sons survived. According to
Thackeray in "The Four Georges," the King's "household
was a model of an English gentleman's household. It was
early; it was kindly; it was charitable; it was frugal; it was
orderly; it must have been stupid to a degree which I shudder
now to contemplate. No wonder all the princes ran away
from the lap of that dreary domestic virtue. It always rose,
rode, dined at stated intervals. Day after day was the same."

The daughters, who were "handsome," "kind, loving and lady-like," "gracious to every person high and low," each had her own accomplishment: drawing, playing the piano, and decorating "whole suites of rooms . . . with their busy little needles."

The three eldest sons, who were in line for succession, reacted against their father's domesticity: they were loud, eccentric, extravagant, and showed poor taste in women.[3] Frederick, Duke of York, had to resign from the army in 1809 because his mistress, Mary Ann Clarke, was convicted of selling commissions. The scandal was intensified by the existence of an observant press and a public that enjoyed seeing how impotent as well as corrupt its royal family was. Charles Lamb reports: "If you see newspapers you will read about Mrs. Clarke. The sensation in London about this nonsensical business is marvellous. I remember nothing in my life like it. Thousands of ballads, caricatures, lives of Mrs. Clarke, in every blind alley" (*Letters,* III, 4). The Duke married an acceptable German princess who shortly after moved to an estate in Surrey where she kept hundreds of dogs, entertained dandies, and introduced England to the practice of giving Christmas presents.

William, Duke of Clarence, was the naval son, who retained the brusque manner and language of the sea long after he had left his ship and taken up life with his mistress, Mrs. Dorothy Jordan, the renowned actress by whom he had ten children. When it appeared that he would have to become king or at least provide an heir who would, he separated from Mrs. Jordan and, two years after she died, married Princess Adelaide of Saxe-Meiningen. In 1830, he became King William IV.[4] Since their children died in infancy, the heir to the throne was sired by Edward, Duke of Kent. This compulsively neat disciplinarian whose fussiness had caused a mutiny in Gibraltar, espoused, to the embarrassment of the profligate aristocracy, the cause of such radical populists as Robert Owen. After separating from his mistress of twenty-seven years, Madame St. Laurent, he married Mary Louisa, sister of Prince Leopold, and fathered a daughter who became Queen Victoria.

But the son who was to inherit George III's throne, first as Prince Regent and then King George IV, was surely the most profligate, foolish, and pathetic of all.[5] Admittedly, in his youth he was as charming a young prince as any in Europe, an affable though self-indulgent, extravagant epicure passing his days at the theater or gambling houses among the dandies and the *demimonde* of Europe. After a two-year liaison with the opulent actress Mary Robinson, nicknamed "Perdita" after her favorite role, he met and married Mrs. Fitzherbert, who, as a Catholic widow with no royal connections, was never legally acknowledged as his wife. Nonetheless, he remained with her until 1803, except for the brief time in 1795 when he lived with his acknowledged bride, his cousin, Princess Caroline of Brunswick, whom he wed reluctantly in exchange for over £600,000 to pay his debts. Nine months after the wedding, when Princess Charlotte was born, he formally separated from Caroline and kept Charlotte to be raised as the heir to the throne. By the time he became Regent in 1811, ruling on behalf of the disabled King, who died in 1820, it was as if Prince Hal had become his own Falstaff: the once florid, chubby, good-natured prince was an overweight, maudlin, impulsive exhibitionist, incapable of directing his private life or a nation at war. In 1812, when the *Morning Post* reported the birthday toasts raised in honor of this "glory of the People," this "Adonis in Loveliness," Leigh Hunt refused to play Emperor's-new-clothes and wrote in *The Examiner* that the Prince was in fact "a corpulant man of fifty . . . a man who has just closed half a century without one single claim on the gratitude of his country, or the respect of posterity!"—for which Hunt and his brother were jailed for libel.

The festivities of 1814, celebrating Napoleon's withdrawal to Elba, illustrated the Regent's capacity for mounting celebrations and his lack of taste. There were processions, parades, illuminations, and banquets at which he was consistently upstaged by the austere King Frederick II of Prussia and the patronizing Czar Alexander I, who chose to stay in a hotel rather than a royal residence. Honors were distributed by the corpulent Prince, who required assistance to invest the even more corpulent Louis XVII with the Order of the Garter, the French King's leg, according to the Regent himself, being the size of a young man's waist. For the people, he turned Green Park, St. James Park, and Hyde Park over to a celebration that included temporary oriental temples, towers, pagodas, bridges, a mock naval battle on the Serpentine, balloon ascents, fireworks, and a grand transformation in which a "Temple of Discord" disappeared in a cloud of smoke and was replaced by a "Temple of Concord." Later, the whole building burst into flames, fell into the lake, killed a lamplighter, and injured five workmen. It was the first of such public celebrations and set new records for public drunkeness. As Lamb described it to Wordsworth, "by the wise provision of the Regent all that

was countryfy'd in the Parks is all but obliterated. The very
colour of green is vanished, the whole surface of Hyde Park
is dry crumbling sand . . . booths & drinking places go all
round it for a mile & half . . . the stench of liquors, bad
tobacco, dirty people & provisions, conquers the air & we
are stifled and suffocated. . . . Order after Order has been
issued by Lord Sidmouth in the name of the Regent . . . for
the dispersion of the varlets, but in vain. . . . The Regent has
rais'd a phantom which he cannot lay. There they'll stay
probably for ever. The whole beauty of the Place is gone—
that lake-look of the Serpentine—it has got foolish ships upon
it—but something whispers to have confidence in nature and
its revival" (Marrs, III, 96).

For himself, the Prince commissioned John Nashe, who
was already remodeling London into what we now call the
Regency style, to create a country house at Windsor. The
architect, busy organizing the urban aristocracy into cres-
cents of stately white stucco rowhouses ornamented with
wrought-iron balconies and plaster statues, turned his talents
to the design of the Royal Lodge, a thatch-roofed cottage
with stained glass windows, plaster walls tinted to resemble
brick, and columns entwined with ivy and honeysuckle. Then
he undertook the final transformation of the marine pavilion
from the farmhouse the Prince first visited in 1783 to the
anomalous mosque, the opulent oriental pleasure dome on
the stony beaches of Brighton. Architects including Henry
Holland, Humphry Repton, and James Wyatt had already
contributed to the Palladian, the gothic, the Chinese, and
Mediterranean motifs of the pavilion. At the expense of another
£155,000 (not including furniture, upholstery, hangings, glass,
linens, and plate) Nashe added battlements, pagodas, minar-
ets, an onion-shaped dome, Indian columns, and stone lat-
ticework, until the outside looked like "a collection of stone
pumpkins and pepper boxes," according to Hazlitt.[6] The inside
resembled a seraglio, with bamboo hangings, silk wallpaper,
lacquered furniture with dragon feet, fanciful chandeliers
resembling waterlilies, and a steam-heated kitchen for pre-
paring the long and unfortunately boring dinners that the
Prince so much enjoyed. It stands now as a frivolous and
melancholy monument to the Regent and his age.

The expense was unconscionable, considering the suffer-
ing of the English people after the war. For example, a miner
earning at best £40 a year would have had to work for 725
years merely to pay for the imitation gold leaf, the ormolu,
on which the Regent had spent £29,000 in 1815. His £49,000

upholstery bill would have taken an agricultural laborer earn-
ing £30 a year 1,633 years to pay for. In a year when a shop-
keeper did well to earn £150 and an artisan was earning a
living at best £55 a year, the Regent's debts amounted to
£339,000.[7] Still, his extravagance stimulated the development
of the decorative arts and he was considered a generous patron.
He commissioned his favorite portrait painter, Sir Thomas
Lawrence, to do the allied leaders in 1914; financed the return
of the Vatican treasures to Rome from the Louvre; supported
Lord Elgin's purchase of the marble friezes from the Par-
thenon; knighted the chemist Humphry Davy and the
astronomer William Herschel; and, finally, made science
fashionable by serving as President of the Royal Institution
and attending the lectures.

His favorite writers were Sir Walter Scott and Jane Austen,
whose novels he kept in each of his residences. In 1815, he
directed his librarian to invite her to tour Clarence House and
give her the liberty of dedicating her next novel, *Emma,* to
him. In March, 1816, the same librarian, J. S. Clarke, wrote
to Miss Austen suggesting that she dedicate her next volume
to the Prince's son-in-law, Prince Leopold, who had married
his daughter Charlotte: "any historical romance illustrative
of the history of the august House of Coburg, would just
now be very interesting." She replied, "I could no more write
a romance than an epic poem . . . under any motive than to
save my life. . . . I am sure I should be hung before I had
finished the first chapter."

Except visually, it was difficult for any serious artist to
relate to the experience of this royal family. When George III
died in 1820, leaving his subjects, as Byron wrote in *The Vision
of Judgment,* "One half as mad—and t'other no less blind"
(ll. 63–64), the Regent feared that Princess Caroline would
expect to be crowned Queen and, the ultimate profanation,
named in the liturgy of the Church and the prayers of
Englishmen. For the previous six years, while the Regent was
having a quiet affair with Lady Hertford with her husband's
assent, this chubby middle-aged princess had wandered around
Europe dressed in abbreviated costumes, odd hats, grotesque
makeup and wigs, her breasts and ankles exposed, dancing
frenetically, exhausting all her hosts, having or trying to have
affairs with everyone from Napoleon's brother-in-law to her
own footman, accompanied by a boy named Willikin who
she claimed was the natural son she had by Prince Louis Fer-
dinand of Prussia—although he was actually adopted from
an unemployed dockyard worker.[8]

While he could not divorce her and beheading her was beyond the constitutional limits of his monarchy, the Regent had her tried on Bills of Pains and Penalties introduced in Parliament whereby the Princess was accused of having engaged in "licentious, disgraceful, and adulterous inter- course" with her courier, Bartolomeo Bergami, the penalty for which was the loss of her titles, her rights to be Queen, and the dissolution of her marriage. Her behavior with him had, in fact, been scandalous, traveling around Italy in a sea- shell-shaped carriage drawn by a child dressed as an angel. Still the trial was even more scandalous.[9] Caroline, hidden in a white veil, dozed while dozens of Italian witnesses using gestures, broken English and Italian, presented evidence from a green canvas bag describing the contents of chamber pots and the stains on her bed sheets. It was all reported to the public within hours, aided by fast, steam-produced mass-cir- culation newspapers. She was defended by Lord Brougham, who had advocated such popular and otherwise respectable causes as national education and the abolition of the slave trade, and she was supported by thousands of working-class fol- lowers who enjoyed embarrassing the Regent. Indeed, the bemused Duke of Wellington was called out to protect the House of Lords from the crowd's enthusiasm. The bill was dismissed, one M.P. concluding "that the Lady was immoral and her husband a fit associate for her." Still the Regent did not invite her to the coronation, and, when she presented herself at Westminster Abbey, the doorkeepers turned her away because she did not have a ticket. She died a month later.

For the rest of his reign, the King remained faithful to Lady Conyngham, another rich, middle-aged, corpulent woman, more religious, petulant, and greedy than the others, whose husband tacitly approved of an arrangment that had many advantages for himself and their children. They spent their time moving from castle to palace, eating large and long din- ners, the King drinking immense quantities of wine, cham- pagne, and brandy, taking laudanum for his hangovers before drinking more, admiring his sloe-eyed giraffe among the 150 animals in his menagerie of exotic pets, inventing a heroic past for himself, and promoting architectural wonders to suit it. He spent £700,000 of public money for Trafalgar Square, Buckingham Palace, and finally Windsor, where in 1830 he died in voluptuous gothic seclusion. He left no heirs; his daughter Charlotte had died in childbirth in 1817, a year after her marriage to Prince Leopold, who later became King of

Belgium. His private legacy, auctioned by his servants, included an immense wardrobe of every costume, fur, uniform, footwear, and decoration he had ever owned, all the coats, boots, and pantaloons he had collected over the past fifty years, five hundred pocket books containing about £10,000 of forgotten money, and countless memorabilia of his love affairs, including love letters and locks of women's hair. When his brother, the Duke of Clarence, became King William IV, his coronation was so informal and on such a reduced budget that some called it the "Half-Crownation."

Given the moralistic attitudes that evolved during the reign of George III, it is difficult to account for the public's tolerance of the Regent and his relatives. However indignant the Hunts were, however contemptuous Shelley and Byron, many, like Scott, were won by his charm and conversational skills: "He is in many respects the model of a British monarch . . . sincerely, I believe, desires the good of his subjects—is kind towards the distressed, and moves and speaks 'every inch a King.' I am sure that such a man is fitter for us than one who would long to lead armies, or be perpetually intermeddling with *la grande politique.*"[10] The middle classes, however circumscribed their own behavior, viewed the Regent with forbearance, as if he were fulfilling their private delinquent fantasies: "They dreamt of sin," John Keats wrote in his satirical fragment *The Cap and Bells,* "and he sin'd while they slept." To maintain such a Regent and aristocracy as a source of ideals, of manners and values, required a capacity for self-deception and hypocrisy that would also carry the middle classes through the false refinements of the Victorian period. Indeed, in Byron's *Don Juan,* his collective self-delusion amounts to a social pathology, the object of his satire.

Beau Brummell

The Regent helped to launch the influential man of fashion called the dandy, embodied in Beau Brummell, a figure who was irrevocably to change the character, appearance, and manners of English gentlemen of all classes.[11] In *Sartor Resartus,* Carlyle defined him as a "Clotheswearing Man, a Man whose trade, office, and existence consists in the wearing of Clothes. Every faculty of his soul, spirit, purse, and person is heroically consecrated to this one object" (p. 272). His style was simple, the opposite of the ornamented satins, the embroidered velvets, the brocades, plumes, laces, braid, and jewels the Prince and his aristocratic friends had enjoyed

wearing before Beau Brummell arrived. The dandy's cos-
tume, which was exactly the same for everyone, consisted of
a blue coat buttoned in brass over the waist, the lapels rising
nearly to the ears and the tails ending just above the knees.
He wore an intricately tied cravat of purest white linen, a buff
waistcoat crossed with a heavy gold watch chain, and closely
fitted trousers tucked into black Hessian boots, which Brum-
mell claimed to polish with the froth of champagne. For eve-
ning, Brummell introduced black and white: a white waistcoat,
black coat and pantaloons buttoning to the ankles, striped
silk stockings, and oval-toed pumps. In place of jewels, coif-
fures, and cosmetics, he engaged in a ritual of personal hygiene
that raised cleanliness to an art, shaving, scrubbing, and
plucking his face until it was pink and childlike, polishing his
teeth and nails, and rejecting all perfumes on the grounds that
he had no smell. He also had no intellectual distinction or
personal accomplishments, no money, occupation, respon-
sibility, function, ambition, passions, connections, commit-
ments, or lineage. In place of conversation, he offered posture,
gesture, and facial expression. He was emotionally detached,
self-involved, and obsessed with appearance: "The ideal of
the dandy," Ellen Moers writes, "is cut in cloth. The dandy's
independence is expressed in his rejection of any visible dis-
tinction but elegance; his self-worship in self-adornment; his
superiority to useful work in his tireless application to cos-
tume. His independence, assurance, originality, self-control
and refinement should all be visible in the cut of his clothes."[12]

Born in 1778, Brummell, son of a civil servant, attended
Eton and Oxford before joining the Prince's regiment, "The
Elegant Extracts," an idle, fashionable, well-born military
regiment, accompanying the Prince on his pleasure trips.
Brummell helped escort the future princess Caroline to Lon-
don, attended the Regent at his wedding and perhaps on the
honeymoon as well, and resigned in 1798 to set up house-
keeping in London. He was instantly popular, invited to the
best clubs and houses. He lived by a mysterious social alchemy
whereby he dictated style to which others conformed, and
their conformity enhanced his influence along with his credit
among the tailors whose merchandise he wore and thereby
endorsed. As long as he was winning, he gambled to pay his
expenses, mostly at Watier's where decks were discarded after
each game until the players were up to their knees in cards.
Inevitably he began to lose, starting with the loss of his good-
luck charm. One night, when his debts had become an
embarrassment, he attended the opera, dined on cold chicken

and claret, and fled to Calais. Visiting him in France became part of the Continental tour until he was confined to debtor's prison where he suffered a stroke. In his final years, he dressed in rags, gossiped obsessively about the ancient and dead friends of his youth, and hallucinated visits from royalty. His appearance was so filthy and his manners so repulsive that the diners in the small hotel where he lived had him removed to the Convent of the Sisters of Charity where he died in 1840.

Brummell's influence on English aristocratic life reveals the insecurity of the upper classes during the early decades of the nineteenth century, the absence of a positive ideal. Their historical and exclusive rights to money and land, the bases of power, challenged by the rising industrial and mercantile classes, the aristocrats responded by creating a new exclusiveness, something they called "society" and the "world," consisting of themselves and characterized by *ton,* an ineffable style or quality they required of those who wanted to participate in it. Brummell, who had little money, breeding, power, intelligence, accomplishment, or talent, merely an exaggerated belief in his own intrinsic superiority, helped to define the style on which this new exclusiveness and snobbery would be based. As Robert Plumer Ward wrote in *Tremaine; or the Man of Refinement* (1825), one of the many fashionable novels in which the Regency dandy became enshrined, "There is something so heroically insolent in an exclusive; such a noble conviction of his or her superiority over all the rest of the human race; such a philosophic independence of everything which people of mere nature look to for happiness. . . ."[13]

Men overcame the loneliness and boredom of exclusiveness with an interest in racing, in violent sports such as ratbaiting, dog fights, and boxing matches, and in slumming, depicted magnificently by Pierce Egan in *Life in London Or, the Day and Night Scenes of Jerry Hawthorn, Esq., and his Elegant Friend Corinthian Tom on their Rambles and Sprees through the Metropolis* (1821), dedicated to the Regent who was then George IV. And women overcame their boredom by overcoming the men, exerting as much power as the Regent himself in drawing rooms and assembly rooms such as Almack's, where even Wellington was denied entrance one night. On long country weekends full of silent and overfed guests, the sleek, self-contained, remote, fastidious dandy was a welcome alternative to the drunken country gentlemen smelling of the stables and the hounds. A passionless, emasculated creature without domestic inclinations, the dandy was an asset in a society where, following the example of the royal princes, families were unfashionable and married couples often led independent social lives. The very opposite of the Man of Feeling who populated eighteenth-century novels, dramas, and drawing rooms, the Dandy's major virtue was composure, self-restraint, avoiding both action and feeling, anything that might be construed as heroic, altruistic, or likely to dishevel his cravat.

Religious Heroes

By 1815, the prestige of institutional Christianity in England, the Anglican Church, had suffered the same decline as the King, who was its supreme head, None of the heroic machinery—miracles, saints, intercessions, private revelations—had survived a hundred years of rational deism, anticlericalism, and middle-class prosperity. Demystified, the church had become a refuge for impoverished or incompetent younger sons of landed gentry. So long as they were politically and socially acceptable, graduates of either Oxford or Cambridge, they were ordained without any theological training, entering a profession which the gentry itself considered only one step above idleness. So Edward Ferrars, a wealthy elder son, explains ironically in Jane Austen's *Sense and Sensibility* that he is "an idle, helpless being," without either business or profession because his preference, the church, "was not smart enough," the army "was a great deal too smart," and he was too old to join the navy, which "has fashion on its side." Those gentry who did enter the clergy brought to it, as Bulwer-Lytton claimed, "a love for decencies and decencies alone" rather than zeal, and were often boring preachers: "It is something disreputable to be too eloquent; the aristocratic world does not like either clergymen, or women, to make too much noise."[14] Had their motives been less worldly, the infusion of retired army officers on halfpay after the Napoleonic wars might have improved the priesthood. But to increase their incomes, they held multiple parishes which they deputized to curates, who in turn augmented their salaries with farming or by engaging in a local craft. Congregations declined and an indifferent clergy, preoccupied with earning a living, tended to keep them that way. "Here the scandal," Elie Halévy writes, "was not that the parsons neglected their flocks, but that the country was burdened by the expense of this enormous ecclesiastical establishment devoid of adherents."[15]

The career of Richard Watson, Bishop of Llandaff, is instructive not only because it demonstrates the nature of leadership and success in the Church of England at the opening of the nineteenth century but also because it impinged on the lives of so many writers of the time. Like Wordsworth, he was from Westmorland, attended Cambridge where he studied science, then obtained the Professorship of Chemistry by writing a series of successful introductory essays on the subject. Acquiring the Chair of Divinity, he tripled his income, married into a respectable family which further increased his wealth, purchased an estate on the shore of Windermere, became a bishop, and ultimately entered the House of Lords. One observer, the chronically impoverished De Quincey, complained: "All his public, all his professional duties he systematically neglected. He was a Lord in Parliament, and for many a year he never attended in his place: he was a Bishop, and he scarcely knew any part of his diocese by sight—living three hundred miles away from it: he was a Professor of Divinity; he held the richest Professorship in Europe, the weightiest, for its functions, in England,—he drew, by his own admission, one thousand per annum from its endowments—and for thirty years he never read a lecture, or performed a public service."[16]

The corruption of the clergy is a familiar literary complaint from Dante to John Bunyan, reaching levels of irreverence in "Monk" Lewis and of comedy in Browning. Traditionally, the substance of the complaint was that clergymen were supposed to lead exemplary lives. If Richard Watson were corrupt, in some ironic way his life was still exemplary—an example of how a clever and industrious son of a schoolmaster could rise in the world by his own wits and sense of timing, setting an excellent example for the new young capitalists, the disciples of Robert Owen and Samuel Smiles. But under the leadership of such men as Watson, the Church became a political instrument which used Christian doctrine to help suppress the growing unrest among the poor, particularly the laboring poor. *The Wisdom and Goodness of God in Having Made both Rich and Poor,* one of the Bishop's old sermons, was reprinted in 1793, when war, bad harvests, and radical agitation had intensified the suffering and deprivation among the poor. The Bishop's complacent defense of the English constitution, social hierarchy, and the judicial system along with his rationalizations for poverty as an expression of Divine Will and a source of virtue so incensed Wordsworth that he wrote a passionate refutation, *A Letter to the Bishop of Llandaff,* which even Joseph Johnson, the radical bookseller, considered too seditious to print. Like Blake, Godwin, and Shelley, among others, Wordsworth decried the self-righteousness of the church and state, their failure to recognize that the official virtues they represented caused most of the misery in the world, a theme Blake had captured in "The Human Abstract": "Pity would be no more / If we did not make somebody poor."

While there were "successful" bishops, such as Richard Watson, there were no leaders who represented the ideals of traditional Christianity. There were fashionable preachers outside the Anglican Church such as the Reverend Edward Irving, a Scottish Calvinist, whose success, according to Hazlitt in the *Spirit of the Age,* illustrated the "preposterous rage for novelty." A consummate actor, he "keeps his public in awe by insulting all their favorite idols . . . and leaves nothing standing but himself, a mighty landmark in a degenerate age, overlooking the wide havoc he had made." But those who attend churches hunger for more than showmanship and relevance; they want their passion directed at the mysterious, the inexplicable, the transcendent. When a cholera epidemic in 1831–1832 killed nearly 60,000 in England alone, and citizens rioted on the basis of a rumor that the graves of victims were being robbed for the purpose of scientific experiment, the parishioners at Reverend Irving's Scotch National Church in Regent Square were ready for a revelation; this fashionable and urbane audience discovered they had the gift of tongues, on the basis of which they founded the Holy Catholic Apostolic Church.[17] In doing so they were following the example of the eighteenth-century Methodists, who, under the leadership of John Wesley and George Whitfield, came close to being the hero-priests for which the working classes longed.

Like the other Dissenters, such as the Presbyterians, Baptists, Congregationalists, Calvinists, and Quakers, the Methodists rejected existing dogma and external authority, proposing that grace is to be found in faith, not works, in private revelation that would turn each believer into his own priest, if not temple. If the hero-priest appeared, he was one favored by God with the eloquence or inspiration to gather a crowd in the fields or marketplace and effect massive conversions. Teaching submission and humility, however, Methodism in the closing decades of the eighteenth century inspired anything but heroic action.[18] The loving, paternalistic God became a holy tyrant whose wrath was inscrutable and whose power was defined by his capacity to ferret out the most private and subtle sins and devise appropriate punishment. A passive and suffering Christ appeared as the effeminate symbol of salvation through pain, of joy in humiliation, of love in sado-masochistic fantasy.[19] The demonism of the Marquis de Sade, the sadistic fantasies of William Beckford, and the necrophilia of "Monk" Lewis reflect the spiritually perverted love cult expressed in the grotesque imagery of such Wesleyan hymns as "O precious Side-hole's cavity / I want to spend my life in thee."[20]

One penalty of this sexual and emotional dislocation was the loss of love as a heroic motive or ideal. With "Thou shalt not," as Blake said, written over the chapel door in "The Garden of Love," the heroes that the middle and lower classes encountered in their reading were dying children, starving parents, sacrificing and suffering servants, neighbors, friends—the mournful population of Mrs. Hannah More's Cheap Repository Tracts from which several generations of English children learned in "Sinful Sally" that reading novels leads to prostitution, and in "Half a Loaf is Better than No Bread" the moral economy of the Evangelical God. Such psychological crimes in the name of spiritual salvation could have been more damaging than the worldly self-interest and social apathy of the Bishop of Llandaff were it not for the curious capacity of the human psyche to generate the fantasies it needs to believe. If the political life sponsored official illusions of heroism, then the religious life inspired subversive ones.

To inspire faith in the heroic potential of man and thereby inspire faith in the God who made him was the common purpose of these subversive illusions. In rare individuals such as Blake, who would and did "Create a System" rather than "be enslav'd by another Man's" (Erdman, 564), the attempt was personal, direct, even extravagant: "Thou art a Man, God is no more, / Thine own Humanity learn to adore" (Erdman, 136). The entire machinery of the church, the confessions, lamentations, self-abasing penances, illuminations, and conversions become irrelevant if "All deities reside in the human breast" (Erdman, 195) and if "God becomes as we are, that we may become as he is" (Erdman, 148). Blake's cosmic humanism, raising believers up off their knees and over their fear and trembling, was influenced, or at least affirmed by Emanuel Swedenborg, a Swedish geologist and philosopher, who had announced that the Last Judgment had in fact occurred and a new age begun in 1757, the year Blake was born. Swedenborg had impressive scientific credentials, offering the first serious post-Copernican speculation on the origins of planets, a theory of explosion through accelerating solar rotation, while English scientists were still trying to justify the Old Testament version of creation with their scientific observations.[21] But his life was devoted to writing out massive Latin tomes in which he explained the correct interpretation of the Bible, an interpretation he acquired from conversations with angels. In 1789, the year in which many saw the world being born again, the Society of London Swedenborgians held its first conference at the New Jerusalem Church, attended by William Blake.

Swedenborg's vision had elevated the human form itself above the heroic into a celestial cartography, a universe designed in the form of a Grand Man to which everything on earth corresponded. Blake's "The Divine Image," written while sitting in the New Jerusalem Church, was inspired by this vision and later grew into the archetypal giant Albion on whom he based his creation myth. Swedenborg's belief in the intuitional nature of faith; in Divine Love as an animating and, expressed in light, an illuminating principle; in the purity of the sexual act; in the divinity of man and the humanity of God, contradicted prevailing pietism and confirmed Blake's own experience, for he also claimed to have conversed with angels, and, a highly visual poet, found God in "the human form divine."[22]

For the majority of people who were neither seers nor prophets, nothing less than a divine intercession could restore them to an original relationship with God and thereby with themselves, a condition basic to heroic experience. A number of self-proclaimed prophets responded to this need and cultivated, primarily though not exclusively among the lower classes, the subversive illusion that such an intercession was in fact at hand. Basing their prophecies on the Book of Revelation, a series of catastrophes (or what we have come to call, strangely, natural disasters) would announce the Last Judgment, and the earth as well as the evil powers which control it would be destroyed; a new Messiah would appear to restore the earth as a paradise for the faithful. Two earthquakes occurring in London within two months early in 1750 gave momentum to millenialist thinking, for, as R. J. White notes, "one quake might be geological but two were manifestly theological."[23] Methodist preachers urged their followers to take heed and repent, while others offered alternative protection by selling "earthquake gowns." When, five years later on All Saints Day, five thousand pious, prosperous, and apparently innocent people were wiped out by the Lisbon earthquake, many others by the attendant tidal waves, while pillagers and looters survived to complete the destruction, it became apparent that repentance was not enough. The oracles had been misread; a new prophet was in order.

And many appeared, popular prophets who answered the immediate needs of the lower classes. By keeping the new order at a constantly receding horizon, they were able to account for such continued and inevitable crises as the Reign of Terror in France in 1793, the food shortages of 1795, the Napoleonic Wars, storms, wayward comets, and eclipses. But more importantly, they appealed, if only subliminally, to the political frustrations of the lower classes. For the impotent and the abused, their visions were irresistible: a God who was their ally, who would revenge their wrongs, destroy their oppressors, and relieve them of the escalating anxiety inherent in such dogma as predestination or salvation through suffering, who, finally, in giving them paradise, would endow them with property and status. Such dangerous political fantasies found refuge in this religious context, for, however radical the prophets, they were protected by the same laws that protected the Methodists. Only once, threatened by the rising revolutionary fervor of 1795, did the government express its discomfort with all this visionary retribution and created a martyr in Richard Brothers (1757–1824). Brothers, a retired naval captain who claimed to be God's nephew, had acquired a large following when his predictions, mostly the meteorological ones, proved alarmingly accurate.[24] Brothers was committed to a lunatic asylum, and his followers transferred their allegiances to Joanna Southcott.

In 1801, Joanna Southcott began a career of writing and preaching the messages that she claimed God had delivered through her. While cleaning out an old house, she discovered an oval seal with the letters "IC," and soon all her correspondence was marked with it, her bearded followers wore it, and the "Sealed People," as those who possessed it were called, anticipated the Final Judgment, when, as the 144,000 elect, they would inherit the earth. In 1814, while Jeffrey was complaining that *The Excursion* was "a tissue of moral and devotional ravings," while aristocratic London gossiped about the Royal family and bought 13,000 copies of Byron's *Corsair* on the day of publication, while all of England celebrated the first end of the Napoleonic Wars, and Napoleon himself on the island of Elba contemplated his own second coming, Joanna, at age sixty-four, announced that she was pregnant, that she had been chosen to bear Shiloh, the son of God. For four months, newspapers reported on her condition, street singers composed ballads about her, and she was inundated with gifts and offers of assistance. Then she died. The Prince of Peace failed to appear although, as directed, her followers kept her corpse warm for four days.[25]

The most eccentric of all the prophets, Joanna's influence lasted longer and spread further than any of the others. In 1825 both Charles Twort and George Turner claimed to be Shiloh; but John Wroe, head of the Southcottians, dismissed them as frauds and set out to convert the Australians. Blake wrote a poem about her, "On the Virginity of the Virgin Mary and Johanna Southcott":

> What'er is done to her she cannot know,
> And if you ask her she will swear it so
> Whether 'tis good or evil, none's to blame,
> No one can take the pride, no one the shame.

Dickens used her as an index to the age at the opening of *A Tale of Two Cities:* "Mrs. Southcott had recently attained her five-and-twentieth blessed birthday, of whom a prophetic private in the Life Guards had heralded the sublime appearance by announcing that arrangements were made for the swallowing up of London and Westminster." She appears in Keats's correspondence and in Byron's, who called her "the real Mrs. Trinity." Hazlitt, reviewing Coleridge's *Lay Sermons,* claims that her "vagaries, whimsies, and pregnant throes . . . were sober and rational" compared with Coleridge's "qualms and crude conceptions" (Howe, 16:101). Joanna Southcott had clearly entered the consciousness of the culture, and even intelligent people were discomforted by the transparency of her illusions. Her very success indicated the need to believe if not in an impending apocalypse—many had promised that—then at least that the affairs of men were not solely in the hands of men, for human beings had proved especially incompetent—as our survey of the monarchy and the established church demonstrated. The virgin birth that she promised reverted to the primitive but compelling idea that God not only appeared in the word or in the light but more immediately in the flesh, that there was still some interpenetration of the human and the divine. Whatever function the god-men of Romantic myth—Shelley's Prometheus, Blake's Albion, or Keats's Apollo—served the poets, Joanna Southcott served for the believing lower classes: proof, however bizarre, that, as Blake wrote in *Milton,* Jerusalem could be "builded here / Among these dark Satanic Hills."

Warrior Heroes:
Nelson, Wellington, and Napoleon

For the English government, both the American War of Independence (1775–1783) and the Napoleonic Wars (1793–1802; 1803–1815) were undertaken basically to protect trade and keep markets open. Against the patriot soldier in America defending his home and the citizen soldier in Europe fighting for his rights, the English sent an army of impressed foot soldiers, which Wellington himself called "the scum of the earth," and a navy of often mutinous and unwilling sailors, kidnapped merchant seamen, smugglers, criminals, and vagabonds commanded by gentlemen with purchased commissions. And though the English civilians had been, as Coleridge said, "clamorous / For war and bloodshed," they preferred to be "Spectators and not combatants!" ("Fears in Solitude," ll.93–95), preferred comfort to glory. Even writers, notably aristocratic and retrospective ones, who admired military virtue, such as Sir Walter Scott and Lord Byron, found in modern warfare, with its vast and distant battlefields, its massive armies and machinery of destruction, an ugly substitute for the chivalric ideal of personal combat, the elaborate rituals of honor and of confrontation. Scott himself joined the Edinburgh Volunteer Light Dragoons, claiming to enjoy the "pomp and circumstance";[26] but his novels depicted the ultimate toll of war on property, on domestic and civil life. While Byron concluded his career seeking "a soldier's grave" in the Greek War of Independence, he was contemptuous of modern warfare:

> Bombs, drums, guns, bastions, batteries, bullets
> Hard words which stick in the soft muses' gullets.
> *(Don Juan,* VII, 78)[27]

Whether surveying the graveyard of Europe after 1815 in *Childe Harold,* III, or exposing the pointless sacrifices for material gain in *Don Juan,* VIII, he memorialized the masses of helpless and often anonymous people whose suffering impugned whatever chivalric values may have survived or been dusted off for expediency. So devastating did modern warfare appear that even victory served at best to illustrate the cynical Malthusian conclusion that war is a human vice which helps keep a check on population. Battles and soldiers, which in the past had inspired Homer, now appeared unceremoniously in the newspapers, a journalistic diversion:

> Boys and girls
> And women, that would groan to see a child
> Pull off an insect's leg, all read of war,
> The best amusement for our morning meal!
> (Coleridge, "Fears in Solitude," ll. 104–7)

The poets came to recognize what all poets have probably always recognized even when their task was primarily to celebrate the military achievements of their patrons, that basically war was a direct threat to the values and occupations on which their art depended.

Attitudes toward the war against France shifted according to class interest. The aristocracy was opposed to Napoleon because he challenged their right to inherited power—even though it meant fighting the country which had been the source of civilized refinements for over a hundred years. The commercial classes realized that the war was being fought to protect their markets, but they resented the heavy taxes required to support it. And "The last to bid the cry of warfare cease," as Byron wrote, "the first to make a malady of peace" (*The Age of Bronze,* ll. 570–71), were the landed gentry who dominated Parliament and supported the war—not victory, just the war, because it kept up the price of grain and permitted them to collect higher rents. But a coalition of writers, radical intellectuals, and the laboring poor withheld their support of the war; for them, Napoleon, at least up until 1804 when he became emperor, was fulfilling the promise of the Revolution. And even when Wellington defeated Napoleon at Waterloo, some such as Leigh Hunt and William Hazlitt went into mourning for what they saw as the ultimate defeat of the Revolutionary ideals and a return to tyranny. The real victims of the war were, as always, the poor: in industry, overworked, taxed, and hungry; in the countryside, dispossessed by increasing enclosures; in the army or navy, flogged and, if they weren't killed, discharged, homeless and unrewarded, to a society that had no facilities for the infirm but the poorhouse or prison.

With such an array of opinions toward the war itself, the warrior heroes who emerged, Horatio Nelson and the Duke of Wellington, were bound to be unique and to serve the public imagination in unprecedented ways. While class friction was rampant among the officers in the navy, the lower ranks offered considerable opportunity for advancement to ambitious and healthy young men. Consequently, although Nelson was only a clergyman's son, small and unimpressive in appearance, after joining the navy at age twelve, he rose through the ranks, acquiring a reputation for kindness to cabin boys, for impatience with ceremony, and for overcoming disadvantages through sheer bravado. After defeating Napoleon in Egypt (1798) and again at Copenhagen (1801), he developed into a vain and often silly egotist, which finally cost him his life. In boyish pride he disregarded his officers' advice at the battle of Trafalgar, and, wearing his many colorful medals on deck, became a moving target: "In honour I gained them," he insisted, "and in honour I will die with them."[28]

However extravagant such a gesture may have appeared, it was in the spirit of the age; and Nelson, very much a public man, reflected its inconsistencies and contradictions far more than he reflected the heroic traditions of his calling. Having neither the cunning of an Odysseus nor the transcendent inspiration of an Arthurian knight, this "darling hero of England," as Southey called him, who "entirely possessed the love of his fellow countrymen," displayed a sober devotion to duty and an admirable capacity for sentiment, which the English novel-reading public had come to prize. Mortally wounded, he directed his officers to send his hair to Lady Hamilton, wife of the British envoy to Naples, with whom he had an extended and public affair, and bequeathed both her and their illegitimate daughter Horatia to England as his "legacy." He died whispering "Thank God, I have done my duty."

Retrospectively we realize that Nelson was among the last English warriors who would appear to, or would even be willing to, slay dragons single-handedly. Less than a month after Nelson's death in 1805, William Pitt, the Prime Minister who had sent him prematurely and unprepared into battle, initiated the modern concept of the collective hero when, honored for having "saved England," he replied: "I return my thanks for the honour you have done me; but England is not to be saved by any single man." What appears as modesty is, in fact, a retreat from personal responsibility for oneself and for the welfare of one's fellows, a retreat into an anonymous abstraction variously known as the State, the People, and ultimately the System. So, Coleridge claimed, "No individual, whether a regent, a general, or a junta, can be representative of a public cause in a season of peril and uncertainty—least of all a general. It is unnatural for individ-

uals to sustain any higher character than that of public func-
tionaries. . . ."[29] It would seem that the very ideal of
leadership, of public action on behalf of others, was being
thrown into question by a society that was evolving on Dar-
winian principles and the laws of the marketplace: *laissez-faire*,
competition, and survival of the fittest. The altruistic goals
of a heroic aristocracy were being replaced by the self-interest
of a power meritocracy. In 1790, in *Reflections on the French
Revolution*, Edmund Burke had lamented that "the age of
chivalry is gone" and with it "heroic enterprise." It was
replaced by the collective identity that would develop, as
Dickens, Dostoevsky, and Kafka were to demonstrate, into
complete moral paralysis, atrophy of will, and the rule of
mediocrity.

The tension between assuming the individual heroic role
which society seemed so much in need of projecting on
someone and withdrawing into the safe anonymity of collec-
tive life characterizes the career of Arthur Wellesley, the Duke
of Wellington.[30] Wellington was born into a moribund tra-
dition, the unimpressive though dedicated son of an impov-
erished Irish gentry which could trace its pedigree back six
hundred years. In manner and appearance, Wellington was
an austere man, private and unapproachable. In battle he was
a tactician rather than a leader, impatient with heroics, repulsed
by the costs of battle, which, by his own admission, was a
last resort: "It was always Napoleon's object to fight a great
battle; my object, on the contrary, was to avoid to fight a
great battle." However reluctant he was to accept a heroic
role, it was repeatedly thrust upon him, Czar Alexander him-
self confiding in him before the Battle of Waterloo: "It is for
you to save the world again."[31] Following his defeat of
Napoleon in 1815, the English showered him with honors,
rewards, even a country estate, but he protested: "I feel I am
but a man."[32] And in the victory painting that Wellington
commissioned, David Wilkie portrayed not the conventional
hero dominating the field of battle but "a closely packed mass
of Chelsea pensioners discussing and celebrating the glad tid-
ings" without him.[33]

In politics this unwilling hero achieved his inverted ambi-
tion. By 1828, having overcome popular mistrust of a mili-
tary figure in government, Wellington became Prime Minister.
Unfortunately, unable to adapt to the collective decisions of
an emerging democracy, he resigned in 1830, another casu-
alty of the reform movement. Wellington's career illustrates
what might be a self-evident proposition: a warrior hero must

have war. Odysseus knew it, as did Napoleon, that feisty little Corsican who was born the same year as Wellington and who in defeat provided that myth of the warrior hero that Wellington as victor never did.

But Napoleon was more than a warrior hero; he was a hero for all people, transcending traditional heroic roles, changing the very definition of heroism itself until it even included his failure, becoming what E. J. Hobsbawm called the world's "first secular myth."[34] Within thirty years he had risen from an obscure and barbaric island off the coast of Italy to become "Emperor of the French," as he preferred to be called; within fifteen more years exiled to the island of Elba; and finally, after another stunning campaign, banished to the island of St. Helena, where he died in 1821, the same year as Queen Caroline and John Keats. A protean figure, endowed with an exceptional array of native talents, energy, ambition, intelligence, and a charismatic personality, he appeared in Paris, glowing from his victories in Italy, at a critical moment when it appeared that the Revolutionary ideals were being lost in the procedural chaos of a citizen governing body, the Directory. To this crisis he brought order, authority, a Civil Code, a reconciliation with the church, a national bank, and security, if not prosperity, to even the poorest French peasant.

His common ancestry, his belief in labor, his efficiency and organizational talents as well as his interest in literature, and his experiments with poetry, recommended him to all the French, from the industrialist to the aspiring artist.[35] Instead of collective life frustrating him, it was through him that it was fulfilled. The English were fascinated by him; he represented that heroic ideal that their own society had failed to provide. In 1801, while deriding Nelson's victory portrait as a "caricature" of a hero, Londoners flocked to an exhibit of Napoleon's portraits, Napoleon who had lost the battle but was winning the peace, who like Byron's Lucifer could claim "I have a Victor—true; but no superior . . ." (Cain, II, ii, 429). In fact, after his death, George IV ordered all the books from Napoleon's library on St. Helena and combed the margins for commentary, so fascinating did he find his old antagonist.

To the English poets and writers, Napoleon represented all that was excessively great and excessively wicked, a Satanic figure for Wordsworth and Coleridge, and a Promethean one for Blake, Shelley, and Byron. He embodied both the energies of the age and the brutal irony of acting upon them: the paralyzing discrepancy between Faustian longings for infinite power and the mortal limitations of a fallen universe. Byron, who seemed of all the poets most preoccupied with Napoleon, dramatized this aspect of his character in both *Childe Harold,* Book III (xxi–xlv) and in "Ode to Napoleon Buonaparte": "extreme in all things," "conquerer and captive of the earth," "a god unto himself" who could "crush, command, rebuild" an empire "but govern not [his] pettiest passion."

In defeat, Napoleon's professed ideal, the Roman hero, had become the Romantic one, the public's ideal, exhibiting that Christian resignation, that submission before authority, and that penitential attitude that had been lately popularized in the eighteenth-century novel of sentiment.[36] Consequently, Sir Walter Scott, who had a keen appetite for such gestures, overcame his youthful aversion toward Napoleon and began in 1825 his most ambitious work: a nine-volume biography completed in two years and selling 4,300 copies out of 5,000 within five days of publication. In 1828, Hazlitt, who had been such an enthusiastic partisan of Napoleon that he went into mourning after Waterloo, began a four-volume biography in defense of his hero. His publisher went bankrupt and Hazlitt was imprisoned for debt. But it was Shelley who in *The Triumph of Life* universalized Napoleon as the embodiment of the heroic dilemma that was to plague public life right up to the present time:

> And much I grieved to think how power and will
> In opposition rule our mortal day,
> And why God made irreconcilable
> Good and the means of good. . . .
>
> (ll. 226–32).

The Byronic Hero

What Shelley saw in Napoleon's defeat—the opposition between "good and the means of good," between, in other words, virtue and power, right and might—was inevitable, given the transitional nature of the culture, the stresses of contemporary life. The heroic figures we have described filled roles, acquired their aura through association. They were conspicuous rather than exemplary figures who derived their authority from the institutions with which they were affiliated or from the acquiescence of those they led rather than from any exceptional personal endowments—with the exception, of course, of Napoleon, whose personal endowments contributed as much to his defeat as his success. The "true" hero, the individual endowed with superior talent, insight, character, will, eloquence, intellect, courage, was unable to perform that public action by which heroism is realized because he was crippled by the institutions where power resided or collective life where it was coming to reside. In spite of the economic and religious individualism that developed during the eighteenth century, the power of collective life, the tyranny of the majority, is not to be underestimated. Moreover, the rise of the social and biological sciences, sciences which seemed so liberating an alternative to religious fatalism, introduced a new and in many ways more inhibiting determinism. While political theorists seemed to affirm individual freedom, their statistical procedures and abstract formulations belittled the individual and finally interpreted all his efforts as culturally, historically, economically, or biologically determined. His identity, his capacity to choose and direct his own life were absorbed in the machinery of society, his achievements interpreted as products of his environment.[37]

The most positive escape from the coercive power of externally defined roles was that of the creative artists, who retreated either to the objectivity of the sociological novelist or to the subjectivity that characterized the Romantic imagination in poetry. From either perspective, they explored the heroic dilemma, what some commentators have called the alienation of the exceptional individual. Shelley, so obviously victimized by it, best conveyed the sense of futility from his self-imposed exile in Switzerland:

> The good want power, but to weep barren tears.
> The powerful goodness want: worse need for them.
> The wise want love, and those who love want wisdom;
> And all best things are thus confused to ill.
>
> *(Prometheus Unbound,* I, 625–28)

In a world so "out of joint" only an original man, a man, to borrow a phrase from Wordsworth's definition of the original poet, creating the values by which he was to be judged, could oppose tradition, collective life, and the institutional habit of mind. Such a self-appointed, indeed self-invented figure, refusing to accept the world on its absurd or contradictory terms, preferring a higher, freer, more logical, humane, or just order, could only appear as a threat to society.[38] When such a heroic figure did appear, he was indeed a threat, an alien, a rebel, even an outlaw with criminal associations, but undoubtedly the most popular literary invention of the Romantic period: the Byronic hero. Here was that "original" man who in literature would redefine the concept of heroism just as Napoleon had redefined it in life.

The Byronic hero first appeared as the narrator in *Childe Harold,* Cantos I and II (1812), a wandering young aristocrat suffering from both unrequited love and an excess of nameless though by implication sexual sins—proud, bored, solitary, cynical, melancholy, self-pitying, a disengaged and passive commentator on the past glories and contemporary compromises of life in Spain and Greece. Byron, having very much enjoyed his own Grand Tour, disclaimed any biographical identification with Harold: "I would not be such a fellow as I have made my hero for all the world" *(L and J,* II, 66), though, ironically, he was creating the only role that he could play when experience caught up with fantasy. The success of Harold encouraged Byron to continue developing his hero in a series of Eastern tales: *The Curse of Minerva* (1812), *The Giaour* (1812), *The Bride of Abydos* (1813), *Lara* (1814), *The Corsair* (1814), *Parisina* (1816), and *The Siege of Cornith* (1816).[39] The heroes of these tales resembled Harold in almost every detail except that, with the advantage of plot, they were active, passionate, adventuresome, even violent. In these tales Byron began to confront that heroic dilemma out of which he would create his more original heroes: the collision between the exceptional individual and a repressive society. These early Byronic heroes were not simply victims of society, as Byron was for a time to portray himself, nor were they villains by default; they were, rather, victims of their own misplaced idealism. Like Keats's Endymion, or the poet in Shelley's *Alastor,* or the Solitary in Wordsworth's *Excursion,* the Byronic hero suffered from an inability to find conceptions equal to desire and to frame desires capable of fulfillment, to paraphrase Wordsworth (IV, 135–39). They were all isolated by their idealism, suffered it as if it were some lingering disease, "a fever at the core, / Fatal to him who bears, to all who ever bore" *(C.H.,* III, 378–79), and the attendant isolation, as if *that* were the crime.

However Byron disowned any biographical identification with Childe Harold, by 1816, the literary invention had become a self-fulfilling prophecy. After his return to England and the publication of the first cantos of *Childe Harold* in 1812, he awoke, he said, to find himself famous, pursued and lionized by Regency society, so preoccupied with mischief and pleasure that it is hard to account for how he found time to write so many tales about lonely and misunderstood adventurers. Finally, he entered an unsuitable marriage to the respectable but sheltered and mathematically inclined Annabella Milbanke. Within a year, after the birth of their daughter, Augusta Ada, Byron's wife left him, claiming that he was mad and having an incestuous affair with his half sister, Augusta Leigh. With Napoleon imprisoned on the island of St. Helena and George IV on the throne of England, Byron, at age twenty-eight, rejected by the society that helped create him, began his exile, moving from the abandoned battlefields of Belgium to Switzerland. Here he joined Shelley, Shelley's wife Mary Godwin, and her half sister Claire Clairmont by whom, after a brief and reluctant affair begun in London, he fathered an illegitimate daughter, Allegra, who died in an Italian convent in 1822. He spent seven years in Italy, writing and drinking, before moving to Greece where he died of a fever before joining the Greek War of Independence, to which he had planned to dedicate the remainder of his life. Byron's own life, then, poignantly illustrates the heroic dilemma, the discrepancy between noble ideals and the physical basis of life, the limited accomplishment of which even the most aspiring and talented individual is capable.

Byron created the "original" man we have been seeking, the consummate expression of the Romantic hero, by shifting the center of value from public life to the human mind, "Our last and only place / Of Refuge" (C.H., IV, cxxvii). Starting with *Lara,* but explicitly in *Childe Harold,* and emphatically in *Manfred,* Byron affirms the life of the mind, particularly the creative mind as opposed to the intellectualism of the traditional meditative life: "The Mind which is immortal makes itself / Requital for its good and evil thoughts,— / Is its own origin of ill and end—And its own place and time . . ."(*Manfred,* III, iv, 129–32). Such a hero endures the most profound isolation, the loss of all social and supernatural guides to behavior, and consolations as well; he leads the "sad unallied existence" Byron ascribed to Prometheus, the ultimate penalty being an intense self-awareness, self-involvement, self-absorption, a paralytic condition from which there was no escape except "oblivion, self-oblivion" (C.H., I, i, 145).

At his best, he achieves autonomy: the dispossessed turns into the self-possessed, an alien and threatening ideal in a society that had lost faith in both a transcendental order and in individual leadership, that was finding refuge in collective life, in the idea of community. But to Byron, and to Shelley and Keats, indeed to many writers of the period, it was not possible to find fulfillment in community, to reconcile "good and the means of good." Consequently, the hero pursued a lonely and joyless quest; his goal, for whatever it is worth, to be as Dickens proposed, at least the hero of his own life: "Lord of himself,—that heritage of woe" *(Lara,* i, 14).

PART II

The Illusion of History

CHAPTER VII

Inventing
the Past

"MAN WAS A creature without history," Loren Eiseley observes of the period before Darwin's theory of evolution: "Man's oldest records told him nothing of himself. They showed him a picture limited, at best, to a few millennia in which he had warred and suffered, changed kings and customs, marked the face of the landscape with towns and chimneys, but, for all that, he had remained to himself unknown. . . . For a thinking being," he concludes, "to be without history is to make him a fabricator of illusions."[1] Perhaps the most tenacious illusion, one in which many people believed well into the nineteenth century, was that the Creation took place at nine A.M. on October 25, 4004 B.C., according to the calculations based on the Old Testament made by Archbishop James Ussher in 1654.[2] Investigations in both archaeology and in the primitive oral cultures associated with the artifacts being exhumed in both England and the Mediterranean helped to undermine the authority of the written record on which such illusions were based. Ironically, however, the developing publication industry quickly created a new written record, translating the preliterate experience into print and endowing it with an equal authority. But without a cosmic history, as Eiseley calls it, a comprehensive theory of nature and human life based on scientific principles, these early historical studies either confirmed existing historical illusions based on the Bible or con-

tributed to new ones: the idealization of ancient Greece in a
Hellenic revival and the idealization of ancient Britain in the
Medieval or Gothic revival. Consequently, while Romantic
writers and painters were the last generation to live without
a cosmic history, they had a wider and richer range of illu-
sions than any of their predecessors. From these they invented
a past that compensated for the absence of both a cosmic his-
tory and a comparatively brief national history, a national
history that appeared even briefer and less significant as sci-
entists discovered a much larger and older universe than any-
one had previously conceived.

For the creative mind, history, even historical inventions,
are dangerous, for it is the tendency of tradition to become
coercive, of custom to become law, and precedence to become
authority. The Romantic writers and painters, however, were
wary of tradition, even the ones they were generating. Many
recognized that they had power over the past, that they were
responsible for the history they were creating, that, as
Wordsworth said in the Prospectus to *The Excursion,* the past
is created out of the present, that origins are defined by ends,
that the creative mind recreates itself, the world, and the past
in its own image:

> Paradise, and groves
> Elysian, Fortunate Fields—like those of old
> Sought in the Atlantic Main—why should they be
> A history only of departed things,
> Or a mere fiction of what never was?
> For the discerning intellect of Man,
> When wedded to this goodly universe
> In love and holy passion, shall find these
> A simple produce of the common day.

> (ll. 47–55)

The Uses of the Bible

Although the influence of religion on social and political
life had declined, for various reasons the Bible became the
single most influential document of the Romantic period, the
most popular book in this first age of popular literature.[3] As
the basic text in a massive campaign by various religious groups
such as the Evangelicals and Methodists to teach the poor to
read, the Bible was placed in millions of households, how-
ever poor or unbelieving. In the first fifty years of the nine-
teenth century, the British and Foreign Bible Society alone

published sixteen million copies and distributed them among Christians, pagans, and infidels, wherever the British lived, traveled, or traded.[4] With the largest audience in history, the Bible had an incalculable influence on both the taste of the reading public and the style of the authors who wrote for that public.

Ironically, the text that many Christians read and taught others to read as a way of achieving grace was as much an invention as the novels and other fictions that were considered so menacing to human welfare. For millions of readers, God, His patriarchs, prophets, and messengers, as well as the mid-Eastern warriors, wisemen, kings, and peasants who spoke with Him, all used an odd archaic vernacular invented in 1611 for the authorized English translation. Overcoming the artificial diction was a small test of faith compared with the challenge, which many poets recognized, of believing that the relevations of a jealous, ill-tempered Shepherd-God to an obscure Hebrew tribe, with its pastoral, agrarian, and primitive economic concerns, could be a major source of truth and a guide to living in this northern industrializing society. But, however, idiosyncratic in style and substance, the diction, idioms, tales, songs, and homilies provided a universal language, a common culture, a center of values in an increasingly diversified society. Such a universality was essential to develop a reading public, an audience with a common ground for the first age of mass communication. And the sheer number of believing readers could turn the illusions of Biblical history, however transparent, into reality.

Illustrating the Bible was itself something of an industry and most painters or engravers, including Blake, Joseph Turner, and John Martin, at one time or other became involved with it. Artists favored scenes of catastrophe such as the Flood, the Parting of the Red Sea, and anything from the Book of Revelation, whatever was grand, mysterious, tempestuous, awesome, terrifying, and demonstrative of God's power, whatever, in other words, displayed qualities of what was called the sublime. However exaggerated, the illustrations were in what was accepted as a realistic style contributing to the documentary quality that the Bible conveyed to those who chose to believe it.[5]

Politically, the Bible served many and often antithetical purposes—from helping to prevent rebellion among the poor to inspiring it.[6] The Evangelicals and Methodists believed that teaching the poor to read the Bible and related tracts and pamphlets would protect them from the incendiary rhetoric of such political radicals as Tom Paine. The lower classes were expected to identify with the patriarchal system of the Bible and to accept their divinely ordained moral and financial dependence on the rich, as the Bishop of Llandaff had argued in his sermon, *The Wisdom and Goodness of God in Having Made both Rich and Poor* (1793). Political radicals, such as the young Wordsworth who answered the Bishop, did not believe that poverty was an expression of God's wisdom nor that the rich were His emissaries. Rather, they invoked the Book of Revelation, the promise that, after a great cataclysmic event, the meek would inherit the earth, of which the French Revolution and smaller popular uprisings were portentious. Blake, along with Byron and Shelley, chose Satan as the hero of this plot, making him the victim of a tyrannical God just as the lower classes were victims of tyrannical rulers; his rebellion and theirs were just ones, and their punishments, victories. At another extreme, Coleridge, following many who had attempted to awaken the consciences of the rich, recommended the Bible as a source of "moral and political wisdom" in his *Statesman's Manual: or, the Bible the Best Guide to Political Skill and Foresight* (1816), which he indicates in the subtitle is addressed to the "Higher Classes of Society."[7]

For the poets, the Bible also provided a number of useful literary models. The simple and increasingly universal idiom was a legitimate alternative to the artificial Latinate poetic diction of the previous generation. Admittedly artificial in its own way, Biblical language offered an uncontroversial norm of purity, transcending class and dialect, and gave the poets, especially Wordsworth, access to the new audiences.[8] As a literary model, the Bible inspired a new wave of devotional poetry, encouraged experimentation with nature lyrics and with the evocative prose-poetry favored by Blake, Lamb, and Carlyle, who often used it humorously. And as poetry was being displaced by journalism, and poets by men of letters, the Bible provided the poets themselves with a personal affirmation, a vision of poets as prophets, individuals who had been imaginatively empowered to speak "of things oracular," as Wordsworth wrote, to be as Shelley aspired in "The Ode to the West Wind," a "trumpet of prophecy." The Biblical language seemed especially appropriate for describing their creative experience as well. So Keats, in a letter to his friend Benjamin Bailey, November 22, 1817, compared the imagination to "Adam's dream," and Coleridge, concluding Chapter

XIII of the *Biographia Literaria,* made what he called the "primary imagination" analogous to "the eternal act of creation in the infinite I AM."

This appropriation of Biblical language, forms, and imagery to describe creativity was symptomatic of a larger displacement of religious experience, especially in England and Germany during the Romantic period, when literature became what M. H. Abrams called in *Natural Supernaturalism* a "reconstituted theology," a "secularized form of devotional experience." Against the chaos of the public world following the French Revolution and the mystery of the inner private world that was just beginning to assert its own claims through the imagination, the Romantics posed the Biblical paradigms, designs, and plots which they adapted to secular life.

While the formal qualities of the Bible had enormous influence, after fifty years of rational theology, of religion based on reason, nature, feeling, or inner light, its spiritual authority had, by 1760, declined—except among the fundamentalist sects who believed in it as the literal word of God. Its spiritual influence was further restricted by the censorship laws that prevented its presentation or any allusion to it on the stage, although historically, among the Greeks and the medieval Christians, the stage was the primary place sacred works could be presented. Consequently, its impact as a central cultural document was limited to a reading public, admittedly the largest reading public in history. To those who could read, the Bible served as much a documentary as a religious purpose; at the very least, they believed that it was an authentic history of the human race disguised in allegory or distorted in oral transmission. Providing explanations for topography, language, class structure, racial differences, sexual relations, and political economy, it served as a comprehensive source book for human, natural, as well as spiritual history.

Some built useful theories on the basis of Biblical lore. In 1786, Sir William Jones, founder of comparative philology, proposed that Sanskrit, Latin, and Greek were related languages; but he claimed that the prototype was lost in the linguistic confusion following the Tower of Babel. Others created totally bizarre theories based on the same Biblical texts, none more exhaustive than Jacob Bryant's *A New System; or, An Analysis of Ancient Mythology* (1774), which appeared in six volumes, engraved by James Basire to whom the young William Blake was apprenticed. Bryant used his analogical skills to develop a universal chronology, illustrating how all myths were derived from the Old Testament, disseminated all over the world after the Flood by a family of Noah's descendents called Amonians.[9]

The Druids

The search for an original Biblical culture and its language took on an especially patriotic dimension in the eighteenth century starting with William Stukely's *Stonehenge, A Temple Restored to the British Druids* (1740), in which he claimed that Druids, reported by Julius Caesar in *Gallic War* to be tree-worshipping savages who engaged in human sacrifice, were actually one of the lost tribes of Israel, descended from Abraham.[10] Brought to England from Phoenicia by Hercules, the great grandson of Noah, after the Flood, according to Stukely, the Druids were learned and civilized, guardians of the true patriarchal religion expressed in their poetry and in Stonehenge, which he claimed they built. A doctor, an ordained minister, founder of the Society of Antiquaries, and friend of Sir Isaac Newton, Stukely's impeccable credentials gave status to the Druidical past he invented: he built what he considered to be a Druid temple, performed what he considered to be Druid rituals, and justified his belief in the Druids by claiming they validated the Bible.

The Druidical theory was a necessary illusion, fulfilling that need for a usable past, a past that gave England a native antiquity, a golden age of its own, and a role in Biblical history, sometimes the major role. Both Rowland Jones in *The Origin of Language and Nations* (1764) and John Cleland (the author of *Fanny Hill*) in *The Way to Things by Words* (1766) identify the ancient Celtic dialect of the Druids as the original language from which all others were derived. And in *Celtic Researches on the Origins, Traditions and Language of the Ancient Britons* (1804), Edward Davies made them the center of all civilization—descended from Biblical patriarchs, guardians of God's revelation, and originators of Greek culture. According to Davies, they provided a sanctuary for the Titans, the primitive Greek gods overthrown by the Olympians in the struggle depicted by Keats in *Hyperion*.[11] Because the Druid Bards specifically were responsible for preserving patriarchal skills, wisdom, and divine knowledge, the role of all poets was enhanced, especially the ancient ones, real and imaginary, such as Gray's *The Bard* and Ossian (whom we shall discuss), and native poetry as well, especially ancient runes, inscriptions, and ballads, genuine and fraudulent.

This association of Druids with poet–priests reflected their evolution in the latter decades of the eighteenth century from symbols of an ideal past to an ideal native type, one that could be emulated. Combining learning, piety, artistic skill, and love of nature, the Druids were an inspiration in a visibly industrializing world of "dark Satanic mills," as Blake called them, where religion offered little more than spiritless ritual or revivalist rhetoric and an oppressive morality. Blake claimed that "All things Begin & End in Albion's Ancient Druid Rocky Shore" (*Jerusalem,* plate 27), that England was the site of Eden, of Jerusalem, that Adam himself, Abraham, Noah, and all the patriarchs were Druids, and that Greek philosophy "is a remnant of Druidism" (*Jerusalem,* plate 52). William Owen Pughe, a Welsh lexicographer and disciple of Joanna Southcott, told Blake that his revelations were the patriarchal truths of the Druids and invited him to participate in the annual rites of the revived Order of Druids which, after 1792, took place on Primrose Hill in London on November 28, Blake's birthday.[12] But to Blake, the Druids were merely the first of a bad thing, priests whom he claimed perverted divine knowledge, as priests will do, creating systems and rituals which they impose on others, best illustrated in their human sacrifice that turned "allegoric and mental signification into corporeal command":

> Druid's golden knife
> Rioted in human gore
> In Offerings of Human Life.
> (*Jerusalem,* Plate 27)

By the turn of the century the symbolic value of the Druids had shifted yet again, from the native but noble and holy savages of Stukely's time, the poet-priests of Blake's, to the teachers, the wizards, the natural philosophers of a still-popular tradition. Wordsworth's "antiquarian dream" of the Druids near Stonehenge, which he recorded in *The Prelude,* XII (1805), represents that popular idealization, one he shared with Southey in *Madoc,* also written in 1805. Having just returned from the Reign of Terror in France, Wordsworth was sensitive to "the sacrificial altar, fed / With living men," but he also saw them as "bearded teachers with white wands / Uplifted, pointing to the starry sky / Alternately, and plain below, while breath / Of music seemed to guide them," and he called them founders of "infant science," their stone circles expressing "knowledge of the heavens" (ll. 340–53). Just as the quest for knowledge itself was passing from the Old Testament to the scientific journals, from the monasteries to the laboratories, from religious to secular authority, so the Druids themselves evolved from a religious symbol to a secular one.

By 1830, when Carlyle composed *Sartor Resartus,* the mythogogues who had created the symbol in the first place, who endowed Druid life with such immense religious and cultural importance, had become objects of ridicule themselves: the protagonist, Diogenes Teufelsdröckh, was writing a universal history of clothes which Carlyle describes as "interminable disquisitions of a mythological, metaphorical, cabalisticosartorial and quite anti-deluvian cast" (p. 37). In 1840, Bellini's opera, *Norma* (1831), based on the love affair between a Druid priestess in ancient Gaul and a Roman soldier during the occupation of 50 B.C., was presented in England, with Stonehenge as a setting, the strange coincidence of a northern setting, primitive Celtic religion, Mediterranean passions, and Italian language emphasizing the absurdity of the historical illusion. In 1871, the mythogogical heir of Jacob Bryant was discernible as Reverend Casaubon in George Eliot's *Middlemarch,* a symbol of superficial, unproductive intellect engaged in the hopeless task of showing "that all the mythical systems or erratic mythical fragments in the world were corruptions of a tradition originally revealed."

The Biblical credentials of the Druids, indeed of all the Greek and Oriental myths that were, according to the speculative mythogogues, derived from the Bible, made a whole new range of materials available to writers and artists. The Bible was also invoked to give legitimacy to a new wave of interest in alchemy and the occult,[13] the pseudo-sciences that emerged with particular strength in the latter decades of the eighteenth century, the transitional period between the decline of the religious interpretation of nature and the development of the scientific one. As the key to all mythologies, however, as well as myth-making, the more meanings or applications that were found in the Bible, the more comprehensive its authority became, the less spiritual impact it had, until it was reduced to little more than a myth itself.

The Hellenic Revival

In 1738, two years before Stukely published his study of Stonehenge, excavations began at Pompeii and Herculaneum, two Greek cities in southern Italy destroyed by the eruption of Mt. Vesuvius in A.D. 79. Like Stonehenge, the discoveries at Pompeii and Herculaneum shifted historical interest from texts to artifacts, from words to experience, from monuments to ruins, from a heroic tradition to a common one. For here among the bones and ashes were the citizens, the domestic refuse, the unfinished business with which their lives had ended on an otherwise ordinary summer afternoon. Based on surviving statues, buildings, mosaics, vases, and fragments, all the silent and unyielding things, writers, scholars, and artists invented a golden age in ancient Greece, which was an extension of Pompeii, an invention reflecting their own need to believe in a sun-filled land of happy, youthful, healthy people, an Arcadia governed by kindly philosophical statesmen and divinely inspired poets.[14] Shelley, who had never been to Greece, studied the statues and architecture in Florence and Rome, studied Plato, Homer, and the Greek tragedians, and concluded, "The human form and human mind attained to a perfection in Greece which has impressed its image on those faultless productions whose very fragments are the despair of modern art" *(Hellas, Preface)*. And he attributed this perfection to living in "perpetual commerce with external nature," as he stated in a letter to T. L. Peacock describing his visit to Pompeii, an external nature that many believed to be more inspiring and congenial to human achievement, even to the development of the human body, than the industrializing countryside and urban pollution of England.

But to the generation that witnessed these discoveries early in the eighteenth century, the new Grecian antiquity offered little of the wonder and admiration that the Romantic poets found in it. Greece was a counter-culture, an alternative to what we now call the neoclassicism, the reason, order, decorum, and abstraction that dominated European thought during the early decades of the eighteenth century, a set of values derived from Roman art and letters during the reign of Augustus (27 B.C.–A.D. 14). These neoclassical ideals were so comprehensive that they became habits of thought; they governed the interpretation of the entire universe and all human experience, applying equally to theology, philosophy, politics, ethics, science, art, music, architecture, gardening, social relations, and literature. Most Englishmen considered Greek art, architecture, literature, and philosophy as inferior with little or no aesthetic value. Alexander Pope translated Homer's *Iliad* (1715–1720) into fashionable and correct heroic couplets, and turned the wild, manipulative, and treacherous Greek warriors into Augustan gentlemen. Greek language, except for its religious uses, was a social accomplishment; and Plato, except for the Christian application of his thought, was nearly unknown—between 1602 and 1804 there were no English translations, and only one complete edition available in Greek. There was a coffee house called the "Grecian" and a drinking club called the Dilettanti Society, comprised of high-spirited and irreverent young aristocrats who had visited Italy (or Avignon) and who began their feats of intoxication with a toast to "Grecian taste and Roman Spirit."[15]

In time the Dilettanti Society grew to include artists, statesmen, and antiquaries, and to promote influential expeditions and publications that helped to educate the public and to develop a taste for Greek art, but it was a taste that reflected its own hedonistic interests. In 1751, the Society sponsored an architectural expedition to Greece by James "Athenian" Stuart and Nicholas Rivett, whose meticulous drawings (published by the Dilettanti between 1762 and 1800) reconstructed the glory that was Greece, right down to the foundations, a glory that was considerably diminished when British architects translated it into banks, hospitals, and ornamental temples. They also conveyed the adventure of contemporary Greece, inspiring young noblemen to defy the heat, plague, and bandits, and travel to Greece, attracted as much by the antiquity as by the danger, the exotic landscape, languages, religious rituals, sexual practices, and political turmoil. On the basis of Lord Byron's adventure in 1809–10, he created the Byronic hero who appeared first in *Childe Harold,* Books I and II, the start of a fantasy literature as intriguing and unrealistic as the romance of the Old West became in modern America.

To the Dilettanti Society and the English aristocrats associated with them, drawing and writing were secondary to collecting. With only a brief history of their own, one that excluded them from the major religious and military events of Western civilization, the English became scavengers of other's history, "marble mongerers," as Byron called them in *The Curse of Minerva,* taking whatever portable relics they could find, to the great despair of later archaeologists. As Robert Wood shamelessly explained in his Preface to *The Ruins of Palmyra* (1755), "Inscriptions we copied as they fell in our way, and carried off the marbles whenever it was possible; but the avarice or superstition of the inhabitants made that task difficult and sometimes impracticable."[16] Great collections were exhibited, sold, or donated to museums, or published in catalogues such as the four volumes devoted to Sir

William Hamilton's collection of vases, published between 1791 and 1795.

And for those who could not collect, there were reproductions and imitations. Josiah Wedgwood adapted Greek designs from Hamilton's vases to the durable and inexpensive dishes, pitchers, gravy boats, salt shakers, sugar bowls, and commemorative platters he produced for middle-class dining rooms at the Staffordshire factory he called Etruria. And the upper classes, including King George's many children, adopted sensuous Greek precedents in carriages, hair-styles, even posture and dress, or rather undress, for, according to fashion, the Greeks celebrated nakedness, enhanced by drapery, which accounts for the costumes in which English matrons liked to be painted. Magazine articles abounded on what was believed to be the Greek fashion in furniture and costumes, codified by Thomas Hope in *Household Furniture and Interior Decoration* (1807) and *Costumes of the Ancients* (1809). This image of Greece was the popular one, promoted by the Dilettanti and affirming their own hedonistic and sexual preoccupations. It falls within what H. M. Jones in *Revolution and Romanticism* called the Anacreontic tradition, named after the sixth-century B.C. Greek poet whose verse celebrated the frivolous pleasures of youth, wine, song, and seduction. Revived by Edmund Spenser and his followers in the Renaissance,[17] from whom many learned their mythology, it was a trivialized form of the Dionysian, Dionysius being that complex god who presided over the irrational aspects of life—love, passion, intoxication, procreation, even madness—all those mysterious and inescapable forces which the Greeks considered natural complements to the Apollonian virtues of reason, order, and serenity.

The Erotic Theme

To those awakened to the depth and mystery of ancient myth, however bizarre the existing speculation, the artifacts being recovered revealed the rituals and iconography of the primitive religious fertility cult Dionysius inspired.[18] With access to Pompeii, Sir William Hamilton, envoy to Naples, described these erotic cults in *An Account of the Remains of the Worship of Priapus* (1777), in which he identified the phallic worship that survived in the superstitious practices of local Italian Catholic peasants. His mistress, Emma Hart (later his wife, and then the mistress of Admiral Nelson), enjoyed imitating the rituals depicted in his collection of vases and bas reliefs in *tableaux vivants,* to the amusement and often the scandal of his guests. In 1786, the Dilettanti published Richard Payne Knight's *A Discourse on the Worship of Priapus,* interpreting paintings and pottery from Egypt and Greece to demonstrate the sexual activity in which he believed all religion originated. His recognition of phallic and vulvular symbolism in Christian as well as pagan ceremony "sexualized," as Jean Hagstrum says, the study of myth, anthropology, and religion: "To read Knight was to eat forbidden fruit."[19]

The explicit illustrations forced Knight to withdraw the book from circulation, for, while the use of Greek erotica was acceptable for decoration or entertainment, Knight's study presented a serious challenge to Christianity, especially the moral and emotional austerity of contemporary Evangelical faith. Attempting to enhance the authority of the Bible, the mythogogues had claimed that all myths, including the Greek, were derived from the Old Testament, that Dionysius and Orpheus, for example, were Old Testament prophets in disguise. Consequently, they made these ancient fertility cults, which were offensive even to Plato, anticipatory forms of Christianity.[20] And in the repressive patriarchal society of George III, the King who issued Proclamations against Vice and enforced them with a vast moral network of churchmen, industrialists' wives, newspapers, Sunday schools, and ladies who wrote books for children, the sacramental role of sex was unthinkable. In 1798, when Thomas Malthus in his *Essay on Population* claimed that war, hunger, plague, and the overpopulation that caused them could be avoided through sexual restraint, the secular role of sex for pleasure or as an expression of freedom became equally unthinkable.

Using the same Greek procreative myths as Payne Knight, Erasmus Darwin sexualized the study of nature, or, rather, used the ancient myths to return sexuality to the realm of nature and to the gods and goddesses who represented its procreative forces.[21] In a series of epic-length poems with massive footnotes—*The Loves of Plants* (1789) and *The Economy of Vegetation* (1791) collected as *The Botanic Garden* (1791) and *The Temple of Nature; or, The Origin of Society* (1803)— he offered encyclopedic surveys of nature, society, animals, plants, diseases, inventions, and contemporary knowledge ranging from creation theory to steam engines. He used common myths such as Cupid and Psyche, Juno and Jupiter, Orpheus and Eurydice, Adonis, Demeter, and Persephone, and obscure ones from ancient Egypt or Rosicrucianism to illustrate his dynamic and evolving view of nature. To him these myths were allegories, as he called them, for the natural processes of metamorphosis, transformation, and sexual selection, as subtle and accurate as his grandson Charles Darwin's were to be. In spite of an often trivial style, his use of Greek mythological precedent helped to emancipate science, natural history, and human history as well from the static classifications based on the Old Testament and perpetuated by the neoclassical ordering that still dominated scientific and philosophical thought.[22]

Darwin was also an erudite and inventive mythographer: he deciphered the Eleusinian fertility ritual represented on the Portland vase, a copy of which Wedgwood had sent him, and adopted the ceremony itself as a structural device for his *Temple of Nature*.[23] Although he was capable of simplistic readings (such as his interpreting the Prometheus myth as a tract against drinking alcoholic beverages because they destroy the liver), and equally capable of silly mythologizing of his own (anthropomorphizing plants as Beaux and Belles wooing their "vegetable loves"), he showed how the whole range of myth could serve and replenish the resources of contemporary poetry and that mythologizing itself was a viable technique for expressing contemporary knowledge and experience in poetry.

Erasmus Darwin was enormously successful as a poet; his verbal extravagance and titillating sexuality were characteristic of the popular Greek style identified with the Regency. In literature, it appealed to that new reading public that arose during this first age of mass publication. Although its tastes were condemned by authors and reviewers alike as vulgar, superficial, and ostentatious, this audience was highly knowledgeable, familiar with the gods, goddesses, heroes, tales, and places of mythic significance, either from recent translations of Homer, in whom there was a great revival of interest, or from a series of popular reference works such as Lamprière's *Bibliotheca Classica* (1788), published in seven editions by 1809; Bell's *New Pantheon* (1790), produced by the resourceful John Bell along with massive and inexpensive volumes of British poets and dramatists; and William Godwin's *Pantheon* (1806) prepared, under his pen name of "Edward Baldwin," for a juvenile audience with the assurance "that nothing will be found in it to administer libertinism to the fancy of the stripling, or to sully the whiteness of mind of the purest virgins," illustrated with statues which in later editions, responding to parental protests, were draped.[24] Moreover, Greek was taught in certain schools, especially to prepare for the clergy, which gave middle-class young men access to the original works. De Quincey and Coleridge both prided themselves on being Grecians, De Quincey translating the morning newspaper into Greek to amuse himself. His opinion that Greek literature was inferior, that the gods and goddesses were amoral, terroristic, and degrading, reflected the way British youth were protected from the pagan implications of the literature while learning the language. Instead, they read patriotic values into Homer, emphasized on very little evidence the moral greatness of his heroes, their rationality and devotion to great causes. If passages showed them as pirates, thieves, liars, and sexually promiscuous, they were clearly not written by Homer, promoting a theory of multiple authorship.[25]

It was the decorative Greek style without philosophical, intellectual, or historical reference that Keats called the realm of "Flora and Old Pan," Flora being the perpetually youthful goddess of flowers and Pan, the simple, goat-footed, bearded god who guided hunters, seduced the mountain nymphs, played his pipes, and spent his afternoons sleeping—the only god to have died. However unfair Wordsworth appeared to be in dismissing Keats's "Hymn to Pan" as a "pretty piece of paganism," his response would have been a conventional one, suited to anyone, however talented, who took this trivial god seriously. Influenced by Spenser, encouraged by Leigh Hunt, and lured by the possibility of popular success, Keats wrote a series of poems in this style culminating in *Endymion*, which incorporated a number of popular myths such as Venus and Adonis, Narcissus, Phoebus, and Endymion himself, the shepherd-king who wins the love of a goddess, a favorite theme among poets. But as Peacock, another poet to work in this style, observed in "The Four Ages of Poetry," "there are no Dryads in Hyde Park nor Naiads in Regent's canal": "In the origin and perfection of poetry, all the associations of life were composed of poetical materials," but the environment of London was inhospitable to the spirits of nature and to the poetry that depended on them. The age required a Dionysius, not a Pan, a more philosophical and abstract god, the one in whose honor the great Greek tragedies were written. After Benjamin Haydon introduced Keats to the Elgin Marbles and Benjamin Bailey introduced him to the Platonic thought that contributed to their significance, Keats turned to this philosophical mode, to what he called "a more naked and grecian Manner."

The Platonic Theme

The origins of this philosophical or heroic style were in Germany, in the idealizing imagination of Johann Winckelmann, the self-educated son of a Lutheran cobbler whose dedication to Greek art led, after his conversion to Catholicism, to his becoming in 1763 the Chief Supervisor of Antiquities in the Vatican. In a series of books starting with *Reflections on the Painting and Sculpture of the Greeks* (1755, translated by Henry Fuseli in 1765, published by Joseph Johnson, with some engravings by Blake), Winckelmann proposed that the greatness of Greek art lay in its "Noble Simplicity and Quiet Grandeur," that it arose from the temperate climate, the democratic government, the inspiring philosophy, and the habit of nakedness which accounted for the beautiful bodies depicted in the statues. Disregarding the dark, irrational, and destructive aspects of Greek culture, the militarism, savagery, slavery, infanticide, chauvinism, and the inevitability even for ancient Greeks of old age and disease, he invented a world of men who were like the statues, like gods, very good, healthy, youthful gods, which he defended in rhapsodic essays based on paintings and statues he had never had seen or, at best, had seen only in copies. His theories were essentially Platonic, based on the assumption that the mortal world is merely a changing and deceptive reflection of a higher reality, an ideal which artists are especially endowed to apprehend, to express and to reproduce in a common idiom. Even working from artistic copies, the artist, according to Winckelmann, is constantly perfecting, abstracting, and moving toward the greater simplification of the ideal. But the major simplification was Winckelmann's. Much of what Plato advocated—the moderation, rationality, other-worldliness—was a reaction against his culture, not a reflection of it: the aesthetic simplicity was a criticism of the clutter, the heaps of painted, gilded, oversized statues of gods and heroes in all the temples and public monuments.[26] As weathered and bleached ruins, the sculpture did at last appear to fulfill a Platonic ideal, but to the culturally disinherited philosophers, writers, artists, and scholars, to Winckelmann and his English disciples who were creating the historical illusions we have been tracing, they served another purpose: whatever was incomplete, broken, imperfect, vague, mysterious, and fragmented provided an imaginative base for the idealizing imagination, a base that was not betrayed by reality.

Winckelmann's idealizing aesthetic found a philosophical

affirmation in Thomas Taylor's equally idealizing transla-
tions and commentaries on Greek texts.[27] His commentary
on the translation of *Mystical Initiation: or, Hymns of Orpheus*
(1787) turned this complex mythological hero-poet, the cen-
ter of a procreative mystery cult, into a "prophet" and a the-
ologian, a precursor of Homer and Plato. Although Taylor
was called "the English pagan" after he sacrificed a bull to
Zeus, which is a fertility ritual, he had no interest whatever
in the sexual role of the gods that his contemporaries were
revealing.[28] He spent his life translating and commenting on
Plato, rescuing him from a personal reputation as a reprobate
and pederast, on the one hand, and a Christian, on the other.
His opposition to reading Plato as a moral or political writer
invoked to justify an elitist society won the approval of the
young liberal writers and intellectuals who were all influ-
enced by Taylor's opinions: Mary Wollstonecraft rented a
room in his house; Coleridge, Shelley, and Blake knew him
personally; and Peacock, whom he called "Greeky Peaky,"
was his special friend. His emphasis on the spiritual Plato
considered in a mystical and polytheistic context was impor-
tant to a generation of imaginative artists who, like Words-
worth, would rather be "A Pagan suckled in a creed outworn"
than live in a society dominated by materialism, as he claimed
in the sonnet "The World Is Too Much with Us."[29]

Although Taylor gave the Romantic poets and artists access
to Plato, he did not make him popular. His fidelity to the
original texts, in what he called "a faithful and animated
paraphrase," produced a very difficult translation, turning,
as Coleridge observed, "difficult Greek into incomprehensi-
ble English."[30] Since Cambridge University did not include
Plato on the syllabus until 1820, nor Oxford until 1847, the
study of Plato required a knowledge of the language, or suf-
ficient money to purchase Taylor's translation at £10 (about
$50) for each of the five volumes in 1804, or attendance at
Taylor's lectures, some of which had been delivered at the
home of John Flaxman.[31]

It was Flaxman, sculptor, engraver, and designer who
interpreted the Platonism of Taylor into visual images, into
the pottery he designed for Wedgwood and the engravings
he designed for editions of *The Odyssey* (1793), *The Iliad,* and
the *Tragedies of Aeschylus* (1795). Using the Greek vases as his
inspiration, he developed a simplified linear style based on
curves and arabesques outlining one-dimensional form. His
neglect of weight, depth, volume, dimension, and perspec-
tive had a philosophical basis in Plato and, of course, Winck-

elmann; his simplifications helped overcome the particularity of the visible world in favor of ideals or abstractions. Copying the disinterred and weathered treasures of ancient Greece, he intentionally created the incomplete, a severe simplicity that appeared late in the nineteenth century as "art deco." Such a style was particularly well suited to engraving and, therefore, publication, which gave Flaxman immense influence: his style became synonymous with the Greek although it was largely an invention and, as John Clay explains, more nearly reflected "industrial expediency," his designs responding to the demands of mechanical reproduction or transformation into a variety of materials.[32] In 1810, as Professor of Sculpture at the Royal Academy, he began lecturing on the history of ancient art, giving it his own Platonic interpretation, and in 1816, testified before the Parliamentary Committee in favor of purchasing fragments from the Parthenon, fragments that would be known as the Elgin Marbles.

The Elgin Marbles

Between 1801 and 1812, while Napoleon plundered Europe and the Mediterranean to fill the museums of Paris, Robert Bruce, Earl of Elgin, British ambassador to Constantinople, convinced the Turks to allow him to remove marble sculptures and bas reliefs from the Parthenon for shipment to England.[33] Although intended to improve public taste, they were kept in a warehouse; artists were allowed to study and copy but not publish them. Before spending three months by himself drawing them by candlelight for up to fifteen hours a day, Benjamin Robert Haydon brought the ill-tempered Henry Fuseli, who in 1778, after translating Winckelmann, had painted "The Artist in Despair over the Grandeur of Antique Fragments," expressing his own sense of impotence before the monuments of Greece. Fuseli was so impatient to see the Elgin fragments that he attacked a flock of sheep that obstructed his path in the Strand, and, swearing "like a little fury," according to Haydon, paced about the room where the marbles were being stored proclaiming " 'De Greeks were godes! de Greeks were godes!' "[34] To a generation of English artists who had taken as their models the badly weathered originals or Roman copies of Greek sculpture, and, following Winckelmann, developed an aesthetic to justify them, the Elgin Marbles were indeed a revelation. The subtle anatomy, the sense of action, the naturalistic detail, and the heroic proportions permanently altered the way the human body was represented in English art.

In 1816, over the protests of Richard Payne Knight, who claimed that the marbles were forgeries, frauds, "Phidean Freaks," the government purchased and placed them on display in the British Museum, hoping to stimulate a national school of historical painting. To adopt a foreign precedent in order to inspire a national school of painting seems very odd indeed except that the inspiration, the Hellenic ideal everyone saw in the marbles, was an English invention, a fiction that artists and writers, cut off by the war from the French and Italian artistic models, developed to fill their cultural vacuum and to compensate for the brevity of British history, of which they were very much aware. Historically impoverished themselves, they had collected the artifacts, appropriated the styles, recreated the myths, assimilated the philosophy, worshipped the icons, and finally projected their own origins on an ancient and alien civilization: "We are all Greeks," Shelley proclaimed in his introduction to *Hellas,* "our laws, our literature, our religion, our arts have their roots in Greece."

Dionysius in England

To other writers, England appeared to be a fulfillment of Greek civilization rather than a derivative. For example, in *Hyperion,* Keats set out to write a British epic by incorporating the structure and syntax of Milton's *Paradise Lost,* the imagery of the Elgin Marbles, and the narrative from Davies' *Celtic Researches,* relating how the Titans, defeated by the Olympians, took refuge in the Blessed Isles, and became the Druids of ancient Britain.[35] But Keats abandoned the poem because structure, imagery, narrative, poetry itself, even epic poetry, cannot convey the "knowledge enormous," the knowledge of human and natural history that deified Apollo and on which the rest of the poem would have depended. The Hellenic movement, of which *Hyperion* is an expression, rested on the assumption that art is history, that from Homer's fantasy one could reconstruct Homer's world, that from statues one could recreate people, from ceremonial objects one could infer spiritual beliefs; but Keats—however eager he was to enhance the value of poetry itself—concluded that art was a poor source of historical information. He not only rejected art as a historical record but also he rejected the influence of history on art, the role of environment that was so decisive to Winckelmann and that was to be even more significant to

Shelley. Poets and artists, according to Keats, are governed by aesthetic rather than social realities; the creation, therefore, takes priority over the creator and over the world he lived in. The true artists, like Keats in *Ode to Psyche,* "see and sing by [their] own eyes inspired." By raising the same historical questions in *Ode on a Grecian Urn* that had yielded so much information about fertility and mystery cults to Knight, Hamilton, and Darwin, he actually ends such historical inquiry: "What leaf-fring'd legend haunts about thy shape," "Who are these coming to the sacrifice? / To what green altar, O mysterious priest, / Lead'st thou that heifer?" Keats, like a priest in a mystery cult, reports the urn's cryptic reply: "Beauty is truth, truth beauty,—that is all / Ye know on earth, and all ye need to know." The answer identifies the flaw behind the Hellenic scholarship and archaeology in which such urns had played a seminal role: an urn as art offers aesthetic experience, not a historical record. Keats's urn is a symbolic representation, a metaphor of the universal human desire for youth, joy, fertility, song, love, and the quest for permanence, a symbol, in other words, for the eternal Dionysian.

Because the Romantic poets without exception believed that the Dionysian, by whatever name they called it, was essential to human experience, believed that a life force permeates man and nature accounting for the irrational, the creative, and the communal impulses in human beings, they required a more comprehensive mythology than could be found in the Old and New Testaments, which rejected everything associated with the Dionysian as part of fallen nature. As Shelley explained in his essay *On the Devil and Devils:* "The sylvans and fauns with their leader, the great Pan, were most poetical personages and were connected in the imagination of the Pagans with all that could enliven and delight. They were supposed to be innocent beings not greatly different in habits from the shepherds and herdsmen of which they were the patron saints. But the Christians contrived to turn the wrecks of the Greek mythology, as well as the little they understood of their philosophy, to purposes of deformity and falsehood."

Drawing on the Greek myths as interpreted through the Hellenic revival of the eighteenth century, Wordsworth, Keats, and Shelley created a synthesis of both traditions, the Platonic or idealistic and the Dionysian or erotic. They evolved an expression that was abstract, generalized, and philosophical, tending toward Platonic idealism, but dealing with specific Dionysian, erotic experience—experience, in other words, relating to love, to creativity, to life, to the animating forces of nature and human beings, and to the new Dionysian realm, the mysterious, elusive, and irrational world of psychological experience from which art is generated. Unlike earlier writers, such as Shakespeare and Milton, who used Greek myths for ornamental purposes, the Romantic writers reverted to the universal human experience that originally gave rise to the myths, to the mysterious powers in mind, nature, and supernature which they hoped through their poetry to illuminate and perhaps to control.[36] Wordsworth, for example, in the ode *Intimations of Immortality,* used the Platonic myth of pre-existence, in which he did not believe, to explain the decline of his visionary powers, an experience he universalized into an explanation of how the human mind matures, its changing perceptions of the natural world, and the development of imaginative powers that are tied to the cycle of life itself, what we have called the Dionysian. Such poetry, overtly adapting Hellenic myths, forms, and themes from both the idealistic and the erotic tradition, was distinguished by its reconciliation of the philosophical and experiential, which was the special achievement of Percy Bysshe Shelley.

Percy Bysshe Shelley: The Hellenic Fulfillment

Like the Dilettanti nearly a century before, Shelley's interest in Greek philosophy, art, literature, and mythology was an expression of rebellion; indeed, most of his extensive readings were from what might be considered the counter-culture of his age. Unlike Coleridge who turned to "abstruse research," as he called it in *Dejection: An Ode,* to escape his feelings, Shelley was a learned poet whose imagination was clearly stimulated by his reading: "A master of seven languages," Stuart Curran wrote in his own learned study of Shelley's use of myth, "his reading was wide and deep, arcane and popular; he was as excited by the first forays into modern physics as by the ancient wisdom of the Greek tragedians."[37] But he was more than a scholar and a poet; he was a political activist, the father of six children, and the center of one of the most notorious and entangled love stories of his generation.

Born into favored circumstances in 1792, the eldest son of a landed aristocrat, he was educated at Eton and Oxford to follow his father as a member of Parliament.[38] But, from the time he was a child, he had an eccentric interest in chemistry, magic, romance, horror stories, and poetry, which became more pronounced as he took his stand against schoolmasters and classmates who bullied him for his effeminate manners (acquired from being raised in a sheltered atmosphere with four sisters) and his lack of interest in sports and games. In writing, indeed in all intellectual pursuits, Shelley found a means of rebellion, retaliation, and control. By 1811, the end of his first term at Oxford, he had published some juvenile verse, two gothic horror novels, poems supposedly written by the insane washerwoman confined to Bedlam after attempting to assassinate George III in 1786, and his first major challenge to authority, *The Necessity of Atheism,* a pamphlet written with his friend T. J. Hogg questioning the possibility of proving God's existence, which led to his dismissal from the university and estrangement from his family.

But Shelley, as he wrote to William Godwin, considered himself a victim, someone who "suffered much from human persecution" but who remained proud and arrogant: "Oxonian society was insipid to me, uncongenial with my habits of thinking. I could not descend to common life. The sublime interest of poetry, lofty and exalted achievements, the proselytism of the world, the equalization of its inhabitants were to me the soul of my soul" (January 10, 1812). He attributed this dedication to reading *Political Justice,* Godwin's influential radical tract of 1793: "I rose from its perusal a wiser and a better man—I was no longer the votary of Romance. . . . I beheld in short that I had duties to perform." Unfortunately, he set out to become a revolutionary when the great old cause, the French Revolution, the cause that had inspired Godwin himself, Paine, Southey, and Wordsworth, his heroes, had turned into Napoleon's war of aggression. The high energy that a revolution requires was being drained by the demands of war and a common external enemy. In England, radical activity had declined into puttering with legislation; occasional libel cases such as Leigh Hunt's for insulting the Regent; and periodic, local, and anonymously led revolts against the price of bread or the threat of machinery.

Shelley began the performance of what he conceived as his duties by eloping with sixteen-year-old Harriet Westbrook, rescuing her from her tyrannical father who preferred that she attend school. Accompanied by Harriet's domineering thirty-year-old sister, Eliza, they went to Dublin, where Shelley distributed his pamphlets advocating Catholic emancipation and Irish independence to government officials and to the working classes who couldn't read at all; to Devon, where he wrote a legally unpublishable pamphlet advocating freedom of the press; and to Tremadoc in Wales, where he tried to help raise money to build an embankment protecting land being reclaimed from the sea. Moving frequently and often pursued by creditors, he dedicated himself to "philanthropy and truth" while he spent his meager allowance and considerable energies on quixotic, trivial, or simply misguided projects.

Shelley was as much a visionary as a reformer, as he reveals in his first major poem, *Queen Mab,* printed in 1813, but not published until 1821, when it was still considered so seditious that the bookseller who issued it was jailed. In nine cantos, 2300 lines, and extensive footnotes, Shelley presented a learned, fanciful, encyclopedic poem placing contemporary radical thought, political and scientific, in a universal context, a universe enlarged by his belief in recent theories of the plurality of worlds. In a dream-vision, Queen Mab reveals to Ianthe, the symbol of the human soul, the past, present, and future, exposing the evils of institutional religion, government, private property, and commercialism; demonstrating the petty, proud, selfish, and loveless nature of contemporary humanity; explaining the advantages of temperance, free love, and a vegetable diet. She envisions a future when mankind, living by reason, uninhibited love, the benign forces of necessity (as defined by Godwin), and the natural evolutionary processes of nature (as defined by Erasmus Darwin) will be redeemed and the earth itself will actually turn on its axis, melting the polar ice cap and producing an eternal summer.

At the time, however, and, except for brief periods throughout his short life, the universal love and rationality Shelley advocated in the poem eluded him personally. Avoiding his sister-in-law, whom he claimed he "abhorred" to the point of "fatigue" but whose presence was required to help care for his pregnant wife and, later, infant daughter, he sought out the company of some French emigrées who lived at Bracknell, about thirty miles from London. At the center was John Frank Newton, millennialist and vegetarian; Mrs. Boinville, a widowed French revolutionary whom Shelley considered "the most admirable human being" he had ever known; her daughter and son-in-law, disciples of Godwin; and Thomas Love Peacock, a self-educated classicist and poet who was to use the Bracknell coterie and Shelley as well in several popular satirical novels ridiculing the excesses of contemporary intellectuals. It was Peacock who helped Shelley overcome his aversion to studying Greek, for he had at one time believed, as he wrote to Godwin, that "the evils of acquiring Greek and Latin considerably overbalance the benefits," that the Greeks themselves were a savage race, and, as the available histories confirmed, incapable of governing themselves. Peacock also introduced him to the Orphic tradition, the tragedies and hymns, and the Plato of Thomas Taylor,[39] the friend who called him "Greeky Peaky." Through Newton, Shelley encountered the eighteenth-century primitivistic Hellenism of Lord Monboddo, who believed that what distinguished human beings from orangutans, which were of the same species, was an innate potential fulfilled in the golden age of Greece. In *On the Origin and Progress of Language* (1773) and twelve volumes of *Metaphysics,* Monboddo presented an ascetic morality fashioned after both monkeys and Greeks, attributing the decline of humanity to such unnatural practices as eating meat, drinking alcohol, wearing clothes, taking drugs, smoking, homosexual activity, masturbation, marriage, living in cities, and using money.[40] Shelley found in Monboddo an affirmation of the moralistic austerity he expressed in *Queen Mab* and, in spite of the chaotic appearance of his sexual relations, in his own life. Newton also introduced Shelley to his special version of Zoroastrianism, which conflated Persian, Indian, and Greek mythology, preserving the Zoroastrian emphasis on free will, morality, and worship in natural surroundings.[41]

Long deprived of intellectually stimulating companionship, Shelley responded intensely, as he often did, to his new friends at Bracknell, especially as he wrote in a letter to Hogg in March, 1814, the "female excellence" he encountered there: "I have escaped in the society of all that philosophy and friendship combine, from the dismaying solitude of myself. They have revived in my heart the expiring flame of life. I have felt myself translated to a paradise." Unfortunately, he also concluded that his marriage had been a "calamity," a "heartless union," a "revolting duty": "I felt as if a dead and living body had been linked together in loathsome and horrible communion." This image of a parasitic relationship between the living and the dead will be relevant to *Frankenstein,* the novel by Mary Wollstonecraft Godwin, whom he met at this time, courted by her mother's tomb, and eloped with to Europe in July, 1814, leaving Harriet and their infant daughter, Ianthe, who had been born the year before. Contributing to the scandal of the elopement, they took along Claire Clairmont, Mary's half sister, which led many to believe that Shelley was having an affair with both of them, and

Godwin (Mary's father and a former advocate of free love) to conclude, "I cannot conceive of an event of more accumulated horror."[42] Returning to England in September, 1814, friendless and pursued by creditors, they continued to explore experimental relationships: Claire became Shelley's companion while Mary, pregnant with their first child (who was to die only a few weeks after his birth in February, 1815) formed an alliance with Hogg, whose attempted seduction of Harriet several years before had angered Shelley. However bereft and impoverished, Harriet, herself pregnant with their second child, conceived during the very spring Shelley was expressing his dissatisfaction with their marriage, rejected his invitation to live with all of them as a sister, and, in June, 1815, found at least financial relief in her small share of Shelley's legacy from his grandfather, who had died in January, an allowance amounting to £200 a year (about $1,000, or $40,000 in contemporary money).[43]

Although Shelley always spent or gave away more money than he had, the remainder of his legacy, £800 a year, allowed him to spend much of nearly three years, until March, 1818, in a scholarly and sedentary life among close friends including Peacock, Hogg, Godwin, and Leigh Hunt. He read voraciously, quickly, and retentively in science, history, philosophy, literature, languages, and for a while, as Peacock recalls, his studies were almost "exclusively Greek." But on some level, his primary concerns were always political. Even his choice of Greek studies expressed the political conflicts within his own life, conflicts he shared with his age and class—those financially independent and educated young men who identified with the lower classes and agitated for political reform. In 1815, the Hellenic movement itself, originally motivated by the interests of the aristocracy and later by an intellectual elite, provided these liberal thinkers and writers with a precedent for a successful pastoral, agrarian, and democratic society even though the possibility of creating such a life in England at the time seemed remote. Moreover, the choice of Greek precedents in architecture, fashion, and literature was an expression of patriotism, an implicit rejection of the Roman models on which the French Revolution and the reign of Napoleon, with whom England had been at war since 1793, had been fashioned. Shelley's political Hellenism reflected the entire range of possible values, however contradictory, from the populist to the elite: in pamphlets he argued for political equality based on principles he derived from Plato and Christ; in *Oedipus Tryannus; or Swellfoot the Tyrant,* he parodied the decadence and ineptitude of the ruling classes; and in *Prometheus Unbound* he addressed "the highly refined imagination of the more select classes of poetical readers," as he claimed in the Preface.

Shelley spent the summer of 1816 with Byron, another young man of privilege with populist sympathies who had actually traveled in Greece and used it as a setting for his popular romances. They were drawn together by Claire Clairmont who convinced Shelley and Mary to accompany her to Geneva so she could be close to Byron, by whom she was pregnant from a brief affair she had initiated and to whom, in her eagerness to please, she had also offered Mary. At the time, Shelley was still an obscure poet having published only one work under his own name, *Alastor, or the Spirit of Solitude* (1816), a fascinating poem reflecting the intellectual ferment and social alienation of the previous year, the penalties he feared from pursuing a self-isolating ideal, and the animosity he felt toward those who had no ideals at all. Byron, on the other hand, was at the peak of his poetic reputation and personal notoriety, having invented Childe Harold, the nefarious hero whose adventures among Mid-Eastern reprobates had captured the public imagination. Byron then became that hero, betraying his conventional and moralistic wife with his half sister, among others, and then exiling himself to escape the social consequences.

They lived close by during that rainy summer and visited often. Byron, having little interest in Claire, allowed her to spend her nights copying out his verses, including *Childe Harold,* Book III, a poem about his being victimized by a society that could not understand his superior nature. Challenged by a ghost-story-writing contest, Mary began *Frankenstein* while caring for her six-month-old son; and Dr. John Polidori, an unstable, young nail-biting physician who served as Byron's companion, wrote *The Vampyre*. Shelley, his perception of the majestic landscape enriched by Byron, by his study of myth, science, philosophy, religion, and Wordsworth, composed *Mont Blanc: Lines Written in the Vale of Chamouni,* in which he claimed that the human mind, participating in the cyclical "everlasting universe of things," gives voice and meaning to the "Power that dwells apart in its tranquillity," an ambiguous celebration of both the Dionysian in nature and Platonic in mankind. But, as he wrote in *Hymn to Intellectual Beauty* while boating with Byron, more often than not his world appeared to be a "dim vast vale of tears, vacant and desolate," a premonition of what awaited them when they returned to England: the suicide in October of Fanny Imlay, Mary's half sister and illegitimate daughter of Gilbert Imlay and Mary Wollstonecraft, and in December of Harriet, who, alone and pregnant, drowned herself in the Serpentine in Hyde Park. Mary Godwin and Shelley were married within the month.

The contradictions in Shelley's life between the lofty and calm ideals he pursued and the stormy realities he endured were reflected in his personality. While some recall Shelley at this period as brave, outspoken, and courageous, others considered him petty and abrasive.[44] In January, 1817, at a dinner attended by Leigh Hunt and Keats, Benjamin Robert Haydon, still flush with success over the purchase of the Elgin Marbles, dismissed him as a "hectic, spare, weakly yet intellectual-looking creature . . . carving a bit of broccoli or cabbage on his plate, as if it had been the substantial wing of a chicken." Haydon continues, "Shelley opened the conversation" by saying in the most feminine and gentle voice, 'As to that detestable religion, the Christian—.' "[45] Such outspoken and remorseless atheism contributed to Shelley's losing custody of Ianthe and Charles, his children by Harriet, to an army doctor and his wife, a respectable couple known for their orthodox religious beliefs. Although Shelley would have been allowed to visit them under supervision twelve times a year, he was so embittered by the decision, disheartened and exhausted by the long custody battle, that he left England in March, 1818, without ever seeing them at all. Suffering from the loss of his children, failing health, financial difficulties, and a sense of persecution provoked by his odd opinions and domestic arrangements, Shelley sought refuge in the mild climate and anonymity of Italy, where he hoped to deliver Allegra to her father, Lord Byron, and relieve his household of one compromising rumor—that he was fathering children by both Mary and her half sister Claire.

On March 11, 1818, Shelley, Mary, Claire, two nurses, and three children—William (age 3), Clara (age 6 months), and Allegra (age 14 months)—sailed to Calais, then traveled overland to Italy where, for four years, they were to move frequently among what Mary Shelley called the "Wonders of Art and Nature," Pisa, Padua, Naples, Rome, Florence, Venice, and Pompeii, for all of Italy "seemed a garden of delight" to Shelley, "placed beneath a clearer and brighter heaven than he had known before" (Prefatory note to *Prometheus Unbound*). But Shelley found little personal solace in Italy. Within months of each other, his two children died:

Clara, just a year old, in Venice, where they had gone so that Claire could visit with Allegra; and William, at three, in Rome the following winter. In spite of the birth of Percy, the one child who was to survive, Mary was desolate, and the marriage suffered, the strain intensified by Claire's continued presence and Shelley's periodic and often disappointing flirtations. Like Pan in Shelley's hymn, he repeatedly "pursued a maiden and clasped a reed / Gods and men we are all deluded thus," although his dalliances produced one glorious poem, *Epipsychidion,* in which he explored the nature of ideal love. Inept and painful treatments for a kidney disorder and his increasing sense of futility as a poet intensified his depression. When Keats died in Rome, February, 1821, reputedly killed by the reviews of *Endymion,* though actually dying of consumption, Shelley identified with him as victim and hero, and depicted himself in *Adonais,* the elegy to Keats, among the mourners as a "frail Form / A phantom among men," "A Herd-abandoned deer struck by the hunter's dart." Before his death in July, 1822, when his boat went down in a squall in the Bay of Lerici, he was working on a poem called *The Triumph of Life,* a poem which expressed his despair over the impotence of virtue and the power of evil, "why God made irreconcilable / Good and the means of good" (ll. 230–231).

But the years in Italy had many compensations. Living frugally—"we eat little flesh and drink no wine" (l. 203), he wrote in his "Letter to Maria Gisborne"—and enjoying the company and often the hospitality of other English expatriates, Shelley was surrounded by the monuments, the art, and the historical settings that had inspired much of the literature that he had read. He began to develop a comprehensive and unique vision, integrating vast learning, personal reflection, and contemporary public life with which he remained, in spite of his self-imposed exile, intensely involved. Overcoming his personal disappointments and his isolation from such expansive libraries as Peacock's, he wrote his most learned and original work: *Prometheus Unbound, The Cenci,* "Ode to the West Wind," *The Sensitive Plant, Witch of Atlas, Epipsychidion, A Defense of Poetry, Adonais, Hellas,* satires, political invective, translations, and philosophical essays.

Shelley's initial literary projects in Italy set the theme for the rest of his work: a translation of Plato's *Symposium;* his own essay, "On Love," which might have served as his contribution to the convivial debate on love of which the *Symposium* consists; and *A Discourse on the Manners of the Ancient*

Greeks Relative to the Subject of Love,[46] designed as an intro-
duction to the *Symposium,* in which he explains that homo-
sexuality existed in Greece because women were too degraded
to inspire heterosexual love. Emancipated by Christianity and
Chivalry from the "degrading restraints of antiquity," Shel-
ley claimed later in *A Defense of Poetry,* women inspired
"the poetry of sexual love": "Love became a religion, the
idols of whose worship were ever present. It was as if the
statues of Apollo and the Muses had been endowed with life
and motion, and had walked forth among their worshippers;
so that earth became peopled by the inhabitants of a diviner
world."

   Shelley's belief that pagan concepts of love were fulfilled
in the unlikely ascetic atmosphere of eleventh-century Chris-
tian Europe was based on a view of history as progressive,
cumulative, cyclical, a view of time as subject to the same
forces as the green and growing landscape.[47] For him, history
followed the recurrent patterns of nature, the past reborn in
the present, like "an inspired rhapsodist" that "fills the thea-
tre of everlasting generations." To Shelley, even the transla-
tion of ancient texts such as Plato's *Symposium* is more than
the substitution of a known language for an alien one; it is a
regenerative act, a resurrection, which he describes in organic
terms: "The plant must spring again from its seed or it will
bear no flower" *(A Defense of Poetry).*[48]

   In this historical process, literature, all imaginative expres-
sions—in which Shelley includes art, music, dance, philoso-
phy, even social institutions—are collective expressions of a
universal body of ideas or archetypes first articulated in ancient
Greek history and myth, a "cyclic poem written by Time
upon the memories of men." Like Pompeii, the "city disin-
terred" that Shelley found so inspiring, ideas, however ancient,
are also excavated, revived by creative minds, embodied in
contemporary language and forms to become new "epi-
sodes" in the endless "cyclic poem" in which he saw himself
participating.

   His *Prometheus Unbound* is such an episode, derived from
both legend and Aeschylus' trilogy recounting an archetypal
struggle between generations: the mischievous Prometheus,
who had created mankind out of clay and water, fools the
petty and tyrannical Zeus with a bony sacrifice disguised in
fat, steals fire, and is punished for refusing to divulge the
secret that Zeus was to be overcome by a son he had yet to
conceive. Even in its original form, the tale had considerable
relevance to Shelley's generation—the rebellion against tyr-

anny, the theme of revolution and revenge, and the heroic posture of Prometheus himself resembling Satan in Milton's *Paradise Lost* (according to the way the Romantics read it), and Napoleon. Starting with this Promethean seed, Shelley invented a four-act lyrical drama, internalizing the struggle, focusing on the role of mind and the subjective life in a collective hero. Prometheus embodies the history of all those god-men, the divinities, who chose to participate in human life and the human beings who were touched by the sacred: Apollo, Dionysius, Orpheus, Buddha, Job, Moses, Christ, Zoroaster, even Satan.[49] But Shelley's Prometheus is exemplary of humanity, rather than divinity, humanity at its most creative, creating not only the gods but also their tyranny, then freeing himself by expelling evil, hatred, and resentment from his own soul. He offers an image of personal autonomy resisting the tyrannical social forces of history and collective life in the opening decades of the nineteenth century. Unlike the self-isolating autonomy of Byron's Manfred, the autonomy Prometheus achieves is expressed in a state of social communion, a prelude to love that redeems both nature and society. The prominence of the love theme in this primarily cerebral work reflects Shelley's Dionysian preoccupation, the influence of Erasmus Darwin's *Temple of Nature* (in which myth also is used to gain imaginative access to contemporary science) and Richard Payne Knight's *An Inquiry into the Symbolic Language of Ancient Art and Mythology* (1818), a new issue of the *Discourse on the Worship of Priapus* with which the Dilettanti Society scandalized the reading public in 1786.[50]

In *Adonais,* Shelley explicitly represents himself among the mourners as a disciple of Dionysius, bearing the thyrsus, the ivy-covered spear topped with a cypress cone. The elegy is based on a fertility myth that also implies resurrection, even immortality: Adonis, killed while hunting a boar, is allowed to spend six months a year on earth with his beloved goddess Aphrodite, the six months that correspond to the growing season. Drawing on this tale, Hebrew and Syrian mythology, Platonic philosophy, an ancient Greek poem by Bion called "Lament for Adonis," and another by Moschus who used it as an elegy to Bion, poems by Spenser, Milton, and Keats himself, Shelley universalizes the death of Keats to represent the death of poetry itself and its renewal, applying the cyclical patterns of nature, which Dionysius governs, to art. *Adonais,* which Shelley considered his finest poem, is such a renewal, and Shelley, in the tradition of Dionysius' most famous disciple, Orpheus, is the fearful instrument of it:

The breath whose might I have invoked in song
Descends on me; my spirit's bark is driven,
Far from the shore . . .

(Stanza 55)

The role of Orpheus had a special appeal to the Romantic poets, for here was the mortal poet empowered with Apollo's lyre to create music and verse that could subdue all of nature. And yet his talent, like theirs, was both a curse and a blessing, isolating him from his community as they were isolated in a materialistic, profit-oriented, and utilitarian society. The ultimate fate of Orpheus and his spiritual allegiances are both ambiguous: after failing to rescue his beloved wife, Eurydice, from the underworld because he turned to see if she had followed him, Orpheus was eventually dismembered by the Maenads, the crazed female followers of Dionysius, either, according to one version, for worshipping Apollo or, according to another, for preaching the advantages of pederasty over the promiscuous heterosexual behavior of the Maenads themselves. His head floated away into the sea and came to rest in a cave sacred to Dionysius, where it continued to prophesy until Apollo, jealous because his oracles were deserted, silenced it. Orphic priests worshipped both Dionysius and Apollo, but the mysteries, the secret rites relating to immortality, were associated with Dionysius, whose seasonal death, dismemberment, and renewal appeared to illuminate the tragic nature of human life with which he became closely allied. He was honored at the spring drama festivals where the great tragedians competed for prizes and ultimately, therefore, was associated with literary creativity. Although Shelley considered the Orphic ritual itself, which he saw depicted on an altar to Bacchus in Florence, to be a "monstrous superstition," testimony to the Greeks' ability to turn everything "prejudice, murder, madness—to Beauty,"[51] the hectic imagery, the caves, the rivers, the madness, the wandering and social alienation, the physical as well as mental anguish suffuse his poetry—explicitly in "Ode to the West Wind" where he becomes an Orphic host praying that his suffering would be the occasion of universal renewal. But to Shelley, all poets participated in the Orphic tradition, for, as he wrote in *Prometheus Unbound,* language itself is "perpetual Orphic song," and "rules . . . a throng / Of thoughts and forms, which else senseless and shapeless were" (IV, 415–17), as Orpheus was reputed to have governed and even rearranged natural objects with his song. Again Shelley is translating natural processes into aesthetic ones.

But more than a divine lyricist, it was also as a prophet that Orpheus served as a model to Shelley and his generation, as he concludes in *A Defense of Poetry:* "Poets are the hierophants of an unapprehended inspiration, the mirrors of the gigantic shadows which futurity casts upon the present, the words which express what they understand not; the trumpets which sing to battle, and feel not what they inspire: the influence which is moved not, but moves. Poets are the unacknowledged legislators of the world." In *Hellas,* Shelley assumes this prophetic role: out of the cycles of the past, the facts of the present, he prophesied a future in which the Hellenic ideal was to be fulfilled.[52] On the evidence of a trivial battle in 1821, which the Greeks ultimately lost, Shelley proclaimed:

> The world's great age begins anew,
>   The golden years return
> . . . .
> Another Athens shall arise,
>   And to remoter time
> Bequeath, like sunset to the skies,
> The splendour of its prime.
>   (ll. 1060–61, 1084–87)

In *Hellas,* Shelley also had an immediate and practical goal: to overcome the image of contemporary Greece as degenerate and, in spite of his pacifism, to win the material support of the European powers. By fashioning his play after Aeschylus' *The Persians,* Shelley placed this often brutal, obscure, and occasionally comic war in the heroic tradition. Relating it to popular uprisings in Spain, Naples, America, Germany, and France, and enriching it with allusions to Christian, Hebraic, Greek, Moslem, Persian, and even Egyptian mythology, he universalized it into another episode in the evolving cycle of human history. He extended his habit of "idealizing the forms of creation," as Mary Shelley described it in her prefatory comments on *Prometheus Unbound,* to "the modern Greek," the "descendant of those glorious beings whom the imagination almost refused to figure to itself as belonging to our Kind." His belief that they had inherited the heroic and intellectual virtues of their ancestors was based on *Anastasius: or Memoirs of a Greek* (1819), a novel published anonymously by Thomas Hope, author of several volumes on ancient Greek fashion and costume.

In Shelley, there were no contradictions between the ideal

and the real in *Hellas* because the ideal he was creating transcended the occasion for which he created it:

> Greece and her foundations are
> Built below the tide of war,
> Based on the chrystalline sea
> Of thought, and its eternity.
>
> (ll. 696–99)

Athens, Hellas, Greece, were his Jerusalem, as Blake called it, Byzantium, as Yeats would call it. It was a metaphor for human perfection, a city of the spirit, or, as Timothy Webb called it in "The Greek Example," his essay on Shelley, "a city of the mind . . . a thought-based monument to human potentiality."[53]

The Hellenic Twilight

The Hellenic revival began with the Dionysian revels of some decadent English aristrocrats in the Dilettanti society, developed into a rich man's hobby, a fetish to some, a source of status to others, but primarily tied to things—collecting, exhibiting, and reproducing them.[54] A Winckelmann or a Richard Payne Knight, the best of the Hellenists, inspired by what Shelley called in the Preface to *Alastor* a "sacred thirst for doubtful knowledge," turned art into history. But the best of this Hellenic revival, the poetry of Keats and Shelley, turned history into art. They endowed the past with aesthetic value using the same perceptual means their whole generation used to turn nature into art—the same imaginative transformations, perceiving and projecting, interacting with the facts, which were few, and the illusions as well: "The Eye altering alters all" as Blake claimed in *The Mental Traveller* (l. 62).[55]

In 1831, the word "classicism" appeared in English for the first time in an essay by Carlyle in which he claimed, "we are troubled with no controversies on Romanticism and Classicism." Although the British knew more about both ancient and contemporary Greece than any previous generation, Greece remained an aesthetic abstraction in both literature and art, often indistinguishable from Roman styles and prototypes.[56] Classicism referred to whatever was good, or typical, or universal, or lasting, and so it remains: classical music and classical cars do not mean Greek music or Roman automobiles. As the idea permeated the culture, the factual basis became increasingly obscure.

In 1834, Pompeii was buried again in Bulwer-Lytton's *The Last Days of Pompeii,* a novel that, like Edward Gibbon's *Decline and Fall of the Roman Empire,* emancipated his generation from anachronistic ideals. Geology now explained the volcanic eruption as a natural event in earth's history, and a revived Christianity explained it as a supernatural event in human history, a divine retribution for the paganism that the Romantics had found so inspiring. The heroes and myths adapted themselves to the times as well.[57] As Pope turned Ulysses into an eighteenth-century gentleman, Tennyson turned him into a Victorian imperialist, the restless visionary, the energetic, morally disciplined embodiment of the work ethic: "strong in will / To strive, to seek, to find, and not to yield." To Matthew Arnold in *Culture and Anarchy* (1869), Hellenism identified a kind of ideal mind, a disinterested intellect, which he felt was lacking in his conscientious and dutiful world. Thus, one of the major contributions of Romanticism, Hellenism and the Greek ideal, originating in a love of human perfection and tending toward the erotic, a renewed appreciation of the physical world and the processes shared by nature and by human beings, had come to mean its very opposite, a disembodied ideal—and Romantic became identified with yet another historical illusion, the gothic.

CHAPTER VIII

Natural History
and Its Illusion

Geological Forces

BY 1760, TELESCOPES and microscopes had revealed a universe infinitely larger and infinitely smaller than had ever been supposed. And travel for both commerce and conquest revealed more diversity and variety in nature and human life than had ever been imagined. Even after 1859, when Darwin published his *Origin of Species*, which distinguished among divine, natural, and human history, there were still those who believed in variations of Thomas Burnet's *Sacred Theory of the Earth* (1681–1689), a narrative of the history of the earth from paradise through the flood to the conflagration and ultimate redemption.[1] According to Burnet, God had created a symmetrical, round, smooth world, with a thin crust covering a subterranean ocean, a paradise where people lived to be ancient in great peace and comfort. Eventually, the earth collapsed from the weight of sin on the surface, releasing the water and creating the irregularities of nature: the mountains, the caves, the winding rivers and wandering shorelines, the odd plants, the slimy animals, all the random, ugly, prickly, fractured things, leaving the world "lying in its own Rubbish," "a great Ruine," a monument to man's sin and God's power.[2]

Although other more optimistic natural philosophers interpreted the irregular or disagreeable features in nature as signs of God's bounty or a failure of human vision, Burnet retained an ardent following, especially among earth scientists who believed in the Flood as a formative influence on the surface of the earth. The theory acquired scientific status from a German mineralogist named Abraham Werner, and, as late as 1811, the Wernerian Society of London had 250 distinguished members all over the world debating not whether there had been a Flood, but whether the water had come from within as Burnet claimed or from without as Werner did.[3] In 1775, Werner had proposed that the water was originally on the outside, that the earth had been soaking in a saline bath, like a giant fetus, out of which four or five layers of sediment settled, punctuated by periods of turbulence or upheaval. The theory was especially appealing because while it did not contradict Genesis, it accounted for the various strata of the earth and such odd distribution of fossil remains as sea-shells in the mountains. Werner's disciples were called Neptunists; his challengers, those who believed that the earth had been formed primarily by heat, were called Vulcanists or Plutonists—the titles being an expression of that mythic revival in which artists, historians, and poets were then deeply engaged.

James Hutton (1726–1797), the most important and complex Vulcanist, claimed that the fires were still inside the earth, an internal source of energy exerted on the surface. Assuming that the laws operating during his lifetime were the same as those that had created the landscape in an unfathomable past, he concluded that the earth was in a continuing state of creation through cyclical or revolutionary processes: the wind and rain eroded the hills, and sediments were carried into the sea, compacted into rocks, rearranged into valleys and hills by occasional trauma such as earthquakes and volcanoes. First presented as a paper to the Edinburgh Philosophical Society (1788), then published as *Theory of the Earth with Proofs and Illustrations* (1795), and finally disseminated to the public in John Playfair's *Illustrations of the Huttonian Theory* (1802), Hutton's work initiated the "golden" or "heroic" age of geology. A shy and pious man, he did not reject God—merely the myths, the supernatural interventions that had been attributed to Him. He studied the landscape, and from the patterns of change, life, and death, he formulated an ecological rather than a moral system, reviving a primitive cyclical pattern of decay and rejuvenation, of death and rebirth, of constant activity organized for the purpose, if any, of sustaining itself, of increasing animal and vegetable life.[4] Believing that it was impossible for a geologist to consider either a creation or a consummation, Hutton replaced six thousand years of earth history with a staggering tract of unaccountable time:

"We find no sign of a beginning—no prospect of an end." For scientists and historians, he shifted the focus from origins to history, to the processes of nature and society, and participated in that secularization of nature and creativity that characterizes Romantic thought. The fires within the earth that to orthodox Christians represented Hell, the symbol of a repressive and punitive God, were to Hutton, as they were to Blake, a major creative force, a symbol of energy.

But Hutton had few advocates, for his ideas were eccentric and his writing obscure. Moreover, he questioned two myths that were a source of great comfort to most people. First, he undermined the idea of a creation, implying that the Old Testament God had been no more powerful than the Greek gods He had displaced, that He was merely another governing rather than a creating god. Secondly, he proposed that the earth was not created for the pleasure and profit of human beings, that it was created long before mankind, and that human beings were in fact strangers, aliens, afflicted with all the anxiety that the concept of a special creation had allayed: no Flood, and for that matter no Eden, none of the engaging fictions that had been based upon them—instead, an impersonal force working through history, sustaining and increasing the material world, an endless future built out of the debris of the present. However much freedom and stimulation such a view of nature offered, Hutton was disregarded (except for a loyal following of Scottish intellectuals including Adam Smith), until Charles Lyell vindicated him in *The Principles of Geology* (1830–1833), "by which time the reading public was satiated with creation theory," as Carlyle complained in *Sartor Resartus* (1833): "of Geology and Geognosy we know enough; what with the labours of our Werners and Huttons, what with the ardent genius of their disciples, it has come about that now to many a Royal Society, the Creation of a World is little more mysterious than the cooking of a dumpling" (p. 4).

In the thirty years between Hutton and Lyell, English geologists concentrated on the study of strata and fossils, carefully avoiding the human implication of their evidence— the age of the earth and of human habitation, using fossil evidence to verify the Creation and the Flood. For example, William Smith (1769–1839) discovered in 1799 that the ages of different strata could be identified by the different marine fossils found in them. Shells, then, became an index of time and could be used to prove either that there was a flood or that the world had in fact emerged from a Wernerian primal sea. By 1815, Smith knew the strata of England and Wales better than any living person, having mapped it and produced a complete geological atlas. A garrulous but uneducated man, Smith, like an Ancient Mariner on an inland sea, wandered about the countryside telling everyone who would listen what he had discovered although he did not understand its significance.[5] When the Reverend J. Townsend published the first interpretation of Smith's discoveries in *The Character of Moses Established for Veracity as an Historian Recording Events from the Creation to the Deluge* (1813), he became head of a geological school called Catastrophism. As he explained in *The Stratigraphical System of Organized Fossils* (1817), each strata was created separately, God having periodically wiped out all the inhabitants of the earth and created new ones. Consequently, the entire earth was a many-layered tribute to a powerful, creative, and governing deity who was also given to violent fits of frustration and anger. The Catastrophists persisted and flourished, their vision appealing to the literary and artistic as well as religious and scientific imagination.

In 1811, the French Baron Cuvier published his *Research in Fossil Bones,* translated in 1817 from the French as *Theory of the Earth* (in an attempt to discredit Hutton) by Robert Jameson, the Edinburgh professor who introduced Werner to England, founded the Wernerian Society, and delivered "incredibly dull" lectures about which Charles Darwin complained as a student. As a comparative anatomist, Cuvier, the handsome and accomplished son of a Swiss army officer, helped found the study of paleontology and acquired the reputation of being able to assemble an entire animal from a single bone. His reconstruction of prehistoric beasts proved that some creatures were indeed extinct, but he did not see any evolutionary stages nor find any fossil he could identify as human, and thereby prove there were earlier creations inhabited by human beings.[6] While retrospectively it appears that scientists could not help but find the history of mankind in the history of the earth, that they could not help but find the outline of evolution and an immensely expanded chronology, Cuvier, like the other Catastrophists, maintained that the earth had been repeatedly subject to violent destruction by flood, by earthquake, by volcanic eruption, and that human beings were indeed a special creation appearing between the last two catastrophes, which, having subsided, were not yet over.

William Buckland (1784–1856) and his friend William Conybeare (1784–1857), ordained ministers, lecturers of international reputation, and geologists, made geology the most popular science in England by concluding from their otherwise reputable studies of fossil remains, of hyena, tiger, and elephant bones, of prehistoric fish and the preserved feces of flying reptiles, that, even in England, there had indeed been separate creations and destructions, some creations including monsters now extinct, and that each creation had exhibited God's purpose—which usually meant that each creature, and each organic or non-organic thing, was designed to prove the existence of God and to serve mankind. To such geologists the existence of suffering or deformity was merely a special intellectual challenge. The theory appealed to the post-war generation of emotionally over-wrought sensation-seekers who were supporting gothic melodrama at Covent Garden, who made Byron a hero, who purchased a record number of broadsides recounting gruesome murders, and who genuinely believed in the apocalyptic yearnings of Joanna Southcott. That first generation of field geologists, a colorful, fascinating, articulate group, invested Catastrophic geology with that same glamour and visibility. Passionate, energetic, idealistic, personable, they traveled, often in pairs, to the Alps, the Arctic, to wherever the configuration of the landscape seemed most interesting, and they wrote long descriptive letters about what they saw. In magazines and reviews, geological reports, especially of unusual sightings, outnumbered all the other sciences. So Conybeare confessed in 1811: "I partake more largely of the spirit of the Knight of La Mancha than of his craven squire and prefer the enterprise and adventure of geological errantry to rich castles and luxurious entertainments."[7] And geology offered an adventure that could be shared, one that could be found in England; it appealed to the same peripatetic instincts as the continental tour did in the eighteenth century, appropriate for young ladies as well as gentlemen, and requiring very little specialized knowledge.

Catastrophism added a great deal of drama to the adventure, for to the fossil-bone hunters scampering over the English countryside, the landscape itself became a graveyard, an accumulation of ancestral bones, an allegory of recurrent sin, failure, and punishment. It offered the same pre-history to the British as Pompeii, Herculaneum, and all the archaeological digs of Greece were giving Mediterranean cultures. And, like the Biblical and Hellenic historical illusions, Catastrophism provided a rich new source of poetic possibilities, stimulating Shelley, for example, to imagine an inner earth as a rich new source of poetic imagery,[8] "the melancholy ruins / Of cancelled cycles":

> The anatomies of unknown winged things,
> The fishes which were isles of living scale,
> And serpents, bony chains, twisted around
> The iron crags, or within heaps of dust
> To which the tortuous strength of their last pangs
> Had crushed the iron crags;—and over these
> The jagged alligator and the might
> Of Earth-convulsing behemoth, which once
> Were monarch beasts, and on the slimy shores
> And weed-overgrown continents of Earth
> Increased and multiplied like summer worms
> On an abandoned corpse, till the blue globe
> Wrapt Deluge round it like a cloak, and they
> Yelled, gaspt, and were abolished. . . .
> (*Prometheus Unbound*, IV, 303–16)

John Martin: Painter of Catastrophism

Catastrophism had its painter as well: John Martin, born in the politically apocalyptic month of July, 1789, in the shadow of Hadrian's Wall (the ancient monument to the northern frontier of the Roman Empire), in the Tyne Valley, where periodic floods had recently disinterred the coffins and bones of his ancestors.[9] One of his brothers lived in the streets of Newcastle selling pamphlets in which he described himself as an "anti-Newtonian philosophical conqueror of all nations." Another spent his life in the army; he served at Waterloo, invented a perpetual motion machine, and published a book of poems, *The Last Days of the Antediluvian World* (1830) with an illustration by John. The third brother, who like his mother claimed to have the gift of prophecy, tried to burn York Minster in a divinely inspired protest against the profligacy of the clergy and, while confined to Bedlam, became the subject of an anonymous pamphlet, *Bits of Biography: Blake, the Vision Seer, and Martin, the York Minister Incendiary*, which, through an error by a French translator, led to the belief that Blake had been confined to Bedlam.[10] His son, a promising young painter who lived with John, committed suicide under the delusion that he had typhus and his breath was turning the family black.

In 1803, when John was fourteen, the family moved to

Newcastle, a hillside city that became the model for many of his later paintings of urban disasters and where he took an apprenticeship first with a carriage maker to learn to paint trim and heraldry and then with an enameler to learn the delicate art of china painting. In 1809, he married a lady nine years older than himself, about whom little is known except that she bore nine children, three of whom died, and read to him while he painted.

To support this family, John moved to London and, in 1812, after much glass-painting and conventional topographic work, he exhibited *Sedak in Search of the Waters of Oblivion*. The massive volcanic mountains luridly illuminated by internal fires, reflected in a strangely placid pool and cascading waterfall, appealed to the same taste as the pantomime, the diorama, the panorama, and the extravagances of Byron. But Martin brought to the genre the intense color and precision he had learned from painting tea cups, demonstrated in the foreground by the tiny, fragile, but luminous figure in a losing struggle against the forces of nature, a figure that will reappear in later paintings as the Last Man, as Macbeth, Adam, Caius Marius, all the heroes and martyrs confronting, even overwhelmed by forces, natural and supernatural, they do not understand. *Sedak* was later engraved for the popular annual, *The Keepsake* (1828), accompanied by a poem by Shelley. After doing *The Bard* in 1817, a figure from Gray's poem that was also done by Blake, de Loutherbourg, and Fuseli, rendered with the characteristic distortions of space and form, Martin began his series of urban disasters, cities or merely buildings destroyed by eruptions, earthquakes, floods, recollecting the ruins of post-war Europe that Byron described in *Childe Harold*. Even falling into oblivion, they resembled the massive country seats that Martin had been painting to support his family, and the elegant, stucco-coated terraces that Nashe was building all over London for the habitation of those patrons who overlooked Martin in favor of more traditional and academic painters. There was, in brief, the painter's as well as God's vengeance in those pictures.

In *The Fall of Babylon* (1819), *Belshazzar's Feast* (1821),[11] *The Destruction of Pompeii and Herculaneum* (1822), and finally *The Deluge* (1826), Martin captured civilization at the moment of destruction, captured the alarm and helplessness of people confronted and defeated by unprecedented power. For architectural detail, Martin studied the Bible, the commentaries, and reports of contemporary excavations, which gave the human dimension of his paintings a documentary quality even though the history he was depicting was derived from the illusions of myth and sacred texts. But the natural world that he placed it in was enlarged, the contexts of space and time expanded, diminishing the human element. It was the image of nature being revealed by contemporary science set around the image of mankind as represented in the Old Testament. Martin's precision, his fidelity to the possible, made *The Deluge* (a commonplace artistic topic during the years of Neptunism and Catastrophism) unique, for while he quoted Burnet in the catalogue of paintings to justify an earthquake with waters erupting from within the earth, he also drew on contemporary scientific speculation proposing that the Flood may have been caused by an inexplicable conjunction of sun, moon, and comet, an idea that Cuvier especially admired in the work when he visited Martin's studio. And in 1833, Bulwer-Lytton, who in *The Last Days of Pompeii* was to illustrate his own fascination with catastrophic events, defended Martin by claiming that the *The Deluge* was "the most magnificent alliance of philosophy and art of which the history of painting can boast."[12]

Although in his paintings he repeatedly destroyed cities and inundated mankind, he invested an enormous amount of energy in proposals for civic improvements, especially in the water supply. He proposed that water be supplied from massive reservoirs on the elevations around London, falling in canals, cascades, and fountains in ornamental parks resembling, with their tropical vegetation, the Hanging Gardens of Babylon, and he urged that human waste be piped back onto the farm land as fertilizer rather than into the Thames, which had become an open sewer contaminating water supplies and causing epidemics in an overcrowded London. However impractical, the projects were important to him. In 1830, he lamented: "If I had only been an engineer. . . . Instead of benefiting myself and a few only, I should have added to the comfort, prosperity and health of mankind in general."[13] The "few only" were the English aristrocracy who were no more educated than during the Regency and may, indeed, have become even more doltish. When, for example, King William IV saw *The Fall of Nineveh* (1828), the most ambitious painting by an artist Bulwer-Lytton called "the greatest, the most lofty, the most permanent, the most original genius of his age," His Highness commented, "How pretty."[14]

A new set of images entered Martin's Biblical epics after 1834, when he first encountered Dr. Gideon Mantell's iguanodon, a prehistoric monster that Martin illustrated accurately for the popular geologist's *The Wonders of Geology* (1838) and later adapted imaginatively to Thomas Hawkins's *The Book of the Great Sea Dragons* (1840). Finally, he reconciled fantasy, science, and scripture by incorporating dragons in his illustrations to Milton's *Paradise Lost* and the Bible, in which Satan is depicted as a dragon that resembles an iguanodon, and in one of his paintings, *The Assuaging of the Waters* (1840), in which an iguanodon creature and some coral shells are visible among the debris of the Flood.[15] Although he represented these creatures with the same attention to detail, the same concern for precision, as he had brought to his tea cups and topographical paintings, Martin, like his contemporaries, continued to affirm scriptural history. Except for a few details, his last paintings, exhibited the year before he died in 1854, adhered to the same interpretation of human history as Milton did in *Paradise Lost*. *The Great Day of Wrath, The Last Judgment,* and *The Plains of Heaven* may be the last monuments to a time before Darwin's *Origin of Species* (1859) when most people, even scientists, believed that the world was "lying in its own Rubbish."

Romantic Melancholy

The ease with which the English, indeed most Europeans, accepted the idea of landscape as a graveyard, of natural history as a succession of failures, may be attributed in part to painters and poets who found inspiration in graveyards, death, and decay. Verse inspired by graveyards usually presents a pensive and solitary speaker reflecting on death among ruins, or in a graveyard, or on a hillside, at twilight or by moonlight, surrounded by cypress or yews or hollow oak trees inhabited by owls or bats, stirred by an impending or departing storm. The speaker usually exhibits that fashionable characteristic called "sensibility," a susceptibility to delicate or tender feeling, an emotional responsiveness expressed either in tears or exaggerated rhetoric. Although sensibility was often aroused by poverty, by ruins, and by other ancient things, it was decidedly an elitist and modern characteristic, a sign of progress and of the emotional superiority of the upper classes.[16]

In *Characteristics of Men, Manners, Opinions, Times* (1711), the elegant and respectable Anthony Ashley Cooper, Third Earl of Shaftesbury had given a philosophical basis to such feeling by offering an ethical system with emotional rather than supernatural sanctions.[17] Shaftesbury's God, "the best-natured being in the world," created human beings in His own cheerful image, and provided them with an aesthetic sense tied to a moral one. The beauty, order, and harmony of the universe as found in landscape, for example, aroused feelings of kindness, pity, generosity, and love, what Shaftesbury called the "natural affections," expressions of kindness and tenderness for orphans, animals, widows, and aged men (aged women, as we noted in our discussion of children's literature, were dangerous and undeserving). In James Thomson's *The Seasons* (rev. 1744–1746), a poem that delighted and fascinated Romantic writers and painters, the cultivation of feeling by studying landscape takes on an elegiac tone. It demonstrates the relationship between man and nature as described by Shaftesbury but taking place in Burnet's universe, a natural world that observation and science would reveal as, at best, indifferent to the needs and comforts of mankind, at worst a stage on which human beings survive only by chance and in great peril.

Following Thomson, most poets believed that tears were more human than laughter, that they were more likely than laughter to lead to benevolent action. But the English were melancholic by nature as well as habit. Consequently, most of the writers following Shaftesbury disregarded the cheerfulness of his Creator, and used nature to cultivate mournful feelings. They ranged from the merely wistful, as in William Collins's "Ode to Evening" (1746) to the genuinely morbid graveyard poets who either preferred to contemplate nature in a graveyard, where the fact of death intensified their feeling, or who saw, with geological basis, all of nature as nothing more than a graveyard, a reminder of God's destructive power. The most prolonged expression of this macabre attitude is Edward Young's *The Complaint: or Night Thoughts on Life, Death, and Immortality* (1742–1746),[18] expressing in nine books "How populous, how vital is the Grave / . . . Creation's Melancholy Vault" (*Night,* I, 115–16); while in *The Grave* (1743), Robert Blair also assumed the self-appointed task "To Paint the gloomy horrors of the Tomb." William Blake later illustrated both of them, and, in the process revised them, for he cheerfully believed in angels and the proximity of spirits with whom he conversed. Life for Blake was a period of dying, essential for reaching a state of higher Wisdom, for fulfilling the cycle. Consequently, in *The Book of Thel,* the unborn spirit, reluctant to enter the world of process, returns to her paradise after a vision of her own grave, preferring never to be born at all rather than to be born and die. The best of mortuary verse in the eighteenth century was Thomas

Gray's "Elegy Written in a Country Churchyard" (1751), a poem that starts with a meditation at twilight and concludes with the observation that "the paths of glory," along with everything else, "lead but to the grave."

The melancholy in poetry and the hypersensitive people who suffered from it reflected a general pathology identified by Dr. George Cheyne as early as 1733 as "The English Malady."[19] Along with contemporary literary portraits of suffering and desolation, gentlemen took interest in medieval tracts on melancholy, spleen, vapors, and hysteria. This preoccupation with ruins, wasted hopes, and decay helped shape one of the great historical achievements of the period, Edward Gibbon's *Decline and Fall of the Roman Empire* (1776–1788), for Gibbon was himself an example of that disaffected, searching, brilliant, and sensitive young Englishman. Unable to marry the woman he loved or to follow the religion he chose, he wandered about Europe until, on October 15, 1764, he opens his history with a description of himself as a gentleman cultivating sensibility: "as I sat musing amidst the ruins of the Capital, while the bare-footed fryars were singing vespers in the temple of Jupiter, . . . the idea of writing the decline and fall of the city first started to my mind." The first volume, appearing on the eve of the American Revolution, offered sobering analogies to the English, a secular prose-poem projecting onto history the melancholy that afflicted the author while those colonial rebels in America were deciding that the pursuit of happiness was an inalienable right.

The Reality of Death

While it had been a religious or artistic convention to focus on death as a subject for art and literature, during the Romantic period, death itself, stripped of its spiritual significance and consolations, became a fact of life, made more poignant and visible by science, politics, journalism, and archaeology itself. Melancholy was attributed to biology, to climate, to diet, to religion, excess and abundance of every sort including spleen, beef, rain, fog, but never to hunger or poverty; for however rich people may have enhanced their melancholy by contemplating the poor, the poor themselves were merely unhappy or discontented. Periodic waves of suicide throughout the century swelled with the failure of the French Revolution when some particularly enthusiastic advocates decided that the world was a "melancholy waste of hopes o'er thrown," as Wordsworth claimed (*The Prelude,* II, 56), and culminated in 1815, coinciding with the final defeat of Napoleon, the post-war economic depression, and the political compromises that came with peace. Byron captured the elegiac post-war mood in his epic graveyard poem, *Childe Harold,* Canto III (1816), in which he toured the battlefields and monuments of Europe from Waterloo, "The grave of France," to Rome while lamenting the lost greatness of civilization.

Other nonliterary events influenced the emotional climate of the English reading public. The long war against France produced unthinkable battlefield casualties, and the names, battles, and fatalities were reported within weeks in every corner of Great Britain by newspapers carried on mail coaches such as De Quincey described in *The English Mail-Coach,* which included a section called "The Vision of Sudden Death." The urban working poor were crowded in unsanitary and poorly ventilated lodgings, where they often slept in shifts, and in damp, cold factories where they labored for too little to nourish themselves, and where they caught one another's diseases. They died in the same crowded conditions without the privacy to protect their dignity or those around them from being in constant contact with death. Years of drought, poor harvests, and enclosures had also deprived the country people of whatever natural advantages they had: they starved amid plenty or were sent by the government to alien countries and climates where they disappeared or died of disease. And even in the best of homes, the understanding of the special needs of women in and after childbirth and of the infants themselves was so limited that they died at an incredible rate for such trivial reasons as the doctors' failing to wash their hands between dissecting corpses and delivering babies. The new and widely circulated newspapers and magazines published obituaries and mortality reports, as they were occasionally called, analyzing the number of deaths, the causes, the locations, the age and sex of the victim. Journalism was making death a public event, another source of statistics, and Malthus was being vindicated: war, hunger, and disease provided a natural check on overpopulation—a predictable number of deaths was essential for the survival of the species.

This new consciousness of death as a secular and impersonal event provoked a plague of meditations, reflections, monodies, and elegies by both major writers such as Coleridge, Byron, and Keats, and popular minor writers such as Tom Moore and Thomas Campbell, leading Peacock in the persona of Mr. Hilary to exclaim in *Nightmare Abbey*: "If we go on in this way we shall have a new art of poetry, of which one of the first rules will be: 'To remember to forget that there are any such things as sunshine and music in the world'." The evolution of attitudes toward death is especially evident over Wordsworth's long career. Writing in *The Prelude* (1805), he recalls when he was a healthy and fortunate young man of twenty, he was as capable as any of the graveyard poets of turning a landscape into an occasion for sorrow:

> Dejection taken up for pleasure's sake
> And gilded sympathies, the willow wreath,
> Even among those solitudes sublime,
> And sober posies of funeral flowers
> Culled from the gardens of Lady Sorrow
> Did Sweeten many a meditative hour.
>   (VI, 483–88)

Acknowledging his own excess, he later offered several correctives, including a parody of the graveyard sensibility in "We Are Seven": the narrator is frustrated in his attempt to indulge his taste for funereal meditation in a country churchyard by a pert child who insists on playing by her dead sibling's graves and eating her dinner there. In *The Ruined Cottage,* Wordsworth is more direct; the philosophical Pedlar, who is his protagonist, regulates the emotional response of the Poet to whom he has told a tale of devastating loss and injustice by observing: " 'My Friend! enough to sorrow you have given, / The purposes of wisdom ask no more' " (I, 932–33). Wordsworth later used the graveyard as an organizational device in Books VI and VII of *The Excursion,* and he undermined the inflated and elaborate vocabulary of grief in his three "Essays Upon Epitaphs" as well as through examples such as "A Slumber Did My Spirit Seal," in which he demonstrated the verbal austerity of genuine mourning.[20] Personal experience as well as taste accounted for Wordsworth's unsentimental treatment of death, for he knew about it as a real rather than literary event, having lost his mother when he was eight, his father when he was thirteen, his brother to the sea in 1805, and two children to disease in 1812.

John Keats:
The Temple of Melancholy

John Keats (1795–1821), perhaps more than any other writer, had reason to believe that the world was "a Vale of Soul-making," a "Place where the heart must feel and suffer in a thousand diverse ways," for by the time he was fifteen, his father had died in a fall from a horse, his mother from consumption; he had lost an infant brother, a favorite uncle, and the grandfather with whom he had been living.[21] His scientific education, however, deprived him of the comfort, the illusions found in fashionable sentimental literature. Apprenticed to an apothecary, he witnessed human suffering on a daily basis, assisting in a number of such minor but disagreeable procedures as bleeding, drawing teeth, setting bones, and attending to infections in the days before anaesthesia and antiseptics. His response to pain and despair intensified when he trained at Guy's Hospital, a charitable institution for incurable diseases, where he attended lectures, observed operations, assisted in the sick wards changing dressings, and dissected corpses that had been stolen from local graveyards by thieves who then sold them to the hospitals. By the time he received his certificate to practice medicine, he had decided he could provide more comfort as a poet than a physician. His exposure to suffering and his immense capacity for it were transformed into an art without precedence, for though it was based in feeling, especially sorrow, it was totally unsentimental. Here science proved to be an excellent training ground for a poet: it developed his capacity for detailed observation,[22] prepared him to attend his own brother Tom, who died of consumption in 1818 at age nineteen, and to interpret the symptoms leading to his own death four years later at age twenty-six in Rome. Experience, then, lay behind his vision of life

> . . . where men sit and hear each other groan;
> Where palsy shakes a few, sad, last gray hairs,
> Where youth grows pale, and spectre-thin, and dies;
> Where but to think is to be full of sorrow
> And leaden-eyed despairs.
> ("Ode to a Nightingale," ll. 23–28)

Beset by illness, pain, and the death of loved ones, Keats was also chronically and unjustly impoverished, for although he had a settlement, Richard Abbey, his legal guardian, prevented his receiving any but the smallest subsidy. Unwilling to practice medicine, Keats believed he could earn his living as a poet, but he was young and lacked the appeal of a Byron or Campbell, so while he continued to write, to plan alternatives—becoming a ship's surgeon at one point, or writing plays or reviews—and to appeal to the obdurate Abbey, his publishers lost money and his debts mounted. And when he was dying of consumption, his friends and publishers raised the money to send him to Italy, where, shortly before his death, he wrote, "O that something fortunate had ever happened to me or my brothers!—then I might hope—but despair is forced upon me as a habit" (*Letters,* II, 352). His wealth, however, was in his friends who were demonstrably loyal to him—Leigh Hunt, Benjamin Bailey, John Hamilton Reynolds, Richard Woodhouse, Shelley, Joseph Severn, William Hazlitt, and his publishers, Taylor and Hessey.

Impoverished, ill, he was also the victim of unrequited or perhaps merely unfulfilled love. According to his letters, Keats had never found women to be especially appealing; he thought they lacked imagination, among other things, and he didn't trust them. Contributing to his discomfort was his sense of physical inadequacy: "I do think," he concludes, "better of Womankind than to suppose they care whether Mister John Keats five feet high likes them or not" (*Letters,* I, 342). In his poetry, Keats depicts women either as silly and self-deluded, or as goddesses who preside over painful initiation rites such as Mnemosyne in *Hyperion,* Moneta in "The Fall of Hyperion," or the seductress in "La Belle Dame sans Merci." Fanny Browne, whom he met in September, 1818, "beautiful and elegant, graceful, silly, fashionable and strange" (*Letters,* II, 8) was neither. Yet, within six months, he wrote: "You cannot conceive how I ache to be with you: how I would die for one hour"; "the very first week I knew you I wrote myself your vassal"; "all I can bring you is a swooning admiration of your Beauty"; "You absorb me in spite of myself—you alone: for I look not forward with any pleasure to what is call'd being settled in the world; I tremble at domestic cares—yet for you I would meet them" (*Letters,* II, 133). Fanny and her mother, a widow with two other children to care for, tended Keats for a month when he became seriously ill, but love and death, however poetic, are impossible companions. When he arrived in Naples in November, 1820, Keats wrote to his friend Brown: "I should have had her when I was in health, and I should have remained well. I can bear to die—I cannot bear to leave her." He was buried with her letters to him unopened.

Keats suffered from the very profession he had chosen. In a world evolving on utilitarian and commercial principles, Keats had chosen to be a poet, and poets were often treated as if they were criminals, or mad, or parasitical, or social deviants. Insecure about his own skill, eager to prove himself to his guardian and friends, with more ambition than experience, he was also particularly vulnerable to the critical attacks on his poetry appearing in the *British Critic, Blackwood's,* and the *Quarterly,* an attack so virulent that the reviewer, John Wilson Croker, was accused of actually causing Keats's death four years later in Rome.[23] But Keats had such an idealized view of poetry and of himself as a poet that he could not expect from a reading public, "a thing I cannot help looking upon as an Enemy" (*Letters,* I, 266), and from a contentious reviewing press the approval he felt he needed and deserved. While setting increasingly lofty goals for himself, he identified with Thomas Chatterton (1752–1770), the misunderstood genius who killed himself at age twenty-two. Keats's rejection, alienation, and withdrawal were typical of high-minded poets during this first age of the literary marketplace, one he shared with Shelley and Wordsworth. But it is also a position that bears with it a terrible penalty, the sense of isolation, futility, and impotence that contributed to his vision of the world as "a Vale of Soul-making," a place where identity is earned through pain.[24] His vision of himself as a wasted talent found expression in his death-bed instructions to be placed in a nameless grave inscribed "Here lies One Whose Name was writ in Water."

Mostly his "leaden-eyed despairs" were temperamental in origin. Although he reveals an appealing sense of humor in his letters and was found by many to be an amusing and genial companion, he confessed to having "a horrid Morbidity of Temperament" that he considered his greatest obstacle (*Letters,* I, 142). To his friend, the young divinity student Benjamin Bailey, he wrote, "I scarcely remember counting upon any Happiness." But he does not consider his personal unhappiness suitable for poetry: "I will not spoil my love of gloom by writing an ode to darkness" (*Letters,* II, 43). Rather, he developed a capacity for self-abstraction, identifying with something outside of himself, literally investing himself in the concrete, the living world: "The setting sun will always set me to rights—or if a Sparrow come before my Window I take part in its existence and pick about the Gravel . . ." (*Letters,* I, 186). Sensibility, the fashionable self-centered emotionalism such as Keats projected on his hero in *Endymion,* is the very opposite of the self-effacement Keats cultivated in himself, the capacity to overcome the limits of self and enter into the being of something else, to experience vicariously, as an actor.[25] This sympathetic imagination may have helped to release him from personal grief, but it did not ameliorate

the sources of grief in the world, and Keats was, in spite of
the popular image projected on him, a worldly poet.

As a student of medicine and an observer of nature, he kept
confronting certain dismal facts that were not easily recon-
ciled with the literary pastoral he cultivated in such early poems
as *Sleep and Poetry*. His training and habit of mind forced him
to see nature as an ecological rather than a moral or aesthetic
system. He saw both the same world of process as Hutton
and Erasmus Darwin and that same competitive world of
interdependencies as Malthus in which the price of life is death.
From Teignmouth, March, 1818, where Keats had gone with
his ailing brother Tom, he describes that world in an infor-
mal rhymed epistle to a friend:

> . . . I saw too distinct into the core
> Of an eternal fierce destruction,
> And so from happiness I far was gone.
> Still am I sick of it, and tho', to-day,
> I've gather'd young spring-leaves, and flowers gay
> Of periwinkle and wild strawberry,
> Still do I that most fierce destruction see,—
> The Shark at savage prey,—the Hawk at pounce,
> The gentle Robin, like a Pard or Ounce,
> Ravening a worm.
> ("Epistle to John Hamilton Reynolds," ll. 96–105)

By the following year this insight into nature had been
extended to all of human life: ". . . Man is originally 'a poor
forked creature' subject to the same mischances as the beasts
of the forest, destined to hardships and disquietude of some
kind or other. If he improves by degrees his bodily accom-
modations and comforts—at each stage, at each ascent there
are waiting for him a fresh set of annoyances. . . ." It is this
vision of life that he considers a "Vale of Soul-making," "a
World of Pains and troubles," "a Place where the heart must
feel and suffer in a thousand diverse ways," to become a soul
(*Letters,* II, 101–2).

Keats's major poetry explores this vision of nature, with
its inexorable and tragic plot, a poetry sufficiently compre-
hensive to include all of human experience but still retain its
aesthetic priorities, a poetry that reconciles beauty and truth
through what he calls "intensity," the capacity to make "all
disagreeables evaporate, from their being in close relation-
ship with Beauty & Truth" (*Letters,* I, 192). The intensity of
art—its energy, its concentration, its complexity, its fascina-
tion, its power of illusion, even deception—overwhelms the

world of pains and troubles that underlies it. Keats's intensity turns a tale dealing with drunkenness, barbarity, hostility, pandering, betrayal, seduction, kidnapping, self-delusion, and even death into *The Eve of St. Agnes,* a poem so flawless that, as Keats says of the Grecian Urn, it "dost tease us out of thought / As doth eternity," turns all the "disagreeables," the coldness, the secrecy, the danger, the deception, into elements that enhance the beauty. It is intensity glutting "sorrow on the morning rose," contemplating "Beauty that must die," "Joy, whose hand is ever at his lips / Bidding adieu; and aching Pleasure high," that turns melancholy into an aesthetic experience. And, finally, it is intensity, that full realization of atmosphere, that distillation of sensuous experience, that turns the elegiac "To Autumn" into a triumph over life so that even the bees "think warm days will never cease," even Autumn herself, the dying figure, sits "Drows'd with the fume of poppies," both the gleaner and the harvest, roused from her patient watching of the cider press, to ask plaintively, "Where are the songs of spring?" The poet, the guardian of illusions, the source of the intensity that will make all "disagreeables evaporate," says as reassuringly as a nurse, "Think not of them, thou hast thy music too." The song is so full, so enchanting, so "intense," that no one would notice it is a funeral dirge, a song, like the Nightingale's, that could lead one to believe: "Now more than ever seems it rich to die." The operational word, of course, is "seems," for intensity, indeed art itself and the special truth that is allied with beauty, is an illusion, a necessary one, in a world of change, of process, where nature survives by an "eternal fierce destruction" and human beings acquire souls, identities, through suffering "in a thousand diverse ways."

Keats, like Erasmus Darwin and Thomas Beddoes, two other poets trained as physicians and scientists, lived in two worlds, each of which he seemed to have observed with exceptional accuracy: the world of art and the world of nature. While his poetry attempts to reconcile the two, it also demonstrates how fundamentally irreconcilable they had become, for during the Romantic period the perception was gradually emerging among philosophers, theologians, scientists, and poets that mankind was destined to work out of his salvation in a natural world, in a landscape that was alien, indifferent, and inhospitable. While his poetic imagination could frequently overcome the emnity between man and nature, between the human need for permanence and the inevitable changes in nature, Keats carried with him a terrible consciousness, heightened by experience, that he was "born for death," that "hungry generations tread" him down.

With this essentially scientific perception of human life as part of a natural as opposed to a human order, the appeal of the graveyard convention declined. While the opening of Keats's *Hyperion* describes the death or rather dethronement of gods who become in their marmoreal splendor their own tombstones, it is not a poem of endings: it depicts gods who fell subject to "Nature's Law," on whose "heels a fresh perfection treads" (II, 180, 214). And it describes the birth of new gods, the Olympians, one of whom is deified by his acquisition of knowledge, of "Creations and destroyings," the same knowledge that was becoming available to John Martin, to the geologists, archaeologists, and paleontologists whose burrowing in the earth had revealed its cumulative history.

Although the knowledge did not deify the scientists, it certainly helped to demystify and desanctify graves and burial sites, giving a different significance to buried things, the animals, plants, the bones and shards of civilization. In natural as opposed to human history, there were no ruins, only, as Robert Chambers was to call it in the title of his book, *Vestiges . . . of Creation* (1844). After Cuvier, even the Catastrophists began to see in the litter and strata of the landscape evidence of creations as much as of destructions. Such science aroused primitive and universal instincts for biological immortality. The opposition to Darwin came from those who were unwilling to believe that some species had disappeared and were extinct, rather than from those who were offended by the idea of human evolution from lower forms of life. Poets and writers conceiving of nature in cyclical terms, either from study, observation, or merely inclination, poets such as Keats and Shelley, turned consciously to those ancient nature myths, especially the seasonal and procreative ones depicting the changing cycles as ritualistic marriage, birth, sacrifice, and death, the very myths the popular writers of romance and drama had unconsciously adopted to deal with their sense of alienation from the scientifically conceived natural world and the dislocated spiritual one.

CHAPTER IX

The Gothic

The Early Gothic Novel:
Horace Walpole and Ann Radcliffe

IN 1747, HORACE WALPOLE (1717–1797), son of the powerful Prime Minister, settled at Strawberry Hill on the Thames near Windsor, and began rebuilding his property into what he called a "little gothick Castel," adopting the style that had become sufficiently fashionable to appear in fiction as the home of Squire Allworthy, Tom Jones's foster father in Fielding's novel. For an age that still preferred regulation to self-expression, Batty Langley had codified and domesticated the gothic in *Ancient Architecture Restored and Improved by a Great Variety of Usefull Designs, Entirely New, in the Gothick Mode, for the Ornamenting of Buildings and Gardens* (1742) and in *Gothick Architecture Improved by Rules and Proportions* (1747).[1] But for Walpole, the appeal of the gothic was its irregularity, its sense of spontaneity and individualism, so he spent the next twenty years personalizing his castle, adding whimsical battlements here, a castellated round tower there, stained glass windows and pointed arches everywhere, breaking up the austere Palladian fronts that had dominated the English countryside. He filled it with relics and memorabilia, armor, weapons, a decorative baptismal font, a mantlepiece designed to look like stone, and wallpaper painted to look like three-dimensional iron fretwork.[2] As a monument, the castle was considerably more fragile than its occupant, for Walpole survived two or three sets of battlements, but periodic collapse enhanced its value, since antique

buildings, especially ruined ones, were supposed to remind
one of the futility of human achievement, stimulating the
agreeable melancholy that English gentlemen, however
favored, enjoyed cultivating. But philosophically, building
ruins and surrounding oneself with the refuse of earlier soci-
eties was merely an accommodation to the natural world as
it was then conceived, an adaptation to "a world lying in its
own Rubbish," as Burnet described it.

A belief in the supernatural seemed to accompany a preoc-
cupation with ruins, as if the instability of the material world
inspired a compensatory faith in another order. But for Hor-
ace Walpole and many of his imaginative contemporaries, belief
in the supernatural was also a reaction to a society that in its
enlightenment had chosen empirical over transcendental truth
and that had relegated the entire supernatural literary conven-
tion to the same position as children's literature. For Wal-
pole, as for many country gentry in the eighteenth century,
gothic architecture and antique collecting contributed to a
fantasy that was preferable to the degeneracy, corruption, and
the visible ruins of politics and the church with which many
of them had been involved. The invisible beings were a bonus.
In the gothic novel the prevailing architecture suggests the
medieval, usually a castle, and the supernatural, usually an
ancestral and avenging ghost. The novels in turn endowed
the buildings with a glamour and mystery they did not oth-
erwise possess.[3]

One evening in 1764, while sleeping among the antiques
in his castle, Walpole dreamt of a giant hand encased in armor
on the staircase, a fairly translucent dream for the compara-
tively hapless son of a tyrannical father. That evening he began
composing *The Castle of Otranto*. He published it anony-
mously two months later and created along the way a for-
mula for a gothic romance which is still in use in the twentieth
century. Claiming to have found the manuscript, Walpole
offered a fast-moving tale in which events take priority over
character, and special effects over events:[4] Manfred, Prince of
Otranto, discovers his sickly fifteen-year-old son dead in the
courtyard, crushed by a giant helmet with waving black
plumes. This scene initiates a novel full of otherwise inani-
mate objects expressing the wishes of the spiritual world: the
nose on a statue bleeds, an armor-clad foot appears in a gal-
lery, a skeleton dressed as a monk offers advice, an ancestral
portrait sighs, descends from its frame, and walks out of the
novel. Along with familiar Greek tragic themes of false
inheritance, blood guilt, retribution, mistaken identity, and

incest, equally familiar Shakespearean ghosts appear in infinite variations.[5]

The gothic, as initiated by Walpole, is an especially revealing example of that illusionary history to which Eiseley refers in the period before Darwin, including the naive supernaturalism, those projections of psychological states on nature and art that offered substitutes for real history. Here, as in subsequent gothic novels, appears the dislocated animation of fairy tale—things rise up and acquire power over people who gradually lose or abdicate control over themselves. A middle-aged bachelor spending his life in a little castle collecting other peoples' used and ancient things, Walpole had himself invested objects with the power to shape his life, to express his needs, to work out his identity, to relate to a society in which he had lost confidence. But the fantasy has social relevance as well, reflecting the middle-class insecurity over property, authority, and social status. In fact, novels and dramas, mostly gothic, dealing with matters of inheritance, increase noticeably in the eighteenth century, expressing the preconscious fears and desires of people living in a society that has suddenly become fluid, in which inherited status is being challenged by merit and money. Finally, *The Castle of Otranto* is a sexual fantasy, primarily masculine and hostile, though appealing to women in that it depicts a dominating and insensitive male villain holding a helpless, innocent, and fearful virgin in subjugation. Some writers would exceed Walpole in writing more demonic novels; others, mostly women, would attempt to domesticate the form.

Although Ann Radcliffe (1764–1823), born the year Walpole wrote *The Castle of Otranto,* lived an especially sheltered life, she was attuned to the tastes of her age, tastes she reflected and shaped as well. Married to the editor of a weekly newspaper and having no children, she was often alone at night and wrote to comfort herself. So reclusive was she that for the last thirteen years of her life she was reputed to be dead, having gone mad from an excess of imagination. In fact, after traveling to some of the landscapes that she had previously imagined, she felt she had no more to say, and stopped writing novels.[6] Starting in 1789, she wrote six major novels, a verse romance, a travel diary, and a collection of poems. They were all placed in some remote, mountainous, moonlit, idealized past. *The Mysteries of Udolpho,* her most influential novel, is set in sixteenth-century France and Italy. Emily St. Aubert is imprisoned in the Castle of Udolpho by the mysterious and morose Montoni, the captain of a band of thieves, who tries to coerce her to give up the property left to her by her late aunt, whom he had married for the same purpose. Menaced with abduction and rape by his bandits and his enemies, most of Emily's terror is nonetheless self-induced, for she imagines supernatural effects that actually have rational explanations. Emily's excessive imagination populates the castle, the major focus of the novel, with spirits and adventures, as if the genuine evil with which she was living were not sufficient. Arriving at Udolpho, just as the sun has sunk behind the mountains, Emily "gazed with melancholy awe"; "lighted up by the setting sun, the Gothic greatness of its features, and its mouldering walls of dark grey stone, rendered it a gloomy and sublime object. . . . Silent, lonely, and sublime, it seemed to stand the sovereign of the scene, and to frown defiance on all who dared to invade its solitary reign." The formal description, the taste for the sublime, and especially the evocation of sensibility contributed to the popularity of Mrs. Radcliffe's novels although they are obvious anachronisms, a projection of contemporary taste and characters on sixteenth-century figures.

Sensibility and the Gothic

Sensibility, as we have seen in our discussion of graveyard poetry, originally had a moral and philosophical basis in the benevolent theories of Lord Shaftesbury. It acquired an intellectual dimension during the middle of the eighteenth century when such philosophers as David Hume attempted to account for human behavior and human relationships without supernatural sanctions, arguing in *An Enquiry Concerning the Principles of Morals* (1751) and *An Enquiry Concerning Human Understanding* (1758), that the origins of morality are in feelings, that virtue is identified with pleasure, and vice with pain. By 1794, however, when Mrs. Radcliffe published *The Mysteries of Udolpho,* the idea of sensibility had degenerated into an "uncommon delicacy of mind," as she called it, "a ready degree of susceptivity," of which Emily St. Aubert and Valancourt, her sweetheart who tries to rescue her, had a considerable share.

Still, sensibility as a definition of character solved a tactical problem, especially for the popular novelists and dramatists; it allowed them to represent good and evil without any religious or spiritual overtones, merely as a capacity for feeling. Like the theater, then, the novel reflected the secularization of experience and contributed to it, offering as models of virtue an emotional elite—anxious, tearful, delicate, high-strung, accident-prone, self-involved men and women of such exquisite sensitivity they could only have inspired a generation of emotional cripples. Typically, the heroine of Henry Mackenzie's *Man of Feeling* (1771) laments: "I love to weep, I joy to grieve; it is my happiness, my delight, to have my heart broken in pieces." And typically, then, like James Thomson, whose poetry often appears in epigrams, Valancourt attributes to the twilight, "that delicious melancholy which no person, who had felt it once, would resign for the gayest pleasures. They awaken our best and purest feelings; disposing us to benevolence, pity, and friendship." And for two hundred years, this passive, tearful, self-regarding, and often useless creature became the popular hero of stage and novel, while the villain—Walpole's Manfred, Montoni/Schedoni in Mrs. Radcliffe's *The Italian,* Oswald in Wordsworth's *The Borderers,* Godwin's Caleb Williams, Shelley's Count Cenci, Maturin's Bertram, Byron's Childe Harold (Canto III)—is someone whose capacity for feeling is dormant, perverted, or depleted.

Although sensibility makes people vulnerable to such creatures, it may be in the end, as the Romantic writers were to illustrate, the major villain. "Those who really possess sensibility," Emily's father advised her before his death, "ought early to be taught, that it is a dangerous quality, which is continually extracting the excess of misery, or delight, from every surrounding circumstance. . . . We become the victims of our feelings unless we can in some degree command them." But she repeatedly pursues sensation for its own sake, believing that "a faint degree of terror . . . occupies and expands the mind, and elevates it to high expectation, [it] is purely sublime, and leads us, by a kind of fascination, to seek even the object from which we appear to shrink." Emily, who is so otherwise mindless, justifies her idle curiosity, the "ill-governed sensibility" against which her father warned her, by alluding to the sublime, an aesthetic category that, like sensibility, had a genuine philosophical and even moral basis but which, like sensibility, had been secularized and popularized.

The Sublime
and the Gothic Romance

The sublime, a term in classical rhetoric describing an elevated style, came in the eighteenth century to describe either a landscape that stimulates spiritual awareness or the literary work or painting that captures this elevating quality.[8] The sublime was chiefly associated with what the Catastrophists found most moving in nature: the volcanoes, the earthquakes, the storms, the mountains, caves, and oceans, reminders of God's power and wrath. But wild animals display sublimity, as do wars, famines, plagues, mysterious phenomena of all sorts that are irrational, inexplicable, powerful, vast, and mostly destructive. In his *Enquiry into the Origin of our Ideas of the Sublime and Beautiful* (1757), Edmund Burke defined the sublime as: "Whatever is fitted in any sort to excite the ideas of pain, and danger, that is to say, whatever is in any sort terrible, or is conversant about terrible objects, or operates in a manner analogous to terror, is a source of the *sublime;* that is, it is productive of the strongest emotion which the mind is capable of feeling. . . ."[9] Gothic architecture evokes sublime experiences in its towers and ruins, reflecting the wild and irregular aspects of nature, the aspirations and failures of mankind, the melancholy, superstition, and weight of orthodox Christianity. Burke's theory of the sublime was more psychological than theological: God was merely one idea that displayed the sublime characteristics of obscurity, power, duration, vastness, infinity, difficulty, and magnificence.[10] Beauty, on the other hand, was its opposite, inspiring love instead of fear and displaying order, proportion, clarity. This regulation and analysis of aesthetic experience, the self-observation it required, became so obsessive in popular literature and among the readers whose interests it reflected that, by 1818, it was merely another fashionable eccentricity parodied by T. L. Peacock in *Nightmare Abbey:* Scythrop, the young hero, having discovered a strange lady in his tower, "either was or ought to have been frightened; at all events, he was astonished; and astonishment, though not in itself fear, is nevertheless a good stage towards it, and is, indeed, as it were, the half-way house between respect and terror, according to Mr. Burke's graduated scale of the sublime" (p. 210).

After Mrs. Radcliffe, the gothic romance would be populated by such delicate creatures in search of sublime experiences. In creating suspense, arousing curiosity, implying supernatural agencies that do not exist and then dispelling all danger by a rational explanation for otherwise mysterious events, Mrs. Radcliffe accomplished in the novel what Coleridge set out to do in the *Lyrical Ballads,* as he recollected in the *Biographia Literaria,* to depict the way a human being would behave "who, from whatever source of delusion, has at any time believed himself under supernatural agency" (p. 168). And she did it well. Her admirers ranged from Sir Walter Scott to Keats, whose *Eve of St. Agnes* was, according to one scholar, influenced by the *Mysteries of Udolpho*,[11] to Jane Austen, whose sensible hero in *Northanger Abbey,* the Reverend Henry Tilney, admits having read all her works, and most of them with great pleasure.

The appeal of Mrs. Radcliffe's novels, like the appeal of the popular theater which they both influenced and reflected, is partly ritualistic, and the myth they represented, a common one, the romance, related, like the pantomime and the melodrama, to the ancient nature myths and the fertility rites they describe: the castle is fallen and sterile earth held in thrall by a serpent/dragon/villain, Montoni, and liberated by Emily the hero/heroine who journeys, suffers, and marries Valancourt, recovering her property, the symbolic start of a new cycle.[12] The symmetry, repetition, formality of language, lack of character development or complication, and lengthy natural descriptions are appropriate to ritual expression, and the myth itself appropriate to the personal situation of the author as well as the times in which she lived. Childless, married to a man who could spend little time with her, often alone, and certainly imprisoned by the social conventions that prevented her from acting independently, the romance provided a means by which she imaginatively overcame the sterility and darkness of a life without progeny that seemed destined for extinction. And on the public level, this recurrent pattern of primitive thinking, appearing during the period from about 1760 to 1830, is symptomatic of the sudden dislocation, challenge to, or loss of faith in the theological interpretation of nature before there was a scientific one to replace it.

Gothic Terror:
William Beckford and Matthew "Monk" Lewis

But not all gothic reflected this romance tradition and the nature myths from which it was derived. In fact, much of what we now consider gothic was at emnity with nature, creativity, and growth. In the hands of a resentful and warped creature such as William Beckford, who referred to Walpole as "the cursed pest of Strawberry Hill,"[13] gothic, the popular acceptance of terror and the supernatural, became a means of escaping from the elementary moral restraints that keep civilized people from torturing, murdering, and mutilating one another out of idle curiosity. Beckford's book, *The History of Caliph Vathek* (1786), while reflecting the popular taste, is intensely personal. Born in 1760, the son of the Lord Mayor of London, grandson of a Jamaican colonialist, Beckford lost his father and gained his inheritance when he was only eleven.[14] A handsome, charming young man, his money was well invested in an education that was privately tailored for him, employing as tutors the best professional in each discipline. He studied music with Mozart, architecture with Sir William Chambers, and painting with Alexander Cozens, while acquiring facility in several modern languages, speaking and writing French with impeccable ease. At eighteen, he fell in love with an eleven-year-old boy, William Courtenay, a relationship encouraged by Louisa Beckford, his cousin's wife, who became his mistress and partner in decadence. For three days, at Christmas, 1781, they gathered an odd assortment of friends at Fonthill, transformed into a palace of sensual delights by Philippe de Loutherbourg, the stage designer at the Drury Lane, with flowers, delicacies, diaphanous drapes, special lighting effects, Italian musicians—an elaborate self-indulgent illusion for the apparent purpose of erotic play.

Shortly after, Beckford wrote *The History of Caliph Vathek* in French in three days, as he claimed, a book so full of mayhem and butchery, so horrid, as he admits in the Preface, that he trembled while relating it. The background is the timeless and imaginary oriental world of the *Arabian Nights,* a twilight zone of time and place that conventionally allowed Europeans a moral holiday. Vathek, along with his many wives, lived in a palace composed of five pavilions, each dedicated to the gratification of a different sense, and a central tower where his mother Carathis, a necromancer with particularly ghoulish tastes, attended by fifty one-eyed-mute negresses and many eunuchs, performed a disgusting sacrifice of skeletons, mummies, and venemous oils while dressed only in her underclothes. One hundred and forty dedicated subjects, fearing that their master would be burned, mount the tower carrying buckets of water. Collapsing at the top from the stench of the sacrifice and from exhaustion, their bodies are added to the fire. Since the novel was not intended for publication (it was printed without Beckford's permission in 1786), it is clearly a private sadistic fantasy that he is here fulfilling. But just as the ending, a conventional one of symbolic retribution, conflicted with the novel itself, so Beckford's conventional side—the one who would marry the loyal and agreeable Lady Margaret Gordon, serve in Parliament, and father two daughters who were devoted to him—seemed constantly in conflict with the deviate.

As a monument to his Christmas revels and to his own past, he built Fonthill Abbey, designed by James Wyatt, whose imperfect understanding of stresses and forces led to its collapse. Five hundred workmen were engaged around the clock in a spectacle of activity that delighted Beckford, especially the torches, the scaffolding, the echoes, and spaces. He engaged Turner to paint it while it was being constructed and Martin to paint it afterward. The completed building had a soaring octagonal tower with four massive transepts, with miles of walls and niches and windows where he could display his many odd mementos. Ultimately, it was surrounded by a twelve-mile wall within which wild animals found refuge along with a series of deformed retainers and a pet dwarf. Beckford lived at Fonthill from 1807 to 1822, when, his financial resources depleted, he moved to Bath where he died in 1844, a contemporary of Robert Browning, in whose dramatic monologues of greed, lust, spite, anger, disappointment, and jealousy he would have found himself reflected.

In 1796, Beckford was replaced in Parliament by Matthew Gregory Lewis, author of *The Castle Spectre* (1797) a gothic melodrama that helped introduce forbidden topics to the English stage. Like Beckford, he was born with many advantages and educated more as a European than an Englishman. In 1792, he was in Weimar learning German, translating the popular ghost ballads inspired by his countryman, Bishop Thomas Percy's *Reliques of Ancient English Poetry* (1765). And in 1794, he held a diplomatic post at The Hague, where he met the French aristocrats who had escaped the Revolution and the Reign of Terror, a time in France when, as Wordsworth described it, "Domestic carnage . . . filled all the year / With feast-days" *(The Prelude,* X, 330–31). The French emigrées carried with them an association with terror, in part because they had escaped the assassinations, arrests, torture, slaughter, and injustice that had been visited upon them as a class but also because of their familiarity with secret and conspiratorial societies, with corrupt clergy, and with an even more decadent nobility about which they enjoyed gossiping, such figures as the Marquis de Sade. When he was in Paris, Lewis had acquired the ten-volume *La nouvelle Justine, ou les Malheurs de la vertu suive de l'histoire de Juliette, sa soeur, ou les prospérités du vice* (1797; single editions of *Justine* and of *Juliette* had appeared in 1791 and 1796). De Sade's lurid philosophy, the exhilaration he found in torture, humiliation, persecution, suffering, and the victimization of women, initiated a new and macabre direction for the literature of feeling.[15] Along with the supernaturalism of contemporary German literature and the depravity of contemporary French literature, Lewis was influenced by the well-plotted native gothic tradition. In ten weeks, while attending to his diplomatic chores, Lewis wrote *Ambrosio; or The Monk,* which appears to be a diabolic answer to the sentimental *Vicar of Wakefield* by Oliver Goldsmith (1766).

Ambrosio, the Abbot of a Capuchin monastery in Madrid, whose eloquence, virtue, and spiritual perfection attract Satan's attention, is turned into a lustful and insatiable fiend when seduced by Matilda, a noble lady who enters the monastery dressed as a young novice, Rosario. He seduces and murders the blameless fifteen-year-old Antonia, and murders her mother only to discover that she was also his mother and that Antonia was, therefore, his sister. Both Matilda and Ambrosio are apprehended, and, as they are about to be burned by the Inquisition, he sells his soul to Lucifer, who flies off with him to a wild moonlit mountainside where he reveals himself as the instigator of all Ambrosio's crimes. Holding Ambrosio in his talons, Satan drops him into a ravine where he lies broken, bleeding, helpless, "venting his rage in blasphemy and curses," for seven days, until, mutilated by insects that devour his flesh and eagles that blind him, he is washed away in a rainstorm. The author implies that Ambrosio is not so much a villain as an instrument of an evil that has become palpable in the world and against which piety offers no protection.

A few reviewers complained about the realism, the fascination with decaying flesh, physical corruption, obscenity, blasphemy, and pollution; but these were the elements that drew the gentry to "Monk" Lewis's dramas where they shrieked, fainted, and applauded what could only have been a vicarious expression of rage against the church, against the entire philosophy of benevolence and sensibility, against the models of virtue being promoted by Hannah More and Maria Edgeworth in their educational pamphlets, against everything else that was being defended by the sanctimonious writers and reviewers who claimed to represent public taste.[16] Lewis himself saw no contradiction between his novel and his role as a gentleman, philanthropist, and public servant; he signed the second edition as a Member of Parliament and enjoyed hospitality at the best houses in Great Britain.

Although the reviewers depicted Beckford and Lewis as

evil, obscene, depraved, or even demonically possessed, they merely represented a public that was being spiritually and aesthetically dispossessed by over a century of rational, empirical, and democratic thinking. Art and even the artists themselves were no longer the heirs of a universal spiritual tradition, transcendental ideals, absolute moral and ethical systems, and supernatural authority. Terror, an aesthetic experience, the major component of the sublime, aroused by reminders of God's power and wrath, had become secularized like the sublime itself, and cultivated for its own sake. After this generation, these dispossessed authors would remain a potent force in English literature, and many whose work would ultimately come to define the central tradition of art and letters, authors such as Wordsworth, Tennyson, and Matthew Arnold, would experience comparable periods of bewilderment, a time when (to paraphrase Thea's description of the fallen Titans in Keats's *Hyperion*) heaven was parted from them, and the earth knew them not (ll. 54–56), a time when, as Keats described it in the epistle "To John Hamilton Reynolds," "imagination brought / Beyond its proper bound, yet still confine'd / Lost in a sort of Purgatory blind, / Cannot refer to any standard law / Of earth or heaven" (ll. 78–80).

The Grotesque: Henry Fuseli's *Nightmare*

The mental phenomenon between sleep and wakefulness described by Keats is the same as the disjointed images, the unlikely associations, confusions, distortions, and exaggerations, the fantasies associated with the grotesque, a style that turns character into caricature. It is the grotesque, rather than the sublime or the pathetic, that we find in the novels of Beckford, Lewis, even Dickens, in the gothic melodrama, and in the cartoon. For the same period that produced the grotesque in the gothic novel also produced the cartoon, both forms acquiring considerable influence through the existence of a popular press. While the engorged, bad-tempered, and bestial Vathek may disgust the readers of Sterne or Goldsmith, he would be familiar to the crowds who huddled in the doorways of the printshops to see the latest irreverent attack on greedy, pompous, and hypocritical public figures by James Gillray (1757–1815) especially, but also William Hogarth, Thomas Rowlandson (1757–1827), and George Cruikshank (1792–1878), who ultimately illustrated the domesticated grotesquerie in Charles Dickens.[17] The grotesque, then, is exaggeration, distortion, and over-simplification in an amoral context. The suffering, mischief, and disorder it depicts arouse neither sympathy nor terror because however much the grotesque resembles social reality in its disregard of consequences and morality, it more closely resembles the amoral world of animals and insects which frequently appear as metaphors for human behavior.

Visually, the grotesque was, perhaps, best represented by Henry Fuseli, born in Zurich in 1741 into a family of artists, and friend of Johann Kaspar Lavater, who was to distinguish himself as a Protestant mystic and the author of *Essays on Physiognomy* (1792), a book on the "science" of interpreting character from facial conformations.[18] In London, he supported himself mostly by doing translations for Joseph Johnson of such works as Winckelmann's *Reflections on the Painting and Sculptures of the Greeks* (1765), which he helped to popularize in England. Through Johnson he met the English radicals Tom Paine, William Godwin, William Blake, and Mary Wollstonecraft, and published an essay in defense of Rousseau.

From eight years of study in Italy, he brought the heroic and historical vision of Michelangelo, which he translated into his own personal and slightly bizarre idiom to illustrate the Biblical and literary themes that the Royal Academy encouraged. Horace Walpole thought his *Satan Starting from the Touch of Ithuriel's Spear* (1780), "Extravagant and Ridiculous"; his *Lady Macbeth Walking in Her Sleep* (1784), "Execrable"; and his *Mandrake* (1785), "Shockingly mad."[19] However shocking his work, he was ultimately elected Professor of Painting at the Royal Academy and given the administrative post of Keeper by George III. Never a great painter, he was learned in theology, classics, languages, English literature, and entymology, an interest he acquired during his childhood and cultivated as an adult, collecting illuminated books on insects, and raising moths, rare ones, in his living room. Eccentric in both appearance and behavior, he was also shy and vain, aloof and aggressive, quick-tempered, sarcastic, vulgar, and insensitive. His beaked nose, bulging blue eyes, slouched figure, trembling hands, and disheveled white hair contributed to the terror he inspired in his students, who suspected him of being a satanist. Benjamin Robert Haydon, who was to become Keats's mentor for a while, recalls going to Fuseli's home in 1805, expecting to meet "a sort of gifted wild beast" and waiting in "a gallery or showroom, enough to frighten anybody at Twilight. Galvanised devils—malicious witches brewing their incantations—Satan briding Chaos, and springing upwards like a pyramid of fire—Lady Macbeth—Paolo and Francesca—Falstaff and Mrs. Quickly—humour, pathos, terror, blood, and murder, met one at every look! . . . I fancied Fuseli himself to be a giant. I heard his footsteps and saw a little bony hand slide round the edge of the door, followed by a little white-headed lion-faced man in an old flannel dressing-gown, tied round his waist with a piece of rope, and upon his head the bottom of Mrs. Fuseli's workbasket."[20]

But he inspired love in Mary Wollstonecraft, who approached Mrs. Fuseli, a former model about whom little is known, with the proposition that she became a member of the household as Fuseli's "spiritual" concubine. Fuseli claimed that she was "a philosophical sloven," when he met her and that he had transformed her into a charming and beautiful woman; she claimed that she had never met a man with such "noble qualities," "quickness of comprehension and lively sympathy."[21] And Blake claimed that Fuseli was "the only Man that e'er I knew / Who did not make me almost spew." But while Blake could cope with Fuseli's irreverence, rages, and profanity, and enjoyed his admiration, he felt threatened by his artistic influence, which was apparently profound.

Because of the particular form of the grotesque with which he worked, the amalgamation of human and animal features, of dream and waking reality, Fuseli is central in our understanding of the particular direction of the gothic in the 1790s. Although he considered dreams "one of the most unexplored regions of art," he did not believe they were suitable subjects for art unless so boldly embodied that they appeared real or unless they were Michaelangelo's, expressing "sublime sentiments."[22] Yet he worked from dreams, rather than life or nature, leading some critics to believe that he was revolutionary as well as disagreeable. His most popular and possibly characteristic painting, *The Nightmare,* represents a dream, a fantasy, and, given the frequency with which it is reproduced, a public fantasy as well. The first of several versions Fuseli was to produce during his career was exhibited as an oil painting in 1781 at the Royal Academy. It depicts a woman sleeping or unconscious or even dead, but clearly helpless, vanquished, exhausted, stretched out on her back across a bed, the covers thrown off, her arms up over her head; squatting on her torso is a dark and simian-like imp, looking out of the picture with an expression that is both angry and surprised, observed from the background by his horse, the "nightmare," peeking through the curtain, curious, impatient, its eyes gleaming. In later versions, the horse-head becomes more central to the picture, brilliantly illuminated, nostrils flaring, pushing through the curtain with vacant eyes and exposed teeth; and the woman appears more voluptuous than in the earlier version, her body too contorted to be alive or conscious, her head hanging down and twisted to the side while her arms, trailing on the floor, appear to be raised in an imploring or submissive gesture. In yet another version, the horse is escaping, the fiend on his back, while two naked women, apparently lovers, stir, one awakened and dismayed. The meaning of the paintings probably depends on whether one sees them as the dreams of a sexually repressed or aroused woman, or as the sadistic and bestial fantasy of the painter; in either case, they reflect that purgatorial state to which Keats referred in the epistle "To John Hamilton Reynolds," one in which the imagination is lost, in a lawless world between earth and heaven, dealing in the images we have called the grotesque.

Fuseli's fantasy, whatever it represents personally, is not a delusion, nor does it depict an emissary, ghost, goblin, or avenging spirit from another world.[23] Rather, at a time when few people even suspected the existence of a secret and secular inner life, its dimensions and power, Fuseli offered a projection of a profound and troubled mind. It was an incarnation of a psychological event, an emanation (to borrow a term from his friend Blake) created by a human being and taking its retribution by haunting him, by requiring the artist repeatedly to give it form over his long creative life. The theme of the artist haunted by his own creation or emanation will appear in Mary Shelley's *Frankenstein,* Polidori's *The Vampyre,* Hogg's *Confessions of a Justified Sinner,* and other major gothic novels of the period.

Shifts in Gothic Taste

Before this particular vision of the inner life found expression in the novel, there was a prodigious change in the consciousness of writers and the reading public. For reasons about which we can only speculate, more than twenty years elapsed between Mrs. Radcliffe's *The Italian* (1797) and the next major gothic novel, Mary Shelley's *Frankenstein* (1818). During that time English life itself acquired gothic dimensions as the war against France escalated, the wounded and maimed returned to a free country where the poor were hungry, often home-less vagrants, and where the children were abandoned, dis-figured, and tormented in factories, workhouses, and mines; where the King was mad, blind, and sequestered in Windsor Castle conversing with the dead while his children, their friends and mistresses, populated the country houses and clubs with other children whose lineage was as mixed and obscure as any gothic hero, or lived in artificial ruins dividing their attention among lapdogs, pet monkeys, and costumes; where an illiterate peasant could be hanged for stealing a turnip or become a prophet by predicting an earthquake; where gas and steam and electricity were animating the inanimate and enslaving the people who created them; where galvanism (battery-generated electricity) made corpses smile and mes-merisim (hypnosis) made people look dead; where Jeremy Bentham, one of the greatest philosophical minds of a gen-eration that sought the permanent destruction of tyranny, spent most of his life designing the perfect prison; where London, Birmingham, and Manchester, the most advanced industrial centers in the world, lay under such a pall of smoke that they were used by Gustave Doré to illustrate Dante's *Inferno;* where graves were robbed on such a regular basis that the London poor suspected medical schools of starting epidemics to replenish their supply of corpses for the dissecting room. In other words, the real horrors had exceeded the fictional ones, and the public needed an adaptive mechanism, not an escapist one; it needed drama, not novels.

During the twenty years from 1797 to 1818 (coinciding incidentally with the last twenty years of "Monk" Lewis's life and his career as a dramatist) gothic melodrama domi-nated the stage, the patent theaters, the minors, and the "blood tubs," both contemporary dramas and Shakespearean or Jacobean adaptations. The gothic, then, found a popular audience, one that responded to the ritual nature of the drama, one that, having learned to read, if at all, from the Cheap Respository Tracts, was starved for the emotional excite-ment of gothic. Gothic drama not only helped them cope with the real world in which they labored, but it also pro-vided, in its representation of the upper classes, an outlet for the rage that was growing among the working and middle classes against the brutally indifferent heirs of the princes and knights, the ladies and maidens who were depicted torturing and destroying one another according to gothic conventions. The gothic also found an audience in the new specialized publications such as the *Lady's Monthly Museum* and the *Lady's*

Magazine[24] that published the romances serially while enterprising publishers offered six penny condensations to clerks, shopkeepers, and schoolboys.

Parodying Gothic:
Jane Austen and Thomas Love Peacock

By 1797, the original audience of educated and middle-class readers that helped create the genre, had become sated, complaining, like Coleridge after writing reviews in the *Critical,* to be "most weary of the terrible," "surfeited with dungeons, old castles, solitary Houses by the Sea Side, and Caverns and Woods, and extraordinary characters and all the tribe of Horror and Mystery" *(CL,* I, 318).[25] Jane Austen responded with *Northanger Abbey,* a parody completed around 1798, when the fashion for gothic novels had peaked. She sold it to a publisher in 1803 for £10, repurchased it in 1816, when the publisher claimed he was under no obligation to bring it out, and died before it was published in December, 1817, the very year when a new and different gothic novel emerged. Miss Austen's parody was directed at the readers as much as the novels, those who became corrupted by them, who developed false expectations of experience from reading them, who lost the capacity to appreciate the commonplace and the genuine pain of ordinary lives.

A learned spectator of fashionable life and letters, Jane Austen was admirably suited to write such a parody.[26] Born in 1775, the youngest of seven children of a country parson, she possessed, according to her brother Henry Thomas Austen, "a most exquisite taste in every species of literature." Aside from an unsatisfactory year away at school with her elder sister, Cassandra, she was educated at home, raised as a middle class lady, attending balls, visiting friends, gossiping, writing letters, and helping to care for her family. In 1801, her father retired to Bath, a provincial city where English people went mostly for fresh air, amusement, flirtation, and the architecture of John Nashe. After his death, she settled with her mother and sister Cassandra at Chawton, a village about fifty miles from London, and spent the rest of her life writing and revising her novels, visiting her brothers, and assisting her family, in the ways expected of a maiden aunt. Henry, who supervised the publication of her novels, lived in London, married to the widow of a French aristocrat who had been guillotined in the Revolution; she visited them often and attended the theater with them. Her brother Edward, who gave them the cottage at Chawton, had been adopted by wealthy cousins, inherited their country estates, and was left a widower with twelve children. According to her brother Henry, in the biographical sketch accompanying the publication of *Northanger Abbey*, "she was formed for elegant and rational society, excelling in conversation as in composition"; "her reading was very extensive in history and belles lettres, and her memory extremely tenacious." His description of her appearance is most intriguing, resembling in its detailed obscurity one of her own heroines: "Her stature was that of true elegance. It could not have been increased without exceeding the middle height. Her carriage and deportment were quiet, yet graceful. Her features were separately good. Their assemblage produced an unrivalled expression of that cheerfulness, sensibility, and benevolence, which were her real characteristics. Her complexion was of the finest texture. It might with truth be said, that her eloquent blood spoke through her modest cheek." She died at the age of forty-one.

Jane Austen had very little to do with literary people, writing for her own amusement, publishing reluctantly, and only in the last six years of her life: *Sense and Sensibility* (1811); *Pride and Prejudice* (1813); *Mansfield Park* (1814); *Emma* (1816); *Persuasion* and *Northanger Abbey,* posthumously (1818). While she was not a professional writer, she held her art in high esteem and was, therefore, legitimately irritated at the delay in publishing *Northanger Abbey* itself, reflected in her "Advertisement": "That any bookseller should think it worth while to purchase what he did not think it worth while to publish seems extraordinary. But with this, neither the author nor the public have any other concern than as some observation is necessary upon those parts of the work which thirteen years have made comparatively obsolete. The public are entreated to bear in mind that thirteen years have passed since it was finished, and many more since it was begun, and that during that period, places, manners, books, and opinions have undergone considerable changes." In fact, the parody has begun: by apologizing for the obscurity of people, places, and fashions that are only thirteen years old, for the delay in publication caused by an irrational bookseller, she has already begun to demonstrate the foolishness of that gothic convention of pretending that the novels were retrieved from ancient manuscripts found in old trunks, or based on stories from the middle ages, but populated by contemporary people with modern tastes and attitudes.

Catherine Moreland, the heroine, raised in a conventional

middle-class family surrounded by "the common feelings of common life," has "by nature nothing heroic about her." Nonetheless, she spent the years between fifteen and seventeen "in training for a heroine; she read all such works as heroines must read to supply their memories with those quotations which are so serviceable and so soothing in the vicissitudes of their eventful lives." Catherine's life is not especially eventful; she goes to Bath for the social season where she acquires a suitor, Henry Tilney, a sensible, rational clergyman who invites her to visit his home, Northanger Abbey. To Catherine's disappointment, Northanger Abbey turns out to be an ordinary country home, comfortably restored with nothing soaring or mouldering.[27] But she assumes the role of gothic heroine, snooping around the house on the suspicion that General Tilney had murdered his wife. "Remember that we are English, we are Christians," Mr. Tilney admonishes her, "Consult your own understanding, your own sense of the probable, your own observation of what is passing around you—does our education prepare us for such atrocities? Do our laws connive at them? Could they be perpetrated without being known in a country like this, where social and literary intercourse is on such a footing; where everyman is surrounded by a neighbourhood of voluntary spies, and where roads and newspapers lay everything open?" (pp. 199–201). Unfortunately, Catherine's education, largely undirected and joyless like most of her generation's, has prepared her for little else but such atrocities; any of the beleaguered populists such as Cobbett, for example, or Shelley, would have answered yes to all the Reverend Tilney's naive questions.

Catherine Moreland displays the mistakes good people make when they judge life by literary standards, a genuine hazard in this first age of the popular press, and of concern to many writers, perhaps none more so than the writers who helped make it possible: Maria Edgeworth, Hannah More, Mrs. Trimmer, Mrs. Barbauld, that "wretched crew" about whom Lamb complained, for their literature was calculated to teach a whole generation of English children how to live in the world and led them to believe they could learn to function in society from reading books. Catherine Moreland, from whatever cause, is simply one of many susceptible to literary influence, someone who was reading the right books for the wrong reasons. Unable to interpret the most common social signals, she becomes vulnerable to the afflictions of real life, to artifice, duplicity, and greed. She learns in the course of the novel to value the ordinary, "to love a hyacinth." "You have gained a new source of enjoyment," Tilney comments, "and it is well to have as many holds upon happiness as possible." At their wedding, "the bells rang and everybody smiled," and the narrator concludes: "To begin perfect happiness at the respective ages of twenty-six and eighteen, is to do pretty well." Catherine does not give up reading novels, for that is an activity Jane Austen values, but she does learn to value the world that she was born into, "the common feelings of common life," "the very world," as Wordsworth said in *The Prelude,* "which is the world / Of all of us,—the place in which, in the end, / We find our happiness, or not at all" (X, 726–28).

Thomas Love Peacock, the other major parodist of the gothic, is more concerned with authors and literature than with the reading public, authors both as readers and writers who reflect such fashionable concerns as medievalism, supernaturalism, sensibility, melancholia, and the sublime.[28] His novels offer personifications of these attitudes, caricatures of the public and primarily literary figures who embody them. His purpose, however, is not at all different from Jane Austen's, from Wordsworth's, from many of the writers and all the humorists of the Romantic period: "to reconcile man as he is to the world as it is," as Mr. Hilary says in *Nightmare Abbey;* and the world, as he saw it, was not quite so gloomy, or philosophical, or sensitive, or passionate, as writers such as Byron, Shelley, and Coleridge had been depicting. These writers bedevil themselves, Peacock says, disregarding the world as it is, setting up false ideals that can never be realized: "To rail against humanity for not being abstract perfection, and against human love for not realising all the splendid visions of the poets of chivalry, is to rail at the summer for not being all sunshine, and at the rose for not being always in bloom" (*Nightmare Abbey,* pp. 225–26).

An unusual combination of experience, education, and friendships led Peacock to a position from which he could view the gothic and philosophical excesses of his contemporaries with amusement and objectivity. Aside from some early poems on ruins and melancholy, Peacock avoided the fashionable excesses of his generation, largely because he was self-educated, mainly in classical literature. In 1812, he met Shelley and through him many of the philosophers, writers, and eccentrics who were to populate his novels, starting in 1816 with *Headlong Hall;* followed by *Melincourt* (1817); *Nightmare Abbey* (1818); *Crotchet Castle* (1831); and *Gryll Grange* (1861). To the life of letters and speculation, he brought the practical skills developed when he joined the East India Company, which allowed him to support his invalid wife, two daughters, and a son. Mary Ellen, his favorite daughter, married George Meredith, whose *Modern Love,* a sonnet sequence published the year after her death, describes the collapse of their marriage and her elopement with her lover.

By the time Peacock died at age eighty-one, he had won the friendship and admiration of an exceptional range of people: he had dined with Jeremy Bentham on a weekly basis in London; worked at East India House with James Mill (and, as an executive, initiated a steamship line to India); and inspired through his playful "Four Ages of Poetry" (1820) one of the most profound aesthetic statements of the period, Shelley's *Defense of Poetry.* Shelley, whose memoirs Peacock published in *Fraser's Magazine* (1858–1862) to correct contemporary gossip, left perhaps the most apt description of him:

> . . . his fine wit
> Makes such a wound, the knife is lost in it;
> A strain too learned for a shallow age,
> Too wise for selfish bigots—let his page
> Which charms the chosen spirits of the time
> Fold itself up for the serener clime
> Of years to come, and find its recompense
> In that just expectation.
>   ("Letter to Maria Gisborne," ll. 237–47)

Although written twenty years later, *Nightmare Abbey* appeared in the same year as Jane Austen's *Northanger Abbey,* 1818, in fact the same year as Mary Shelley's *Frankenstein,* a novel that would make both their complaints obsolete. The novel is set at Nightmare Abbey, "a venerable family mansion, in a highly picturesque state of semi-dilapidation." It is inhabited by Christopher Glowery, Esq., a widower, and his son, Scythrop, named after an ancestor who had hanged himself out of boredom and whose skull had been made into a punch bowl. They are attended by servants selected on the basis of "a long face and a dismal name," Raven, Crow, Skillet, Mattocks, Graves, and Diggory Deathshead, who was dismissed when Mr. Glowery discovered that he had been cheerful. We first meet Scythrop, who represents Shelley, sitting under a tower "ruinous and full of owls," reading *The Sorrows of Young Werther,* and suffering from unrequited love, and so he is again at the end of the novel, in spite of meeting the very suitable Celinda Toobad, "a lovely, serious creature, in a fine state of high dissatisfaction with the world, and everything in it." Such creatures, Peacock illustrates, how-ever obsessed they are with love, are too self-involved to actually experience it.

Both Jane Austen and Peacock explain indirectly the shift of taste in the gothic novel when it reappears after 1817. The kind of evil explored in the eighteenth-century gothic romance, the depravity and satanic forces invoked both by novelists and by gothic melodramatists, were no longer effective. Such evil had no spiritual, no metaphysical status; rather, it was equated with a defect of character, misapplied intelligence, a temporary lapse of will, a negative environment, or simply an inappropriate social or political context. The supernatural element had come to express a psychological or sociological rather than a spiritual state.

The Psychological Gothic:
Mary Shelley

In many ways no less ridiculous, Peacock's *Nightmare Abbey* had a contemporary analogue in Villa Diodati on Lake Leman in Switzerland, temporary residence of Lord Byron, now a notorious outcast from English society; Percy Shelley, a poet who was hardly known at all; his mistress, Mary Godwin and their six- month- old son; Claire Clairmont, Mary's half sister pregnant with Byron's child; John Polidori, a preco-cious young physician and Byron's traveling companion; and, for a brief visit in August, "Monk" Lewis. There they passed the long rainy days and nights in conversation about philos-ophy, science, religion, and literature; they rowed, walked, told tales, and proposed a contest in which each would write his own ghost story.[29] Two major gothic works resulted: Mary Shelley's *Frankenstein: or The Modern Prometheus* (1818) and John Polidori's *The Vampyre* (1819), both exploring the per-petuation of biological as opposed to spiritual life. The idea of biological immortality was nearly as interesting scientifi-cally and philosophically as creation theory, for the study of fossil remains led inevitably to the study of inherited charac-teristics and evolution, or biological survival. Mary Godwin and Polidori, like Beckford, Lewis, Fuseli, Keats, Byron, and Shelley lived in that long transition period when the world and human experience were explained by two irreconcilable histories, natural and spiritual, lived, like Keats's Titans in *Hyperion,* parted from heaven but aliens on the earth. While Wordsworth, Jane Austen, Peacock, and even Keats tried to reconcile "man as he is to the world as it is," the others, as

Keats said, could not "refer to any standard law / Of earth or heaven." Southey, a rational deist and wary of religious superstition claimed poignantly, "in flying from idolatry, what a fearful chasm we have left between man and God! What a void we have made in the universe," a void haunted by satanic dreams, charnel visions, live burials.[30] Some writers filled that void with god-men, Promethean figures, even Lucifer himself, figures who were immortal, who possessed both human and divine knowledge, but who were aliens in both realms.

Frankenstein had a personal dimension as well, one that has piqued the curiosity of many,[31] for Mary was just a young mother of eighteen when she wrote the novel, and she had little writing experience. Her mother, Mary Wollstonecraft, died eleven days after giving birth to her in 1797, the year of the last major gothic novels. Raised by William Godwin, the resourceful but impatient Mary Jane Clairmont whom he married, Mary's childhood was confused and unhappy, beset by financial and familial difficulties. Nonetheless, by age sixteen she was sufficiently educated and charming to win the love of Percy Shelley, age nineteen, a disciple of Godwin, an atheist, a vegetarian, with a small income, a pregnant wife, a child, and a history of dedicating himself to idealistic but losing causes. They courted by the grave of Mary's mother, eloped, endured separation, poverty, and the death of an infant child, before retreating to Villa Diodati with their second child. Returning to England with an unfinished *Frankenstein,* they encountered two suicides, Fanny Imlay, Mary's other half sister, and Harriet Shelley, several months pregnant, drowned in the Serpentine in Hyde Park. Within less than a month, Mary and Percy were married, and while awaiting the birth of their third child, she completed *Frankenstein,* published the following March (1818). Over the next five years, Shelley drowned; two more children died; and Mary, a widow at twenty-five, returned to England with their one surviving child. *Frankenstein* had already been adapted for the stage.

Mary Godwin seemed to have born in a cycle of birth and death, a cycle in which death was repeatedly overtaking birth, in which one life was gained at the expense of another. To Mary Godwin, to her mother, to most women of hers and succeeding generations, birth was often a fatal event, and if the mothers survived, it was often only to bury their own dead children. The fantasy of an unmarried man creating life in a laboratory must have been a very appealing one. Creating life out of death, assembling his being out of corpses, reversing the life processes, Dr. Frankenstein, a student of natural philosophy, shapes the monstrous creature who then plagues and destroys everything he loves. The monster escapes from his creator and educates himself by reading *The Sorrows of Young Werther,* from which he acquired the refinements of sensibility; Plutarch's *Lives,* from which he acquired a concept of nobility; and *Paradise Lost,* from which he recognized the difference between himself and the true Adam, envying his perfection. Measuring himself against alien fictions, he assumes them as his own, and concludes that although he is innocent, he is a "fallen angel" driven "from joy for no misdeed."

Along with her intense personal experience, Mary Godwin brought a great deal of learning, especially in literature, to her novel, reading in classical, Biblical, and gothic texts, the *Arabian Nights,* Milton, Rousseau, Goethe, Coleridge, Beckford, Scott, Mrs. Radcliffe, "Monk" Lewis, Byron, Shelley, and Godwin, her father, leading one critic, Robert Kiely, to conclude, *"Frankenstein* seems a little book to have born up under such a mixed and mighty company of sponsors, midwives, and ancestors."[32] So many obvious sources demonstrate how inadequate the existing literature was to contemporary experience, certainly to a contemporary woman's experience, for her sympathies in the end lay with the monster, as much a victim of literary experience as Catherine Moreland.

John Polidori's *The Vampyre*

Although *The Vampyre* (1819), the other product of the writing contest at Villa Diodati, also demonstrates the penalties of biological immortality, the interpenetration of life and death, it does not offer such an original conception as the monster in *Frankenstein,* and its debts are to folklore rather than to the literary tradition. Originating in the Mideast, the idea of the vampire arrived in Western Europe offering a plausible explanation for many physical or psychological disorders,[33] such as tuberculosis, anemia, cancer, stroke, and depression. According to legend, the vampire is possibly a suicide, a heretic, or someone victimized by another vampire, whose body is possessed by an evil spirit that perpetuates itself through sucking blood from otherwise innocent people, usually close friends, family members, or lovers, who invite him to enter their homes. Arriving at midnight by the light of a full moon, the source of his energy, he transfixes the victim with a hypnotic stare and, after drawing blood, usually from the neck, leaves the victim exhausted, possibly dead, and often a vampire as well. A vampire can be overcome by a religious icon, garlic or any other handy magical herb, sunlight, or, in Christian countries, by a priest. He must then be destroyed in his grave by driving a stake through his heart, decapitating him, burning his body, or simply turning him over so that he faces downwards. Metaphorically, as Fuseli's visual representations indicate, the vampire explained nocturnal sexual experiences and was often associated with sexual initiation.

The vampire first appeared in German literature in 1748, and came to England by way of the popular ghost ballads. It appeared in Southey's *Thalaba the Destroyer* and in Coleridge's *Christabel*.[34] The idea was certainly in the air at the Villa Diodati for when Byron recited the yet unpublished *Christabel,* the impressionable Shelley suffered such a hideous vision that he fled shrieking from the room. By 1819, then, when the first full-length treatment of a vampire myth appeared in the *New Monthly Magazine,* the image had acquired immense popular appeal; the fact that the story was signed "Lord B," leading the public to believe it was by Lord Byron, contributed enormously to its appeal.

Polidori (1795–1821), like Erasmus Darwin, Keats, and Beddoes, was trained as a physician, indeed at age twenty-one, the youngest to be graduated from the University of Edinburgh. As a traveling companion to Lord Byron, he was sullen, moody, competitive, and abrasive, leading Byron to dismiss him. He went to Italy where he was jailed after challenging an Austrian officer to a duel for obstructing his view of the stage at the opera house in Milan. Byron arranged for his release and he returned to England in the spring of 1817, with an outline of the vampire story that Byron had intended to write as his contribution to the ghost-story contest. Along with the magazine appearance in 1819, Polidori published the story as a pamphlet with a scholarly introduction on vampires. It was instantly successful, and, like *Frankenstein,* soon appeared on the stage as a gothic melodrama. Polidori himself committed suicide in 1821, at age twenty-six, believing enough in his own myth to use death as a means of acquiring a power over the living that he never had in life.

Polidori was exploiting his association with Byron in calling his vampire Lord Ruthven, the name Lady Caroline Lamb used in *Glenarvon,* her satiric novel about Byron, and his description recalls the features of the popular Byronic hero, a mysterious stranger who appears in Regency society, "a nobleman, more remarkable for his singularities than his rank" (p. 266).[35] He acquires a young traveling companion named Aubrey who promises, after Lord Ruthven nurses him through an illness, not to reveal anything about him for a year and a day. But Ruthven is released from his promise too late to save his own sister who marries and is destroyed by the vampire. The vampire remains free, both a menace and temptation, to wander the countryside, the salons, and the dreams of English virgins.

Charles Maturin's *Melmouth the Wanderer*

Yet one more figure representing biological immortality, this time as a curse, appears in gothic novels during the period, most successfully in Charles Maturin's *Melmouth the Wanderer* (1820).[36] The alien wanderer had appeared in Oriental literature, in Hebraic lore as Cain, and in Christian lore as Ahasuerus, the Wandering Jew, actually the Roman who, having denied Christ a resting place on the way to the Crucifixion, is condemned to wander the earth afflicted with sorrow and guilt until the Second Coming. During the eighteenth century he appears in ballads, dramas, comedies, and gothic novels such as *The Monk,* Godwin's *St. Leon* (1799), Shelley's *St. Irvyne* (1811), and Southey's *Curse of Kehama* (1810). In each version, responding to the social and political circumstances, he becomes less an eternally suffering sinner and more a rebel against divine tyranny, taking on the characteristics of Lucifer, of the rebellious Cain, of Prometheus, and of Faust, defiant, learned, dangerous, and secularly motivated. In Maturin's version, he offers his soul to Satan in exchange for eternal life, a bargain he can only escape by finding someone else to take on his fate. The Wanderer is a fictional device allowing Maturin to explore "life in its extremities," as he claims in the Preface, "those struggles of passion when the soul trembles on the verge of the unlawful and the unhallowed," struggles depicted in precise, even journalistic detail. He pauses at times to explain the atrocities that human beings inflict on one another in terms reminiscent of the Marquis de Sade: "It is actually possible to become *amateurs in suffering,* . . . You will call this cruelty, I call it curiosity that brings thousands to witness a tragedy, and makes the most delicate female feast on groans and agonies."

To put such a passage in its proper perspective, it is difficult but necessary to recall that it was written by a Protestant minister, one of the most popular in Dublin, a successful dra-

matist who had won the admiration and assistance of Sir Walter
Scott, composing his novel in his sitting room surrounded
by his family. This same minister had an incredibly lurid mind
fascinated by the very things humane and civilized individu-
als are supposed to detest, as his description of the tortures
inflicted on a young novice by a group of sadistic monks
demonstrates: "No ancient sculptor ever designed a figure
more exquisite and perfect than that that they had so barbarously
mangled." For romance, Marturin allows Melmouth to find
and love the ideal of his generation, a child of nature named
Imalee who lives on a deserted island; he takes her to Spain,
marries her at night in a ruined church attended by a ghost,
kills her brother when he pursues them, and leaves her to die
along with their child when she refuses to share his fate. Even
nature is ugly, deformed, that world in ruins and twilight
described by Burnet without any of the sublime connotations
it acquired during the eighteenth century. The book ends with
Melmouth's return to the ancestral castle where he is flung
into the sea by demons, having been released after only 150
years of eternal life from a world that was absolutely joyless.
In the curious logic of sado-masochism, his death is a reward.
Just as the popularity of gothic melodrama declined on the
stage, with the publication of *Melmouth the Wanderer* the pop-
ularity of the gothic romance declined; the genre had become
too sensational, introverted, humorless, burdened with lit-
erary allusion, and inappropriate for the new reading public.

James Hogg's
Confessions of a Justified Sinner

One novel, *The Private Memoirs and Confessions of a Justified
Sinner* (1824) by James Hogg,[37] offers a transition from the
gothic novel that was primarily a public statement, reflecting
contemporary tastes and affirming the values of the com-
munity, such as *The Castle of Otranto,* to a private statement
exploring the psychological aberrations, crises, or collapse of
a unique individual in opposition to his community, such as
Dostoevsky's *Notes from Underground. The Private Memoirs* is
based on just such an opposition between an individual's record
of his experience and the way it is observed by the public, in
this case an editor—a new character to enter literature, cre-
ated by the popular press. The work retains the historical
reference common to the gothic story, for the Editor has
gathered his version, according to the subtitle, from "curious
traditionary facts and other evidence."

In the public version of the story, George Colwan, the good-natured and uncomplicated son of the Lord of Dalcastle, is murdered by his "brother," Robert who, it is implied, is the illegitimate son of the Reverend Robert Wringhim, their mother's confessor. Robert, like his father, whose name he assumes, is a dour, sullen, self-righteous bigot. He believes that he is justified, that he is predestined to be saved no matter what he does, that he is among the elect, and, even in murdering his brother, serves as an instrument of God. After inheriting the estate, he is captured temporarily by the late laird's housekeeper and a prostitute, who conclude that he is a demon. His ultimate disappearance supports that interpretation. To the superstitious, caught between an ineffectual church and an inept judicial system, fiends and demons offer the only explanation for the mysterious and threatening events that beset them.

The second half of the book reproduces Robert Wringhim's version of the same events recovered in a manuscript found in his grave. He attributes much of his bizarre behavior to Gil-Martin, an unaccountable companion who has the unusual ability to disappear or to take on the appearance of others, even Robert himself. Robert vacillates between a supernatural and a psychological explanation both for what happens and how he feels about it: "Either I had a second self, who transacted business in my likeness, or else my body was at times possessed by a spirit over which it had no control, and of whose actions my own soul was wholly unconscious. . . . To be in a state of consciousness and unconsciousness, at the same time, in the same body and same spirit, was impossible" (p. 165). Pursued by those who thought he was a criminal, by those who thought he was a demon, pursued, he thought, by demons, by angry peasants, and equally angry fiends, he flees only to meet Gil-Martin, who convinces him to commit suicide. At no point does Hogg reveal whether Robert is in fact a victim of demons and those who believe in them or of his own insanity aggravated by religious fanaticism. Perhaps both are true; for neither the modern, rational, and secular explanation nor the primitive, subjective, and superstitious one can account on its own for the mysteries of human behavior.

Hogg was especially well qualified to represent both points of view, for, like his countryman Robert Burns, he lived in two worlds, a pastoral world of poverty and superstition and an urban world of letters.[38] His father was a shepherd; his mother, a descendant of minstrels, was interviewed for contributions to Sir Walter Scott's *Minstrelsy of the Scottish Border* (1802); and his grandfather claimed to be the last man in the region to have conversed with the fairies. In 1797, after hearing a "half daft man" recite *Tam O'Shanter,* he decided to become a poet. Only four years later, the young shepherd who had taught himself to read, write, and play the fiddle published his first collection of poems, *Scottish Pastorals* (1801), followed over the next thirty-four years by at least twenty-five volumes of poems, novels, narratives, verse dramas, Highland songs, anecdotes, sermons, parodies, a treatise on diseases in sheep, at least a hundred contributions to *Blackwood's,* and even a weekly paper called *The Spy*. He married at age fifty and fathered five children, whom he supported largely with his writing, while living on an especially unproductive farm. In 1832, at age sixty-one, he made his first visit to London, where he was honored at a large and formal dinner, but he preferred the annual boozy gatherings in Edinburgh with the kind of friends who accosted him on the street and called him a "d—d stupid poetical devil." He seems to have been on familiar terms with a number of the major literary figures of the day, including Wordsworth, Scott, Southey, and Byron, who thought his originality, like Burns's, came from drinking whiskey, but that "he and half of these Scotch and Lake troubadours, are spoilt by living in little circles and petty societies. London and the world is the only place to take the conceit out of a man" *(L and J,* IV, 152).

With the splendid conceit of the urban literati, Byron overlooked the source of Hogg's strength, the close connection with his origins, the poise he maintained between the worldly and the naive, represented in the two parts of *The Private Memoirs and Confessions of a Justified Sinner,* and in the two parts of his career, writing a treatise on diseases in sheep and anecdotes of Sir Walter Scott, writing *Blackwood's Magazine* and performing bawdy songs in dialect. The world to which Hogg was reconciled was far more complex and interesting than the one Peacock had in mind when he claimed, through his classicist Hilary in *Nightmare Abbey,* that the function of literature was "to reconcile man as he is to the world as it is" (p. 54). Living in two such different worlds, the poise it required, was also a great source of anxiety for Hogg, an anxiety he turned to account, expressing it with power and precision in his description of Robert Wringhim's identity crisis, his sense of doubleness, and ultimately disintegration.

The Role of the Gothic

Between Horace Walpole, the cultivated gentleman writing about a fragmented ghost in his elegant little castle, and James Hogg, the self-taught peasant writing about a fragmented mind on his dilapidated farm, an entire social and political system had changed, a new reading public had emerged, and a new concept had evolved of the natural world and man's place in it. The terrors that once lurked in the ruins and the landscape were now found lurking in the mind, just as mysterious, inescapable, and isolating. The countryside, the cottages, the factories, the urban chapels, slums, schools, poorhouses, orphanages, the kitchens, sitting rooms, and bedrooms of the working and middle classes held greater and more authentic terror than the monasteries and haunted palaces of the eighteenth century which they replaced on the stage and in the novel. The medieval setting and architecture are important but not definitive characteristics of the gothic just as the historical association of the ballad, that we shall discuss next, is an important but not definitive characteristic. Manfred, Frankenstein, Robert Wringhim, even David Copperfield, Captain Ahab, and Lord Jim shared an emotion, not a period or a setting, shared with each other and their authors the terror, the sense of helplessness, of being manipulated by forces—natural, supernatural, psychological, social, historical—one does not understand. While such monumental figures in the nineteenth century as Darwin, Marx, Fraser, and Freud would soon begin to illuminate the processes of nature, of human behavior, and of history itself, while they would "empty the haunted air," as Keats said in *Lamia,* none of them would explain the mysteries of evil, suffering, tyranny, injustice, and death, the themes of the gothic. Science, philosophy, history, would merely deprive literature of certain explanations for them. But the role of gothic, I believe, has been to invent new mysteries, mysteries that like Gil-Martin take on the appearance of the environment in which they occur, perhaps a frontier tale, or a detective story, or a sea saga, or even science fiction.

CHAPTER X

Bards
and
Minstrelsy

WHILE FICTIONAL MEDIEVALISM started in Walpole's dream, medievalism in Romantic poetry started with a genuine interest in history and custom, a belief that poetry would provide access to that past, either as recorded in manuscripts or as preserved in the oral culture of contemporary rural life. The period of interest ranged from tribal Britain through the reign of Elizabeth, and the materials the aniquarians collected included Celtic lays, French minstrelsy, folk songs, metrical romances, work songs, sea chanties, ballads, runic verses, street literature, and political broadsides. Some, such as Richard Hurd, in his *Letters on Chivalry and Romance* (1762), and Thomas Warton, Professor of Poetry at Oxford, advocated the study of chivalry and the courtly tradition, while others found inspiration in the poetry of preliterate contemporary rustic communities where ancient folk legends and customs in vernacular verse survived. Scotland, especially as represented in William Collins's "An Ode on the Popular Superstitions of the Highlands of Scotland" (1749; first published 1788), sustained its own cult of balladry and folk song, for to contemporary poets and scholars it appeared to be a naturally poetic country, "Fancy's land," "Where still, 'tis said, the fairy people meet," a land where battles, wizards, lovers, mourners, bards, and kings survived in ancient tales and living superstitions. The poets themselves, especially the ancient bards, fascinated historians such as Thomas

Gray, a classicist and Professor of Modern History at Cambridge University, whose poem, *The Bard,* recounted the legendary confrontation on Mount Snowdon between the last bard and King Edward I, who conquered Wales and decreed that all the bards were to be destroyed. It inspired paintings by Fuseli, Martin, even Turner. To contemporary poets who also felt that they had lost their position at court, the poem had political relevance.

The Appeal of Antiquarianism

The antiquarian movement in poetry had political and certainly nationalistic relevance, although the scholars and clergymen who collected the manuscripts, broadsides, and oral performances, and who traveled over the countryside like the geologists, botanists, and bird-watchers were not especially political creatures. The courtly tradition, originating in Southern France and Italy, idealized that aristocratic political system disrupted by the Revolution of 1688 in England and the Revolution of 1789 in France. Appealing to a William Cobbett as well as an Edmund Burke,[1] the courtly tradition preserved a vision of a paternalistic society of kings, aristocrats, and peasants bound by necessity, by faith, by oath, and by blood. The folk tradition, on the other hand, was based mainly on an idealization of agrarian or even pastoral societies, populated with innocent, spontaneous, simple, virtuous, intuitive, innately musical and wise peasants who lived in tune with their natural environment and in close proximity to the fairies and demons that were the major source of their charm. However much scholars idealized and misrepresented these traditions, they justified their research by treating the literature as sources of historical information about events, customs, manners, ceremonies, and language, as well as sources of mystery, ritual, and belief in which their own culture had become so impoverished. Not only did they misinterpret the poetry and the poets, they recorded it badly as well, having little interest in authenticity.[2]

Consequently, however artificial, contrived, and even fraudulent, James Macpherson's Ossianic verses were immensely successful, depicting in misty prose-poems, of which he was unable to produce any of the purportedly third-century originals, "the deeds of days of other years": ancestral battles, love affairs, and betrayals as told by Ossian, the blind minstrel. Starting with *Fragments of Ancient Poetry, Collected in the Highlands of Scotland, and Translated from the Gaelic*

or Erse Language (1760), *Fingal* (1762), and *Temora* (1763),
Macpherson offered to an eager and believing public adven-
tures, battles, ghosts, fogs, melodrama, and fine speeches in
an unlikely combination of corrupted Homer (a "white-
bosomed Moina" waited for a "dark-bosomed ship") and an
inflated Bible (the blind Ossian crying plaintively, "O thou
that rollest above, round as the shield of my fathers! Whence
are thy beams, O sun! thy everlasting light"). Macpherson
found an especially ardent audience on the continent where
such passionate heroism was much admired: Goethe used
Ossian in *The Sorrows of Young Werther;* Napoleon slept with
a volume of Ossian under his pillow; symphonies, operas,
plays, and babies were named after him.[3]

Macpherson provided evidence for a theory of natural or
original genius in which many people wanted to believe: that
primitive, postdiluvian man was naturally poetic, that his
language was metaphoric, that he knew a simplicity, tran-
quility, and faith that was no longer possible, and that prim-
itive minds—whether of a Greek poet, a Hebrew prophet, a
Celtic bard, or a contemporary rustic—were analogous
wherever they were found. In 1767, a series of Scottish intel-
lectuals published influential works exploring different facets
of this primitivism, both chronological and cultural: Adam
Ferguson, *History of Civil Society,* Adam Smith, *Considera-
tions Concerning the First Formation of Language,* and William
Duff, *Essay on Original Genius,* an unoriginal but representa-
tive essay summarizing most people's thoughts on the sub-
ject of natural or original genius: "in the earliest and most
uncultivated periods of society, Poetry is by one great effort
of nature, in one age, and by one individual brought to the
highest perfection to which human Genius is capable of
advancing it. . . . [Thus] Ossian composed *Fingal* and *Temora*
when none of the Arts, whether liberal or mechanical, were
known in his country." Such original poetic genius, the abil-
ity to see "something new and uncommon in every subject"
depends on an "uncultivated" environment:

> The undisturbed peace, and the innocent rural pleasures [are]
> congenial to its nature. A Poet of true Genius delights to con-
> template and describe those primitive scenes, which recall to our
> remembrance the fabulous era of the golden age. Happily
> exempted from that tormenting ambition, and those vexatious
> desires, which trouble the current of modern life, he wanders
> with a serene, contented heart, through walks and groves con-
> secrated to the Muses; or, indulging a sublime, pensive, and
> sweetly-soothing melancholy, strays with a slow and solemn step,

through the unfrequented desert, along the naked beach, or the bleak and barren heath. . . .[4]

However absurd, enough readers believed in the possibility of such original talent to create cults around Henry Jones, the Poetical Bricklayer; Mary Collier, the Poetical Washerwoman; Stephen Duck, the Thresher Poet; Ann Yearsly, the Poetical Milk-Maid; Robert Bloomfield, Henry Kirke White, Joseph Blacket; and, finally, the genuinely talented though hardly tranquil and uncultivated Robert Burns, who collected taxes but was depicted as a plowman ("in glory and in joy / Following his plough," as Wordsworth described him in *Resolution and Independence*, ll.45–46), and John Clare. The fabrications of Macpherson, then, stimulated thought on the nature of originality, creativity, and genius that would be more useful and lasting than the Ossianic poems themselves.

Percy's *Reliques*

In 1815, Wordsworth claimed that the Ossianic poems "have been wholly uninfluential upon the literature of the country," whereas "there is not an able writer in verse of the present day who would not be proud to acknowledge his obligations to the Reliques,"[5] namely Thomas Percy's *Reliques of Ancient English Poetry: Consisting of Old Heroic Ballads, Songs, and Other Pieces of our Earlier Poets (Chiefly of the Lyric Kind), Together with Some Few of a Later Date,* first published in 1764. For Percy, a poet himself as well as a cleric (later chaplain to George III and ultimately a Bishop), a collector, and editor with ranging interests, the *Reliques* was an expression of his taste for the novel and exotic. His sources included a manuscript about to be used for tinder in a Staffordshire country house, broadsides he found in the ballad stock in a warehouse, recent political street songs, contemporary imitations, his own original verse, and anything else that interested him.[6] Here are such well-known songs as "The Ancient Ballad of Chevy-Chase," "The Wife of Usher's Well," "Sir Patrick Spens," "Edward," a whole series on Robin Hood, and others on King Arthur and the Round Table. If the versions were rough, Percy polished them; if they were unfinished he completed them, justifying such tampering on the basis that the poems were anonymous, that multiple versions already existed, and that he was merely altering them to conform with public taste.[7] He retained, however, the symmetry, the incremental repetitions, the nonsense refrains, the verbal formula, and the

unadorned vernacular diction, the characteristics of oral per-
formance. Percy overlooked, along with communal author-
ship, the ritualistic function of the ballads, their relationship
to animistic beliefs, to fertility rites, and to the vulgarity of
country lore. Instead, he emphasized individual authorship,
themes and types that had moral or social relevance, tales of
love, fidelity, betrayal, separation, jealousy, reconciliation,
relationships, identity, revenge, ghosts that rise up to accuse
a murderer, spirits that haunt a rival or an inconstant mate,
dogs and birds that carry messages or lead people away from
danger or toward treasures, trees and plants that grow as
memorials to crimes or to loyalties, dreams, omens, charms,
enchantments, riddles, and supernatural creatures who pro-
tect, admonish, or advise people. Percy revived the supernat-
ural machinery and basic emotions that had been displaced in
fashionable literature by theories of decorum and imitation,
by reflections, meditations, effusions, didactic or philosophic
musings, and occasional verse.

Percy's collection may not have preserved an authentic native
ballad tradition, but it did provide a new voice to contem-
porary poetry, a complex one combining the folk and courtly
tones with the educated, regulated ones of an eighteenth-cen-
tury gentleman-cleric, introducing to a largely middle-class
urban reading public some of the concerns and attitudes of
lower-class country people and their vision of the governing
class. And his influence on the subsequent generation of poets
is incalculable. Burns, Scott, Wordsworth, and Byron
expressed their debt to him. Coleridge used many details from
the *Reliques* in *Christabel,* including the heroine's name,
his debts being primarily to Percy's additions rather than to
the original ballads. After publishing his first volume of poetry
in 1820, John Clare received a copy of the *Reliques* and found
versified "all the stories of my grandmother and her gossip-
ing neighbours." Four years later, this poet who had the
advantage of maturing in a world where the ballads were liv-
ing and genuine, claimed that Percy's tales and ballads offer
"the essence and simplicity of true poetry that makes me regret
I did not see them sooner as they would have formed my
taste and laid the foundation of my judgment in writing and
thinking poetically. As it is I feel indebted to them for many
feelings."[8] The artificial ballad had become the "true poetry,"
an inspiration to other poets to write what then were called
literary ballads.

The Minstrel:
James Beattie and Thomas Chatterton

In the minstrel bard Percy also introduced a new hero, essentially a European figure appearing in England primarily as a jester, a vagabond, a rogue who performed familiar ballads and bawdry at the taverns and fairs. By the seventeenth century he had become a pedlar, a ballad monger who wandered over the countryside and through the city streets selling broadsides that he sang, teaching his customers the tunes of what he offered as new and often political and satirical songs.[9] Throughout the eighteenth century, the pedlars, concentrated on the lower classes, selling such ballads and tales as "Tom Thumb," "Robin Hood," and "Guy of Warwick," the very ones banished from the nurseries. By the end of the century, even though they were still considered and often behaved as rogues, they served an essential educational function by bringing literacy and news to the rustic areas—for example, Wordsworth's Wanderer or the aged woman described in the *Prelude* arriving annually with "books, pictures, combs and pins" (VIII, 29). In 1818, Wordsworth, describing the interest with which country people read "halfpenny Ballads, and penny and two-penny histories in great abundance," confessed that he had "many a time wished to produce songs, poems and little histories, that might circulate among other good things in this way," concluding: "Indeed, some of the Poems which I have published were composed, not without a hope that at some time or other they might answer this purpose."[10]

Surrounded by the living heirs of the minstrel tradition, writers nonetheless preferred to believe in the fictional bards of Macpherson, Gray, and Percy, apotheosized by James Beattie's *The Minstrel: or, the Progress of Genuis* (1771–1774), a poem in Spenserian stanzas describing the youth and education of Edwin, a medieval poet, and his encounter with a recluse who teaches him about human life and how to become reconciled to an imperfect world.[11] Beattie was not himself a minstrel. He was Professor of Moral Philosophy at Aberdeen during the most exciting period in Scottish intellectual history, and author of the "Essay on the Nature and Immutability of Truth" (1770) that won the admiration of Thomas Gray, Dr. Johnson, and George III. Through intelligence, self-discipline, and industry, he had raised himself from the poverty of his youth to professional distinction, although his personal life was a series of disappointments. Shortly after his marriage at age thirty-two, his wife began to show signs of a mental disorder that became so threatening to Beattie and his children that she was ultimately confined. After the death of his sons, one in 1790, at age twenty-two, and the other in 1796, at age eighteen, he was inconsolable, suffered a stroke, and, after four years of paralysis, died in 1803.

Drawing in part on his own experience and in part on existing literary convention,[12] Beattie created in *The Minstrel* a poet that would serve as a model for both the lives and the fantasies of those subsequent poets, gifted or not, who felt misunderstood, isolated wanderers in both the natural and social world: "The neighbors star'd, yet bless'd the lad: / Some deem'd him wondrous wise, and some believ'd him mad" (I, xvi). While Beattie's young minstrel lived under "the influence of a malignant star," overcome by poverty, pining and dropping "into the grave, unpitied and unknown," the figure of Edwin was, in fact, immensely influential, appearing in Wordsworth's *Prelude* and *Excursion,* in Shelley's *Alastor,* in Byron's *Childe Harold's Pilgrimage,* in Keats's *Hyperion* and *Endymion,* in Scott's novels, and in the popular image of the youthful, natural, and obscure genius whose talents are wasted and who dies unfulfilled. Such a contemporary figure, whatever his credentials, had as much appeal as authentic medieval manuscripts or unpublished songs, which explains the impact of the life, but mostly the death, of Thomas Chatterton.

Thomas Chattterton (1752–1770) was a young man of such talent that before the age of twelve he was capable of convincingly fabricating poems by the fictional fifteenth-century Bristol monk, Thomas Rowley, whose work he claimed to have found among the illuminated parchment manuscripts in St. Mary's Redcliffe.[13] The poems circulated for some time among the citizens of Bristol but the two publishers to whom they were submitted rejected them as forgeries, and not very good ones. To convey a sense of the antique, he borrowed from Spenser, from neo-Spenserian imitations, and from Chaucer and Percy; he disordered the syntax, distorted the spellings, and made the poems nearly unreadable. Since contemporary interest in ballads was based on their simplicity and artlessness, Chatterton's contrivances were clearly self-defeating. In 1770, Chatterton moved to London where, unable to survive on the pennies he earned writing for magazines, he composed "An Excellent Balade of Charitie," and then committed suicide, becoming the symbol of high but unfulfilled genius destroyed by an insensitive society. Seven years after his death, in 1777, the poems were published, edited by

Thomas Tyrwhitt (whose edition of Chaucer appeared between 1775–1778). Coleridge wrote a monody on his death, depicting him as the "Sweet harper of time-shrouded minstrelsy," and Wordsworth described him in "Resolution and Independence" as "the marvellous Boy / The sleepless Soul that perished in his pride"; Keats dedicated *Endymion* to his memory; and Shelley, in *Adonais,* his elegy to Keats, described him as among the "Inheritors of unfulfilled renown."

Robert Burns

When Robert Burns (1759–1796), a genuine contemporary minstrel, appeared, "His Bardship" or "Bardie" as he called himself, bore no resemblance to the literary symbol: he was convivial, lusty, irreverent, sentimental, raucous, outspoken, patriotic, sociable, and beset by problems more economic than philosophical.[14] Born to a stern but affectionate tenant farmer, he was, in an irregular fashion, more educated than the normal rustic bard, learning math from his father, grammar and French from a local schoolmaster, and dancing at a village school. His reading included Calvinist theology, Greek and Roman religion, history, geography, eighteenth-century novels such as Mackenzie's *Man of Feeling* and Sterne's *Tristam Shandy,* poetry by Thomson, Shenstone, Goldsmith, Gray, Young, Blair, and Beattie, proving that original genius can survive exposure to even the least inspired literature. Nor did pastoral life, with its illusion of abundance, innocence, beauty, and contentment, of a surviving paradise, contribute to the fulfillment of Burns's genius, for, like Hogg, who was to model himself after Burns, he spent his life failing at farming, worrying about the weather, and arguing with landlords. He studied surveying until "the sun entered Virgo, a month which is always a carnival in my bosom," he confessed, and never finished the course. He became partner to a flax-dresser, but during a drunken New Year's celebration, his partner's wife burned down the shop. Finally, he became a tax collector, and did very well, supporting his growing family while writing verse and collecting songs.

He was neither the lonely ascetic depicted by Beattie, nor was he restlessly searching for an ideal goddess, for he loved often, intensely, and in a variety of ways, bedeviled by his own lusty nature and by the many women who found him attractive, flirted with him, entertained him, and bore his children. His affairs ranged from the married Agnes M'Lehose to a serving girl named Meg Cameron, who supposedly bore his triplets; to Elizabeth Paton, Ann Park, and Jenny Clow, each of whom had one of his children. Ultimately he married Jean Armour, who bore two sets of twins and several more children as well, the last born on the day Burns was buried: "I married 'my Jean'. . . not in consequence . . . of romance perhaps; but I had a long and much-loved fellow creature's happiness or misery in my determination, and I durst not trifle with so important a deposite."[15] His sense of responsibility for the women he loved extended to their children, and he did his best to see that they were sheltered, sometimes with his wife or mother, and provided for.

Unlike any original genius depicted in literature, he disliked being alone and avoided it as much as possible, explaining in an autobiographical letter a "constitutional hypochondriac taint which made me fly solitude." This same convivial nature often led to excessive drinking: the night he sold his first crop, thirty people engaged in a three-hour drunken brawl while the rest lay sick on the floor in the house: "You will easily guess how I enjoyed the scene."[16] But, if the occasion required, he could summon tact and charm to excuse himself: "O all ye powers of decency and decorum! whisper to them that my errors, though great, were involuntary—that an intoxicated man is the vilest of beasts—that it was not in my nature to be brutal to anyone—that to be rude to a woman, when in my senses, was impossible."[17] Finally, Burns, the rustic bard whose amorous successes, sociable nature, and consummate diplomatic skill violated all preconceptions of the favored though melancholy being so popular among the writers of sensibility, was capable of writing the most colorful bawdry, equal to anything in a vernacular tradition famous for sexually explicit verses.[18]

Like Hogg and Scott, he had a vast store of native Scots lore acquired mostly in childhood from his mother and from a servant "remarkable for her ignorance, credulity and superstition—she had, I suppose, the largest collection in the county of tales and songs concerning devils, ghosts, fairies, brownies, witches, warlocks, spunkies, kelpies, elf-candles, deadlights, wraiths, apparitions, cantraips, giants, inchanted towers, dragons, and other trumpery."[19] While Burns believed in God and may even have had a religious crisis at one time, he had his reservations about the Scottish Kirk, where he had been publicly rebuked and forced to confess to fornication when Jean Armour's parents refused to give them permission to marry, a humiliation he accepted in order to be certified as a bachelor, free, if he chose, to marry someone else. The admission, the hypocrisy of the elders, and the self-righteousness of the parishioners motivated Burns to write several religious satires such as "The Holy Fair," "Address to the Deil," "The Fornicator," and "Holy Willie's Prayer," all of them implying that since God created people to be imperfect and pleasure-loving creatures, the Kirk should be more tolerant of them. His rebellion against the church became part of his general resentment of authority, position, pretension of any sort.

Little of Burns's poetry is polemical, although he did write some election ballads and broadsides, some patriotic verse such as "Scots Wha Hae," and songs that serve political purposes such as "Is there for Honest Poverty." Mostly, he preferred to write about "the amours of my Compeers, the humble Inmates of the farm-house and cottage. . . . To the sons and daughters of labor and poverty they are matters of the most serious nature: to them, the ardent hope, the stolen interview, the tender farewell, are the greatest and most delicious part of their enjoyments!"[20] Like Wordsworth, his topic is "the common growth of mother earth," universal passions as they are felt and expressed by ordinary, humble, and particular people, those commonplace sights and experiences that bind one to the earth and to one's fellow man. And like Wordsworth he made up a diction suitable to it, colloquial, unadorned, melodious with more dialect than Wordsworth, but artfully assembled from general Scots and general English to create a language of conversation that no one in fact ever spoke.[21] While other poets may have been finding divine analogies in nature, Burns found, characteristically, human ones; turning up a mouse with his plough, for example, he concludes, "The best laid scheme o' mice an' men / Gang aft a-gley." Or, while sitting in church watching a louse climb up a lady's bonnet: "O wad some Pow'r the giftie gie us / To see ourselves as others see us."

In 1786, *Poems Chiefly in the Scottish Dialect,* his one major collection, appeared to great acclaim in Kilmarnock. When he went to Edinburgh to arrange for a second edition, he was treated as a hero and visited the drawing rooms of such provincial aristocracy and erudition as Dr. Adam Ferguson, the historian, where he met the fifteen-year-old Walter Scott. Burns was twenty-seven. He spent the next ten years composing, collecting, and editing songs for the *Scots Musical Museum* (1787–1803) and *Select Scottish Airs,* over three hundred of the best-known songs in the world including "Green Grow the Rashes" (in polite and bawdy versions), "Comin thro' the Rye," "Auld Lang Syne," and "Sweet Afton." He wrote lyrics, and sometimes the music as well, on love, friendship, separation, pleasure, seasons, aging, drinking, and Scotland. In 1795, when Great Britain was threatened with invasion by France, he joined the Dumfries Royal Volunteers, and when he died the following year, at age thirty-seven, he was buried with full and solemn military honors.

"Burns's achievement," David Daiches writes, "was astonishing. At a time when Scottish culture was split into a genteel anglicizing stream (by far the most influential), a half-antiquarian, half-debased vernacular stream, and a current of fragmented and often corrupted folksong, Burns was able to weld together elements from all three to produce a body of poetry which has no equal anywhere for vigour, individuality and powerful human appeal."[22] And his successor, Sir Walter Scott, confided in his journal, "Long life to thy fame and peace to thy soul, Rob Burns. When I want to express a sentiment which I feel strongly, I find the phrase in Shakespeare or thee" (p. 252). Yet this iconoclast, the man who destroyed the sentimental, fashionable, and artificial symbols of the rustic bard, became, much like Chatterton, just such a symbol. Everyone visited his grave, and otherwise sensible poets like Keats and Wordsworth indulged in that self-induced melancholy that Burns found so ludicrous. Although Wordsworth disapproved of Hazlitt's, Coleridge's, and De Quincey's excesses, he defended Burns's: "It is the privilege of poetic genius to catch . . . a spirit of pleasure wherever it can be found,—in the walks of nature, and in the business of men the poet, trusting to primary instincts, luxuriates among the felicities of love and wine . . ." (*A Letter to a Friend of Burns* [1816], *Prose*, III, 124).[23] Carlyle, who wrote Burns's memoirs, and Keats, who claimed after visiting the cottage that Burns's misery kept him from writing anything at all, considered Burns's Scottish background—the poverty and vulgarity—to be his major misfortune, although Burns, especially in collecting and editing songs, saw it as a great advantage. Unlike the scholars, he knew that authentic simplicity was often vulgar, that pastoral innocence and Christian virtue often had little in common. In his concern for authenticity, the reconstruction of the old in the spirit of its time rather than contemporary taste, Burns was opposing Percy, Macpherson, Gray, all those gentlemen scholars who had contributed to the cult of original genius and made an unlikely alliance with the collectors and antiquarians represented by Francis

Grose, Joseph Ritson in England, Herder and the brothers Grimm in Germany for whom accuracy was a passion.

Collectors and Antiquarians

Francis Grose was an industrious and convivial archaeologist, social historian, and friend of Burns. His *Classical Dictionary of the Vulgar Tongue* (1785) and his *Provincial Glossary* (1787), including *A Collection of Popular Superstitions,* provided the basic materials for anyone who wanted to read or, as historical novelists were to do, write in an authentic colloquial dialect. In *The Antiquities of England and Wales* (1787) and *The Antiquities of Scotland* (1791), he set out to provide such an inventory of British monuments and remains as Johann Winckelmann had provided for Greece in *Reflections on the Painting and Sculpture of the Greeks.* In exchange for including a sketch of Alloway Kirk, where Burns's father was buried, Burns wrote "Tam o'Shanter" for a footnote and later memorialized Grose's cheer and amiable curiosity in "The Late Captain Grose's Peregrinations Through Scotland."

Joseph Ritson (1752–1803), on the other hand, had a morose and contentious disposition that some attributed to his diet of milk and vegetables.[24] He was a spelling reformer who proposed banishing the capital "I," an ardent disciple of the French Revolution who associated with Blake and Godwin, and a lawyer enraged by the forgeries and idiosyncratic editing procedures of his predecessors. As a scholar, he was tireless and implacable, producing collections of local verse and traditional children's rhymes called *Gammer Gurton's Garland: or the Nursery Parnassus: A Choice Collection of Pretty Songs and Verses for the Amusement of all Little Good Children Who Can Neither Read nor Run* (1784, 1799, 1810, and on and on), *Pieces of Ancient Popular Poetry* (1791), *Ancient Songs* (1792), and *Robin Hood: A Collection of All the Ancient Poems, Songs, and Ballads now Extant Relative to that Celebrated Outlaw* (1795). Working mostly from manuscripts, previous collections, or broadsides, Ritson's books were meticulously produced, with engravings or woodcuts by Blake or Bewick. Attacking the aging Percy for misrepresenting the poetry and attributing folk ballads to courtly minstrels, among other things, he established the importance of objectivity, of authenticity and accuracy. He "ought to be canonized by the lovers of the ballad," Francis Gummere wrote, "if only for his indomitable zeal in editing and his passionate accuracy. Full of evil were his days, and his end was dark indeed; but his services to sound learning should never be forgotten."[25]

However inaccurate and even fraudulent the Ossianic poems and Percy's *Reliques,* they inspired German scholars such as Johann Gottfried von Herder to collect and interpret their native folklore, believing that it held the key to racial character and national identity. Their theories of communal as opposed to individual authorship were disputed for nearly one hundred years in libraries, scholarly journals, and at dinner parties, for educated gentlemen were reluctant to give up the divine origins of the Bible and divine inspiration of Homer, both of which, Herder claimed, were originally collective expressions of a primitive culture.[26] Poets were especially unhappy about losing the ideal of natural genius, of individual achievement, the potential of favored beings to arise periodically and inexplicably within a society, someone with the vision and verbal power to articulate its needs and ideals, to record its accomplishments, to represent its character, to serve as a mediator between the secular and the sacred, some special creature who even then could be plowing, milking cows, or making shoes. Such speculations on authorship coincided with and contributed to a growing interest in language itself, its nature and history. Adam Smith in *Considerations Concerning the First Formation of Languages* (1767) and Lord Monboddo in *The Origin and Progress of Language* (1773) claimed that primitive language, whether found in early texts or among contemporary uncultivated people, was naturally poetical, precise, passionate, and metaphoric.[27] These theories of primitive language assisted poets as different as Wordsworth and Shelley in defending specific poetic practices and poetry itself, Wordsworth adapting them in the Preface to *Lyrical Ballads* to justify his using the language of rustics in poetry, and Shelley in *A Defense of Poetry* asserting that "Every original language near to its source is in itself the chaos of a cyclic poem."

Sir Walter Scott: Minstrel Historian

The supernatural and sentimental dimension of German folklore and balladry had an immediate impact on English poetry.[28] Just as the 1823 translation of fairy tales collected by the brothers Grimm, published as folk tales in Germany in 1812, contributed to the rehabilitation of children's literature, the publication in 1796 of Gottfried Bürger's "Lenore" in the *Monthly Magazine,* translated by William Taylor, awakened a native strain of "spook" balladry, at a time when an interest in gothic horror had reached a peak in both the novel and the drama. "Lenore" describes the abduction of a young woman by the ghost of her lover, who had been killed in the Crusades, and the consummation of their marriage in his tomb. Southey, Lamb, Coleridge, and Wordsworth, read, translated, and imitated it. Scott translated all sixty-six stanzas in one night after hearing it recited and claimed it inspired him to become a poet. While awaiting its publication as "William and Helen," he began raiding the countryside, collecting native ballads for *Minstrelsy of the Scottish Border* (1803), a collection of ballads with learned annotations emphasizing his interest in customs, manners, and superstitions, in historical rather than literary values.[29]

At the time, Scott's historical contributions were as valuable as his literary ones, for, in spite of the monumental *History of England* by David Hume (1754–1761), the *History of the Anglo-Saxons to the Norman Conquest* (1799–1805) by Sharon Turner, or even the fascinating *Complete View of the Dress and Habits of the People of England* (1796–1799) by Joseph Strutt, the writing of native history was barren and uninspired. Blake complained that there was too much opinion: "Tell me the Acts, O historian," he writes, "and leave me to reason upon them as I please" (Erdman, 534). Wordsworth observed that "high-wrought modern narratives" were "Stript of their harmonizing Soul, the life / Of manners and familiar incidents" (*The Prelude,* VIII, 773–75). And in Jane Austen's *Northanger Abbey,* Catherine Moreland dismisses history as nothing but the "quarrels of popes and kings," "wars and pestilences,": "the men are all so good for nothing, and hardly any women at all . . . And yet I often think it odd that it should be so dull, for a great deal of it must be invention." In such ballad collections as *The Lay of the Last Minstrel* (1805) and historical romances starting with *Waverley* (1814), Scott brought to life fifty years of scholarship in England, an amalgamation of the documentary history, of the oral history that had grown up around the ballad revival, and of the imaginative history associated with the gothic romance. As Hazlitt wrote in *The Spirit of the Age,* "Sir Walter has found out (oh, rare discovery) that facts are better than fiction; that there is no romance like the romance of real life; and that if we can but arrive at what men feel, do, and say in striking and singular situations, the results will be 'more lively, audible, and full of vent,' than the fine-spun cobwebs of the brain."

Born in 1771, Scott first encountered the ballads and tales of the Border wars, the customs and superstitions of rural Scotland, when as a child he was sent to live with his grandfather to recover from infantile paralysis. Back in Edinburgh, he enjoyed the normal comforts and discipline for the son of a successful advocate and strict Presbyterian, a dour gentleman who enjoyed going to funerals. Young Scott avidly read through Shakespeare, Spenser, volumes of chivalry and romance, and Percy's *Reliques,* while amusing his friends with tales of his own invention. At age twelve he entered the University of Edinburgh, and two years later became an apprentice in his father's law office, passing the bar at age twenty-one. As both Sheriff of Selkirkshire and Clerk of Sessions, and throughout his long and respectable legal career, he defended the ancient Scottish legal system against the English influences that were permeating all levels of Scottish civil life. Although lame from a childhood illness, he matured into a tall, vigorous, cheerful, and sociable man, attending dances and dinner parties, riding around the countryside hunting, visiting old castles and battlefields, and collecting ballads. His patriotism, his delight in physical accomplishments, and perhaps some vanity led to his joining the Royal Edinburgh Volunteer Light Dragoons in 1797, when Scotland appeared in danger of invasion from France. He loved to parade and drill on his fine horse, named Lenore after Bürger's ballad, and designed a red-coated uniform with silver lace and silver epaulettes, white leather breeches, black boots with spurs, and a helmet trimmed with leopard and red and white feathers. Two years after a searing rejection from his first love, he courted clumsily, then married Charlotte Carpenter, a swarthy, orphaned, French emigrée with a small allowance, a heavy accent, and odd European ways, who bore him five children, of whom four survived.

In 1805, Scott entered a secret partnership to publish his books with James Ballantyne, an old school friend and printer, the intent being to allow Scott to keep more of the profits from his work. In 1811, he acquired Abbotsford, another expensive hobby, to which he added two adjoining estates, remodeled the buildings into his own modest castle, and added appropriate but expensive furnishing and ornaments. To cover losses incurred by Ballantyne and expenses at Abbotsford, in 1814, he began writing novels, along with reviews and poems. He seemed indefatigable and probably would have managed to pay for Abbotsford when, in 1825, a severe economic depression led to the failure of a number of publishing houses including Ballantyne. As a silent partner, Scott was responsible for over £100,000 in debts. The Trustees allowed Scott to keep Abbotsford, the library and furniture, and a small allowance so long as all the proceeds from his writing were used to pay off the debt. Scott accepted the alternative: "to save Abbotsford I would attempt all that was possible. My heart clings to the place I have created. There is scarce a tree on it that does not owe its being to me and the pain of leaving it is greater than I can tell" (*Journal*, pp. 40–41).

Scott had always worked under enormous pressure, including periodic illness and melancholy: "What a life mine has been," he reflected in 1825, "Half educated, almost wholly neglected or left to myself—stuffing my head with most nonsensical trash and undervalued in society for a time by most of my companions—getting forward and held a bold and clever fellow, contrary to the opinion of all who thought me a mere dreamer—Broken-hearted for two years—My heart handsomely pieced again—but the crack will remain till my dying day—Rich and poor four or five times—Once at the verge of ruin yet opened new sources of wealth almost overflowing— now taken in my pitch of pride and nearly winged" (*Journal*, pp. 42–43). The following year he was devastated by the death of his wife, "who could always talk down my sense of the calamitous apprehensions which always break the heart that must bear them alone" (*Journal*, p. 145). Through it all he fulfilled his legal responsibilities, raised his four children (his daughter Sophia married John Gibson Lockhart, the editor of the *Quarterly Review*, and his sons Charles and Walter had careers in the foreign service and the military), paid off enormous financial obligations, and, in spite of his extraordinary literary reputation, retained his modesty and wit. He was kind to poor, struggling young poets and helped his friends and neighbors acquire for themselves or their children positions, pensions, subscriptions—indeed, however beset he was with his own financial difficulties, he was an extremely generous man and a tolerant one as well. He enjoyed the company of James Hogg, the Prince Regent,[30] Joanna Baillie, and Lord Byron, the admiration and friendship of Maria Edgeworth, "Monk" Lewis, Princess Caroline, Southey, Wellington, Haydon, and Sir Humphry Davy, with whom he climbed Helvellyn in 1805 along with Wordsworth. People dropped by for breakfast and stayed for dinner or a weekend, but Scott continued writing although children, dogs, and guests trooped by his desk, lured him out for long walks, and kept him talking late into the night. He had an aversion to foreigners—

"fine waistcoats and breast pins upon dirty shirts" (*Journal,* p. 10)—and foreign literary correspondence except with Goethe, in whose friendship he took particular pride (p. 279).

Scott had not begun his literary career with any aspiration to fame. He had collected ballads as a hobby; he enjoyed roaming the countryside, interviewing such fine old ladies as James Hogg's mother (who feared that printing the ballads would break their charm), corresponding with Bishop Percy, or Ritson, or George Ellis, the founder of the *Anti-Jacobin Review* and editor of *Specimens of Early English Poets* (1790). Then, in January, 1805, Scott published *Lay of the Last Minstrel,* an original poem "intended," according to the Preface "to illustrate the customs and manners, which anciently prevailed on the Borders of England and Scotland." It was followed by *Marmion* (1808), a historical poem relating to the defeat of the Scottish army at the battle of Flodden in 1513, and *The Lady of the Lake* (1810), a topographical poem. Weighted with names, places, customs, and events, all these metrical romances were annotated as meticulously as the *Minstrelsy,* the factual base appealing to a reading public that preferred history and archaeology to the now-declining gothic romance. Despite the cost, each volume set astronomical publishing records. The reviewers complained, however, that the books were overpriced, that Scott's diction, verification, and grammar were sloppy and set a bad example for the young.[31] *Rokeby, The Bride of Triermain* (1813), and *The Lord of the Isles* (1815) were less successful, as Scott's style and subject became familiar, and Byron's exotic narratives competed for an audience that craved novelty.

To pay for Abbotsford, Scott had to keep writing while continuing his legal career. In 1814, the year Wordsworth published *The Excursion;* Jane Austen, *Mansfield Park;* Byron, *The Corsair;* when England was paralyzed by frost and snow, when Napoleon abdicated and the Prince Regent mounted the greatest public celebration in history; when London was inundated with foreign dignitaries, ceremonies, and parades; and when Joanna Southcott expressed the apocalyptic yearnings of the lower classes by announcing at age sixty-four that she was about to give birth to the Prince of Peace, Scott published anonymously *Waverley or 'Tis Sixty Years Since.*[32] In his Preface, Scott explains how his novel differs from the gothic of Walpole's *Castle of Otranto,* the horror stories of "Monk" Lewis, and contemporary novels of fashion. By offering a realistic rather than fantastic picture of a recent and not very glamorous period, Scott claims, he can concentrate on "the characters and passions of the actor;—those passions common to men in all stages of society, and which have alike agitated the human heart, whether it throbbed under the steel corslet of the fifteenth century, the brocaded coat of the eighteenth, or the blue frock and white dimity waistcoat of the present day." Like Wordsworth, then, and Jane Austen, he gives priority to "the common growth of mother-earth" ("Peter Bell," ll. 133), the "common feelings of common life," to community, the shared feelings and ideals that bind people together over time as well as geography or social class. His historical perspective emphasizes what Jane Austen and Wordsworth can only suggest: how much diversity and contradiction may exist within the common and therefore within the community.[33]

The traumatic events of recent Scottish history explained his interest in the past, an interest Scott shared with such Scottish intellectuals as Adam Smith, David Hume, James Hutton, even Burns. "There is no European nation," he continued in the introductory notes, "which within the course of half a century or little more, has undergone so complete a change as this kingdom of Scotland. . . . But the change, though steadily and rapidly progressive, has, nevertheless, been gradual; and like those who drift down the stream of a deep and smooth river, we are not aware of the progress we have made until we fix our eye on the now distant point from which we have been drifted." But that point was within memory, for Scott's grandfather and his contemporaries, whom he had met as a child, recalled participating in Prince Charles' ill-fated attempt to recover the throne in 1745, his leading 5,000 Highlanders on an unopposed march all the way south to Derby, and his defeat at Culloden the following year. While the English victory put an end to the patriarchal power of the Highland chiefs and their tribal organization, and the feudal power of the landlords, placing them all ostensibly under English law, the old ways and preferences survived as a counterculture, pagan in orientation, passionate, and anti-authoritarian, opposed to the rational, pious, self-disciplined, and self-denying Presbyterian Lowlanders. For Scott, writing in the introduction to *The Fortunes of Nigel,* this sudden juxtaposition between the civilized and the primitive, between culture and nature, produced "the most picturesque period of history . . . when the ancient rough and wild manners of a barbarous age are just becoming innovated upon and contrasted by the illumination of increased or revived learning and the instructions of renewed or reformed religion." It also produced some unusual creatures, such as Rob Roy, the ban-dit-hero of one of his novels, whose fame is attributed to his living, as Scott claims in the introduction to *Rob Roy,* "on the very verge of the Highlands, and playing such pranks at the beginning of the eighteenth century as are usually ascribed to Robin Hood in the middle ages, and that within forty miles of Glasgow, a great commercial city, the seat of a learned university. Thus a character like his, blending the wild vir-tues, the subtle policy, and unrestrained license of an Amer-ican Indian, was flourishing in Scotland during the Augustan age of Queen Anne. . . ."

As history as well as fiction, these observations are extraordinary; from ballad collecting and reading, Scott had observed that history and circumstance shape character, that there was a difference between the character of his contem-poraries and those of the previous generation; that a High-land chief who is a hero in one age can become an outlaw in another and a criminal in a modern one, or he can be a pro-tector to his own people, but a villain, mysterious and terri-fying, to everyone else; and, finally, that the great heroic virtues of loyalty, courage, and honor are often found among the lawless, while the civilized are motivated, as Bentham claimed, by self-interest. Scott's sympathies lay with the outlaw, the bandits, the gypsies, pedlars, smugglers, poachers, all the mis-fits that as Sheriff he was supposed to be protecting the land-lords of Selkirkshire from. He found in the outlaws, the dis-possessed, and the rustics that same spontaneous expression of feeling in a strong and uncorrupted language that Words-worth chose to celebrate in his poetry. To Scott, the assim-ilation of these people, of their customs and manners into modern, urban, and Anglicized society meant the loss of an entire emotional dimension and manner of expression, a loss to Scottish national life, and to himself.

As a historical novelist, then, he resembles the wandering minstrels, bards, and balladeers, providing a record not so much of the events as what the events meant, how they were perceived by the people most affected by them—not the great public figures who inspire chronicles, not the ones who ini-tiate actions and are responsible for their success or failure, but the ones who participate and live with the consequences, the ones who do not leave records or memorials. The narra-tives—episodic, improbable, anecdotal, pictorial, often out of proportion—reflect this interest in what is remembered rather than what happened, how the "lower orders," his "principal personages," and the quite ordinary heroes and heroines who survive, how they perceive reality, rather than how it is officially recorded.[34]

The paradigm, one with considerable autobiographical significance, appears in *Waverley,* when Edward after many adventures with bandits, patriots, traitors, and thieves, marries the ordinary Rose, finding his place in "the quiet circle of domestic happiness, lettered indolence, and elegant enjoyments, of Waverley-Honour." Describing a future for him that is much like Scott's, Flora, the Jacobite heroine, predicts, "And he will refit the old library in the most exquisite Gothic taste, and garnish its shelves with the rarest and most valuable volumes; and he will draw plans and landscapes, and write verses and rear temples, and dig grottoes; and he will stand in a clear summer night in the colonnade before the hall, and gaze on the deer as they stray in the moon light, or lie shadowed by the boughs of the huge old fantastic oaks; and he will repeat verses to his beautiful wife, who will hang upon his arm; and he will be a happy man" (Chapter 52). In *Waverley,* Scott reveals the secret of his strength, his discovery of the "romance of real life," as Hazlitt called it, at that reconciliation between man and the world, a world over which one has little control, a world subject to the inexorable laws of history, nature, society. His novels offered a view of life that balanced the personal desire for freedom with the social necessity for order. He showed that to live in a world where history is destiny, human beings must adapt to survive, change, and diversify, act as if they were free, master themselves, and bring their own desires into line with existing necessities or, like his rebels, his Rob Roys and Meg Merrilies, choose goals other than happiness.

His novels not only helped him fulfill his own personal fantasies, but they suited the fantasies of his audience, an audience that chose to accept his subjective view of history. In the long economic depression and unrest that followed the peace of 1815, years when events supported and affirmed the theories of social scientists such as Bentham and Malthus, years when, as Shelley wrote in *The Triumph of Life,* it seemed that "God made irreconcilable / Good and the means of good" (ll.231–32) and all individual aspiration seemed futile, years when Byron's defiant but important heroes continued to divert the idle rich while the defiant poor were being ignored, shot, imprisoned, or deported by their own government, Scott's vision of the inevitable justice of history, the human potential for adapting to restrictions, provided comfort and a certain edifying illusion to the thousands of novel readers who purchased his books.

If he manipulated history to fulfill his own needs, if by placing his values, his conflicts, his solutions, in an historical setting he endowed them with anachronistic authority, he was far more artful and subtle than the eighteenth-century gothic novelists whose anachronisms, especially of character, so offended him. In the process he altered the course of historical writing. As Carlyle wrote in the *Edinburgh Review* (January, 1838), Scott's historical novels "have taught all men this truth. . . . : that the bygone ages of the world were actually filled with living men, not by protocols, state papers, controversies and abstractions of men. Not abstractions were they, not diagrams or theorems; but men in buff or other coats and breeches, with color in their cheeks, with passions in their stomach, and the idioms, features, and vitalities of every man!"

However prolific as a novelist and poet, and industrious as a lawyer, Scott was still unable to pay off the monumental debts that threatened his ownership of Abbotsford. He reviewed for the *Edinburgh Review,* and then for *The Quarterly,* as well as his own *Edinburgh Annual Register* (1808–1816).[35] He prepared editions of Swift, Dryden, Anna Seward, letters, papers, novels, biographies, even a history of Scotland that he had written in three volumes for his children. His major historical work, *The Life of Napoleon,* was an incredible performance—nine volumes completed in only two years, including interviews with those who knew Napoleon and research in newspapers, government documents, and journals. Scott was so prolific that, excluding the many works that are not in the major collections, his miscellaneous prose, published in 1871, came to thirty volumes; his letters, published from 1932 to 1937, came to twelve volumes; and the Border edition of the novels, published in 1893, came to forty-eight volumes. Yet he berated himself at the slightest sign of sloth, entering in his journal such invigorating notes as "If you once turn on your side after the hour at which you ought to rise it is all over. Bolt up at once" (p. 102). Some claim that his death in 1832, after a series of strokes, was caused by overwork.

Thomas Carlyle:
The Historian as Bard

If Scott was the minstrel of the Romantic period, Carlyle, born in 1795, the same year as John Keats, was its bard. His task was complex and often joyless: the historian–poet–priest–prophet, so described by Blake is the one who "Present, Past and Future sees," "Whose ears have heard / The Holy Word." Like Scott, indeed like Hazlitt in his role as annalist, Carlyle shared the Romantic impatience with literary conventions and the tendency toward incarnating ideas and forces, seeing people at the center and source of events. Adopting the odd exclamatory style, the prose-poetry of classical and Biblical derivation used by his fictional predecessor, Ossian, he set out to identify those who reveal God through their lives, the Heroes, the Great Men. Like Blake and Wordsworth, he believed they were everywhere, that history itself, another revelation of divine purpose, was merely an accumulation of their biographies. Using periodicals, pamphlets, lectures, and historical evocations that defy analysis, using the very machinery of publication that he abhorred, as bard and prophet, Carlyle set out to redeem his community by identifying human greatness, its relationship to the sacred, and the relationship between past and present.[36]

A product of the same Scottish intellectual climate with its peculiar combination of skepticism, superstition, historicism, common sense, and passion that produced Adam Smith, David Hume, James Hutton, Robert Burns, Sir Walter Scott, and James Hogg, Carlyle had a predisposition to find value in the past and, from his Calvinist faith in an elect, to believe in great men, an aristocracy of the spirit. He was born in Ecclefechan, a lowland village in the West of Scotland in 1795, one of ten children of a poor and pious stonemason. But, like Burns, he was educated far better than his English counterparts, for in Scotland even the children of peasants had been receiving free education for at least one hundred years.[37] In 1809, just before he turned fourteen, Carlyle walked the hundred miles to Edinburgh University to begin preparing for the ministry. Industrious, bright, frugal (living mostly on the turnips and oatmeal periodically sent from home along with his clean laundry), socially uncultivated, Carlyle was one among many of the poverty-stricken students who had come to the University to improve themselves and had little access to the riding, hunting, nocturnal drinking parties, and balls that diverted wealthier students such as Walter Scott. Taking the required curriculum, he became absorbed in mathematics and natural philosophy or science, especially geology, which at the time was taught by the aging John Playfair,[38] defender of Hutton's uniformitarianism.

While teaching school at Kirkaldy, Adam Smith's birthplace, he met the mercurial Edward Irving, a young minister who was to be his most loyal friend, depicted by Hazlitt in *The Spirit of the Age* as the fashionable London preacher whose success illustrated a "preposterous rage for novelty." Irving lent Carlyle a copy of Gibbon's *Decline and Fall of the Roman Empire* and introduced him to Mary Gordon, who inspired him to find a new occupation so he could afford to marry her. Returning to Edinburgh, he wrote some biographies for the *Edinburgh Encyclopaedia,* studied law, in which he had little interest or confidence, and decided to learn German so he could read the Neptunist Abraham Werner in the original and solve to his own satisfaction the debate between Playfair, representing Hutton, and his colleague Jameson, representing Werner. After Mary Gordon rejected him, he spent several despondent years reading German literature, undecided about his future until Irving introduced him to Jane Welsh, whom he courted for the next five years. In 1822, on the eve of Sir Walter Scott's ceremonial extravaganza to welcome George IV, the first Hanoverian to set foot in Scotland, Carlyle experienced the spiritual conversion recorded in *Sartor Resartus,* a work that expressed his contempt for all the outworn and extravagant symbols of power and belief, the spectacles, parades, costumes, formalities, and dinner parties, with which the reluctant, corpulent, and tearful king of England was so lavishly entertained.

Unable to earn a living in Edinburgh because of the same publishing depression that overcame Scott, Carlyle withdrew to Jane's ancestral farm, Craigenputtock, where Jane, overcoming her genteel upbringing by reading Cobbett's *Cottage Economy,* baked bread, and Carlyle wrote *Sartor Resartus.* From his own austere rural retreat, he exhorted the British public to abandon the materialistic philosophy of Bentham and the utilitarians, the worn-out symbols of religion, literature, and government, to overcome the self-centered emotionalism of the Byronic, and to explore "the region of the Wonderful," to see and feel that "life is girt with wonder and based on Wonder, and thy very blankets and breeches are Miracles" (p. 269). Since "man must work as well as wonder," he also advocated duty, obedience, and productivity as more appropriate goals than the pleasure or happiness that Hume and Bentham had claimed as motivating mankind, for in pursuing happiness "Always there is a black spot in our sunshine: it is . . . the *Shadow of Ourselves*" (p. 190). *Sartor Resartus* demonstrates the power of the human mind, the "wonder-working" or "Thaumaturgic art of thought," as he called it, by which one can give meaning to life, bring order out of chaos, and recognize the "natural supernaturalism," the spiritual force that inheres in nature, and the divinity with which man is endowed.[39]

This book, in itself a glorious excess, is also a parody of contemporary fashionable and intellectual excess, deflating the philosophical and emotional pretention, the worn-out beliefs and customs that afflicted European man with helplessness and depression in the opening decades of the nineteenth century. The title, cryptic Latin meaning "the tailor re-tailored" or even edited, refers to the project of the book: the life and works of Diogenes Teufelsdröckh ("God-born Devil's-dung") Professor of Things-in-General at Know-not-Where University, the author of *Clothes, Their Origin and Influence*. The narrator, an anonymous English editor, assembles the biographical remains of Teufelsdröckh from paper bags full of incoherent scraps, notes, and bills marked with signs of the zodiac, sent to him by Hofrath Heuschrecke (Councillor Grasshopper). It parodies both German scholarship, the intelligence invested in the history of trivia, and parasitical English scholarship, its devotion to the detritus of German scholarship, which the Editor does not understand. The fictional autobiography of Teufelsdröckh, his spiritual crisis, wandering, and recovery, his passage through the "Everlasting No," the "Centre of Indifference," and the "Everlasting Yea," recapitulates the experience of several generations of poets: Blake, Coleridge, Wordsworth, Byron, Shelley, and Keats followed similar patterns though for different reasons—excessive faith in the French Revolution and its subsequent failure, excessive faith in the creative imagination and its subsequent failure, excessive faith in nature, love, God, and subsequent disappointment.[40] Carlyle attributes the experience to excessive faith in the forms of things, the clothes, the institutions, symbols, laws, conventions, beliefs, all kinds of false expectations, and the brooding introspection that characterized those who were addicted and then alienated from them.

However lucid and practical his alternative—altering one's perspective, assuming command of one's life, engaging in a course of action—the style of *Sartor Resartus* seemed impenetrable as, through the voice of the Editor, Carlyle conceded: "Of his sentences perhaps not more than nine-tenths stand straight on their legs: the remainder are in quite angular attitudes, buttressed-up by props (of parentheses and dashes), and ever with this or the other tagrag hanging from them; a few even sprawl-out helplessly on all sides, quite broken-backed and dismembered" (p. 31). And yet it is precise, concrete, evocative; it resembles Scott's historical novels, rather than philosophy, which had become especially abstruse, or the passionate, evangelical sermons of Carlyle's friend Edward Irving, or even the critical journalism of Hazlitt himself, shrewdly alternating formal and colloquial diction and syntax.

Unable to find anyone to publish it as a book, Carlyle convinced the editor of *Fraser's Magazine* to publish it as a serial (1833–1834), an unpopular one in the end, although it attracted the attention of Ralph Waldo Emerson in America who wrote an introduction and had it published as a book. But Carlyle, moving to Chelsea, a fog-bound suburb of London, was already at work on the history of the French Revolution, an ill-fated work the first volume of which was burned accidentally by John Stuart Mill's maid. Like the phoenix, he began again, from memory, for he had already destroyed his notes, a prodigious act of will further inspired by another great conflagration of that year: the burning of the Houses of Parliament, and the elation with which it was greeted by the poor and the unemployed who interpreted it as divine retribution for the Poor Law of 1834, a law that threatened to confine them in workhouses. So while Bulwer-Lytton, making use of a century of archaeological research, aroused the public's appetite for historical and retributive catastrophe with *The Last Days of Pompeii* (1834), Carlyle, in an even more vivid style, began again to depict the French Revolution as divine justice, punishing the profligate and irresponsible aristocracy, an omen and admonition to the English ruling classes to whom the book, given its expense, was addressed.

Partly to compensate for the lack of research material, Carlyle imaginatively recreated events in a style he had learned from Scott, depicting the Revolution from within, from the perspective of the common people themselves, interpreted from time to time by a spectral voice: "Hunger whets everything, especially Suspicion and Indignation. Realities themselves, in this Paris have grown unreal, preternatural. Phantasms once more stalk through the brain of hungry

France." It appeared in 1837, the year "the poor little Queen," as Carlyle called her, ascended the throne at an age when, he claimed, she could hardly be trusted to choose her own bonnet. His friend, John Stuart Mill, identified Carlyle's role as bard: "This is not so much a history as an epic poem; and not withstanding or even in consequence of this, the truest of histories. It is the history of the French Revolution, and the poetry of it, both in one. . . ."[41] While few could quarrel with his method, some took exception to his interpretation. Wordsworth, for example, who had been in France at the time, witnessed the bloodshed, deplored the ideology that justified it, and suffered an emotional crisis as a consequence, objected to interpreting human violence as a divine instrument: "Hath it not long been said the wrath of Man / Works not the righteousness of God?" ("Dedicated to Liberty and Order").

To supplement his earnings as a writer, between 1838 and 1840, Carlyle offered a series of lectures on literary history, modern revolution, and on heroes, the latter published as *On Heroes, Hero-Worship, and the Heroic in History* (1841), offering an eccentric selection of figures—Odin, Mahomet, Dante, Luther, Samuel Johnson, Robert Burns, and Oliver Cromwell—who were divinely inspired and overcame great obstacles. The lectures were about heroes rather than heroism, for they seem to have accomplished very little. The portraits, in some ways reminiscent of *The Spirit of the Age,* offer symbols or incarnations of those attributes Carlyle considered necessary when the world is inhospitable to spiritual guidance. He identified the modern hero, the one who had replaced divinities, prophets, poets, rulers, as "a Man of letters," a creature made possible by the existence of printing and mass publication: "Much had been sold and bought, and left to make its own bargain in the marketplace; but the inspired wisdom of a Heroic Soul never till then in that naked manner. He with his copy-rights and copy-wrongs, in his squalid garret, in his rusty coat; ruling (for this is what he does), from his grave, after death, whole nations and generations who would, or would not, give him bread while living, is a rather curious spectacle!" (p. 154). His bitterness arose from the disappointment he had recently shared with Wordsworth, Southey, and Dickens, with whom he had agitated for copyright reform in England to extend protection to an author's heirs, and in America to extend international protection of literary properties against piracy.

Actually, Carlyle enjoyed a great deal of prestige as an

author, for, with the periodical press, the extension of literacy, and inexpensive publication, an author could live very well by his pen alone. When London replaced Edinburgh as a center for publication, it attracted literary talent as well as an educated middle and upper class that courted literary people, for whom they served as social advantages. In spite of his pedantic, broody, and irascible manners, Carlyle enjoyed the friendship not only of Ralph Waldo Emerson, John Stuart Mill, and Leigh Hunt, an unlikely combination, but also the new generation of Victorian writers such as George Meredith, Browning, Tennyson, Dickens, Arnold, Ruskin, and Harriet Martineau. Among the aging generation of Romantics, he considered Coleridge overrated and self-involved; Hazlitt, "thickheaded"; Lamb, a drunken fool and possibly insane; Hogg, vain and pretentious; Scott, greedy; and Wordsworth, aloof. While Carlyle found fashionable aristocrats, the combination of power, breeding, intelligence, wealth, and beauty irresistible, he lived modestly, refusing a baronetcy and pension on the grounds that he did not need the money. He and Jane maintained their provincial habits, both of them smoking a pipe, and, in spite of dyspepsia, maintaining a peasant diet of meat, potatoes, and porridge. He enjoyed swimming in icy northern rivers well into old age, but urban noises so offended him that he required a sound-proof study.

The decade following the publication of *The French Revolution* in England was so volatile that Carlyle's book appeared prophetic.[42] Twenty-five years after the war, it did indeed seem as if the population had exceeded the resources for supporting it: the English working-class was miserable and exploited, while capitalists, manufacturers, mine- and mill-owners, disregarding the human cost of their success, prospered. Improved travel and communications helped unify the country but they also contributed to the agitation that led many, like Friedrich Engels in *The Condition of the Working-Class in England in 1844,* to believe that revolution was at hand. Carlyle's solution was *Past and Present,* a moving and eloquent work in which he juxtaposed a twelfth-century monastery with a contemporary workhouse, recommending the revival of medieval paternalism and of communal life, the position held by Cobbett, Owen, and Southey, and the vision that lies behind Marx's *Communist Manifesto* (1848).[43]

As Carlyle grew older, although he had established his position as public prophet, historian, and bard, he invested immense energy in unrewarding biographies such as those of Oliver Cromwell (1845), John Stirling (1851), and finally, consuming thirteen years of dedicated and meticulous research, six volumes on Frederick the Great, someone he did not even like. In 1866, the boy who had walked next to a potato cart to get to Edinburgh fifty years before, returned triumphantly to accept an honorary post as Rector of the University. But his excitement was tempered by his wife's illness and news of her death, news communicated by telegraph, another measure of the technological progress during his lifetime.

For the last fifteen years of his life, he mourned her loss and lived on as "the sage of Chelsea," a disheveled prophet in a musty and disorganized house, visited by friends and dignitaries whom he would unpredictably charm or insult, who would overlook his anti-Semitism, his racism, and his fascism, the inevitable result of hero-worship. Carlyle, who, like Dostoevsky's Underground Man, would rather be free than happy, rejected the evidence accumulating around him that every aspect of life is guided by some version of Adam Smith's invisible hand, that history is destiny, and every act or form is somehow determined by an antecedent. Appealing to origins and history, Darwin (whose theory of human evolution Carlyle, for all his enlightened view of natural history, rejected) showed how human beings, even the best, are biologically determined; Marx, how they are economically determined; Tylor, in *Researches into the Early History of Mankind* (1865) and then James Frazer, how they were culturally determined; and Freud, how they were environmentally determined by early childhood experience.[44] While bards are allowed to shape experience to meet aesthetic standards, historians are not.

History and Poetry

The gradual fragmentation of human knowledge, the development of various disciplines, with specialized and often opposing methods and values, the collapse of the artificial eighteenth-century synthesis of human experience coincided with the Romantic period. Social science (formerly moral philosophy), natural science or natural history (formerly natural philosophy), history, philosophy, theology, and aesthetics, once part of a single body of knowledge, all sharing religious assumptions, became irreconcilable when the empirical method—the study of concrete evidence, experience, and experimentation—revealed how unrelated were the different compartments of knowledge, revealed, for example, that while Malthus's theories of population may be true, they were not beautiful, that Keats's poetry may be beautiful but not relevant, and that Hutton's geology may be both beautiful and true, but sacrilegious. The alliance between poetry and history lasted well into the nineteenth century in part because during earlier periods all the scholars—Warton, Percy, Macpherson, Ritson, Scott, Herder and his German disciples—believed that literature, especially ancient epics and ballads, offered an uncorrupted source of historical information. Certainly novelists and such topical poets as George Crabbe, Thomas Campbell, and James Montgomery continued to believe that their fictions also reflected manners and therefore provided a historical record. And finally, the alliance worked because many believed that to be a good historian, to apprehend, recreate, and convey the past, required as prodigious an act of imagination as writing poetry. For most poets, however, the singing was more important than the song; the journalist gradually replaced the bard as the recorder, the historian of his times.

Other forms of historical writing, however, did become possible with the extension and diversification of print and audiences: writers of all sorts published memoirs, reminiscences, and diaries recording the lives of shoemakers, booksellers, clergymen, of interesting people such as Charles Dibdin, successful ones such as Samuel Smiles, or sociable ones such as Henry Crabb Robinson. Not only did they record what happened to them but also how and where their private lives intersected with public events, providing an especially vivid social as well as intellectual history of the period. The *Monthly Review,* the *Annual Register,* the reviews and magazines consciously assumed an historical role, reflecting the events of the age and recording them for the future. Along with the periodicals, the press also published the results of the many inquiries and surveys, often statistical, that the British especially valued and on which much of our knowledge of the period is based. Surveys of prisons, poverty, child labor, schools, churches, transportation, agriculture, and trade influenced legislation and became historical documents.

Such information was unsuited, however, to the skills and purposes of imaginative writers, the memorialists of their times. So far had public life, however well recorded, drifted from the ideals of the past as preserved in literature, so far was it removed from aesthetic concerns, that it was difficult to find a poet who would serve as Poet Laureate, as an official bard: Scott turned down the post, Southey accepted it for the income, and Wordsworth accepted it so long as he was not expected to write anything. However grand, the events of this revolutionary age generated no contemporary epics except comic ones such as Byron's or mythic ones such as Blake's. Consequently, the French Revolution, to which M. H. Abrams attributes the Spirit of the Age,[45] did not have a historian until Carlyle wrote about it in 1837, the year Victoria ascended the throne unofficially ending the Romantic period. Although the Revolution and the long war that followed generated more records and reports, more printed material than librarians knew how to store and retrieve, a mass of uncatalogued, unclassified, and inaccessible primary sources accumulating in the British Museum, and in spite of having more written evidence to work from than previous historians, Carlyle wrote a history of the French Revolution that was much like Gibbon's *Decline and Fall*,[46] inventing probable characters and speeches, animating them with appropriate reactions and gestures, endowing his narrative with the purposeful shape of fiction or drama that real events seldom demonstrate. Romantic historicism, then, began with illusions represented as realities and culminated in realities represented as fiction, for fiction had become a way of coping with experience.

PART III

The Experimental Arts: Poetry, Painting, Science

CHAPTER XI

The Poetry of Life: The Philosophical Background

Tradition and Creativity

ALONG WITH THE fabricated Biblical, Hellenic, and gothic pasts, several other forms of history became available to the English Romantic writers: the documented public history, the organic record of natural history, and individual human memory or private history that became the special concern of artists and writers. This private history was potentially more deterministic than any other, for it was based on the belief that, as Wordsworth said, "'The Child is Father of the Man,'" history is destiny. However, the exploration of memory and the inner life released the creative energy that was a genuine source of freedom in a deterministic world. Moreover, the search within led to the realization, as Northrop Frye wrote in *A Study of English Romanticism* (1968), that human civilization itself—language, music, art, laws, religious and political institutions—was a human creation, not a divine gift, and that the continued influence of the mind could change them. Out of the various historical conventions grew a belief in progress, in the "March of Mind," as it was everywhere called, the spirit of improvement. "The 'good old times'," Byron writes sardonically, "all times when old are good":

> Great things have been, and are, and greater still
> Want little of mere mortals but their will.
> (*The Age of Bronze*, ll. 1, 3–4)

The belief that human energy, intellect, and vision could lead to the conquest of all ills and to a mastery of the environment inspired eloquence in many different and otherwise cautious thinkers such as Thomas Malthus, who opened his *Essay on Population* (1798) with the following:

> The great and unlooked for discoveries that have taken place of late years in natural philosophy, the increasing diffusion of general knowledge from the extension of the art of printing, the ardent and unshackled spirit of inquiry that prevails throughout the lettered and even unlettered world, the new and extraordinary lights that have been thrown on political subjects which dazzle and astonish the understanding, and particularly that tremendous phenomenon on the political horizon, the French Revolution, which, like a blazing comet, seems destined either to inspire with fresh life and vigour, or to scorch up and destroy the shrinking inhabitants of the earth, have all concurred to lead many able men into the opinion that we were touching on a period big with the most important changes, changes that would in some measure be decisive of the future fate of mankind.

As Malthus's statement indicates, to this generation progress did not mean freedom; many already saw an insoluble conflict between the belief that human beings are intellectually free enough to improve their lives, to provide themselves with what they need for wealth, pleasure, or comfort, and the belief that they are also bound by some form of natural law, necessity, or historical determinism that limits or shapes their choices, or even defeats them. Keats, for example, attributing Wordsworth's being "deeper than Milton" to "the grand march of intellect," to a freedom from superstition, concludes that "a mighty providence subdues the mightiest Minds to the service of the time being, whether it be in human Knowledge or Religion" (*Letters,* I, 282).

Most of the poets, however, the artists and scientists as well, considered the limitations of progress to be self-created, "Mind-forged manacles," as Blake called them. The study of origins had verified that mankind had the power of creation, a power that in its noblest function had created the gods themselves. Unfortunately, they invented gods that in turn enslaved them. "The Ancient Poets," Blake wrote in *The Marriage of Heaven and Hell,* "animated all sensible objects with Gods or Geniuses, calling them by the names and adorning them with the properties of woods, rivers, mountains, lakes, cities, nations," forming "a system" of priests and rituals:

And at length they pronounced that the Gods had ordered
such things.
Thus men forgot that All deities reside in the human
breast.

In spite of the power to liberate themselves, human beings
had a tendency to invent new forms of coercion in customs,
laws, traditions. Even the French Revolution, the great asser-
tion of liberty, was interpreted as inevitable. So Carlyle, among
others, recognized that losing freedom to a secular philoso-
phy was even more demeaning than losing it to a religious
one: "How changed in these new days! Truly may it be said,
the Divinity has withdrawn from the Earth; or veils himself
in that wide-wasting Whirlwind of a departing Era, wherein
the fewest can discern his goings. Not Godhead, but an iron
ignoble circle of Necessity embraces all things; binds the youth
of these times into a sluggish thrall, or else exasperates him
into a rebel" (*Characteristics*, 1831).

That same inner creative life, however, was the great if not
only source of freedom. Following John Locke's *Essay Con-
cerning Human Understanding* (1690), English philosophers as
diverse as Bishop Berkeley, David Hume, David Hartley,
Joseph Priestley, Jeremy Bentham, and William Godwin
claimed that there were no innate ideas, that human beings
were not born ignorant but free, that they learn only from
experience, that what they know, and do, and even become
in maturity is determined by what happens to them in their
youth or in the environment in which they are raised.[1] To
political scientists such as Bentham, Godwin, and Owen, to
the Edgeworths and other educational theorists influenced by
Rousseau, and to Coleridge, Southey, and the others plan-
ning ideal communities such as Pantisocracy, an ideal adult,
a happy, productive, contented, honest, loving, and cooper-
ative citizen was made by manipulating the environment of
children. Freed of the innate idea of natural depravity, chil-
dren would retain their natural innocence if they were pro-
tected from adult corruption, isolated in a rational and
antisceptic environment from urban, political, and religious
superstition.

Empiricism:
Hartley and Wordsworth

David Hartley's *Observations on Man, His Frame, His Duty
and His Expectations* (1749), based on Locke's psychology, had

such an influence on Coleridge that he named his son after
him, and Wordsworth, under the influence of Coleridge,
adopted many of his concepts and vocabulary to describe the
development of the human mind.[2] Starting with Locke's
assumption that there are no innate ideas, that all knowledge
is acquired from transactions between a human mind and the
external environment, Hartley developed a mechanical sys-
tem that accounted for the development of moral ideas from
these transactions, physical sensations that register as vibra-
tions in the brain. According to Hartley, sensations from the
external world are registered on the human mind; through
repetition, they become associated with other sensations; and
upon reflection, they develop into ideas of increasing com-
plexity, moral attitudes and insights, and finally spiritual
intuitions. If they are not totally corrupted by their environ-
ment, individuals can initiate this progress from feeling to
spiritual awakening at any time in life: acquire new sensa-
tions, reflect on them, associate them, until they ripen into
moral attitudes and spiritual insights. Some of Wordsworth's
nature lyrics written in the spring of 1798 are so uncritical of
Hartley's psychology that they appear to illustrate it. In "To
My Sister," for example, Wordsworth invites Dorothy to
join him on "the first mild day in March" to gather sensa-
tions, to share "the hour of feeling": "One moment now may
give us more / Than years of toiling reason." In "The Tables
Turned," he reveals the anti-intellectual biases of association-
ism, preferring sunshine to books:

> One impulse from a vernal wood
> May teach you more of man,
> Of moral evil and of good,
> Than all the sages can.

And in "Expostulation and Reply," he describes the "wise
passiveness," "a heart / That watches and receives" as con-
ditions for learning:

> 'The eye—it cannot choose but see,
> We cannot bid the ear be still;
> Our bodies feel where'er they be
> Against or with our will.'

The simplicity of Hartley's system was appealing to those
who, like Wordsworth, had lost touch with their own expe-
rience, who had become caught up in the subtle and abstract
intellectualism of such contemporary social theorists as Ben-
tham, Godwin, Malthus, and the French philosophers.

The simplicity was misleading. As research and historical records were essential to a society that believed its nature, function, even its destiny could be explained by its past, so memory and recollection were essential to an individual who believed that his past explained who and what he was. Moreover, the proliferation of printed records was making the collective memory obsolete as a means of preserving culture. Memory was becoming a personal faculty with strong psychological connotations. Confessions, memorials, histories, each attempting to explain the adult by the experiences of the child, inundated the magazines and booksellers, tales of success, of crime, and of sorrow. One common theme was nostalgia for the time in childhood before character was irrevocably established, when sensations were especially vivid, a time "Of splendour in the grass, of glory in the flower," as Wordsworth alludes to it in the Intimations Ode, contributing to the popular sentimentalism associated with childhood. Another common theme was helplessness, the sense of being a victim of early experiences over which one had no control, a theme that is especially evident in contemporary melodrama. If the events that ultimately determine character are all in the past, if many of the most significant ones are obscured by memory, then, like the monster in *Frankenstein,* like the growing child around whom the "Shades of the prison-house begin to close" in Wordsworth's Intimations Ode, we are all prisoners of our history.

Relief is to be found in recollection, in memory, in the reconstruction of the past as an act of will. Wordsworth, who explained learning as the unconscious assimilation of sensations and perceptions, and was especially favored by his childhood environment, had considerable difficulty in making the connections between his adult mind and his early experiences. In *The Prelude,* an epic exercise in recollection, he asks:

> Who knows the individual hour in which
> His habits were first sown, even as a seed,
> Who that shall point as with a wand and say,
> 'This portion of the river of my mind
> Came from yon fountain'?
>
> (II, 208–12)

After testing it against experience, Hartley's lucid and mechanical description of intellectual development as a process in the association of ideas appeared to Wordsworth as "a dark / Inscrutable workmanship that reconciles / Discordant elements, makes them cling together / In one society" (I, 341–44). Believing in recollection, habitually writing from "emotion recollected," as he claimed in the Preface to *Lyrical Ballads,* attributing to "shadowy recollections" in the Intimations Ode "the fountain-light of all our day," he was bewildered by the transformations of memory, by its relationship to his most significant imaginative experiences: "O! mystery of man, from what a depth / Proceed thy honors. I am lost, but see / In simple childhood," he carefully qualifies, "something of the base / On which thy greatness stands . . . (*The Prelude,* XI, 329–34). He accounts for the power of some memories through what he calls "spots of time," moments of intense experience recurring from earlier childhood that have the power to renovate, nourish, and repair the mind in maturity, to stimulate creativity. These "spots of time" are found

> Among those passages of life in which
> We have had the deepest feeling that the mind
> Is lord and master, and that outward sense
> Is but the obedient servant of her will.
> (*The Prelude* XI, 270–74)

In other words, those memories that are most significant occur when the mind is not passively feeding on sensation but is engaged in interpreting events. To account for those recollected experiences which cannot be attributed to childhood sensation, he revives the notion of innate ideas, represented in the Intimations Ode by the Platonic myth of pre-existence, the belief that the soul exists before it enters the body:

> Our birth is but a sleep and a forgetting:
> The Soul that rises with us, our life's Star
>   Hath had elsewhere its setting,
>   And cometh from afar:
>   Not in entire forgetfulness,
>   And not in utter nakedness,
> But trailing clouds of glory do we come
>   From God, who is our home.
>   (ll. 58–65)

His concern, as he explains in the preface to the poem, is the initial sense of glory, "the vividness and splendour which invest objects of sight in childhood" itself, a "visionary gleam" that cannot be accounted for by any mechanistic psychology. Wordsworth's concern with the functioning of the human mind, whether the creative or the criminal, and his careful analysis of memory are rare among his generation. Poets and critics disapproved of what appeared to be an excessive and brooding preoccupation with oneself, what Keats called the "egotistical sublime" (*Letters,* I, 387).

Idealism:
Berkeley and the Poets

Bishop Berkeley, a disciple of Locke, was concerned with the logical problem of how the mind, being immaterial, can know the external world. Rejecting the mechanical explanation of Hartley, he concluded that the external world exists only in perception, that, to cite a common example, if a tree falls in the forest and no one hears it, it makes no noise. Whether or not the external world exists may have been a silly problem, but by denying its independent existence, by making the reality of the world depend upon its being perceived, Berkeley and later David Hume elevated the mind itself, emancipated it from its passive dependence on environment. The mind became the origin of meaning and value. This idealism appealed to such Romantic poets as Blake, who claimed that "Mental things alone are real: what is called corporeal nobody knows of its dwelling place" *(A Vision of the Last Judgment),* and Shelley invoked "human thought" to give meaning to "The Everlasting universe of things," as he called the world in *Mont Blanc,* and a "dark reality," "life's unquiet dream," as he called it in *Hymn to Intellectual Beauty.*[3] Wordsworth found the mind itself "A thousand times more beautiful than the earth / On which he dwells," "Of substance and of fabric more divine" (*The Prelude,* XIII, 447–52). By elevating the mind over nature, by recognizing that it was the source of meaning and value, Wordsworth overcame the final vestiges of that passive mechanical role Hartley and the other empirical philosophers had assigned to it.

The skeptical and idealistic reaction to Locke's empiricism had denied significance to the external world, the world of nature and society, the traditional sources of artistic inspiration. But the same response endowed the mind with creative power and emancipated the artist from his servile role of imitating the world as it is known by most people. For the Romantic poets, seeing was creating, perception was invention; meaning, beauty, significance were conferred on the world by the observer, by his imagination, not simply received as part of the observation.[4] As Blake concluded in *The Marriage of Heaven and Hell,* "Where man is not, Nature is barren." Or Shelley, after exploring his vision on Mont Blanc and all the power it represents, concluded:

> And what were thou, and earth, and stars, and sea
> If to the human mind's imaginings
> Silence and solitude were vacancy. (ll. 142–44)

Not only are beauty and meaning conferred on the world by the observer, but also the world itself takes on the character of the observer: "As a man is, so he sees," Blake wrote, "As the eye is formed, such are its Powers." In his depression, Coleridge complained that he had lost the "shaping spirit of Imagination": "I may not hope from outward forms to win / The passion and the life, whose fountains are within" ("Dejection: An Ode," ll. 45–46). The world reflected his own depleted resources, his inner void: "we receive but what we give, / And in our life alone does Nature live" (ll. 46–48). Wordsworth agreed that the imagination is the source of meaning, value, even joy; he believed, as he wrote in *The Prelude*—addressed to Coleridge—"from thyself it is that thou must give / Else never canst receive" (XI, 329–30). And, dealing with loss in the Intimations Ode, also addressed to Coleridge, he concluded that the imagination is altered by grief not destroyed, that perception is conditioned by experience not obliterated:

> The Clouds that gather round the setting sun
> Do take a sober colouring from an eye
> That hath kept watch o'er man's mortality.

Such responses made a virtue of the subjectivity, the relativity that Locke and his followers had considered obstacles to knowledge and contributed to what now appears to be a perpetual debate between the truth of art and the truth of science.

The Common Sense Philosophers

The belief in both an active mind and the reality of the external world found ample support among the Scottish Common Sense philosophers—Thomas Reid, James Beattie, Adam Smith, and Dugald Stewart, who indirectly had an enormous influence on British aesthetics—although their initial concern had been the contemporary moral degeneration of Edinburgh, which they attributed to the skeptical philosophy of David Hume. Reid shifted the focus of discussion to the mind, visualized spatially as a set of faculties or powers, such as memory, imagination, parental love, similar to the innate ideas that Locke and his followers had discarded, faculties that predispose the way people respond to experience. He dismissed Hartley's process of association and proposed that knowledge comes from the direct apprehension of the external world, which is real enough not to require verification. This is the major point of Beattie's *Essay on the Nature and Immutability of Truth* (1770), for which George III gave him a pension and because of which Sir Joshua Reynolds depicted him allegorically in a painting called *The Triumph of Truth*. On an issue relevant to aesthetics, the Common Sense philosophers agreed with Hume, who employed imagination not as an inventive or poetic faculty, but as a connecting or social faculty. Described by Adam Smith in his *Theory of Moral Sentiments,* this imaginative faculty had a positive social function enabling people to anticipate the consequences of their actions and to identify with one another, both of which were essential for the complex democratic community that was evolving. This idea of imagination influenced Hazlitt's aesthetics and, ultimately, Keats's concept of "sympathetic imagination," the poet's special ability to invest himself in his creations. Hazlitt and Keats gave the concept a curious turn by making this imagination amoral: "The Poetical Character," Keats writes, "is everything and nothing—It has no character—it enjoys light and shade; it lives in gusto, be it foul or fair, high or low, rich or poor, mean or elevated—It has as much delight in conceiving an Iago as an Imogen. What shocks the virtuous philosopher, delights the camelion Poet" (*Letters,* I, 387). Through Dugald Stewart's lectures on moral philosophy at the University of Edinburgh, the same principles of common sense shaped the aesthetics and social philosophy of a diverse set of writers ranging from James Mill, the utilitarian; Carlyle, a transcendentalist; and Frances Jeffrey, the founder of the *Edinburgh Review,* who had an immense influence on public taste.[5]

Physiognomy and Phrenology

Yet one more philosophical reaction against both Locke and the skeptical reaction to him appears in a bizarre but influential set of theories advocated by the physiognomists and phrenologists. Their origins were in folklore, popular superstition, and religion, in any belief that physical deformity or beauty reflects the state of the soul or one's relationship with a powerful supernatural being. The "Science" of physiognomy was invented by Fuseli's friend Lavater, who believed that the body is inhabited by God and that facial characteristics reflect its character or spiritual nature. Many authors had used physiognomic principles in presenting their characters—Chaucer's pilgrims and Shakespeare's villains, for example. It was suited to the stage, especially the simplifications of pantomime and melodrama where villains could be identified by complexion and heroines by the color of their hair. And with the rise of print, which increased the value of visual signals, physiognomy provided the basic vocabulary for cartoons and decorative engravings. Even after the Romantic period it found such ardent disciples as Robert Fitzroy, Captain of the *Beagle,* who considered rejecting Charles Darwin as his naturalist on his trip to South America in 1831 because Darwin's nose did not exhibit "energy and determination."[6]

Following F. J. Gall and his disciple J. C. Spurzheim, the phrenologists believed that the shape and contours of the skull reflect not a spiritual state but an organic and intellectual one. They visualized the brain itself as a collection of organs representing intellectual or moral faculties such as parental love, friendship, pride, memory, aesthetic talent, piety, wit, and so on, many of which were the innate ideas that Locke had banished and that the Scottish Common Sense philosophers had revived. Common Sense philosophy and phrenology had much in common and ought to have complemented one another, but, when Spurzheim visited Edinburgh and in public dissections attempted to locate the powers or faculties in specific areas of cerebral anatomy, the Scots rejected him, for he was merely exchanging one form of materialism and its fatalistic consequences for another.[7] Coleridge considered Spurzheim "a good man," but "dense, and the most ignorant German I ever knew. If he had been content with stating certain remarkable coincidences between the moral qualities and the configuration of the skull, it would have been well; but when he began to map out the cranium dogmatically, he fell into infinite absurdities. You know, that every intellectual act, however you may distinguish it by name in respect of the originating faculties, is truly the act of the entire man; the notion of distinct material organs, therefore, in the brain itself, is plainly absurd."[8]

In localizing certain responses in the brain, Gall and Spurzheim contributed to the development of neurology, but their fame arose from rather frivolous associations. Spurzheim's mobility, his lectures in Great Britain and America, his phrenological heads and charts suitable for the drawing room, and his concession that character could be amended helped to popularize phrenology and augmented the symbolic vocabulary for conveying character that painters and novelists had acquired from physiognomy. As a parlor amusement, the best-known incident concerning phrenology took place at what Benjamin Robert Haydon called his Immortal Dinner on December 28, 1815, when the drunken Charles Lamb took a candle to examine the "phrenological development" of a comptroller of stamps who had tried to engage Wordsworth in conversation by asking, "Don't you think Newton a great genius?" "Do let me have another look at that gentleman's organs," Lamb exclaimed before being rushed out of the room by a very amused John Keats and Haydon.[9]

Fragmented Philosophy and Philosophical Poetry

Idealism, skepticism, mysticism, common sense, phrenology were all in some way reactions against the materialism of Locke and the associationists. After studying Locke, Berkeley, and Hartley, Coleridge questioned in *Biographia Literaria*, Book XI, if it were even possible to have "a system of philosophy" aside from "mere history and historical classification," as if "the sole practicable employment for the human mind was to observe, to collect, and to classify," activities he considered a "wilful resignation of intellect." It was even harder to reconcile these philosophical systems with poetry, for they rejected the creative imagination as misleading, as an inappropriate use of the human mind.[10] Nonetheless, the empiricists, the ones most opposed to imagination, served the poets, indeed, the painters and scientists as well, for Locke turned their attention from the world above, the supernatural, to the world around them as a source of knowledge and inspiration. After Locke, as Basil Willey indicates, a poet had to "either make poetry out of the direct dealings of his mind and heart with the visible universe, or . . . [to] fabricate a genuine new mythology of his own."[11] The poets in turn were emancipated from the "visible universe," from the power of the environment which had become as tyrannical as the superstition it replaced, by those active-mind philosophers, the skeptics and idealists who were also stimulated by Locke. These philosophers identified the world within, the mind and the imagination, as the source of energy, of value, meaning, and knowledge. Consequently, by 1818, a poet such as Keats could exclaim, "I see, and sing, by my own eyes inspired" ("Ode to Psyche," 1.43), and lament that so few know they have "original minds" and "are led away by Custom": "almost any man may like the spider spin from his own inards his own airy Citadel" (*Letters,* I, 231–32).

Unfortunately, the philosophers themselves knew little of such creativity, seldom enjoyed the freedom to build their own "Citadels," for, like the historians, they were constrained by their method or by tradition, by Blake's "Mind-forged manacles." Philosophy made enormous contributions to the understanding of human experience and behavior during the eighteenth century, but it was essentially cheerless, bound by some idea of necessity, and illustrating what Byron called "the fatal truth": "The tree of knowledge is not that of life" (*Manfred,* I.i.12). While traditional concepts were becoming obsolete, overtaken by the March of Mind, by technical and intellectual achievement, philosophical inquiry had become timid and irrelevant. Philosophers were debating the reality of the external world while engineers were building iron bridges, Captain Cook was exploring new continents, and the astronomer, William Herschel, was naming the stars and speculating on the existence of remote galaxies. Even philosophical writing held little appeal for a reading public that preferred romances, poetry, political pamphlets, religious inspiration, a reading public that, as the contents of the magazines reveal, would read about any useful subject, however abstruse, including contemporary theories of electricity, chemistry, animal diseases, and mathematical computation.

Like many disciplines, after the brief and artificial coherence of the Enlightenment, philosophy appeared fragmented and specialized. Natural philosophy became concerned with what we now call science, and each of the sciences in turn developed special vocabularies, methods, and problems in such areas as physics, botany, zoology, anatomy, and geology. Moral philosophers developed the special perspective and statistical interests that we now associate with the social sciences, history, and such historical studies as philosophy, archaeology, and anthropology. The philosophy we have been describing, epistemology, the study of knowledge and how it is acquired, became psychology, developing principles and laws to explain not only the nature of knowledge but also its limits and acquisition, perception, relationship, motivation, and character as well. As information about knowledge of mankind and nature expanded, it not only lost touch with a central core of values through specialization but also it lost touch with life itself. As Shelley claimed in *A Defense of Poetry:* "We have more moral, political and historical wisdom, than we know how to reduce into practice; we have more scientific and economical knowledge than can be accommodated to the just distribution of the produce which it multiplies. The poetry in these systems of thought, is concealed by the accumulation of facts and calculating processes. . . . We want the creative faculty to imagine that which we know; we want the generous impulse to act that which we imagine; we want the poetry of life" (pp. 68–69).

If philosophy became fragmented, uncreative, and uninspired, literature, especially poetry, became more philosophical, more comprehensive. Blake, for example, who was especially critical of contemporary materialistic philosophy, declares through Los, the figure representing human imagination in *Jerusalem:* "I must create a system or be enslaved by another Man's / I will not Reason & Compare; my business is to create." Wordsworth, at Coleridge's urging, spent much of his life writing what was to be a great *philosophical* poem. In *The Excursion,* one part that he completed, he recommends philosophical speculation as a cure for despondency:

> If tired with systems, each in its degree
> Substantial, and all crumbling in their turn,
> Let him build systems of his own, and smile
> At the fond work, demolished with a touch!
> (IV, 603–6)

And Keats, who admired the philosophical poetry of Wordsworth, and who appeared often on the verge of speculation himself, claimed at one point that poetry is "not so fine a thing as philosophy—For the same reason that an eagle is not so fine a thing as truth" (*Letters,* II, 81). Fortunately, he believed most of the time that truth is "what the imagination seizes as beauty," that aesthetic integrity takes priority over analysis and reasoning.

The Imagination

"The poetry of life," as Shelley called it, had little to do with verse, rhyme, and diction. To the Romantic generation of writers, scientists, painters, to anyone who had an interest in human experience that existing knowledge did not account for, the poetry of life was any experience that inspires a creative response, displays aesthetic values, arouses the imagination, and provides pleasure, a sense of coherence and harmony. It is found in those perceptions, to quote Words-worth, where "the mind / Is lord and master," and "outward sense / Is but the obedient servant of her will" (*The Prelude,* XI, 271–73). The poetry of life may be found in the landscape, in the human body, in human relationships, in natural forces, supernatural visions, concepts, beliefs, and dreams. It may be expressed as poetry itself or as painting, music, history, landscape gardening, even science, all those human endeavors that reveal the creative powers of the mind being asserted over the mindless, the animating power of the imagination over the lifeless and inert.[12]

The key to the poetry of life is the imagination, both as a human faculty and as a quality of human expression. During the Romantic period, the poets and the literary critics who wrote about poetry became both advocates and witnesses of the imagination. They endowed it with a special literary significance while redeeming it from traditional associations with madness, irrationality, and deception, which had become exaggerated in the eighteenth century when so much value had been placed on reason. Whatever the prevailing philosophy maintained, writers such as Cervantes, Shakespeare, and Swift, to name a few, had always known that rationality, not imagination, is the source of madness, evil, even violence. From about 1760, however, shortly after Bishop Young's *Conjectures on Original Composition,* and, incidentally, coinciding with that vast reinterpretation of human experience we found in the historical revivals, the imagination began to acquire positive associations. In *Zoonomia* (1794–1796) Erasmus Darwin claimed that the sex of an unborn child is determined by what the father is imagining at the moment of fertilization. By 1826, when Lamb wrote "The Sanity of True Genius," it had become a commonplace that imagination was universally shared and among poets a sign of their sanity as well as genius, for, unlike the lunatic and the dreamer, a poet "is not possessed by his subject, but has dominion over it."

During the Romantic period, writers attributed to the imagination many functions that had been in the past and would become again, perhaps under other names, the proper concerns of philosophy, psychology, theology, science, sociology, as well as poetry. It could invent, interpret, order, create, and perceive relationships—relationships between language and experience, form and function, the internal and external world, the human and the natural, the human and the supernatural, individuals and society, the sacred and the secular, the past and the present, the present and the future, the public and the private or inner self. To everyone, not just poets, it offered an extension of rather than an alternative to common experience, a way of perceiving that clarifies and enriches life, that gives significance to the ordinary and makes the exceptional seem familiar. Many of these functions were identified by Wordsworth and Coleridge when they set out to write the *Lyrical Ballads* (as Coleridge recorded it in the opening of Chapter XIV of the *Biographia*), and were shared by their contemporaries. Coleridge, primarily interested in the supernatural, was "to transfer from our inward nature a human interest and a semblance of truth sufficient to procure for these shadows of imagination that willing suspension of disbelief." But Wordsworth was to choose things from "ordinary life"; "to give the charm of novelty to things of every day, and to excite a feeling analogous to the supernatural, by awakening the mind's attention from the lethargy of custom and directing it to the loveliness and wonders of the world before us; an inexhaustible treasure, but for which, in consequence of the film of familiarity and selfish solicitude, we have eyes yet see not, ears that hear not, and hearts that neither feel nor understand."

However diverse in style and ideology, all the major poets, and the prose writers from Hazlitt to Carlyle, believed that humanity as a whole, and Englishmen certainly, were too enthralled by contemporary systems of thought, by history, by philosophy, by custom. They believed that everyone could be liberated through an awakening of imagination that was their common goal: "What we have loved," Wordsworth tells Coleridge in his dedicatory conclusion to *The Prelude,* "Others will love; and we may teach them how" (XIII, 444–45).

A source of invention, of freedom, of community, the imagination acquired a religious function as well, creating as God created, and bringing divinity, the sacred, however it was conceived, back into human affairs. The Anglican church, institutional Christianity, was spiritually depleted, a source of income for younger or improvident sons, a source of social or political credentials. Empirical philosophers, as well as the believing deists and the unbelieving skeptics, had denied the intervention of God in human affairs, and repudiated the possibility of miracles, revelations, and intercessions. And the popular cults, the followers of Richard Brothers, Joanna Southcott, and the many derivatives of popular Methodism, encouraging an apocalyptic hysteria, belittled the value of worldly experience. The poets, whose inspirations were worldly but whose aspirations were not, responded by reviv-

ing their ancient priestly roles as mediators between the sacred
and the secular, interpreting the supernatural as an extension
of life allied with the imagination. Literature became a reli-
gious surrogate, or, as M. H. Abrams writes in *Natural
Supernaturalism,* a "displaced and reconstituted theology," "a
secularized form of devotional experience."[13] To Blake, "The
Eternal Body of Man is the Imagination, that is, God himself
. . . It manifests itself in his Works of Art . . ." *(The Lao-
coön).* In *Biographia Literaria,* Chapter XIII, Coleridge dis-
tinguished a special form of imagination, the "primary"
imagination as a divine analogue, "the living power and prime
agent of all human perception, and as a repetition in the finite
mind of the eternal act of creation in the infinite I AM." Shel-
ley claimed in his *Defense of Poetry* that it "redeems from decay
the visitations of the divinity in Man." Keats, defending "the
Holiness of the Heart's affections" to his friend, Benjamin
Bailey, a divinity student, assigned it a prophetic or prefigur-
ative function: "Imagination and its empyreal reflection is the
same as human Life and its spiritual repetition" *(Letters,* I,
185). Wordsworth, describing the developing mind of a child,
depicts it as helping to fulfill a divine intent:

> his mind,
> Even as an agent of the one great Mind
> Creates, creator and receiver both,
> Working but in alliance with the works
> Which it beholds.—Such verily is the first
> Poetic spirit of our human life. (II, 273–76)

And in the Prospectus to *The Excursion,* the text Abrams
explicates in *Natural Supernaturalism,* Wordsworth describes
the imagination as redemptive, restoring the lost paradises of
pagan and Hebraic-Christian belief, mediating between the
divine and the natural:

> Paradise, and groves
> Elysian, Fortunate Fields—like those of old
> Sought in the Atlantic Main—why should they be
> A history only of departed things,
> Or a mere fiction of what never was?
> For the discerning intellect of Man
> When wedded to this goodly universe
> In love and holy passion, shall find these
> A simple produce of the common day.   (ll. 47–55)

The imagination also served as mediator between man and
nature. To idealists such as Blake and Shelley, to whom nature

was itself lifeless and the source of much error, the landscape responded to the imagination and provided symbols, correspondences, and analogies. Objecting to Wordsworth's dependence on nature, claiming "natural Objects did & now do weaken, deaden & obliterate Imagination in Me," in his own verse, Blake used clouds, clods of clay, pebbles, roses, lilies of the valley, worms, sun flowers, and thistles in symbolic roles in the continuing dialogue between spirit and matter. He saw "a World in a Grain of Sand," "Heaven in a Wild Flower," and "Israel's Tents" shining in the "Atoms of Democritus / And Newton's Particles of Light" ("Auguries of Innocence," ll. 1–2; "Mock on, Voltaire, Rousseau," ll. 9–12). Shelley often conceived of nature in a similar fashion as, in *Hellas* for example, an expression of imagination but without any reality in itself:

> Thought
> Alone, and its quick elements, Will, Passion,
> Reason, Imagination, cannot die;
> They are, what that which they regard, appears,
> The stuff whence mutability can weave
> All that it hath dominion o'er, worlds, worms,
> Empires, and superstitions   (ll. 795–801)

And Wordsworth, who at one time believed, following Hartley, that the mind is formed passively by impulses from the vernal woods, described his observations in "Tintern Abbey" (ll. 106–7) as half-perceived and half-created. The imagination, as he writes in *The Prelude,* is "creator and receiver both, / Working but in alliance with the works / Which it beholds" (II, 274–76). Sustaining his faith in this interchange was a belief that "man and nature [are] essentially adapted to each other," as he wrote in the Preface to *Lyrical Ballads* (1802), a belief he shared with geologists, anatomists, and botanists, who also recognized

> How exquisitely the individual Mind
> (And the progressive powers perhaps no less
> Of the whole species) to the external World
> Is fitted:—and how exquisitely, too—
> Theme this but little heard of among men—
> The external World is fitted to the Mind;
> And the creation (by no lower name
> Can it be called) which they with blended might
> Accomplish.   ("Prospectus," ll. 64–71)

Although Wordsworth's attitude toward nature is different from Shelley's and Blake's, and although their attitudes very much differ from those of Coleridge, Keats, and Byron, the lyrical poems in which natural objects are the subject are similar, for the poets' interests were not in external nature itself but in how the mind relates to it.[14] Whether the poet is Blake talking about lambs and tigers, Coleridge confined to a lime-tree bower, Wordsworth recollecting a field of daffodils, Shelley meditating on Mont Blanc, or Keats addressing a nightingale, the poems have a common concern: how the poet feels about the external world, how he relates to it, and what it means to him as an occasion, a metaphor, or a symbol.[15] Art and theater criticism as well as history reflect the same attitude: how the mind, the imagination, is affected, how it responds to an event, and how the response is more important than the event itself.

More political than aesthetic in origins, the sympathetic imagination relates human beings with one another, with the external world, and with the consequences of their own actions. But it also was the basis for a special poetic form: a narrative that was both dramatic and subjective. It is characterized by a clearly developed narrative voice representing a point of view other than the author's. The subject of such a poem is neither the action nor the narrator himself, but the way he perceives and responds to events or to the world around him. Identifying the nature of the narrative voice, determining if it is reliable, sane, naive, deranged, and what it is responding to in the fictional environment is absolutely crucial in interpreting such poetry. For example, in *Songs of Innocence*, Blake represents the same fallen world as he represents in the *Songs of Experience*, but it is viewed by a naive or a series of naive narrators.[16] The primary narrator, the Piper, differs from the Bard, the narrative voice in the *Songs of Experience*, because he sees by a "celestial light." He moves about, as Wordsworth described that same state in Intimations Ode, "in worlds not realised" (l. 144), or, like the young Apollo in Keats's *Hyperion*, "In fearless yet in aching ignorance" (III, 107). The instructed mind or the awakening consciousness were especially attractive points of view for the Romantic poets, who literally reconstructed the naive perspective from their own past, often idealized but sometimes brutally honest. They were also fascinated by the insane point of view. In *The Rime of the Ancient Mariner*, Coleridge was more interested in how his deranged narrator, the crazed old sailor, remembers what happened than in what actually happened, but he had to educate his audience, providing them with the cues in notes and glosses, to appreciate this imaginative point of view. Similarly, because Wordsworth's readers believed "The Thorn" was about a demented mother who had murdered and buried her child by a storm-blasted tree, he wrote a headnote to explain that it was about the narrator—"a Captain," he writes explicitly, "of a small trading vessel," "past the middle age of life," "credulous and talkative from indolence," and "prone to superstition"—and the way he views the tree.[17] And in *Childe Harold*, Byron invented the persona he finally became, claiming it as his motive for writing:

> 'Tis to create, and in creating live
> A being more intense, that we endow
> With form our fancy, gaining as we give
> The life we image. . .
> (*Childe Harold*, III.46–49)

For Byron, the poet became the poem; the creator, the creation.

The same sympathetic imagination that allowed an author to identify with external nature, with art, with history, to identify with his own artistic creations, with other versions of himself, and with his own inner lives, also held great perils for the poet whose visions became nightmares. Prometheus, in Shelley's *Prometheus Unbound*, besieged by furies who embodied his hatred of Jupiter, learned how a wayward vision could overcome the visionary: "Methinks I grow like what I contemplate / And laugh and stare in loathsome sympathy" (I, 450–51). Or the vision could seem to take on an independent life and become repellent to the poet, an experience Keats described in "Ode to a Nightingale" when his imagination led him to "faery lands forlorn," and the spell, originating in the song of the nightingale, is broken: "Forlorn! the very word is like a bell / To toll me back from thee to my sole self!" Or in Coleridge's "Kubla Khan," the poet is enchanted with his own vision and becomes intoxicated and isolated by it:

> Beware! Beware!
> His flashing eyes, his floating hair!
> Weave a circle round him thrice,
> And close your eyes with holy dread,
> For he on honeydew hath fed,
> And drunk the milk of Paradise. (ll.49–54)

The poets were so fascinated by imagination that they often wrote poems about it, such as "Kubla Khan," poems describing their own generation, or the creative experience in general, or, ironically, the failure of that experience. Coleridge's "Dejection: An Ode," a dirge over the loss of the "shaping spirit of Imagination," is one of his most successful poems, as is Shelley's "Ode to the West Wind," in which he laments his loss of inspiration.

In order to write about the imagination, poets had to create symbols for it. Blake and Byron described it as a source of energy such as a volcano or the sun. Others represented it as a bird, the isolated and invisible nightingale singing, as Shelley claimed in the *Defense of Poetry,* to cheer itself, or as the skylark soaring over its nest, as Wordsworth described it, in a "privacy of glorious light": "Type of the wise who soar, but never roam; / True to the kindred points of Heaven and Home"—an image that captures the terrestrial biases of even the most visionary verse of the period. Like Coleridge in his youth, they could compare imagination to an Aeolian harp, passively responding to the inspiration found in nature, represented by the wind.[18] Or, more assertively, it was identified with light—from within, from above, or, as Wordsworth wrote in "Peele Castle," the "light that never was" at all. Such light imagery not only suffuses the poetry but also preoccupied the painters, scientists, and divines, for all of whom it not only represented the traditional idea of truth, divine as well as secular illumination, but also, when viewed as atoms, waves, spectrums, reflections, or refractions, offered an example in nature of that similitude in dissimilitude that Wordsworth claimed in the Preface to *Lyrical Ballads* is "the great spring of the activity of our minds." The most appealing form of light was moonlight, for its mystery, its shadows, its transformations most nearly resembled the activity of the imagination itself, represented magnificently in Wordsworth's extended analogy in *The Prelude* (XIV, 63–87) between the moon on Mount Snowdon and the creative mind.

Except in certain religious moments, there was no precedent for the imaginative experience among rational people, and few understood its nature. What the poets knew of imagination was gained from studying its action and interaction, from self-observation and self-consciousness, from the same scientific inquiry to which it also applied. Consequently, poems and paintings, as well, were creative experiments, providing information about the imagination itself that altered or enlarged the artist's or poet's understanding of it. The Romantic poets offer in their poetry a record of their creative life, the life of the imagination. Few were as meticulous and conscientious as William Wordsworth, who recognized that the value of his vision would depend upon his validating the nature of the visionary, that, along "with the thing Contemplated," as he wrote in the Prospectus to *The Excursion,* he must "describe the Mind and Man / Contemplating; and who and What he was," "when and where, and how he lives," as part of the vision.

William Wordsworth

Born in 1770, Wordsworth was sent after his mother died to Hawkshead with his brothers to be raised by a Quaker, Dame Tyson, among the gently rolling hills around the placid lake in the Vale of Esthwaite.[19] An active, even volatile child, he recalls this time with pleasure, a time when "I breathed with joy" (II, 194). In 1787, he entered St. John's, Cambridge, prepared in math and science above his peers, appropriately clothed in powdered hair, a velvet coat, and silken hose, as he ironically depicts himself in Book III of *The Prelude.* Amid the clatter of the college kitchens beneath his rooms he could hear "Trinity's loquacious clock" and see

> The antechapel where the statue stood
> Of Newton with his prism and silent face,
> The marble index of a mind for ever
> Voyaging through strange seas of Thought, alone.
> (1850, ll.60–64)

Wordsworth claimed to have been a dilatory student, wavering between idleness and introspection, critical of the institution, the examinations, the academic politics, and the lazy and uninspired faculty. He felt he was different from the others, "not for that hour, / Nor for that place," perhaps in some ways superior, "a chosen son," a "Freeman" "otherwise endowed," inhabiting other and private worlds: "I had a world about me—'twas my own; / I made it, for it only lived to me, / And to the God who looked into my mind" (III.142–44). Separated from his origins and the expectations others had for him, he discovered an inner solitude, a psychological identity, and something of its power: how "each man [becomes] a memory to himself," the "points . . . within our souls / Where all stand single" (III, 189, 186–87). Returning from a country dance at sunrise, during the summer holiday

when he was eighteen years old, he discovered his vocation
as a poet:

> My heart was full; I made no vows, but vows
> Were then made for me; bond unknown to me
> Was given, that I should be, else sinning greatly,
> A dedicated Spirit.   (IV, 340–45)

In the summer of 1790, along with his friend Robert Jones,
he went on a walking tour of the Alps to collect material for
his poetry, and he found it not so much in the scenery itself
as in his response to it, a response he was not to understand
until almost fifteen years later when he completed the first
long version of *The Prelude* in 1805. He was, he recalled, dis-
appointed in Mont Blanc, a huge, silent, glaciated peak that
most poets addressed at one time or another, because in com-
parison with his expectations it was merely a "soulless image,"
that had "usurped upon a living thought / That never more
could be" (VI, 454–56). At Simplon Pass he encountered a
similar discrepancy between what he anticipated as the spec-
tacular experience of crossing the Alps and the reality of
crossing without even being aware of it. From both experi-
ences he learned that the recollections from which his imagi-
nation would create poetry were not to be gathered like
souvenirs. Poetry, he concluded, did not arise from encoun-
ters with conventionally poetic occasions.[20]

A careful and reflective observer, Wordsworth gathered
information about nature that he would later interpret with
the eyes of a painter, and the insight of a scientist; he saw the
world of process that natural scientists were also discovering
in the laboratories, in museums, and among the mountains.
He saw, as they did, that nature was a self-perpetuating sys-
tem of forces: "woods decaying, never to be decayed," "sta-
tionary blasts of waterfalls," "Winds thwarting winds,
bewildered and forlorn," "types and symbols of Eternity, /
Of first, and last, and midst, and without end" (VI, 557–
72). James Hutton, the geologist, studying the same features
of the landscape, the winds, clouds, vegetation, and the
waterfalls, arrived at the same observation: "We find no sign
of a beginning—no prospect of an end"—which made him a
heretic among those geologists who were still busy finding
verification of Genesis in the landscape. Similar forces so fas-
cinated Constable and Turner that they tried to arrest the
running waters, the passing seasons, the changing clouds
without losing the vitality, Turner going so far as to depict
energy, motion, force, even speed itself in a visual form.

Although Wordsworth's vision was a contemporary one, in 1790 he did not have the poetic voice, the understanding, or perhaps the confidence to express it. He stood bewildered and disappointed at Simplon Pass and wrote the conventional topographical poem, *Descriptive Sketches* (1793).

This first visit to France coincided with the anniversary of the fall of the Bastille, a moment when France was "standing on the top of golden hours," "benevolence and blessedness everywhere" (VI, 353, 368–69). Returning in 1791, he met Michael Beaupuy, who awakened his political conscience, and Annette Vallon, by whom he fathered a child, Caroline. In spite of the September Massacres in which Robespierre slaughtered thousands of political prisoners, Wordsworth left France still an advocate of the Revolution. Within months, a formal declaration of war between England and France decisively separated him from Annette and Caroline and divided his loyalties between the ideals of the Revolution in a country which was at war with England and threatened to invade and destroy it. The final failure of the Revolution in the Reign of Terror, the realization of his personal guilt in leaving Annette, led to his final despair and to his walking tour of England. He lingered several days on the barren and uninhabited Salisbury Plain, where the contemporary vagrants and the relics at Stonehenge awakened his imagination. Among visions of warlike ancient savages, the altars of human sacrifice, and the Druid priests in "the obscurities of time," he came to believe that he could create a work "from the depth of untaught things, / Enduring and creative," with a "power like one of Nature's" (XII, 310–12). He made his poetic commitment not to the past, an "antiquarian's dream," but to the new world he found in "life's every day appearances," (XII, 347, 369) and dedicated himself to "making verse / Deal boldly with substantial things" (XII, 233–34).

In 1795, he began to share his life with his sister Dorothy, "the Beloved Woman" who, he later wrote in *The Prelude*, "in midst of all, preserved me still / A Poet" (IX, 909, 919–20), and his friend Coleridge, first at Racedown and later at Alfoxden where they planned and wrote most of *The Lyrical Ballads*. Published anonymously in September, 1798, by Joseph Cottle, *The Lyrical Ballads* gradually found an audience, passing through four editions by 1805, in part because they resembled contemporary magazine poetry and the primitive colloquial style that rustic and provincial poets such as Burns managed with such consummate skill.[21]

The Lyrical Ballads appeared one month after Dorothy,

William, and Coleridge left for what would be a cold and lonely winter in Germany, where they had gone to learn the language, before settling in Grasmere for fourteen crucial and exciting years, nine of them at Dove Cottage. Here Wordsworth prepared two more editions of *The Lyrical Ballads,* and here he wrote the magnificent set of nature lyrics, odes, and sonnets that appeared in his *Poems in Two Volumes* (1807), such poems as the Intimations Ode, "Resolution and Independence," "I Wandered Lonely as a Cloud," and "Elegiac Stanzas." To prepare himself to write the great philosophical poem of which Coleridge thought he was capable, Wordsworth began a poem retracing his mental development to find out how, if at all, he was suited to write a philosophical poem. He completed a version in two books in 1799, a version in five books in 1804, and thirteen in 1805, believing it "a thing unprecedented in literary history that a man would talk so much about himself" (*EY,* 587).[22] He set the poem aside in 1839, sealed it, and directed that it not be published until after his death to provide a source of income for his heirs. It was entitled *The Prelude* by his widow Mary when she published it in 1850. *The Recluse* was never finished although, as Kenneth Johnston points out, the combined parts are longer than *Paradise Lost* and *Paradise Regained* together, "somewhat too large to be invoked as evidence of failure."[23]

It was a great deal to have accomplished during years of turmoil and change. At age thirty-two, he married Mary Hutchinson, who was suited by temperament and experience to the modest and often difficult cottage life she expected to lead, sharing her husband with poetry and with Dorothy.[24] Although depicted as withdrawn from the world, Wordsworth was surrounded by children, by adoring and compatible women, and by a vast library, many friends, and visitors. Adam Sedgwick, the geologist and Charles Darwin's mentor, considered Wordsworth "the best talker" he knew,[25] and, while introducing him to the controversies of this Golden Age of geology, discovered the aesthetic values Wordsworth found in the landscape. Walter Scott and James Hogg shared his interest in country lore and landmarks, and Humphry Davy climbed Helvellyn with him while discussing contemporary science. Sir George Beaumont and his wife encouraged Wordsworth's interest in painting and gardening, and he in turn designed their winter garden at Coleorton.[26] Politically, Wordsworth became more conservative by standing still in a changing world; but he maintained friendships with Thomas Clarkson, the abolitionist, Robert Owen of New Lanark, and

Lord Lonsdale, the son of the man who had employed his father. Although he later quarreled with Coleridge, Hazlitt, and De Quincey because of what he considered to be their irregular habits, among literary people his friends included Lamb, Southey, Godwin, Henry Crabb Robinson, and Samuel Rogers, the banker poet.

The years in Grasmere were also marked by anxiety, crisis, even tragedy, and his ability to cope with the problems he confronted was a tribute both to the strength of his imagination and the strength of his character. Being a poet carried with it certain predictable problems: "Solitude, pain of heart, distress, and poverty," he explained in "Resolution and Independence," problems exemplified in the lives of Chatterton and Burns:

> By our own spirits are we deified:
> We Poets in our youth begin in gladness;
> But thereof come in the end despondency and madness.
>
> (ll. 47–49)

His whole life had been haunted by visions of poverty, for while he had been educated as a middle-class gentleman, he was dependent, like Keats, on insensitive relatives, who had no sympathy with his calling, and a reading public that was satisfied reading *The Monthly Magazine* (5,000 copies in 1797), the *Morning Post* (4,500 copies in 1803), the *Evangelical* and *Methodist* magazines (18–20,000 copies in 1807), the Cheap Repository Tracts, Scott's *Lay of the Last Minstrel* (1805),[27] and Samuel Rogers's *Pleasures of Memory* (1792), which passed through nineteen editions by the time Wordsworth published *The Excursion* in 1814. In spite of his inheritance and the generosity of the Beaumonts, who gave Wordsworth a small farm on which he could build, he could not, however frugal and industrious, afford to live on his income as a poet.

Moreover, writing was difficult for him. Fearing the loss of his imaginative power, he confessed, "I see by glimpses now; when age comes on, / May scarcely see at all" (*The Prelude*, XI, 338–39), and he forced himself to write so long as the vision remained. This fear had a basis in reality, for it appeared at times that he was literally going blind as well, his sensitivity to light forcing him to abandon reading in his later years and to wear a green eyeshade. Moreover, the nervous headaches and pains in his stomach and sides that had plagued him since boyhood, especially when he was writing, became more intense in the industrious years from 1797 to 1814, requiring Dorothy, Mary, or Sarah to take down his verses in dictation and make all the copies for him. Yet he avoided medication, for he saw how laudanum or opium, which was as common as aspirin for pain at the time, had destroyed Coleridge and his neighbor, DeQuincey, as well.

The first great tragedy occurred on February 2, 1805, when his beloved brother John went down with his ship, the *Earl of Abergavenny,* in a freak storm in Weymouth Bay.[28] John was a good-natured, even-tempered, attractive, and by all accounts totally virtuous creature. His loss embittered Wordsworth, who dismissed his early faith "that Nature never did betray / The heart that loved her" ("Tintern Abbey," ll. 122–23) as a "fond delusion" ("Elegiac Stanzas," l. 39). His faith in nature and the feeling it inspired were tempered by this loss, and he began to cultivate the more Stoic virtues of "fortitude," "patient cheer," shifting his allegiance from nature to, as he concluded in the Intimations Ode, the "human heart by which we live."

Long before his brother's death, Wordsworth had explored extremes of emotion in his poetry, especially grief, anguish, and regret, in part building an idiom of genuine emotion to replace the rhetorical extremes of fashionable sensibility.[29] In preference to the tearfulness and exaggeration of contemporary literature and the stage, he offered the "still, sad music of humanity," the reality of silence and isolation in *The Borderers* and *The Ruined Cottage,* of reticence and restraint, in "A Slumber Did my Spirit Seal," and "She dwelt among the untrodden ways," of stoic calm and brave submission in "Ode to Duty," and "Character of a Happy Warrior." With the death of his brother, however, he came to know what he had before only imagined: a grief beyond words, beyond sympathy, "Beyond participation" and "beyond relief," as he had described it in "The Affliction of Margaret": "If any chance to heave a sigh, / They pity me and not my grief" (ll. 71–74). His faith already shaken, even worse disasters, common ones for his times, were to befall him. In 1812, he lost his daughter Catherine, age four, and his son Thomas, age six and a half. Like Coleridge in "Dejection: An Ode," he survived by insulating himself against all feeling.

Even during the good years, however, Wordsworth's poetry, his character and personality, elicited such negative reviews that, after the volumes of 1807, containing some of his most poignant reflections on his experience, he decided he would never publish again, and, indeed, except for a political tract, *The Convention of Cintra* (1809), he avoided publication until *The Excursion* in 1814. Since the first edition of

The Lyrical Ballads (1798) anteceded the founding of the *Edinburgh Review* (1802), and the other reviews that were to follow, it escaped the attention of those tyrannical reviewers who, when reviewing later editions of his poetry, measured his poetry against the eighteenth-century ideals of sentiment, decorum, and virtue, and found it infantile, vulgar, provincial, and trivial, ridiculing Wordsworth as humorless, egotistical, pedantic, aloof, or trivial. The liberals attacked him for abandoning the ideals of the French Revolution and the conservatives for his sympathy with the poor. And his preference for the Lake District over London or Edinburgh alienated him from everyone, for writers were supposed to move toward urban centers. Although he dismissed the reviewers as "Men of palsied imaginations and indurated hearts" in the Essay, Supplementary to the Preface of 1815, he still did not have the audience he set out to create, an audience he attempted to educate or at least to convert in his many Prefaces, for he knew that he was among the first generation of poets to address the new and anonymous middle-class reading public. This audience was vastly expanded from the one Beattie, Cowper, and Thomson addressed, expanded by improved means of printing and distribution and by literacy, but not necessarily education or taste. This was an audience that had been raised to distrust the imagination, to prefer the useful or decorative arts, an audience whose taste was formed by reviewers, not poets.

His claim that the language of poetry was no different from the language of prose, to which Coleridge legitimately objected, and that the poet was merely a "man among men," ought to have given him a common base with this audience. And, like every worldly philosopher in the eighteenth century who defined pleasure as the primary motive for human action, so Wordsworth in the Preface to the edition of 1802 invoked the pleasure principle to justify his poetry, appealing to "the grand elementary principle of pleasure . . . by which [mankind] knows and feels, and lives, and moves."[30] Wordsworth's concept of pleasure was more spiritual and aesthetic than that of the utilitarians, but it was within their range of understanding. Unfortunately, the reviewers, even Coleridge, misunderstood the purpose of his Prefaces: to "create the taste by which he [was] to be relished," "teach the art by which he [was] to be seen," which, as he explained in a letter to Lady Beaumont after the disappointing reception of the 1807 volume, was the responsibility of an "original" poet (*MY*, I, 125–31). Like Blake, Byron, Keats, and Shelley, he came to believe that his lofty aspirations were wasted on an incorrigible reading public: rejected, he became defensive, and ultimately even hostile toward the very audience he had dedicated himself. In 1815, the poet whom he had defined as "the rock of defence of human nature; an upholder and preserver, carrying everywhere . . . relationship and love" (Preface, 1802), dismissed the reading public entirely and addressed himself to posterity, "the People, philosophically characterized and to the embodied spirit of their knowledge."[31]

In 1813, to escape from the sorrowful sight of their children's graves, the Wordsworth family moved to Rydal Mount, a spacious, airy, magnificently situated house near Grasmere, and William became Distributor of Stamps, an occasionally arduous job involving the collection of duties levied on wills, licenses, publications, and legal documents, an inland version of Burns's position as an exciseman. The following year, he gathered together material he had been working on since 1795 as part of *The Recluse* and published it as *The Excursion*. John Wilson of *Blackwood's* called it "the worst poem, of any character, in the English language," while Francis Jeffrey began his review with a dictatorial, "This will never do," observing that Wordsworth was "hopeless," "incurable," "beyond the power of criticism."[32] But high on the hillside at Rydal overlooking Windermere and Rydal Water, Wordsworth was becoming inured to criticism, for, given the philosophy of that amazing poem, it was merely a trial that would contribute to his strength, a test of faith.

In nine books of over 9,000 lines, *The Excursion* presented a vision of survival in a Malthusian world, a world in which virtuous men and women can be destroyed by poverty, disease, and war, while their memories are obliterated by nature's "calm oblivious tendencies," by "plants and weeds, and flowers, / And silent overgrowings." However inhospitable, mysterious, and even unjust the world of man and nature, "the secret spirit of humanity," he affirms, "Still survived." ("The Ruined Cottage," I, 927–30). *The Excursion* offered a myth of psychological redemption; it demonstrates how the sorrows, struggles, and uncertainties of human life can be converted to personal and ultimately social salvation. In *The Excursion,* Wordsworth showed individuals dealing with the remote, anonymous, and collective authority that had replaced the tyranny of kings and priests, dealing with the helplessness and despondency that afflicts human beings in a world governed by inexorable, mysterious, and disembodied power, both natural and political. Placing his faith in "the individual

Mind that keeps her own / Inviolate retirement, subject there / To Conscience only" (Prospectus, ll. 19–22), he affirms the existence of an *"active* Principle," a principle of life which the scientists were even then attempting to identify. It was a principle that pervades the universe—the stars, clouds, plants, stones, water, air—"that knows no insulated spot, / no chasm, no solitude," unfolding itself everywhere. Obeying that law, a law that takes precedence over all others, the "law / of life, and hope, and action" (IX, 127–28), human beings can generate the order, harmony, and direction they need to survive, the myths they need to believe in, the means (and they are many, for "manifold and various are the ways of restoration" [IV, 1112–1113]) to become reconciled with the world, "the place in which, in the end, / We find our happiness or not at all" (*The Prelude,* X, 727–28).[33]

The Excursion was Wordsworth's last major contribution to the verse we have called the poetry of life, but he continued to be productive and experimental, bringing his imagination to other areas of experience, bringing poetry to life. In 1815, in his collected poems he designed a classification that still bewilders scholars, for he claimed that, among other things, the poems were presented to reflect the various powers that dominated in each stage of his life, powers such as fancy, imagination, reflection, and so on.[34] The classification, which was maintained in later collections with some alterations and additions, expresses his belief that single poems are only partial statements, that the meaning of a poem depends on the context in which it was written, and that it can be altered by the context in which it is read. This principle influenced his two experimental sonnet sequences, the *River Duddon Sonnets* and *Ecclesiastical Sketches,* a sonnet sequence tracing the history of the Church of England from its impact on the native Druid cults through the Reformation up to the building of new churches. Doing much of his own scholarship, Wordsworth approached the past as he did the landscape: with an imagination that receives and endows, that observes and animates, presenting every event or monument in relation to its impact on the human community.

Wordsworth and the Guidebooks

Wordsworth brought all these imaginative powers to bear on a relatively minor genre, the guidebook, which he raised to an art form. In the middle of the eighteenth century the guidebook became an indispensable tool to young men on their educational tour of the Continent. Thomas Gray, William Gilpin, Thomas West, Thomas Pennant, Arthur Young, Ann Radcliffe, and other travellers and authors described their favorite places of visual interest, analyzed them on the aesthetic principles derived from the landscape paintings of Salvator Rosa, Claude Lorrain, and Nicholas Poussin. They distinguished sublime effects, the large, irregular, mysterious, and lawless ones, from the picturesque, the composed, domesticated, and contrived.³⁵ They identified prospects, "stations" or vantage points, the best time of day or season for the view, and appropriate comparisons with other famous views. Along with a reputable guidebook a tourist carried a Claude glass, an oval, smoked glass in which he viewed a reflection of the scene to which his back was turned; the glass made the scene resemble a painting. Many travellers rode in carriages from station to station sketching scenes and recording impressions in journals and letters. But they were spectators, observers, as alien from nature as if they had never left their parlors. Wordsworth himself fell victim to this artificial aesthetic, "a strong infection of the age," one of the imaginative impairments he suffered after his return from France (*The Prelude*, XI, 152–176). And Jane Austen in *Northanger Abbey* parodied this fashionable excess as early as 1798 when her heroine, Catherine, having listened to "a lecture on the picturesque," on "foregrounds, distances, and second distances—side-screens and perspectives—lights and shades . . . voluntarily rejected the whole city of Bath, as unworthy to make part of a landscape."

During the war against France, the English gave up continental travel to discover England, and in the landscape, the topography, they discovered their own special character. The countryside was transformed from a social wilderness to be crossed on the way to London, from a source of servants, bread, or beef, from a place to hunt or hold balls, to a series of distinct regions with topographical features, special dialects, customs, and ceremonies that they found necessary to preserve. The recognition of cultural diversity within England itself, defined by geography, contributed to the regional pride that was threatened when railroads and improved communication appeared to turn England into one large community later in the century. At first the guidebooks reflected the middle-class interest in markets, products, industry, churches, architecture, manners, "curiosities," and economy, not in scenery.³⁶ John Housman's *Journal of a Tour Through Scotland* (1798), for example, begins, "Turnips are much cultivated here as a fallow crop by every farmer, and generally in drills or flitches from two to three feet wide, and properly hoed." By 1810, there were engraved books of selected "beauties," tours designed for families, foreigners, children, young ladies, and "walks" through such otherwise inconspicuous provincial centers as Litchfield, Stamford, and Mansfield. The aesthetic category of the sublime once confined to the Alps was now applied to industrial smoke, and the picturesque was applied to tenant farms. Nature, in guidebooks, was a resource for products, commerce, and industry, not a source of religious or aesthetic experience. By 1810, when Wordsworth first considered writing a guide, the production and sale of guidebooks had reached an absurd proportion, parodied in pantomimes and by Thomas Rowlandson, the caricaturist, and William Combe in *The Tour of Doctor Syntax in Search of the Picturesque* (1809) in which a scrawny, feckless country parson in need of money decides to "make a Tour" and then write about it:

> I'll prose it here, I'll verse it there
> And picturesque it everywhere.

Wordsworth's *A Guide Through the District of the Lakes for the Use of Tourists and Residents,* first published in 1810, was written, unlike other guidebooks, by a native with lofty motives: to identify the special beauty of the Lake District and to try to preserve it from the impact of tourists, settlers, and improvers. Retaining the vocabulary of picturesque travel literature, Wordsworth views landscape in the context of nature, not painting, or scripture, or commerce. The first part, "A View of the Country as Formed by Nature," offers a definition of the sublime suited to the natural world, not the industrial revolution or Italian landscape painting: "Sublimity is the result of Nature's first great dealings with the superficies of the earth . . ." (*Prose,* II, 181).[37] In the second part, "Aspects of the Country as Affected by its Inhabitants," he offers a historical survey of how human beings used the land and the landmarks they left from ancient times, still emphasizing nature, its "silent overgrowings," as he called it in *The Ruined Cottage,* reclaiming the land, repossessing it. The houses built of native rock altered by succeeding generations seem "a production of nature," "to have risen by an instinct of their own, out of the native rock," while the "rough and uneven" tiles and rocks "have furnished places of rest for the seeds of lichens, mosses, ferns, and flowers. Hence buildings, which in their very forms call to mind the processes of nature, do thus clothed in part with a vegetable garb, appear to be received into the bosom of the living principle of things, as it acts and exists among the woods and fields" (*Prose,* II, 202–3). The third part, "Changes, and Rules of Taste for Preventing Their Bad Effects," was designed to defend the integrity, what we now call the ecology of the area. To preserve the character of the area as a retreat for future generations, Wordsworth discourages importing foreign plantings such as Scotch firs and larch trees, cutting down the native forests, white-washing houses, and inappropriate southern architecture. As a model, he designed the gardens of Rydal Mount, gardens that still exist in essentially the form he planted, the trees, steps, terraces, ferns, and mosses, another contribution to the poetry of life.

Wordsworth's poetic career spanned almost sixty of his eighty years, a career that is synonymous with Romantic poetry. He began as an eighteenth-century loco-descriptive poet in *An Evening Walk,* achieved that "union of deep feeling with profound thought" that Coleridge believed characterized his genius (*Biographia Literaria,* Chapter XIV), and developed as early as 1820, when he wrote "To Enterprise," that ceremonial and hortatory voice that was to endear him to the Victorians. In 1825, Hazlitt claimed he was "the most original poet now living, and the one whose writings could least be spared" *(The Spirit of Age);* that was twenty-five years before publication of *The Prelude,* his most original poem. The colloquial diction, which reviewers considered his original contribution and for which he was ridiculed was, in fact, anticipated by Chaucer, whose poetry Wordsworth translated, and by Burns. It was, as Wordsworth claimed, a universal language, validated in principle by the Bible, and more recently, by journalism, the theater, and popular literature.

What was truly original, what he shared with other Romantic writers as well as painters and scientists, was a way of seeing, a mode of perception that endowed the world, the self, and the relationship between them with human value, human meaning. His concentration on "common life" altered it, as he celebrated the capacity of the human mind to transform the ordinary into art. His experiments with language and form rejuvenated the aesthetic tradition, and his adaptations of public forms, such as drama, epic, and ode, for private purposes contributed to the development of new forms expressing the intersection between public and private experience. In brief, Wordsworth discovered the poetry of life, the imaginative essence expressed in living poetic forms analogous to the living forms of nature. In a sonnet on an obscure northern river, he powerfully expressed that poetry of life in what many have considered, ironically, one of the finest epitaphs in the language: "The Form remains," he concluded his sonnet sequence on the River Duddon, "the Function never dies":

> Enough if something from our hands have power
> To live, and act, and serve the future hour.

CHAPTER XII

Painting and the Other Visual Arts

The Awakening of the Visual Arts

"It is very extraordinary," William Blake wrote in July, 1800, "that London in so few years from a City of meer Necessaries or at least a commerce of the lowest order of luxuries should have become a City of Elegance in some degree & that its once stupid inhabitants should enter into an Emulation of Grecian manners. There are now I believe as many Booksellers as there are Butchers & as many Printshops as of any other trade. We remember when a Print shop was a rare bird in London & I myself remember when I thought my pursuits of Art a kind of Criminal Dissipation & neglect of the main chance which I hid my face for not being able to abandon as a Passion which is forbidden by Law and Religion but now it appears to be Law and Gospel to . . ." (Erdman, p. 679). As Blake's observation suggests, the first great age of British painting, engraving, and visual arts coincided with the Romantic period: the intellectual, economic, and emotional transformations in the latter decades of the eighteenth century stimulated crafts, industry, and commerce in general, publishing, political, social, and natural sciences, and the theater, all of them ultimately impinging on the visual arts.[1] Because the artistic community was concentrated in London and its productions localized around a few exhibition halls, the characteristic diversity that we have observed in other disciplines is especially evident. Indeed, after 1770, this comparatively small and insular community of artists, patrons, and critics generated the same variety as appeared in the literature, theater, architecture, and philosophy. There were advocates of convention and innovation, realism and fantasy, science and superstition, the commonplace and the exotic, the sentimental and the sadistic, the beautiful and the grotesque, the terrestrial and the sacred, and even an aesthetic philosophy that claimed such oppositions enhanced artistic experience. To explain the wildness, terror, and disorder they enjoyed, they invoked a classical aesthetician, Longinus, and called the pleasure sublime. While they disliked religious art and resisted decorating their churches, they developed a lively school of Biblical painting, lived in new or restored abbeys, and put miniature decorative chapels or ornamental hermit cells in their gardens. While they disliked monumental public art of all kinds, they decorated their parlors with views of public buildings and bridges. And although, after 1800 especially, they advocated the development of a native British style, the Regent built an Oriental pavilion at Brighton and an immense *cottage ornée,* an artificial peasant hut, at Windsor. His subjects filled the countryside with Italian villas and the cities with Greek revival town houses, churches, and banks embellished with freizes depicting contemporary military leaders dressed in Roman togas.[2] Like the writers, some artists found a usable past in the Bible, native literature, and classical myth, as well as in ruins, the antiquities of the countryside. Others found a usable present, the poetry of life, in the contemporary landscape or social world.[3]

William Blake

Blake found inspiration everywhere, and everything contributed to his art. Born in the London neighborhood of Carnaby Market in 1757, he was surrounded by tradesmen like his father, a hosier, as well as a slaughterhouse, a workhouse, dissenting chapels,[4] a community so diverse that even a child who claimed at age four to see God looking through his window and a tree full of angels could find refuge. To his pious, industrious, affectionate, and tolerant parents, however, he was too vulnerable for the discipline of regular schooling and was educated at home until the age of ten, when his father sent him to drawing school. Four years later he was apprenticed as an engraver to acquire a marketable skill, a lucrative one if he were willing to subordinate himself to drawing diagrams for anatomy books, specimens for herbals, illustrations for other poets, reproductions of portraits, ornaments and costumes for contemporary magazines. In the process he would acquire an education from whatever subject he was engraving.

His own powerful style was rich in cultural allusion for it combined both Greek and gothic, a pagan delight in the naked body and a Christian spirituality. For example, the figures he designed for Blair's "The Grave" combine the mortuary sculptures of Westminster with the Greek figures he engraved for Erasmus Darwin's essay in *The Botanic Garden* (1791) on the Portland Vase, the design representing the Eleusinian Mysteries, an ancient rite conducted annually to commemorate the return of Persephone from the underworld.[5] The myth associating fertility and death appealed especially to Blake, who had been acquiring an impressive familiarity with occult philosophers such as Paracelsus, Boehme, Plotinus, Swedenborg, Thomas Taylor the Neo-Platonist, as well as with alchemy, physiognomy, astrology, and speculative mythology.[6] From such reading and engraving, from friends, and from his own special visionary experiences, he developed a vast complicated myth of transformations, metamorphoses, cycles, and processes, along with Christian patterns of fall and redemption which he expressed in a series of illuminated books, the most palpable expression of his gothicism, intergrating text and ornament in one hand-colored engraving.

Assisted by his wife, Catherine, the illiterate daughter of a gardener whom he married in 1782, and inspired by the ghost of his brother Robert, who supposedly had revealed the process in a vision in 1788, he began etching and printing his visions and prophecies: "All Religions are One" and "There is no Natural Religion," 1788; *Tiriel, Songs of Innocence,* and *The Book of Thel,* 1789; *The Marriage of Heaven and Hell,* 1790–1792; *The French Revolution,* 1791; *Visions of the Daughters of Albion,* 1793; *America: A Prophecy,* 1793; *Songs of Innocence and of Experience, Europe: A Prophecy,* and *The First book of Urizen,* 1794; *The Song of Los, The Book of Los,* and *The Book of Ahania,* 1795; *Milton,* 1804; and *Jerusalem,* 1820. The texts were so impenetrable, the designs so feverish, and the names so bizarre that no one noticed how heretical and seditious they really were; in fact, few ever even saw them.

Often composed at night, after the meticulous engraving he did to earn a living, these visionary works express, among other things, Blake's creative response to his deep resentment of authority, his belief in the power of the human mind either to enslave or free itself. By an imaginative awakening, individual men and women, he believed, can overcome all forms of tyranny, starting with the self-imposed tyranny, the "mind-forged manacles," by which they create and then enslave themselves to unworthy institutions and ideals. Reflecting the political turmoil around him, the French and American revolutions he endorsed, he created myths of political as well as spiritual revolution, myths populated with shackled spectres and angry prophets whose visions of redemption (though more gorgeous and interesting) resembled in terror, brooding, fear, tumult, fire, and anguish the contents of Revelation, resembled, in fact, the apocalyptic rhetoric of Joanna Southcott, Joseph Brothers, all the radical dissenters who found that particular Biblical text so appealing. While natural philosophers were radically distorting available evidence to support the creation myth of Genesis, Blake simply invented a new one, freeing himself from the tyranny of the Judeo-Christian universe and its definition of time, space, and morality. At the center of Blake's vision, however, is humanity, the God within not above, a god he associates with poetic genius and the imaginative faculty. On the expression of this genius, personal, indeed national, salvation depends. A religious Christian without a church, except for a brief affiliation with Swedenborg's New Jerusalem Church,[7] Blake was a patriot in opposition to his government, a husband who disapproved of marriage, a learned man opposed to education, an artist who rejected art. In a society evolving toward collective activity, such individualism would be as great a handicap as the incommunicable nature of his vision.

Some of Blake's artistic work was more conventional. In 1779, he began attending classes and lectures at the Royal Academy and for a while exhibited paintings on Biblical, historical, and literary themes. In 1826, he even sold two of his paintings to Sir Thomas Lawrence, the embodiment of contemporary fashion and President of the Royal Academy. But by temperament and talent he was not suited to that community. He disliked oils, landscapes, and portraits. As an engraver, he was committed to detail at a time when Sir Joshua Reynolds' neoclassical aesthetics of generalization prevailed: "To Generalize is to be an Idiot," he wrote after reading Sir Joshua's *Discourses* (1798), "To particularize is the Alone Distinction of Merit" (Erdman, 630). Again, as an engraver, his particularities depended on outline, a priority he found confirmed in classic Greek forms and in gothic, but disparaged by his contemporaries in favor of color, form, and *chiaroscuro* (the interplay of light and shade): "The great and golden rule of art, as well as of life, is this:" Blake wrote in his *Descriptive*

Catalogue, "The more distinct, sharp, and wirey the bounding line, the more perfect the work of art; and the less keen and sharp, the greater is the evidence of weak imitation, plagiarism, and bungling."

While it was possible, as John Martin's career illustrates, to survive without the Royal Academy, it was not possible to be a painter without patrons, and Blake was politically opposed to the aristocracy that was the major source of patronage. His friend Flaxman, along with the Reverend and Mrs. Matthews, financed the publication of his juvenilia, *Poetical Sketches,* in 1783; he ridiculed them and the entire fashionable world they represented in *An Island in the Moon.* Dr. Trusler, a clergyman from Surrey who wanted to commission some moral paintings for a book, complained that Blake's "Fancy" is obscure; Blake tactlessly replied "What is Grand is necessarily obscure to Weak men. That which can be made Explicit to the Idiot is not worth my care." Under the patronage of William Hayley, a minor poet, he moved to a cottage in Sussex, where, for three years, he did miniatures and designs for popular trivia. Resentful and frustrated, he longed to do the visionary and historical works dictated, he claimed, by his personal angels: "I am under the direction of Messengers from Heaven Daily and Nightly," he explained to the patient Dr. Butts, for whom he painted small water colors on Biblical subjects. He demonstrated his aversion to more terrestrial authority by assaulting a soldier who refused to leave his garden, and, according to the soldier, making treasonous remarks about the King—such as that English citizens would prefer being governed by the French, should the impending invasion everyone feared in 1803 actually occur. Blake was brought to trial and however suspicious his behavior and conflicting the reports, however nervous the population was about spies and traitors, he was acquitted.

In London, he turned against the competitive artistic community completely and held his own exhibition at his brother's shop in 1809, attended by the kindly Lamb, Southey, and Henry Crabb Robinson, as well as Robert Hunt of *The Examiner* who dismissed Blake's work as symptomatic of the insanity of his age. But Blake, resigned to poverty, felt superior to such judgments:

> I have Mental Joy & Mental Health
> And Mental Friends & Mental wealth;
> I've a Wife I love & that loves me;
> I've all But Riches Bodily.
> (Erdman, 472)

He did the designs, drawings, and watercolors on those literary works that appealed to him: the *Book of Job, Paradise Lost, Paradise Regained, The Divine Comedy,* and *Pilgrim's Progress.* He even acquired disciples, a group of young painters including John Linnell and Samuel Palmer who, calling themselves the Shoreham Ancients, claimed that Blake taught them how to see nature but in their odd communal behavior indicated how little they understood of the Blake they claimed to admire. Blake died at age sixty-nine, singing of heaven, leaving a legacy of anecdotes that supposedly illustrated how demented he was, and of visions that in time would tell more about the great awakening in English art than all the flaking and fading canvases of his more successful contemporaries.

The State of the Arts

Blake's new methods of printing contributed to the already rich array of media available to artists, encouraging the spirit of experimentation and flexibility with which they worked. An artist could do traditional sculpture in real or synthetic stones, watercolor, oil, crayon, chalk, engraving, mezzotint, lithograph, woodcut, or any combination of them. Among the many possible subjects, the Romantic painters excelled at genre painting and landscape. Genre painting, in part derived from the French and in part from Hogarth, presented anecdotal, domestic, usually rural scenes, commonplace events and people's responses to them, from a sentimental, pathetic, or comic perspective. Adaptable to Biblical and historical subjects, and appealing to the same taste as the melodrama and the ballad, genre paintings were especially well-suited to the democratic inclinations of the middle classes, the sentimental primitivism of the philosophers and nobility, and the narrative or documentary interests of the working classes, with which most painters were affiliated. It is this documentary function that made Joseph Wright (1734–1797) of Derby's industrial genre so useful as well as artistically successful. The faces, the scenes, the settings are from the provincial middle class whose interests included contemporary scientific experimentation, a setting from which many of the major discoveries of the Industrial Revolution emerged. But while Wright was painting a lecture on the use of the orrery, a model of the universe, or an experiment with an air pump, he was himself experimenting with painting artificial illumination. His effects translated successfully to engraving for popular publication, itself an experiment in form.[8] Genre acquired a second and very prosperous life with the publication of popular illustrated novels, anthologies, and magazines.

The isolation of England during the war was an advantage to the landscape painters, for it helped emancipate them from Mediterranean ideals of scenic beauty and from the abstract theories of the picturesque which originated in the experience of European artists such as Claude Lorrain, Salvator Rosa, and Nicolas Poussin. Instead of following their travels, copying their landscapes or their paintings of landscapes, English painters, including Constable, Turner, and Martin, took their easels and sketchbooks to the English fields, mountains, and seaside. Like the poets, the painters found new inspiration in the data of experience, viewing the landscape with an imaginative eye, and experimenting with techniques for representing their personal perception of the natural world. Through their experimental attitude and careful observation, their landscapes acquired that empirical weight we saw in such poets as Wordsworth and Keats, reflecting that scientific interest in the forces behind phenomena, the principles within natural events.[9]

Since it evolved from the craft tradition rather than the courtly tradition, the artistic community was closer in origins to the scientific community than it was to the literary one. In fact, the distinction between fine and applied arts did not even become significant until the second decade of the nineteenth century.[10] Until then, the role of the artist was well defined: he expressed rather than formed or reformed the tastes and values of his patrons. New wealth had created an exceptionally receptive audience for painters and craftsmen of all kinds, while new technology provided them with more varied materials and means of dissemination. To a society made up of an insecure aristocracy and a wealthy middle class, who believed they could be perpetuated by their possessions and symbolized by their clothes, whose aspirations were embodied in their gothic windows, whose character was assessed by the pitch of the nose, whose quality was represented in trophies and door knockers, whose virtue was equated with a carpet or glove, and whose status could depend on a button, to a society, in other words, that functioned, as Carlyle claimed in *Sartor Resartus,* on symbols rather than realities, the symbol-makers, the artists, were indispensable. It was a society, as we discovered in our discussion of the theater, that by education and habit was addicted to spectacle, that was visual but not imaginative.

Anyone with artistic skills, anyone capable of drawing, painting, engraving, enameling, or carving, anyone with a sense of color, line, or form could find employment. He could illustrate herbals, anatomy books, poetry annuals, fashion magazines, travel guides, or Bibles. He could paint murals in country houses, stage sets, carriages, shop signs, or tea cups. He could design coats of arms, jewelry, tapestries, mouldings, medallions, furniture, garden statuary, table settings, and tombs. He could do the very popular portraits, busts, silhouettes, and miniatures on ivory, parchment, brass, or even woven in hair. He could do architectural renderings of buildings, views of them during construction or in ruins. He could recreate past events or commemorate contemporary ones such as coronations, battles, and weddings. Much of this work, however trivial or decorative, was willingly undertaken by otherwise fine artists to finance their study and their original work, for while it was possible to be a painter or a sculptor in England, it was very difficult to be an artist.

The Professionalization of the Fine Arts

There was, then, no tradition of fine art in England. Europeans such as Winckelmann believed that the English were not even capable of original painting because of the damp climate, which was also thought to account for melancholia. An aspiring painter had to go to Paris or Rome not only to study but merely to see the French, Italian, and Dutch masters, for until 1837, when the National Gallery was opened, the only access to the great European paintings was by invitation to a private collection. Located on the country estates of the aristocracy that owned them, these collections removed painting further from a public that had not learned to value painting as a form of collective expression and from the young art students who could have learned to provide that expression for them. Constable, for example, was nineteen years old before he saw a painting, Claude's *Hagar and the Angel,* which Sir George Beaumont was so fond of that he always carried it with him in a special case even when he went to visit his mother in Dedham, where Constable met him. After the founding of the Royal Academy in 1768,[11] there were annual exhibits of native artists, but their work expressed the preferences of Reynolds, West, and Gainsborough, among others, for portraits and for the mythological landscapes, the burnished tones and artificial lights of the Mediterranean.

By offering lectures and free classes to anyone who showed the aptitude, the Academy did contribute to the development of an English school of painting. In studio classes, supervised by mature painters and often attended by their peers, students drew from antiquities, nudes, and still life; and in lectures by senior members they learned about aesthetics, art history, perspective, and architecture. A faculty of non-painters included William Hunter (brother of John) as Professor of Anatomy, Samuel Johnson as Professor of Ancient Literature, Oliver Goldsmith as Professor of Ancient History succeeded by Edward Gibbon. Between 1769 and 1790, the first President, Sir Joshua Reynolds, delivered annual discourses institutionalizing a set of neoclassical, European aesthetic principles which dominated the early years of the Academy, principles that were even then being undermined by the experience of English students enmeshed in contemporary life. Reynolds' belief in generalization, in ideal types, in training over inspiration, in craft over performance, in imitation of other painters, in fidelity to external reality, and his advocacy of the Venetian painters so angered Blake that among his many incisive annotations to *Discourses* he claimed they were the "Simulations of the Hypocrite," that "Insulted and Degraded" "True Art & True Artists" (Erdman, 631). However critical, young, poor, or obscure, anyone, even Blake, could participate in the annual exhibitions if his work showed sufficient skill to be chosen by the committee. Exhibition at the Royal Academy was essential; it provided access to commissions, patrons, and the reading public as well, for reviews, as lively and polemical as theater and literary reviews, appeared in magazines and newspapers such as *Le Beau Monde, La Belle Assemblée, The Examiner, Blackwood's,* and *London Magazine.*

Many painters such as Martin, Constable, Blake, and Haydon resented the power of the selection committee, especially its arbitrary way of arranging the paintings in the exhibition halls. Because such public exhibitions were fairly recent phenomena, the logistics, courtesies, and rituals were ill-defined and, to an artist eager for an audience, appeared inscrutable. Exhibited in the crowded and dimly lit rooms of Somerset House, the handsome but disorderly building where the Academy was located, and placed in unlikely juxtapositions, the paintings were lost in a visual clutter along with the purpose of the exhibit: to display the best work produced in England over the previous year. In 1808, Martin Archer Shee, President of the Royal Academy, instituted varnishing days, which allowed the members to adjust the tone of the paintings to the exhibition walls. Some merely heightened their palettes, producing the characteristic brilliance of British painting during the period; others completed their work; and J. M. W. Turner often did his entire painting just before the exhibition opened, intent not only on overcoming the environment but also on surpassing all the other paintings in the room. "The study of an exhibition effect," as Shee complained in *Elements of Art* (1809), "is now indeed an Art in itself, an art also, which occupies the attention to the prejudice of nobler objects . . , everything to be forcible must be violent—to be great must be exaggerated—in which all delicacy of expression, detail of parts, and discrimination of hues, are laid aside as useless particulars, or lost in the formless void of general masses."[12]

Recognizing the limitations of the Academy, in 1802, Benjamin West advocated a National Association for the Encouragment of Works of Dignity and Importance in Art. It was followed in 1806 by the more successful British Institution, and in 1823 by the Society of British Artists with its own journal, the *Annals of Fine Arts*. Stimulated by competition and the power of exclusion, increasingly specialized clubs, committees, and societies proliferated; each representing different orientations and practices helped to diversify taste and to emancipate painting, drawing, and engraving from Continental influence. But such specialization also removed these otherwise popular arts from their familiar place among the accomplishments of an enlightened society and conferred on them that special language and ritual of professionalization. In 1826, following a new exhibit at the Institute for the Encouragement of the Fine Arts in Edinburgh, Sir Walter Scott, whose novels and poems had provided inspiration for many painters, observed:

> It is all become a mystery the secret of which is lodged in a few Connoisseurs whose object is not to favour the productions of such pictures as produce effect on mankind at large but to class them according to their proficiency in the inferior rules of the art which though most necessary to be taught and learned, should yet only be considered as the . . . steps by which the higher and ultimate object of a great popular effect is to be obtained. They have all embraced the very stile of criticism which induced Michael Angelo to call some Pope a poor creature who turning his attention from the general effect of a noble statue his Holiness began to criticize the hem of the robe (*Journal,* pp. 87–88).

While fine art developed late in Great Britain and became professionalized within an especially short period, it remained remarkably open socially, a nearly classless profession in which a young man with industry and skill could acquire wealth and even a title simply by associating himself with the Royal Academy—which itself remained admirably free from political influence. Often artists from humble origins acquired titles: Sir Joshua Reynolds (1723–1792), son of a school teacher; Sir William Beechy (1752–1859), son of a house painter: Sir Henry Raeburn (1756–1823), son of a Scottish miller; Sir Francis Chantrey (1781–1842), son of a Sheffield farmer; Sir Thomas Lawrence (1769–1830), son of an indigent inn-keeper; Sir David Wilkie (1785–1841), son of a Scottish minister; and Sir Edwin Landseer (1802–1873), son of an artist in what was the first generation in which one could be identified as a professional artist. Nonetheless, Blake, among others, complained that the aristocratic influence on the art world favored manners over ability: "The Enquiry in England is not whether a Man has talents. & Genius But whether he is Passive & Polite & a Virtuous Ass: & obedient to Noblemen's Opinions in Art & Science" (Erdman, 632).

But most artists were neither polite nor virtuous: their personal lives ranged from conventional to scandalous to squalid, and their eccentricities endeared them to a public that delighted in gossip. Richard Cosway, for example, a favorite of the court, was an extravagant dandy who delighted in gathering fashionable people to his studio, where he painted miniatures for the Prince Regent and his friends, and claimed that the Virgin Mary sat for him. Blake depicted him in his satirical *Island in the Moon* as Mr. Jacko, a monkey in Astley's Circus. Many, like Blake, were Swedenborgians: Cosway, John Flaxman the sculptor, William Sharp the engraver, and De Loutherbourg, the landscape painter and scene designer who later became a follower of Richard Brothers and a faith healer until an angry mob stoned his house. Fuseli, as we have seen, was pathologically obscene and associated with such politically disreputable people as Tom Paine who gathered at Joseph Johnson's bookshop. Yet he became, with the approval of George III, Keeper at the Royal Academy, and, along with Blake, Constable, and Haydon, joined the menagerie of artists Lord Egremont gathered at Petworth.

Lord Egremont was representative of that generation of wealthy landed aristocrats who patronized the arts and the artists, whom they often exceeded in eccentricity—except perhaps for Wordsworth's friend, Sir George Beaumont, a polished and urbane nobleman, whose eccentricity was his own ambition to be an artist.[13] At Petworth, a massive and productive estate, Lord Egremont mounted annual birthday celebrations for the poor in which he entertained up to 6,000 people with beef, pudding, and fireworks. Surrounded by rustic and peculiar servants, reputed to be rude, abrupt, impatient with ceremony, he attracted, nonetheless, a collection of lords, ladies, dandies, and retired military officers, along with painters, and his many children, all illegitimate, borne by the mistress he married in 1801. But he did give Blake commissions and after Blake's death bought some paintings from his widow. At Petworth, Haydon claimed "The very flies . . . seem to know there is room for their existence, and that the windows are theirs. The dogs, the horses, the cows, the deer & pigs, the Peasantry & the Servants, the guests & the family, the children & the Parents, all share alike his bounty & opulence and luxuries. . . . Everything solid, liberal, rich, English."[14]

Benjamin Robert Haydon: Exemplary Failure

Haydon's failure in spite of the existence of patrons such as Egremont, in spite of his ability to ingratiate himself with nobility and people of fashion far less tolerant than Egremont, in spite of his dedication, piety, and industry, illustrates how someone with great visions but limited powers could end up a suicidal bankrupt because he did the right things but at the wrong times—starting with his protest against the Royal Academy for hanging his picture in what he considered to be an inappropriate place. The son of a bookseller, he arrived in London with more education than most painters, studied with Fuseli, befriended Keats and Lamb, tutored the wood engraver Thomas Bewick and the animal painter Edward Landseer, offered hospitality to Wordsworth, and borrowed money from, among others, Sir Walter Scott, who considered him a great genius. Haydon preferred the tragic and the grand to the humorous, and chided his friend David Wilkie, the genre painter, for choosing to see the pantomime *Mother Goose* over *Macbeth*. His infatuation with the broken statuary brought back from the Parthenon by Lord Elgin led to his crusade for the purchase of the Elgin Marbles by the British government. Feverishly studying and copying them, he believed they would be instrumental in starting a new era in painting that would renovate the classical heroic ideal, an era which he intended to initiate single-handedly. His heroic longings, however out of date, were infectious, inspiring one of Wordsworth's most pretentious sonnets, "High is our calling, Friend," and one of Keats's silliest lines in which he claims that the Elgin Marbles made him imagine his dying "Like a sick Eagle looking at the sky." To recreate the heroic models of the past in an unheroic age, Haydon concentrated on size: *Christ's Entry into Jerusalem,* in which he depicted Wordsworth, Keats, and Voltaire among the spectators, was so large that it had to be exhibited in Egyptian Hall, where the panorama appeared. A labored cliché, it was too large for a painting, too dull for a spectacle.

Haydon was capable of painting the portraits by which most artists earned a living, and, for a time, supported his wife and five children by painting portraits of Napoleon, nineteen of them. In his later years, in spite of being imprisoned for debt, he became absorbed in patriotic subjects advocating the decoration of the Houses of Parliament, rebuilt after the fire of 1834, with scenes from British history. While his proposal was accepted, he lost the competition, and directed his unfashionable but patriotic enthusiasm toward a massive and unlikely painting of George IV and Wellington inspecting the field of Waterloo, for which he borrowed the General's boots. In 1846, having failed to reach his unrealistic goals, he committed suicide, leaving behind a rich and fascinating diary that reveals, ironically, how out of touch he was with himself and his age.

Illustration and Portraiture

While Haydon's knowledge and enthusiasm for the native literary tradition endeared him to contemporary writers, he avoided literary illustration where the heroic, if it existed at all, survived. Scenes and characters from Chaucer, Spenser, Shakespeare, Milton, Thomson, Gray, and Scott had considerable appeal to a public that was becoming conscious of its literary heritage through the popular theater and inexpensive publication. Painters found a usable past in literature, Shakespeare and Ossian especially. In 1798, the year of the *Lyrical Ballads,* the Royal Academy, in recognition of that alliance between literature and art, allowed artists to attach literary quotations to their paintings or in the exhibit catalogues.

While literary illustration was eventually dismissed as a trivial occupation, at the time it offered fresh sources of inspiration and necessary alternatives to historical painting. Historical painting, like the theater, performed more of a ritual than a documentary function, preserving the collective and necessary illusions of the past. The development of archaeology, however, raised standards of authenticity that threatened these historical illusions. Literature, on the other hand, offered a one-dimensional timeless past, idealized figures in anachronistic splendor, human forms arrayed in flowing armor and calcified drapery who could pass as Homeric warriors, Shakespearean kings, and Miltonic angels. Among the favored scenes: dying heroes, partings, reconciliations, oaths, battles, confrontations between mortals and ghosts or malevolent spirits, extended arms, gaping mouths, grasping hands, bulging eyes, all the terror and intensity of the melodrama and the gothic novel. In fact, theater managers often reproduced famous paintings for the scenes or tableaux at the end of acts. This creative freedom and the promise of a wider audience through illustrated publications attracted prominent artists to contribute hundreds of paintings to Boydell's Shakespeare Gallery, Macklin's Gallery of Poets, and Fuseli's Milton Gallery. The galleries themselves had only limited success but the promise of catalogues based on them stimulated engraving as an art form, the engravings often surpassing the originals in quality and detail.[15]

Sir Joshua Reynolds, as the President of the Royal Academy and certainly the most influential painter in England, had always encouraged artists to read literature for inspiration, especially classical and mythological literature. Even in the portraits for which he was famous, the literary and classical allusions helped him in idealizing, generalizing, and abstracting the plump, pock-marked ladies who sat for him, turning them into playmates for the graces and their squinting, chalky children into dimpled cherubs. Up to 150 people a year came to him for his transformations, which were accomplished largely by assistants and disciples who collectively created, if not a representation of the age, at least a representation of how affluent people preferred to see themselves. While they were often depicted individually with their houses, pets, or symbols of their status or profession, they were also represented in groups called conversation pieces, engaged in characteristic activities, in conversation, or riding to the hunt, but surrounded by their possessions and looking interesting. These groups emphasize the social and journalistic preoccupations of the artists in the early years of the Royal Academy while creating, almost incidentally, a great age of portraiture.

The popularity of portraits coincided with the rise of biographical interest in literature. It was this period that produced the *Biographical History of England* (1769), in which James

Granger introduced engraved portraits of dead people by contemporary artists, a process still called "grangerizing."[16] Just as James Boswell's *Life of Samuel Johnson* (1791) is a subjective interpretation expressing Boswell as much as it depicts Johnson, so portraits by Reynolds (who was a good friend of both Johnson and Boswell) reflected the tastes and ideals of the painter as much as the subject. Consequently, Reynolds' views of George III, Samuel Johnson, Mrs. Siddons, John Hunter, James Watt, and the Duchess of Devonshire all share an unlikely family resemblance. Part of the resemblance may be attributed to technique; there was a flesh tone, a way of doing hands, or ears, the conventionally enlarged eyes and heads that, with minor adaptations, suited everybody, whatever the rank or occupation. But believing they were inappropriate to portraiture, Reynolds consciously eliminated idiosyncrasies and personal expressions, preferring an inanimate composure, detachment, even vacancy, to achieve what he considered beauty. While the middle and upper classes wept in public, collapsed in tearful fits in theaters all over Britain, and encouraged the emotional excesses of the gothic industry, while they endorsed if not created the sensitive, lachrymose hero of sensibility and purchased landscapes designed to evoke terror and awe, they had their portraits done by a painter who believed that "perfect" beauty, as Reynolds wrote in his fifth discourse, was incommensurate with "the passions, all of which produce distortion and deformity, more or less, in the most beautiful faces"—to which Blake replied: "What Nonsense. Passion & Expression is Beauty Itself—The Face that is Incapable of Passion and Expression is Deformity Itself . . ." (Erdman, 642).

His popularity and the popularity of his followers—James Northcote, John Opie, Sir William Beechey, and even Sir Thomas Lawrence—indicate that right through this period of intellectual, political, and scientific ferment, the lords and ladies, industrialists, politicians, performers, bankers, and authors, the subjects of these portraits, liked to think of themselves in these mindless and inert attitudes. The frozen stares and marmoreal postures appeared on library and drawing-room walls, and in gothic novels as well, where portraits, serving as revelations of identity or tokens of love, had, like the ghosts of melodrama, become ubiquitous. Influenced by literature, the theater, the taste for the Byronic, the Napoleonic wars, and his own unfulfilled passions, many of Sir Thomas Lawrence's portraits have more interest than those of his predecessors. His slightly wistful men, many of them statesmen and royalty, suggest concealed desires, and the slightly wasted women suggest concealed diseases from which they, like his first loves, Mrs. Siddons' daughters, would die at an early age.

The alternative to such portraits offered more objectivity, though even less expression: the silhouette or "shade," occasionally created with such ingenious machinery as an Ediograph, a Prosophographus, or a Physionograce, exactly reproduced a profile. While such devices produce an exact copy that in some ways foreshadows photography, when exhibited in a large number, as Piper observes in his study of English portraiture, the silhouettes offer the poignant image of shadows, lost souls, in search of people to possess them.[17] The life mask, on the other hand, offering the most accurate representation of all, appeared to be a face in search of a soul. And perhaps because it required several uncomfortable hours of sitting while the plaster dried, it was indistinguishable at times from the death mask, which was also popular.

Physiognomy, Natural History, and Animal Painting

However accurate these representations, they all concealed, if not disregarded, the inner life, the psychological as well as physiological processes that went on under the carefully applied flesh tones, an inner life with which the philosophers, scientists, and poets were obsessed and to which the painters had considerable access. Lavater's physiognomy, for example, was well known to the students at the Royal Academy through his friend Fuseli, and he had used art as well as artists to illustrate his belief that the conformations of the human skull, especially the face, reveal character and the state of the soul. Blake extended physiognomy to explain his politics: "I can't help being [Republican], any more than you can help being a Tory: your forehead is larger above; mine, on the contrary, over the eyes."[18] Lavater's vocabulary was popular enough to be incorporated into popular novels, both in prose descriptions and in the illustrations that accompanied them. He believed that a precise representation of the human face, as in a silhouette, would reveal the analogues between human beings and animals, and thereby account for bestial characteristics in people, their lust, greed, secrecy arising from their resemblance to goats, pigs, and rodents. These animal analogues influenced the Romantic caricaturists, James Gillray, Thomas Rowlandson, and George Cruikshank who in turn influenced the way ordinary people, who may not have been familiar with Lavater, viewed public figures that were the subjects of these caricatures.[19]

Painters became aware of contemporary theories of anatomy as well from John Hunter's popular presentations in his dissecting theater, the exhibition in his museum, and his brother William's lectures on anatomy at the Royal Academy. From the time John arrived in London, a gifted but uneducated Scottish peasant, until his death in 1793, he dissected over 500 species of animals ranging from barnacles to a seventeen-foot whale he had delivered to his home in Earl's Court, and an eight-foot Irish giant who tried to avoid such a fate by asking to be buried at sea. In his museum Hunter arranged the parts of all specimens in ascending orders of complexity: fossils, embryos, arms, hearts, with corresponding parts in different animals illustrating an evolutionary history (from polyps to human beings) in which all life forms appeared to develop through common stages. Sir Joshua Reynolds depicted him alongside a series of skulls to which he bears an especially simian resemblance, and Blake portrayed him in *An Island on the Moon* as Jack Tearguts.[20]

Unfortunately, like much of the life science in the eighteenth century, Hunter offered a demonstration without a principle. Although he had all the evidence to account for the survival of animal characteristics in human beings, Hunter was unable to conceptualize the biological commonplace, formulated only a few years later by Erasmus Darwin in *Zoonomia* (1794–1796), that the human race had actually evolved from the lower life forms it resembled. Moreover, the formal analogies he revealed were threatening to the prevailing idea of what constituted being human, for they shattered the boundary between people and animals. At worst, they gave substance to the persistent belief in the possibility of human as well as animal transformations, such as lovers turning into werewolves, that were so fascinating in novels, toads into princes, thieves into mice that were so hilarious in the pantomimes, and infants into rabbits, a danger that terrified the credulous into joining bizarre religious cults. On a rational level, Hunter's exhibitions gave a physical basis to Lavater's theories on the appearance of animal characteristics in adults, the porcine appearance of gluttons, the mulish appearance of the stubborn, and conversely, to the appearance of human characteristics in animals, such marketplace oddities as the learned pig, the musical dog, and other curiosities of nature.

Painting Animals and Illustrating Natural History

However amusing and interesting, such natural history was a great source of anxiety to human beings who discovered how much they shared with sheep, and monkeys, and mollusks. By excluding both anatomy and psychology, portrait painters isolated their subjects from natural history and kept them firmly in social history, among their human ancestors and heirs. But the same anatomical knowledge that threatened human dignity contributed to an extraordinary school of animal painting at which the English excelled, for they were genuinely fond of animals, especially horses.[21] George Stubbs (1724–1806), one of the most influential animal painters of the period, began as the son of a tanner with a special interest in anatomy, which he was demonstrating to medical students in York when he received a commission to illustrate a book on midwifery (1751), for which purpose he dissected a human fetus and learned engraving.[22] In 1766, after months in an isolated farmhouse dissecting horses, studies in both Italy and at the Royal Academy, and meticulous engravings, he published his indispensable *Anatomy of a Horse,* applauded by both scientists and artists who depended on it for their popular hunt scenes, and for historical, allegorical, and even literary paintings, all with their inevitable horses. The animals were far more successful, certainly more animated and realistic than the human subjects with which they often appeared.

In fulfilling a commission for one of his many aristocratic patrons, Stubbs began painting a series of horses attacked by lions, the anatomically perfect horse caught in a moment of confusion, anger, and terror, set in an anonymous moonlit mountainside such as those made familiar by Rosa, Ossian, and the gothic novelists.[23] The interpenetration of fantasy and fact, of terror and beauty, of invention and representation places the paintings in the same imaginative sphere as the *Lyrical Ballads* or *Childe Harold,* conveying that interaction between a creative mind and the forces of nature that we have called the poetry of life. In his careful observation, his recognition of the art that is in life, his exertion of intellect over nature, Stubbs overcame many of the artistic clichés, but he perpetuated others. His anthropomorphism, his projection of human emotions on animals, expressed the age of sensibility in which he lived; sentimentalized and popularized in literature and on the stage, it made Sir Edward Landseer, one of

Stubbs's disciples, perhaps the most successful painter in history.[24]

However artificial the human figure in English painting, the authentic, or what they thought was authentic, depiction of animals was sanctioned by an ancient convention of illustrated natural histories going back to the second century, moralized in the Christian bestiaries of the medieval period, and ultimately secularized in the eighteenth century.[25] The initial impulse was to observe, describe, collect, classify, and exhibit specimens in museums, out of their living habitat. But, as travel and publications became more accessible, an immense amount of artistic energy was devoted to drawing these specimens, often from life in a natural environment. While European artists were developing theories of what the landscape would look like if God had been an Italian painter, and Englishmen, who studied in Europe, imported theories of the picturesque to imitate in the studios of the Royal Academy, native artists employed to illustrate, often anonymously, natural histories were acquiring far more valuable representational skills: how to draw, engrave, and color the butterflies, birds, wild flowers, fish, and animals in the world they inhabited; how to represent water, scales, fur, petals, bark, and even insects.[26]

Illustrated versions of such books as Thomas Pennant's *British Zoology* (1761–1762), with 132 pages of colored plates, were seldom out of print in the eighteenth century. They were followed in the nineteenth century by, among others, Edward Donovan's natural histories of insects in sixteen volumes with 569 colored plates, of birds in ten volumes with 244 colored plates, of shells in five volumes with 180 colored plates, fishes in five volumes with 120 colored plates, and quadrupeds in three volumes with seventy-two colored plates—all published by Rivington between 1792 and 1820. Some illustrated natural histories were prepared for children, others for ladies; some were abridged and others were original pocketbooks. Anything about birds or accompanied by verse or with the word British in the title would, like Bewick's *History of British Birds* (1797–1804) with its charming woodcuts, find an appreciative audience.[27] The vegetable world was represented by gorgeous hand-colored herbals, mammoth productions such as John Hall's twenty-six-volume *The Vegetable System* (1759–1775) with 1,549 plates, and fanciful ones such as Erasmus Darwin's *The Loves of Plants* (1789), a poetic inventory of plants classified by the Linnaean system of sexual parts, published by Joseph Johnson with some illustrations by William Blake.

Exhaustive illustrated regional natural histories of areas in Britain start in the seventeenth century with those of Oxfordshire (1677), Staffordshire (1686), Northamptonshire (1712), Surrey (1719), Cornwall (1758), culminating though hardly ending with Gilbert White's *The Natural History and Antiquities of Selborne* (1789), which has never been out of print. There were similar regional natural histories of foreign countries, also based on first-hand observations, such as Mark Catesby's comprehensive *Natural History of Carolina, Florida, and the Bahama Islands* (1729; 1781). Out of these first-hand regional or specialized natural histories grew the compendious *History of the Earth and Animated Nature* by Oliver Goldsmith, eight volumes and 101 plates, first appearing in 1774, and in at least twenty-eight editions over the next century. Goldsmith, in turn, inspired many imitations and rivals such as George Shaw's *General Zoology,* published between 1800 and 1826, in twenty-eight volumes with 1,217 plates. Legions of artists and engravers were occupied with these productions, many of which survive in exceptionally good condition while the more prestigious though derivative landscapes that were being exhibited at the Royal Academy have deteriorated, originally darkened by varnishes and later by the aging of unstable, bituminous-based paints, for most artists understood neither the natural world they lived in nor the materials with which they painted.

John Constable: Painting as Earth Science

It was in the tradition of Gilbert White, the field naturalist, affectionately observing the processes of nature and their interrelationships, from the large meteorological events to the most obscure tracings on the bark of a tree, that John Constable started painting, long before he saw his first Claude or received his first instruction at the Royal Academy at age twenty-four.[28] Born in June, 1776, in East Bergholt, Suffolk, the son of a prosperous corn merchant, Constable began his life as a miller learning to read the winds and clouds on which his livelihood would depend. The settings and tone of the fields where he did oil sketches became a life-long preoccupation: "The sound of water escaping from Mill dams, . . . Willows, Old rotten Banks, slimy posts, & Brickwork. I love such things. . . . As long as I do paint I shall never cease to paint such Places. . . . Painting is but another word for feeling" (letter to John Fisher, October, 1821). His emphasis on memory, feeling, and fresh observation, especially of the commonplace, are among the many parallels between Constable and Wordsworth,[29] with whom he became acquainted through Sir George Beaumont, painter, collector, patron. However kindly and generous, Beaumont represented all the artificial conventions that Constable was rejecting. The brown trees and russet foliage, the mythological creatures and ruined temples, the abstract idea of beauty codified in the picturesque were to Constable what personification and poetic diction were to Wordsworth—barriers between art and experience.

But Constable's concept of experience was extremely limited: it was what he knew and saw in the Stour Valley, or Salisbury, or Hampstead, on the banks of the Thames, at the seaside in Brighton. He disliked the Lake District because it lacked "human association" and the solitude weighed upon him, according to his friend and biographer, C. R. Leslie. And he never visited continental Europe at all. His explorations of the inner life were similarly limited: his paintings, however precise and original a response to the external world, exhibit little of the reflectiveness and spirituality of Wordsworth. If Wordsworth's clouds, as he said in the Intimations Ode, "took a sober colouring from an eye / That hath kept watch o'er man's mortality," Constable's reflect the weather, the wind, his reading in contemporary meteorology,[30] his training as a miller, and his talent as a naturalist. In his essays on English landscape painting, a copy of which he gave to Wordsworth,[31] Constable wrote, "I hope to show that landscape painting is a regularly taught profession; that it is scientific as well as poetic; that imagination alone never did, and never can, produce works that are to stand by a comparison with realities."

Constable shared Wordsworth's delight in the natural world, his view that it is full of radiance whether one perceives it or not, his belief that the artist can awaken the sense of wonder to be found in familiar objects, their textures and conformations. But he disparaged such impalpable elements as genius and inspiration, values that the contemporary artistic and literary community held in great esteem. When Blake saw one of his studies of trees on Hampstead Heath, and commented reverently, "Why this is not drawing, but *inspiration*," Constable replied, "I never knew it before; I meant it for drawing."[32] For Constable, creativity required perception, not inspiration; viewing his work required a mind as creatively engaged as the artist's, an imaginative response that completed the work. His task was more complicated than, say, Blake's or Wordsworth's, who also claimed that their work required an imaginative response: if the way an object appears is conditioned by the eye of the perceiver, as the poets and philosophers believed, a painter must, first, either compensate for or represent the distortions of his own vision; secondly, translate it into the limited dimension of canvas and pigment; and, thirdly, overcome the predisposition and context of a viewer who may be accustomed to an entirely different representation and who may be viewing the painting in unfavorable light. How, for example, can an urban gentleman appreciate the freshness and color of a sun-drenched meadow just before harvest when he is viewing it in the middle of winter by the gas light introduced at the Royal Academy in 1817, surrounded by paintings of battles, murders, cherubs, and Biblical disasters?

To control this complicated transaction, to compensate for the various distortions, Constable developed several interesting techniques that both amused and irritated his colleagues. Fascinated by the light reflected off the surfaces of water and leaves, refracted through moisture, distributed by trees, and showering directly onto the landscape at his favorite and luminous moment of noon, he invented representations of it such as white spots on the surfaces of foliage and grass, a mannerism his colleagues called "Constable snow." He was equally interested in levels of shadow cast by clouds, on themselves and on the earth, by and within trees, and within the low-lying shrubbery, how they influence the way color is perceived from the pale hues in the sunlight to the jewel tones, the intense greens, blues, reds, and whites in the shade. He applied these experiments in optics, as Wordsworth applied his experiments in diction, to commonplace and primarily rustic scenes: *The White Horse* (1819), *Stratford Mill* (1820), *The Hay Wain* (1821), *View on the Stour* (1822), *The Corn Field,* and *Hampstead Heath* (1828). By manipulating light and shade, Constable integrated the skies, meadows, woods, and waters with the human associations he required, the subtle assertions of mind over nature. He found them among the windmills, canals, locks, towpaths, wagons, cottages, distant church spires, and bridges, which especially interested him, from the chain pier at Brighton opened in 1823, a suspension bridge exhibiting intricate Regency art work, to the stately stone bridge at Waterloo opened in 1817. He also found this association between man and nature in places of worship ranging from the soaring Salisbury Cathedral, of which he completed many studies, and of nearby Stonehenge with its primitive pagan associations. Occasionally dominated if not subdued by a rainbow, they expressed Constable's priorities. When human beings do appear, they are dwarfed by clouds, trees, and expanses of meadow, assimilated into the landscape and the seasons.

Constable did nothing of literary or historical association, abandoned portraits early in his career, and avoided the conventional images of the sublime in nature, although his seascapes are by association uncharacteristically troubled. The barren sand and menacing sky of *Weymouth Bay,* begun on his honeymoon in 1819, reminded him of Wordsworth, "for on that spot perished his brother in the wreck of the Abergavenny."[33] Similarly, his seascapes at Brighton, where he had moved his family in a hopeless effort to save his wife Maria, who was dying of consumption, are often storm-tossed and mysterious. But his habitually sedate subjects, his acerbic personality, his unwillingness and perhaps inability to court critics and patrons, and his reluctance to part with his paintings even when he had sold them impeded his career. He was not elected an associate of the Royal Academy, a position he needed for financial as well as personal reasons, until he was forty-three, twenty years after Turner, his contemporary. As a painter without prospects, he had been prevented from marrying his childhood sweetheart until he was forty years old. And twelve years later, she died of consumption, leaving him inconsolable with seven children to raise, a task he carried out with warmth, energy, and devotion. In 1829, at age fifty-three, several years after he began exhibiting in Paris, where his work had been enthusiastically received, he was grudgingly elected to full membership in the Royal Academy. Founded to promote a British school of painting, the Royal Academy under Reynolds and his successors encouraged the pursuit of alien and anachronistic ideas of history and heroism while disregarding this native-born and educated artist who had spent his life enshrining the golden moments of English country life.

Starting in 1833, Constable gave a series of lectures on the history of landscape painting at the Literary and Scientific Society of Hampstead, of Worcester, and at the Royal Institution, lectures in which he explicitly stated the importance to painters of natural history as well as aesthetics: "Painting is a science, and should be pursued as an inquiry into the laws of nature. Why, then, may not landscape be considered as a branch of natural philosophy of which pictures are but experiments? In such an age as this, painting should be *understood,* not looked on with blind wonder, not considered only as a poetic aspiration, but as a pursuit, *legitimate, scientific, and mechanical.*"[34] His youthful fondness for music and poetry, he recalls in 1835, "have less hold on my mind in its occasional ramblings from my one pursuit than the sciences, especially the study of geology, which more than any other, seems to satisfy my mind."[35] After a lifetime of observing the weather, the clouds, the contours of the landscape, the movements of rivers and tides, the quiet shaping powers of wind and water, Constable's concept of nature coincided with Hutton's, whose uniformitarianism was just then being vindicated.

J. M. W. Turner:
Painting as Physical Science

Born in London, in the teeming marketplace around Covent Garden, J. M. W. Turner (1775–1851) also exhibited an affinity with contemporary science and came to believe in the scientific basis of painting. As one astute critic in the *Literary Gazette* (May 14, 1831) noted, "If Mr. Turner and Mr. Constable were professors of geology, instead of painting, the first would certainly be a Plutonist, and the second a Neptunist . . . the one all heat, the other all humidity."[36] But Turner was more of a chemist or physicist than a geologist, focusing on the forces, the elements, rather than the forms of nature. He was preoccupied especially with motion and energy expressed in light, color, water, fire, steam, storms, avalanches, and floods, a preoccupation for which he would be criticized. Turner is the "ablest landscape painter now living," Hazlitt wrote in a *Round Table* essay (1816), many years before Turner's most original and abstract paintings, but he indulges in "too much abstraction of aerial perspective," "representations not properly of the objects of nature as of the medium through which they were seen."

Turner was also more versatile than Constable, possibly more versatile than any other painter of his generation,[37] capable of doing whatever was necessary to earn a living as well as the experimentation necessary to make a life—except for portraits, for, like Constable, he had difficulty with the human face.[38] His single-minded industry and his adaptable

talents allowed him to achieve at an early age all the recog-
nition that Constable found so elusive. Enrolled at the Acad-
emy schools at age fourteen, in 1789, he exhibited his first
painting the following year, became an associate in 1799, and
a full academician in 1802, when he was only twenty-seven.
During that period he supported himself by coloring archi-
tectural drawings and copying famous European landscapes
from which he learned the conventions of the picturesque.
He also began those energetic sketching tours that ultimately
led him all over Great Britain, France, the Alps, and Italy,
yielding thousands of pencil sketches and notes, scenes of
famous castles, abbeys, churches, country houses, the Lake
District, Oxford, the rivers and mountains of England and
France. His topographical interests led to his designing a pan-
orama, the *Battle of the Nile,* at the Naumachia in 1799, influ-
enced by the son of the inventor, Robert Barker, who studied
with him at the Royal Academy, and by de Loutherbourg,
whose combination of action and scenery in the Eidophusi-
kon had fascinated him.[39]

However attuned he was to profitable fashions in publish-
ing and technology and to the ways of luring commissions,
he was also learning to work in those conventions that would
bring him prestige as an artist. Views that he sketched for
engravings became the backgrounds for *The Holy Family* (1803)
and *Venus and Adonis* (1803)—pagan and Christian sources
being interchangable for him—or tailored to the picturesque
epic of *The Goddess of Discord Choosing the Apple of Contention
in the Garden of the Hesperides* (1806). The objective and accu-
rate topographical drawings he completed at one stage in his
career reappeared in imaginative explosions of angry storms
and avalanches annihilating people, cottages, ships, and for-
ests. Drawings of scenery appeared to rise up and revert to
disorganized nature, an adversary of mankind, a retributive
force that Turner knew from both the Biblical and the geo-
logical catastrophic tradition of deluge and plague verified by
his own experience. An alpine view, a storm in Yorkshire, a
fiercely cold winter in London, and Napoleon's foolish con-
frontation with the Russian winter came together in *Snow-
storm: Hannibal and His Army Crossing the Alps* (1812), to which
he appended a passage from his poem "The Fallacies of Hope,"
a long and pessimistic catalogue of defeated aspiration.[40] In
spite of wealth or success, he continued to work in all these
styles, however contradictory, throughout his career. His
charming drawings for *Picturesque Views of England and Wales*
(1832) were adapted to the imaginative Mediterranean setting

of *The Parting of Hero and Leander* (1837) and served the same year as the basis for *Snowstorm, Avalanche, and Inundation*.

Turner is chiefly remembered as a landscape painter, but his repertoire included many scenes of documentary, historical, or social significance, such as his patriotic *Battle of Trafalgar as seen from the mizen starboard shrouds of the 'Victory'* (1805–1808) showing Nelson dying on the deck, or the brilliantly illuminated but inanimate *George IV at a Banquet in Edinburgh* (1822) commemorating the ceremonial visit orchestrated by Sir Walter Scott, or the ominous *Burning of the Houses of Lords and Commons* (1834), sketched from among the crowd on the banks of the Thames during the fire. His favorite, though derivative, *Dido Building Carthage* (1815), in the manner of Claude Lorrain, was followed by the sombre boredom of *The Decline of the Carthaginian Empire* (1817). He did two genre pieces, both based on arguments over debts; a series of iridescent interiors at Petworth, the home of his patron, Lord Egremont; a silent elegy for a warship being tugged to her last berth in 1838; a stormy elegy in 1840 for some anonymous black slaves thrown into the sea half a century before; and the sea-burial of his colleague David Wilkie in 1842. Although anecdotal, or narrative, even political in subject, in execution the forms, the literal meaning, disappears; atmosphere, largely expressed through color and texture, takes priority over form.

As Professor of Perspective at the Royal Academy between 1807 and 1828, Turner read extensively in optics and chemistry, a field stimulated by the needs of the textile and ceramic industries to develop a standard and communicable system of color and pigments. However well-informed, Turner's terse elliptical speaking style and lower-class accent were handicaps, and his lectures were dismissed as unintelligible, enigmatic, and disorganized, although magnificently illustrated. Turner was almost as eclectic intellectually as he was artistically. He began and possibly ended his career still believing, like his friend de Loutherbourg, in alchemy as an explanation for the power of certain colors and the power of light, an idea that in later life he found confirmed in the invention of photography.[41] Like Coleridge and Shelley, he learned from Joseph Priestley's *History and Present State of Discoveries Relating to Vision, Light, and Colours* (1772) about phosphorescence, a luminous glow produced by fish, a natural phenomenon especially well suited to his painting, but he was equally fascinated by a mechanical phenomenon that coordinated light and movement, the kaleidoscope, an immensely popular "Romantic Toy," invented in 1814 by Sir David Brewster, an otherwise serious scientist who used it to demonstrate his theory of optics, the organizational role of the mind in visual events.

By 1830, however diverse the subjects of his paintings, however remote the references, Turner's work displayed an integrity of style, a unity of vision based on his preoccupation with light not only as an agent to illuminate, unify, and transform, but especially as a creative force, the very subject of the painting itself, whatever the occasion. In 1843, he portrayed the Deluge, a Biblical scene often chosen by painters to express the sublime. But Turner's Deluges, *Shade and Darkness—the Evening of the Deluge* and *Light and Color (Goethe's Theory)—the Morning After the Deluge,* had little to do with either spiritual or natural history; rather, he invoked the most universal of myths to illustrate the color of darkness in relation to the color of light, in part attempting to refute Goethe's *Theory of Colors,* a work that, among other things, deprived all nature of color and placed it in the human eye. Turner thought it was a poor exchange.[42] In a similar style Turner turned to contemporary expressions of technology, which he verified through his own experience, to illustrate the same phenomena of color, light, and elemental force in *Snowstorm—steamboat off a harbour's mouth making signals in shallow water, and going by the lead* (1842), for which he had himself tied to the mast of a ship during a storm; and *Rain, Steam and Speed—The Great Western Railway* (1844),[43] for which he poked his head out the window of a speeding train, to the consternation of his fellow passengers. The diffusion of light and color to represent motion, force, even temperature, obscures the subjects of the paintings. Noah's Ark in the Deluge would be interchangeable with the Great Western Railway had Turner not appended detailed captions in the manner of topographical poetry or the topographical drawings with which he started his career. In these late paintings his imaginative and interpretive commitments take priority over his topographical ones. Like Wordsworth, for example, in "Lines Written a Few Miles Above Tintern Abbey," Turner provides a precise location to externalize an otherwise mental event, one that could have occurred anywhere.

Except for a few erotic drawings John Ruskin found among Turner's thousands of sketches and then suppressed, little of Turner's work is personally revealing. He seemed to work equally well in everybody's garden, and his own flourished without his palpable presence. His mother, who had an ungovernable temper, died in an insane asylum in 1804. His loquacious and good-natured father, whom he resembled in temperament, lived with him until his death in 1829, at age eighty-five. In 1799, the year he became an RA, he took as his mistress Sarah Danby, the widow of a musician with four children. After 1833, he lived anonymously in Chelsea, assuming the name of Admiral Booth, the late husband of his mistress and housekeeper. Although he was immensely wealthy for a painter, he was miserly and distrustful. He wore ill-fitting and uncoordinated clothes, his coattails nearly reaching the floor, enormous buttons, umbrellas, hats, and long scarves. With his ruddy face, large nose, and ill-kempt hair, his appearance in the age of Beau Brummell was unforgivable. He was dedicated to the Royal Academy, which he often referred to as a substitute mother. But he was even more dedicated to his paintings, which he considered his children, and he built two galleries so they would be properly displayed. The second gallery, opened in 1822, was equipped with a high skylight, tissue, and fishnet to filter the sun's rays and show his increasingly radiant paintings to advantage.[44] Competitive by nature, he was disconsolate at the loss of his rivals, Constable in 1837, and Wilkie in 1842. And to defend himself against bad reviews, about which he was extremely sensitive, he often bribed critics with drawings. Circumstances and rapacious relatives prevented the fulfillment of his will, in which he left his wealth to educate indigent native-born artists, and his paintings, many of which he had repurchased in his later years, as a bequest to the nation.

Turner's ultimate preference for light and color over form, his tendency toward abstraction, and his delight in energy would, if he were a religious man, suggest the spirituality, even mysticism of a Blake. But Blake, like most spiritualists, was totally committed to outline, to precision of form, to the literal translation of the ineffable—even his drawing of the ghost of a flea is as precise as any of Stubbs's anatomies. His adherence to "the bounding line," as he called it, expressed both his habits as an engraver and his sense of divine mission: to incarnate the spiritual world, to make it visible and known. However secular and empirical by nature, Turner rejected form; his reasons were scientific, however, not transcendental. From his studies in chemistry and physics, he recognized the priority of energy or force over matter, and for what the eighteenth-century natural philosophers called "imponderable" or "subtle" fluids, the animating juices that accounted for phenomena such as electricity, magnetism, life itself and whatever held it together, whatever scientists could not weigh or measure. Having become totally familiar with God, having painted all His acts, dominions, and agents, the painters like the poets found in this vitalistic, anti-Newtonian science a new ineffable spirit, often identified with nature, one that, like God, could not be named except obliquely, could not be seen except by its effects, "An *Active* Principle," as Wordsworth called his version of it, for there were many,

> —how'er removed
> From sense and observation, it subsists
> In all things, in all natures; in the stars
> Of azure heaven, the unenduring clouds,
> In flower and tree, in every pebbly stone
> That paves the brooks, the stationary rocks,
> The moving waters, and the invisible air.
>   (*The Excursion,* IV, 3–9)

Turner was perhaps the first painter to concern himself with depicting this new divinity, this life force identified with light and permeating the universe.

CHAPTER XIII

Science

D URING THE ROMANTIC period, many scientists, or nat-
ural philosophers as they were called, abandoned the
conventional metaphysical and theological questions
concerning the purposes and goals of life and explored secu-
lar explanations of life itself, its origins, conditions, and char-
acteristics. Although narrower and more specialized than the
philosophical perspective out of which it grew, this secular
investigation of life became the special concern that we now
call science. Like the religious and philosophical interpreta-
tions of life and nature that it displaced, some science, such
as physics and chemistry, dealt with what were called invisi-
bles, the intangible and inaudible forces behind and particles
within the processes and forms of nature. Influenced by the
same theological and philosophical assumptions, by the same
succession of ideas starting with the experimentalism of Bacon,
the empiricism of Locke, the idealism of Berkeley, the asso-
ciationism of Hartley, the skepticism of Hume, and the fac-
ulty psychology of the Scottish Common Sense philosophers,
their creative processes were also similar to artists' and writ-
ers', elevating experience over convention, mind over nature,
or merely affirming the reciprocity of mind and nature, the
"ennobling interchange / Of action" (XII, 376–77), as
Wordsworth described it in *The Prelude*—although the writ-
ers were, ironically, more preoccupied than the scientists with
the world of experience, the visible, tangible, and audible

universe, choosing, like Wordsworth, to "Deal boldly with substantial things" (*The Prelude,* XII, 234). Nonetheless, in 1830, the British Association for the Advancement of Science acknowledged the similarities, coining the name "scientist" as an analogy to "artist."[1] By then, however, art, literature, science, even religion had become differentiated, professionalized, developing special vocabularies, procedures, and credentials.

The Chain of Being and the Chain of Life

The lost coherence provoked much nostalgia during the nineteenth century, but it was a coherence based on a fiction, a religious though not necessarily Christian view of the universe traditionally represented as a Great Chain of Being.[2] This view, encompassing God, mankind, nature, morality, politics, the entire range of visibles and invisibles, was replaced by a less comprehensive secular view limited to man and nature bound in a chain of life.

The Chain of Being, a useful and tenacious metaphor going back to antiquity, described a vision of a hierarchical or vertical universe with God and other supernatural agents at the top, human beings distributed according to status in the middle, followed by brute creations, the animals, birds, fish, and insects, the eagles, lions, pigs, and gnats giving way to such transitional figures as hydras, polyps, and carnivorous plants descending to the vegetable kingdom that included, according to some, minerals and fossils growing in the earth, and coming finally to rest on inanimate nature, the earth, air, fire, and water out of which many believed God had created everything else. The Great Chain of Being was a static and immutable representation of the world as it was created according to Genesis, containing everything it was possible to create, with nothing altered, introduced, or lost. Because it made the right to govern part of the order of nature, because it made, according to the Bishop of Llandaff, wealth and power, poverty and suffering an expression of God's wisdom, the Great Chain of Being carried political as well as theological sanctions. It was with more than scientific ardor, then, that natural philosophers employed themselves with filling the interstices of the Great Chain of Being, assigning a proper place to each thing from the remotest stars to microscopic creatures. Believing that the world was complete from its creation, natural philosophers defined their functions as observing, discovering, naming, and classifying.

When natural philosophers working in fields that were to become chemistry, biology, physiology, and physics began to question these abstract and restrictive theories along with their implicit religious and political constraints and, like the poets and painters, turned to the world of experience, they turned the Chain of Being into a chain of life. Overcoming their ideological biases, they discovered an evolving system of processes, forces, interdependencies, growth, potential, and diversity. This gradual almost imperceptible shift took over one hundred and fifty years of isolated insights. While Locke and his disciples, for example, worried about how human beings can know the natural world, several investigators, working independently, discovered that merely breathing involves human beings in a far more intricate and binding relationship with nature than could have been philosophically conceived. In 1771, Joseph Priestley, a Unitarian minister who enjoyed experimenting with gases, observed that mice placed in a bell jar depleted the air and suffocated while sprigs of mint refreshed the air and made the mice especially frisky. In *Observations upon Different Kinds of Air* (1772), he concluded that the air consisted of different kinds of gases[3] and that one of them, oxygen, was essential to animal life. In 1780, Antoine Lavoisier, a brilliant French theoretician who earned his living collecting taxes, interpreted Priestley's data into what ultimately became that splendid symbiotic formula that now seems self-evident: life is dependent on the production of heat through respiration; respiration is the consumption of oxygen and the release of carbon dioxide; plants use carbon dioxide that would otherwise be poisonous to produce the oxygen essential for human life. In *Phytologia: or the Philosophy of Agriculture and Gardening* (1800), Erasmus Darwin offered as complete a description as was possible at the time of the plant chemistry that was to be called photosynthesis, adding that the plants also convert starch to sugar, which is essential for human nourishment.[4]

The idea, then, that human beings were dependent on plants to produce the air and even the carbohydrates on which life depended had become available in both popular and experimental science in Europe and Britain at a time when writers, painters, and philosophers were especially receptive to information about the natural world, the landscape to which many, following Shaftesbury, had already attributed their moral ideas and others of religious inclination attributed their sacred ones.[5] Photosynthesis, respiration, the very breath of life itself orig-

inating among the green and growing things offered an
empirical basis, a literal meaning to what philosophers, art-
ists, and poets already believed abstractly and metaphori-
cally: that human life exists in a productive, progressive, even
reciprocal relationship with the natural world.[6] Certainly, they
were eager to find new values in the verdant and sunlit land-
scapes they toured, painted, and described. As the ancient
gods inspired art and poetry while breathing life into man-
kind, so the trees, gardens, and meadows both stimulated
their imaginations and purified the air they breathed. Here
was the most vivid demonstration of a transfer of power from
the divine to the secular, from the supernatural to the natural
world.

The scientists, unfortunately, had some difficulty accept-
ing a theory that made man dependent on the vegetative world.
In 1830, fifty years after this analysis of respiration first
appeared, and seventeen years after he described it himself in
Agricultural Chemistry (1813), a book that influenced both
Coleridge and Shelley, Sir Humphry Davy, the greatest
chemist and, as President of the Royal Society, certainly the
most influential scientist in England, still doubted its valid-
ity,[7] rejecting the notion that human physiology had a chem-
ical basis, that life itself was sustained by the "plants, and
weeds, and flowers, / And silent over-growings" of nature
(*The Excursion,* I, 928–30). Such a dependency was as repug-
nant to those natural philosophers whose assumptions were
based on the hierarchical view of nature, on the Great Chain
of Being, as the analogies between human beings and animals
had been to portrait painters. Although it clearly offered the
potential for a new, coherent, and secular view of nature,
chemistry was slow to acquire authority, for it was burdened
with occult and alchemical origins that lingered in its proce-
dures. Priestley himself was unable to see the significance of
his discovery of oxygen because he believed, as many
enlightened people did, in phlogiston, a substance or activat-
ing agent released by burning objects. Consequently, although
Priestley observed the effects of oxygen on mice and plants,
he thought it was "dephlogisticated air."

Analogical Thinking

Revolutions and innovations, new perspectives on nature
and human experience in political and economic theory had
gradually undermined the significance of the Great Chain of
Being in most fields. The up-down universe, as Northrop

Frye calls it,[8] gave way to a horizontal one of relationships between man and nature, man and society, man and himself. Still, the habit of analogical thinking that went with the Great Chain of Being, arguing from the known to the unknown, projecting human characteristics on both the supernatural and natural world, continued to influence and unfortunately to retard the development of the life sciences especially.[9] For example, breathing, indeed nutrition, in plants and animals had always been considered as analogous; the new descriptions of these life processes were unacceptable for they were based on concepts of conversion, transformation, and interdependency and could not be interpreted analogically. Similarly, while analogical thinking had been useful to Hunter, his comparative studies of anatomy, producing a huge body of otherwise unavailable evidence, it also prevented him from seeing the evolutionary theory that his evidence demonstrated, for the idea of evolution also depended on conversion and transformation. Instead, scientists and painters used Hunter's information to demonstrate the human characteristics of animals, the bestial characteristics of people, and the generosity of God in creating all possible forms of life in the most subtle gradations. In economics, Adam Smith demonstrated this analogic thinking by adopting the popular French physiocratic analogy between the economy and the human body, money circulating like blood. And German *naturphilosophie,* epitomized in Laurenz Oken's *Compendium of the System of Nature Philosophy* (1809–1811), revived the alchemical and hermetic concept of the universe as an analogy to the human body, formed originally as a Grand Man from which individual creatures had fallen into sin, error, division. Swedenborg, himself a scientist before his private illuminations made him a religious mystic, also conceived of the universe as analogous to a giant man, on which Blake later elaborated.[10]

As analogical thinking had led the physiologists and physiognomists to humanize animals, so it led the naturalists to humanize or personify plants. Taking special interest in the mimosa, or sensitive plant, which Shelley was to use as a metaphor for the sensitive artist, natural philosophers assumed that to some degree all plants slept, ate, perspired, breathed, and even experienced pleasure or suffering just as people do.[11] Erasmus Darwin's apparently frivolous attribution of sexual feelings to plants, then, was merely the expression of a popular philosophical opinion. Similarly, Wordsworth, influenced by Erasmus Darwin and a host of other contemporary writers on natural history, was expressing a popular and pervasive attitude when he claimed " 'tis my faith that every flower / Enjoys the air it breathes" ("Lines Written in Early Spring," ll. 11–12.).[12] But his use of analogy was in part a youthful inclination to observe, as he recalls in *The Prelude,* "affinities / In objects where no brotherhood exists / To common minds" (II, 404–6).

To every poet going back to Homer, analogy and personification were legitimate figures of speech. They help to personalize alien forces, to familiarize and even domesticate threatening natural phenomena, and to extend the human community into the world of nature. Personification also asserts that human, not sacred values and characteristics, are a universal norm. For a while, then, scientific speculation gave a new philosophic value to a common poetic device, analogy and personification, a device that was even then being revived by the Ossianic poems, by Burns, and by other rustic or primitivistic poets as indicative of the naive mentality. But as scientific investigation made natural phenomena more familiar and predictable, as more rigorous empirical methods showed the absurdity of explaining plant life by analogy with human, and as scientific publication made the distinction between animal and vegetable physiology common knowledge, analogy and personification lost favor even as a poetic device. By 1856, John Ruskin in *Modern Painters* dismissed the projection of human emotions on plants as a "pathetic fallacy" to which the Romantic poets, he claimed, were especially susceptible.

Electricity

Eighteenth-century speculative biologists found analogy especially useful for exploring the otherwise undemonstrable origins of life, a problem with which they were as deeply concerned as geologists were with the origins of the earth. Most scientists identified life as a power such as electricity or galvanism, permeating living things in the form of a fluid called subtle or imponderable because it could not be weighed or measured but was known, like the invisible world of the supernatural, only by its effects.[13] Collected and stored in Leyden jars, these electrical currents had no purpose; they were used as convulsives in pointless demonstrations involving army regiments and a whole monastery full of monks holding hands and responding to shock. Mostly, however, electricity was used for healing. Mrs. Blake had electrical treatment to reduce the swelling in her legs, and Scott was subjected to it as a child to correct a deformity. Dr. Graham's Celestial Bed was supposed to use electricity to cure impotence and sterility, while John Wesley claimed it had the power to cure the blind. Natural sources of electricity had similar applications: in America, slaves suffering from fever and their owners from gout were submerged in whole vats full of electric eels, which shocked but did not cure them.

In 1752, when Benjamin Franklin, using his famous kite and key apparatus, demonstrated that electricity had celestial origins, it became associated with the Promethean myth, identified with that celestial fire stolen by a god for human beings for which they were all to suffer endlessly. In the Romantic versions of this myth, appearing in many disguises in Blake's, Byron's, Keats's, and Shelley's poetry, as well as in Mary Shelley's *Frankenstein* (subtitled *The Modern Prometheus*), the Promethean figure, whether depicted as rebellious or martyred, was primarily human, an example of the divine aspirations that plague human beings limited by their mortality. Electricity had both awakened these aspirations and frustrated them, for it still belonged to the sky, to the gods, its sources mysterious, uncontrollable, healing and blasting arbitrarily, like Shelley's West Wind, as destructive as it was creative. Franklin's efforts to attract this atmospheric electricity, however menacing, to harness its power and find an appropriate application for it, expresses that determined anthropocentrism of Romantic science that made Prometheus into a human hero rather than a fallen god. Joseph Priestley's *History of Electricity* (1767; 1966), written at Benjamin Franklin's suggestion, documents this assertion of mind over nature, which made the book, however dated the information, especially appealing to the Romantic writers and painters who conceived of creativity in just such terms.

In 1800, the study of electricity shifted to an exclusively human level when an Italian named Volta explained in a letter to the Royal Society how to generate electricity by a chemical reaction in a primitive battery called a Voltaic pile. Instead of being a source of life, of energy, transcendental in its origins, electricity became a product like steam or heat that could be known and directed toward human ends. Now that human beings could produce electricity, they encountered the awesome fact that they had all along been capable of producing the celestial fire that was once believed to have been stolen on their behalf by a divine rebel from the omnipotent and obdurate gods. Here was one more piece of evidence that, like Prometheus in Shelley's *Prometheus Unbound,* human beings had within their own intellects the power to free themselves, proof that they were the origins of the myths they believed and, as Blake claimed in *The Marriage of Heaven and Hell,* of the gods in whom they believed.[14] Like artists and poets, then, scientists participated in the recovery of those creative powers restoring them to the human mind where they originated.

The discovery that electricity could be generated by human beings using simple apparatus, that it was, as Sir Humphry Davy discovered, a common and accessible transforming agent, helped emancipate scientists from a whole collection of undemonstrable theses about the nature and origins of life as well as from the subtle or imponderable fluids that supposedly explained them. In fact, there were few imponderables left. By the end of the eighteenth century, the components of water were identified as specific gases, not imponderables, and heat, the ultimate imponderable, was known to be available through friction. Finally, John Dalton's speculations on matter revealed that chemical compounds, particles, atoms— invisibles but not imponderables—underlay all of nature. Since these atoms were too subtle for human perception, the scientists who worked with them required a special capacity or instinct for invisibles, an instinct with which Quakers such as Dalton who had built a religion on them, were particularly favored, accounting for the large number of Quakers who were active scientists during this decidedly empirical and materialistic period of British science.

Naturphilosophie

But imponderables, analogy, and imminences, forsaken, as Philip Ritterbush explains in *Overtures to Biology,* by the scientific community as inadequate for explaining objective reality, found a second life in painting, poetry, and philosophy, where they served moral and aesthetic ends. Indeed, much of the science that Romantic writers such as Wordsworth, Coleridge, and Shelley approved was either foreign or obsolete.[15] German *naturphilosophie,* in which Coleridge claimed to have found a "genial co-incidence with much that I had toiled out myself"[16] offered an imaginative alternative to the discredited speculation of eighteenth-century British life science. More philosophic than scientific, *naturphilosophie* maintained as its priority a unified theory of life based on a force that was constantly fulfilling itself in nature. Everything, however inert, was potentially alive, participating in the endless polarities by which the universe is sustained. Derived from the mystical philosophies of Boehme, Paracelsus, and the more objective and rational philosophers such as Leibniz, Kant, Herder, Goethe, Schelling, and, finally Oken, this amazing philosophical explanation of nature turned mankind from an afterthought in the creation to the glory and fulfillment of it, possessing a mind through which the divine spirit is most fully realized, a microcosm, a perfect representation of the world. As a system it inspired passionate disciples and contributed interesting though not always useful insights into the study of electricity, galvanism, magnetism, and embryology. Believing in the existence of certain archetypal creatures from which all others were differentiated, *naturphilosophers* contributed what is called the law of parallelism to the nascent field of embryology, a phenomenon first described by Erasmus Darwin: the development of the individual (ontogeny) recapitulates the development of the race (phylogeny). In other words, every animal in its development passes through the stages of all the animals that anticipated it; mankind, the epitome of nature, passes through the most forms from simple water creatures to the simian forms of maturity.

What Is Life?

In Britain, physiologists who had abandoned the idea of electricity as an imponderable fluid accounting for life nonetheless continued to debate the related question of whether it was a force conferred upon form or form to which vitality was added.[17] The debate was ancient, implicit, and unresolved in Genesis, which offers both versions: in the first, God created man in His own image in a series of commands (1:26) and in the second He formed him of dust and then breathed life into him (2:7). John Hunter had concluded to the satisfaction of most that life is a force separate from organization and not the result of it. Believing he represented Hunter, John Abernethy, lecturing before the Royal College of Surgeons between 1814 and 1819, disregarded all available evidence from chemistry and physics, and defended the proposition that there is a life principle analogous to electricity, a force added to organization, a soul, in other words, added to the body. His position was popular, and his advocates included Coleridge. His former disciple, William Lawrence, on the other hand, a distinguished surgeon specializing in eye diseases, maintained that human activity could be explained by chemical analysis and required no such life principle separate from organization, that mental activity was the function of the brain and had nothing to do with an immortal soul. Logically, though not actually, Lawrence's position would allow life, it if were knowable through chemistry, to be superimposed on a corpse, as Victor Frankenstein animated his monster in Mary Shelley's *Frankenstein,* written about the same time as the lengthy and widely reported debates between Abernethy and Lawrence. Although he did not deny the spiritual dimension of life, Lawrence objected to all religious influences on science just as he had objected to political ones. Finally, in his *Lectures on Physiology* (1819) and later in a popular encyclopedia, he concluded that human understanding is so limited that any knowledge of life's origins is "forever beyond our reach."[18] The opposition between religion and science was firmly defined.

Science and Poetry

The many meanings that accrued to the concept of life, like the concepts of nature, energy, imagination, and culture, reflect the changing attitudes of the period, the healthy diversification of meanings within and among such disciplines as theology, philosophy, art, history, literature, and the various sciences. And yet, in spite of this differentiation, art, religion, and science retained much in common—a vocabulary, an audience, even a view of creativity. All the poets, for example, at one time or another, like Coleridge in "The Destiny of Nations," condemned the "subtle fluids, impacts, essences, / Self-working tools, uncaused effects, and all / Those blind Omniscients" because they threatened the spiritual dimension of life, "Untenanting creation of its God" (ll. 32–35). At other times, the same poets invoked scientific principles and ideas for imagery and authority. Keats, for example, drew on his medical studies and his reading of Davy's *Elements of Chemical Philosophy* (1802), to explain "Men of Genius" as "great as certain etherial chemicals operating on the Mass of neutral intellect."[19] And Coleridge believed that to write an epic poem he would need to be "a tolerable Mathematician," to know "Mechanics, Hydrostatics, Optics, and Astronomy, Botany, Metallurgy, Fossilism, Chemistry, Geology, Anatomy, Medicine—the *mind of man* then *minds of men*—in all Travels, Voyages, and Histories . . ." (*CL,* I, 320). Blake learned anatomy from Hunter, biology from Erasmus Darwin, physics from Paracelsus and Jacob Boehme, and, although he condemned the influence of Newton's materialism, he found beauty in contemporary science. And it was this most religious as well as imaginative poet who offered what would eventually become the secular and scientific definition of life based on metabolism. "Energy is the only life and is from the body," he wrote in *The Marriage of Heaven and Hell* (1790), exemplifying yet another of his aphorisms: "What is now proved was once only imagined." Wordsworth, in the Head-note to "The Thorn," even defined poetry itself as the "history and science of feelings," the two suggesting a comprehensive theory. At one point, according to Coleridge, he considered engaging in chemical experiments to help "moderate" his feelings just as he had found solace in mathematics, rescuing Euclid's Elements along with poetry in his dream of the Del-uge (*The Prelude*, V, 70–139 for the entire dream). As we noted in our discussion of geology, Wordsworth was also an especially acute observer of natural processes, forms, and the forces that shaped them. And, "if Shelley had been born hundred years later," according to Alfred North Whitehead, "the twentieth century would have seen a Newton among chemists": "What the hills were to the youth of Words-worth, a chemical laboratory was to Shelley."[20]

In spite of the inspiration writers derived from science, it nonetheless appeared to be most often in opposition to poetry, especially after 1800, when experimental and mechanistic models replaced the analogical and fluid ones. Wordsworth, for example, claimed that scientists were constantly employed "picking up things about their feet, when thoughts were per-ishing in their minds," "gross, definite, and tangible objects . . . putting on more brilliant colours" while "the splendour of the imagination has been fading" ("The Convention of Cintra," *Prose*, I, 324–25).

Humphry Davy: Poet Scientist

The conflict between the claims of science and of imagi-nation, specifically the poetic imagination, appears vividly in the life of Humphry Davy. Coleridge believed he was "the Man who *born* a Poet first converted Poetry into Science and *realized* what few men possessed Genius enough to fancy," "realized," as he wrote in another context, "poetry . . . in nature."[21] His birth and childhood did indeed seem auspi-cious for a literary career, perhaps as an untutored rustic such as Burns. Born in Cornwall, he spent his youth hunting, fishing, wandering about the countryside learning supernat-ural lore from his grandmother and amusing the neighborhood children with tales of his own. Apprenticed to an apothecary surgeon at fifteen, he set out, like Coleridge, indeed, like Franklin, on an ambitious scheme of self-education including theology, language, philosophy, and science. In 1798, he found an ideal mentor in Dr. Thomas Beddoes, a physician and political activist who hired him to work in the Pneumatic Institute in Bristol, founded for the study and treatment of various diseases through gases. Trained in London and Edinburgh, former lecturer on chemistry at Oxford, Beddoes' friends included Priestley; Josiah Wedgwood, the industrialist; Erasmus Darwin, whose poetry inspired him to write his own *Alexander's Feast;* and Richard Edgeworth, whose daughter he married and by whom he fathered the dramatist and eccentric Thomas Lovell Beddoes. Along with expanding Davy's interests and sympathies, Beddoes was receptive to his young protegé's poetic inclinations. In his poem "The Sons of Genius," with its lofty, grim, and overblown heroics, Davy endeared himself to the ambitious young intellectuals of Bristol such as Coleridge and Southey, who published the poem in the *Annual Anthology* (1799):

> Like yon proud rock, amidst the sea of time,
> Superior, scorning all the billows rage
> The living Sons of Genius stand sublime,
> The immortal children of another age.

Davy developed an intense and working relationship with a number of contemporary authors: he supervised the publication of Southey's *Thalaba, the Destroyer,* assisted Wordsworth with *The Lyrical Ballads,* and accepted Coleridge's help in publishing *Researches, Chemical and Philosophical Chiefly Concerning Nitrous Oxide* (1800).

He brought the same enthusiasm to his chemical studies and, after only five months, in the spirit of a "philosophical Alchemist," as Coleridge called him, he concluded in his "Essay on Heat, Light, and the Combinations of Light" (1799), "No more sublime idea can be formed of the motions of matter, than to conceive that the different species are continually changing into each other." On the assumption that changes in feeling and thought were accompanied by changes in the body, he anticipated a day when chemistry could be used to increase pleasure and reduce pain. Two years later, after nearly killing himself in his own experiment, he discovered nitrous oxide, laughing gas, but it was not adopted as an anaesthetic until 1844.

His major work began when he joined the Royal Institution, founded to promote inventions for "domestic comfort and economy," especially in "the management of heat." Assisted at one time by Michael Faraday, he experimented with compounds and chemical reactions, using the voltaic pile, a primitive battery, and delivered his popular lectures to the fashionable urban audience whose subscriptions paid for his research. A handsome, articulate, vivacious man with an expressive face, a quick wit, and considerable charm, he investigated, interpreted, and explained combustion, mete-orology, agriculture, medicine, textiles, tanning, glass-mak-ing, processes of generation, respiration, motion, and decay, contributing to the popularity of chemistry. In a country dependent on coal for light, locomotion, and heat, his most significant invention was the safety lamp (1816), allowing miners to see without being exploded or suffocated by their own sources of light. From such contemporary concerns he turned his attention in 1818 to antiquity, advising the schol-ars excavating at Herculaneum how to unroll the papyrus scrolls without damaging them.

In 1812, Davy married Jane Kerr Apreece, a spirited and clever widow who had already been courted by John Play-fair, the Edinburgh professor and biographer of James Hut-ton. According to her cousin, Sir Walter Scott, she was "most actively ambitious to play a distinguished part in London society," but she forced herself beyond her intellectual limits, for she had no accomplishments of her own and "no great taste either for science or letters" (*Journals,* pp. 78–80). They quarreled often and in public, embarrassing, among others, Davy's talented protegé and traveling companion, Michael Faraday, whose experiments with electromagnetic induction led to the development of the dynamo. In 1812, the year they were married, Davy was knighted by the Prince Regent: "Alas!," Coleridge lamented, "Humphry Davy has become Sir Humphry Davy and an atomist," referring to his belated acceptance of atomic theory proposed by John Dalton in 1803. In 1812, in spite of the war, he was invited to France to receive a medal from Napoleon. And in 1820, this self-educated son of a Cornish widow was elected President of the Royal Soci-ety.

Following a stroke in 1825, he wrote *Salamonia,* a rumi-native work about fishing, his favorite sport, and in 1830, an intriguing philosophical essay, *Consolations in Travel; or the Last Days of a Philosopher* (1830), both of which were more popular than any of his scientific works. *Consolations* was a philosophical essay, a colloquy dominated by the mysterious but clearly autobiographical Unknown whose vision of the origins of both nature and society celebrates the diversity and fecundity of life.[22] He began with a description of tropical forms emerging as the earth cooled and solidified; shellfish, corals, insects, reptiles, turtles, and crocodiles, all destroyed in time by volcanic eruptions. He lingered over a second climactical equilibrium in which human creatures appeared, brutish, deformed savages surviving on maggots, worms, and the carcasses of rotting whales, creatures who evolve economically through pastoral, agricultural, and finally industrial stages. To this fascinating reconciliation of contemporary economic, scientific, philosophical, and religious attitudes, Davy added his special faith in a plurality of worlds, a universe full of infinitely diversified spiritual life passing through natural forms and planet systems. This imaginative leap is characteristic of his later years, when he attempted to endow chemistry with the poetic dimension he had forsaken early in his career and with a moral dimension as well: "Whilst chemical pursuits exalt the understanding, they do not depress the imagination or weaken genuine feeling; whilst, they give the mind habits of accuracy by obliging it to attend to fact, they likewise extend its analogies; and, though conversant with the minute forms of things, they have for their ultimate end the great and magnificent objects of nature." He concluded, "The true chemical philosopher sees good in all the diversified forms of the external world."[23]

Science and "The Household of Man"

Responding to Davy's scientific claims at the Royal Institution early in his career, Wordsworth had magnified the distinction between poetry and science in the Preface to *Lyrical Ballads* (1802) and presented what has since become a commonplace:

> The remotest discoveries of the Chemist, the Botanist, or Mineralogist will be as proper objects of the Poet's art as any upon which it can be employed if the time should ever come when these things shall be familiar to us, and the relations under which they are contemplated by the followers of these respective sciences shall be manifestly and palpably material to us as enjoying and suffering beings. If the time should ever come when what is now called science, thus familiarised to men, shall be ready to put on, as it were, a form of flesh and blood, the Poet will lend his divine spirit to aid the transfiguration, and will welcome the Being thus produced as a dear and genuine inmate of the household of man.
>
> (*Prose*, I, 141)[24]

In fact, the major contemporary scientific work was still "familiar," "palpably material," in the "form of flesh and blood," and, like Wordsworth's poetry, still written in "the real language of men." Indeed, it took more learning to read some of Wordsworth's poetry, especially the Intimations Ode, *The Excursion,* and *The Prelude,* than it required to read in contemporary science, which was rarely as speculative as Davy became in his later years. Contemporary science was largely concerned with pedestrian matters, with problem solving, although on a theoretical level great advances were being made. Shelley, for example, whose poetry was permeated with the most esoteric scientific allusions, found inspiration in Davy's description of plant metabolism, noting from *Elements of Agricultural Chemistry:* "The earth is a laboratory in which the nutriment of vegetables is prepared. Manure is helpful and may be converted into organized bodies. . . ." And Priestley, whose work with gas, light, and electricity would have made him one of the foremost scientists of any age, acknowledged the social basis, the common, familiar, and human significance of scientific speculation: ". . . the immediate use of natural science is the power it gives us over nature, by means of the knowledge we acquire of its laws whereby human life is in its present state, made more comfortable and happy, but the greatest philosophical speculation is the discipline of the heart, and the opportunity it affords of inculcating benevolent and pious sentiments upon the mind."

Reporting on experiments, inventions, and discoveries, the periodical press helped to introduce contemporary science to "the household of man." Stimulating popular interest in contemporary scientific activity were specialized journals for the general public such as *Nicholson's Journal of Natural Philosophy, Chemistry and other Arts,* founded in 1797; *The Annals of Philosophy; or Magazine of Chemistry Mineralogy, Mechanics, Natural History, Agriculture, and the Arts,* founded in 1813; and *The Philosophical Magazine,* founded in 1798, with the "grand object" of diffusing "Philosophical Knowledge among every class of society and to give the public as early an Account as possible of everything new or curious in the scientific world. . . ." The first volume offered an account of the "first mechanical invention of modern times," Cartwright's steam engine; instructions on how to dye cotton red according to the American method, how to fireproof writing paper, how to taste wine, descriptions of the telescope at Kiel, of a Javanese swallow that builds edible nests, of navigation by bats, and of sugar maples in America accompanied by the following

advice from the prominent Dr. Benjamin Rush: "A diet con-
sisting of a plentiful admixture of sugar has many advan-
tages. . . . The author of nature seems to have implanted a
love for sweets in all children for their growth, and to ward
off the disease of worms." He concludes with the comforting
observation: "It has been said that sugar injures the teeth; but
this opinion now has so few advocates, that it does not merit
a serious refutation." The editors noted that because the natives
of Cornwall lacked a knowledge of mineralogy, they could
not identify their natural resources and what to do with them.
Consequently, they were discarding valuable minerals such
as cobalt. Within a decade, the able and prolific Dr. Arthur
Aiken published for popular consumption *A Dictionary of
Chemistry and Mineralogy with an Account of the Processes
Employed in Many of the Most Important Chemical Manufactures*
in two six-hundred-page volumes.

   Works of scientific interest also appeared in reviews,
reflecting the ranging interests of middle-class readers, their
concern with assimilating scientific skills as well as informa-
tion. In 1808, for example, *The Annual Review of History and
Literature* covered nine books on voyages and travel; five on
geography; ninety-seven on theology; along with Scott's
Marmion; Francis Bailey's *Doctrine of Interest and Annuities; A
Short Practical Grammar of the English Language;* Drummond's
translation of Lucretius; Kirwan's *Essay on the Elements, Prin-
ciples, and Different Modes of Reasoning;* and the annual trans-
actions of the Royal Society, featuring an essay on the functions
of the heart and a report on the dissection of a fetus born
without one. Reflecting the same range and integration of
science with the general knowledge expected of an educated
person were such encyclopedias as Abraham Rees's *New
Cyclopaedia or, Universal Dictionary* (1802–1820),[25] where along
with the history of Spain, the functions of verbs, and the use
of percentages, an analysis of the Arabic language, and an
introduction to medical instruments, Lawrence offered his
startling definition of life as a chemical process. Such scien-
tific interest even penetrated the fashionable world of Ack-
erman's *Repository of Arts, Literature, Fashions, Manufacture,*
where in 1816, along with plans for building a *cottage ornée*
and a dairy, illustrations of carriages and fireplaces, opera,
wedding, and morning dresses, are instructions on determin-
ing the authenticity of wine, vinegar, and pepper, and the
alcoholic contents of various "spirits," how to distinguish
iron from steel, how to dye feathers, how to waterproof
leather, and how to restore "whiteness" to linens and cot-

tons, remove coffee, wine, fruit, and tea stains (ink being ineradicable), concluding with advice on why young ladies should avoid chemicals in curling their hair. Here, as in many other periodicals, contemporary chemistry was being used to protect consumers and improve domestic life; science clearly was "familiar," an "inmate of the household of man."

The Professionalization of Science

Between 1754 and 1831, between the founding of the unspecialized Royal Society for the Encouragement of Arts, Manufacturers, and Commerce and the British Association for the Advancement of Science, science, technology, and natural philosophy belonged to the people, not professional scientists. Public lectures, provincial learned societies, and Mechanics' Institutes assisted in making science popular, practical, and "palpably material to . . . enjoying and suffering beings." Because universities showed little interest in science until the middle of the nineteenth century, only the major figures, and not all of them, even considered themselves scientists, for they were not educated as such and often had other vocations. For example, when Wordsworth's friend and Darwin's mentor, Adam Sedgwick, an ordained minister and President of the Geological Society in England, was elected Woodward Professor of Geology at Cambridge, he proudly admitted that he knew absolutely nothing about geology, and claimed this ignorance gave him an advantage over his rival who "knew a great deal—but it was all wrong."[26] By the turn of the century, even the Royal Society, dominated by the agricultural interests of the politically conservative landed gentry, had more social than scientific prestige, serving as a not always reliable or discriminating clearinghouse of information relevant especially to natural history.

With the same organizational fever that characterized contemporary religion, politics, charity, art, even literature during the period, those interested in science and scientific experiments who were unable or unwilling to participate in the proceedings of the Royal Society held meetings, formed associations, and published magazines.[27] In Birmingham, Erasmus Darwin, Richard Edgeworth, Josiah Wedgwood, Thomas Day, Joseph Priestley, James Watt, the dissenters, the politically liberal industrialists, the writers, physicians, poets, a priest, a naturalist, and a printer, met between 1766 and 1791 at one another's homes whenever the moon was full to discuss papers and invent projects. They called themselves

the Lunar Society.[28] By 1847, the Reverend Hume, who wrote
what constituted a handbook to learned societies, noted that
there were more than 20,000 members of learned societies,
"the choice spirits of the age, the intellectual men in their
various localities, the ablest in their respective depart-
ments."[29] The Mechanics' Institutes, originating in Scotland
to provide lectures on science for artisans and craftsmen,
proliferated at an even more astonishing pace than the philo-
sophical societies, influencing the style of scientific presenta-
tion, the kinds of problems scientists chose to explore, and
ultimately, an audience for scientific literature. Between 1823,
when Dr. George Birkbeck opened the first in London, and
1850, six hundred such institutes were founded all over the
country with more than 100,000 members who received a
scientific education that exceeded anything available at the
major universities.[30]

In representing the charm as well as utility of scientific
inquiry, the Royal Institution, serving an urban middle class,
was perhaps the most successful of the societies. It was founded
by the idealistic, energetic, and adventurous American-born
Count Rumford, who acquired his title through marriage to
a widow in Concord, Massachusetts, where he had settled
after receiving a degree from Harvard. After his imprison-
ment in America for his sympathy with the British, he moved
to Bavaria, where he contributed to the organization of the
army, the relief of the poor, and where he developed a theory
of heat as a mechanical process rather than an imponderable
or subtle fluid. Moving to London, he combined his scientific
and charitable interests in creating the Society for Encourag-
ing Industry and Promoting the Welfare of the Poor (1798),
which in turn sponsored the Royal Institution, a "Public
Institution," as he described it in the prospectus, "for diffus-
ing the knowledge and facilitating the general introduction
of useful mechanical inventions and improvements, and for
teaching by courses of philosophical lectures and experiments
the application of science to the common purposes of life,"
the most common purpose being to provide information to
the poor on how to keep warm. Here Humphry Davy pur-
sued his electro-chemical research while lecturing to an
enthusiastic and fashionable audience that might otherwise
have been at the theater. In 1805, when the popularity of the
lectures overshadowed the humanitarian purposes for which
the Institution was founded, Count Rumford left for France,
where he married the widow of Lavoisier and continued his
philanthropic work. With Coleridge's lectures on poetry,

Constable's on landscape, and Dr. George Shaw's on zoology, the Institution continued to offer a broad range of liberal and humane learning to an audience whose access to contemporary thought was primarily the periodical press.

At a more learned level, "departmental societies," as the Reverend Hume called them, devoted to such special and emerging disciplines as geology, chemistry, horticulture, anatomy, and ornithology, held meetings, funded research, promoted cooperative experiments, published magazines, and sponsored outings, exhibitions, gardens, libraries. Young ladies and gentlemen, who once might have undertaken picturesque travel, explored the countryside collecting specimens of rocks, herbs, or butterflies, or exchanged shells and fossils, and even contributed their botanical, geological, and entomological observations to the societies and the publications they sponsored.[31] Largely because of its social implications, ornithology became the most popular scientific discipline. As ornaments or status symbols, birds had been bred, hunted, stuffed, and cooked; they had appeared caged in libraries and ornamental gardens, in poetry, heraldry, hats, porcelains, and textiles.[32] Gilbert White's *Natural History and Antiquities of Selborne* (1788), Thomas Bewick's *A History of British Birds* (1797–1803), and George Montague's *Comprehensive Ornithological Dictionary; or Alphabetical Synopsis of British Birds* (1802), along with inexpensive and widely distributed handbooks and periodicals, helped educate a reading public in the procedures and pleasure of observing birds in their natural setting while encouraging the exchange of information.

Such collective activity, characteristic of the age in all fields, reflects in part the open and participatory basis of natural history as well as scientific inquiry in the early decades of the nineteenth century before the various fields were professionalized, before they developed the specialized languages and complex procedures that accompany intellectual progress. Investigators shared their experience in correspondence, lectures, publications, visiting one another's laboratories and collections, contributing to one another's work. Nonetheless, the Faustian image of the scientist as an isolated, disheveled, deranged, self-involved, criminal dabbler in the occult, incapable of the love that could redeem him, persisted in gothic novels, melodrama, and even the critical prose of such otherwise enlightened authors as Wordsworth, who, in the Preface to *Lyrical Ballads* (1802), not only claimed that scientific knowledge was out of touch with human needs but also that its very acquisition was isolating, "personal and individual," "slow to come to us, and by no habitual and direct sympathy connecting us with our fellow-beings" (*Prose,* I, 141). Other authors invested these otherwise modest and self-effacing scientists with supernatural powers. For example, in 1813, the poet Thomas Campbell reported a conversation with William Herschel: "He said, with a modesty of manner which quite overcame me, when taken together with the greatness of the assertions: 'I have looked further into space than ever human being did before me. I have observed stars, of which the light, it can be proved, must take two millions of years to reach the earth.' I really and unfeignedly felt at this moment as if I had been conversing with a supernatural intelligence."[33]

But to the ordinary, believing, provincial middle classes depicted fondly by Joseph Wright of Derby, science and natural philosophy offered a social ritual binding them in new ways to their "fellow-beings," a source of strength and wealth. In paintings such as *An Experiment on a Bird with the Air Pump* and *A Philosopher Giving a Lecture on the Orrery,* Wright captured that rare combination of superstition and intelligence, of faith and curiosity, with which the open-faced citizens in the industrial midlands responded to popular science.[34] Surrounding his figures with darkness, their faces irradiated with light from a center of contemplation, Wright appropriated the format of traditional religious painting, reviving in a northern and secular context the themes of light, the bringing of light and life, the fellowship of faith. In *Alchymist in Search of Philosopher's Stone Discovers Phosphorus and Prays for the Successful Conclusion of His Operation, as was the Custom of the Ancient Chymical Philosophers,* he depicted not only the proximity of science and religion, but also the latent appeal of magic behind both of them.

Science and Technology

At the center of the paintings are the instruments that were at the center of Joseph Wright's world, instruments that made the industrial revolution and that brought science into the parlors, the nurseries, and even the palace. The British took great pride in their instruments, many of them designed and constructed by simple provincial craftsmen who understood little of scientific theory.[35] The initial thrust of the industrial revolution, for example, may be attributable to a Dartmouth blacksmith, Thomas Newcomen who, more interested in draining the mines than in the nature or origin of heat, invented a machine, a primitive steam engine, for converting heat to energy, a machine fueled by the coal that it was making possible to mine. The idea was refined and made applicable to industry by the equally humble James Watt, a Scottish instrument maker, funded by John Roebuck, who had a large iron works, and Mathew Boulton, who had started as a buckle manufacturer.[36] Such ordinary and on the whole unphilosophical, even unscientific craftsmen, relying on common sense, on problem-solving skills, in one generation translated the mechanistic Newtonian universe into the factories of northern England, translated the facts of nature into the facts of life.

For a time this technology exceeded scientific knowledge, indeed exceeded the social, philosophical, and psychological understanding that would integrate it into the human community. Consequently, like Frankenstein's monster, the inventions overtook the inventors; the machines came to dominate human life, to impose regularity, repetition, and depersonalization on those they were intended to serve.[37] Even such an enlightened and humane manufacturer as Robert Owen explained in *A New View of Society* how to motivate workers by equating them with machines: "When you shall acquire a right knowledge . . . of their curious mechanism, of their self-adjusting powers; when the proper main spring shall be applied to their varied movements, you will become conscious of their real value, and you will be readily induced to turn your thoughts more frequently from your inanimate to your living machines. . . ." The Romantic generation, then, the contemporaries of Wordsworth and Keats, the first generation of industrialists, may have been the last to know that "man is not the creature and product of mechanism; but in a far truer sense its creator and producer," as Carlyle reminded his readers in 1829, in *Signs of the Times*. Writers and artists especially lamented the analogy between humans and machines, because machines, instead of humans, became the norm—instead of humanizing the machine as nature had been humanized in a comparable analogy, human beings were mechanized. And this analogy excluded the special human attributes: the capacity to create, to feel, to love, to choose.

This opposition between the organic and the mechanical view of life was only one among many to emerge during the period. By 1830, science, technology, art, philosophy, history, literature, psychology, religion, politics, and economics were being professionalized, and certain antagonisms, now commonplace, emerged, antagonisms between the organic and the mechanical, theoretical and applied knowledge, the spiritual and the material, individual and collective needs, rational and imaginative truth, objective and subjective verification. While Joseph Wright, living in a more coherent age, could reconcile religious, scientific, technological, aesthetic, and human values on one canvas, when later painters such as Turner and Constable tried to adapt scientific knowledge to art, the human content was either very much diminished or lost.

The Limits of Knowledge

While some scientists continued to argue that science and the machinery that made it possible enhanced the sense of human power over nature and natural forces, a few isolated but significant observers were discovering the limits of human knowledge. The universe began to unfold as vaster and more complex than anyone had previously conceived. As natural philosophers continued to discover and name new life forms and processes, as inventors and machines continued to harness various forms of natural power for travel, communication, and industry, other scientists inadvertently discovered that the unknown may also be unknowable, that the complexity of the universe may well be greater than the capacity of human beings to know and master it. Independently, these scientists, attacked often for their deviant views, discovered an alien, inscrutable, timeless, boundless, secular universe, a universe that was simultaneously more immense and more minute, certainly more subtle and mysterious than had ever been imagined, a universe that existing theology and the Great Chain of Being could not explain. Among the first to challenge traditional concepts of time and earth history, James Hutton claimed in a paper presented before the Edinburgh Philosophical Society in 1788 that, given the available data, the chronology of Genesis was unverifiable, creation itself inexplicable, the landscape offering "no sign of a beginning—no prospect of an end."[38] Twenty years later, reviving the ancient theory of atoms attributed to Democritus, John Dalton in a *New System of Chemical Philosophy* (1808) was "confounded with the thought" that the particles, the building blocks of the perceptible world, were smaller than had ever been conceived, infinitesimal, and numerous as the stars.[39] Having spent most of his life counting and charting those stars, in 1818 William Herschel acknowledged that space also was infinite, "fathomless," to use his word, as inconceivable as time had appeared to Hutton thirty years before. And the following year, 1819, William Lawrence, concluding his long argument with Abernethy on the relationship between form and life, described in the influential *Cyclopaedia Universal Dictionary of Arts, Sciences, and Literature* the same essential mystery as Hutton, Dalton, and Herschel: "So narrow are the limits of human understanding that the knowledge of first causes seem[s] placed forever beyond our reach. The thick veil which covers them envelopes in its innumerable folds whoever attempts to break through it."[40] Given the amazing dissemination of scientific ideas in journals, periodicals, lectures, and here, in this popular encyclopaedia, ordinary men and women, as well as philosophers and scientists, were encountering a new idea of infinity, a staggering expanse of space and time packed with innumerable and invisible particles of energy. Moreover, from the clash of various mental philosophies starting with Locke, philosophies that made the human mind the source of all value and meaning, the world within, the human mind, also seemed boundless, mysterious, a greater source of "fear and awe," according to Wordsworth, than "worlds / To which the heaven of heavens is but a veil" (Prospectus, *The Excursion,* ll.29–30).

This concept of an alien and inaccessible external universe, a world created long before and with little relevance to human beings, without regard for their comfort, prosperity, or moral condition, and an equally mysterious and inaccessible inner universe, had a certain disquieting appeal to a generation that cultivated in art and literature a taste for the sublime, for the terror, awe, and expanse of the unknown. It had, however, little impact on scientists, except for a few, such as Hutton, who gave up speculative questions about origins in favor of such demonstrable issues as function, process, and a palpable reality—the visible, tangible, audible world of Wordsworth, Keats, and Constable, on the one hand; on the other, the invisible but equally palpable energies and forces of Blake, Shelley, and Turner. The most influential figures, ranging from Humphry Davy to Jeremy Bentham, maintained the conservative view of a finite, stable, purposeful, knowable, rational, providentially created universe functioning like a giant, self-sustaining machine to which human beings, their bodies, abilities, and inclinations were admirably suited. They found support in the reigning psychology of Hartley and in the theology of William Paley's *Natural Theology: or Evidence of the Existence and Attributes of the Deity Collected from the Appearances of Nature* (1802), required reading at the major universities. Consequently, most scientific investigation remained in the experimental and empirical tradition of Bacon and Locke, "Dull and inanimate," as Wordsworth, among others, complained, "Chained to its object in brute slavery" (*The Excursion,* for entire passage read IV, 1251–63). Equipped with the scales, clocks, thermometers, chronometers, chronologies, all the "philosophical apparatus" that eighteenth-century ingenuity had developed, scientists measured the earth, its age, weight, density, even its wobble, its distance from the stars and the speed at which light travels among them, believing that such calculations would help them master nature and perhaps themselves. These same calculations affirmed and elevated to a state of law a set of rational principles identified with nature, a divinely sanctioned hierarchical order represented in the Great Chain of Being, on which their most treasured social and political institutions had been based.

The new vision of a boundless universe of infinite potential endlessly fulfilling itself in diverse ways threatened, first, the belief that scientific knowledge would one day lead to the control of nature and, second, that it could justify and perpetuate those social organizations based on natural law. In place of the Christian creation myth represented in the Chain of Being with its justification of an inherited aristocracy, the new science revealed a chain of life as represented in ancient cyclical earth myths, myths that were more suited to the contemporary revolutionary climate. This shift in metaphor from a Chain of Being to a chain of life reveals a profound shift in the conception of life itself, of nature, and of society. During the transitional period we have been investigating as Romanticism, it appears as a shift of interest in such diverse fields as science, religion, philosophy, aesthetics, politics, history, painting, and poetry, a shift from origins to history, from product to process, from status to contract, from mechanics to relationships, from form to function, from matter to force, from substance to energy, from the world theoretically conceived to a world of experience,[41] and, most importantly for our purposes, from the creation of the world to the perception of it, from the awakening of life itself as described in Genesis, which, scientists were learning, could not be known, to the awakening of the individual consciousness.

Enfranchisement of the Human Imagination

In this transition, poetry and painting played a special role, for they helped to enfranchise the imagination, raising it from a faculty associated with fantasy, falsehood, even insanity to one that could, for artist, philosopher, and scientist, overcome the limits of observation and intellect; mediate between the known and the unknown; discern common principles among the variety of natural phenomena that preoccupied scientists, painters, and writers alike; formulate responses to change; anticipate consequences; and establish relationships among the increasingly diversified members of the social and intellectual community. Writers were as fascinated with this mysterious faculty, its functions, failures, and triumphs, as scientists were by light and energy.

Although the imagination was as essential to scientists as to artists, except as a subject of inquiry, they were uncomfortable with it, for they pursued objective and universal principles, while the imagination, as it was usually understood, was associated with subjective and idiosyncratic experience. To extricate their discipline from both its magical and philosophical associations, scientists single-mindedly tried to objectify the study of nature and of mankind as well, to refine observations until they appeared independent not only of spiritual agency but also of human agency, uncontaminated by human values, feelings, perceptions, until, in other words, they appeared absolute, indeed oracular. While artists and writers chose to represent the world as it is perceived, scientists were intent on representing it as it is, the "true" world, abstract and mathematical.

The quest ultimately was futile, for, however accurate the instruments, however sophisticated the technology, a human mind identifies the problems to be studied and interprets the data. As Werner Heisenberg, that formidable modern physicist, pointed out in an essay contrasting Goethe's subjective theory of color with Newton's objective one, pure objectivity, like pure subjectivity, may even falsify nature: "Our experiments are not nature itself, but a nature changed and transformed by our activity in the course of research. . . . It was originally the aim of all science to describe a nature as far as possible as it is, i.e., without our interference and our observation. We now realize that this is an unattainable goal."[42] Here Heisenberg acknowledges, as Einstein acknowledged in his theory of relativity, that the self, its preferences, biases, and interpretations, is inescapable; that, as Blake claimed, "As a Man is, so he Sees." Moreover, all nature, all phenomena, however remote from human experience, can only be known in terms of a human context, a point of view, a perceiver. Again, quoting Blake, "Where man is not, nature is barren."

To artists and poets during the Romantic period, to philosophers, historians, and scientists as well, the human context, the expression of the human mind through nature, the assertion of the imagination over all that is meaningless, lifeless, and inert, the simultaneous perception of natural objects, the unseen principles that shape and govern them, their history, potential, relationships, origins, ends, and analogues, the fullness and diversity of the living world both within and without, the "capacity to imagine what we know," as Shelley claimed, constitute their common pursuit, constitute the "poetry of life."[43]

Notes

For the convenience of the readers, I have cited the most accessible editions of primary works, reliable though not necessarily definitive texts such as the Everyman editions of Hazlitt's *Spirit of the Age* or Coleridge's *Biographia Literaria,* the Penguin editions of Jane Austen's novels, the Oxford paperbacks, the Riverside, or the Norton Critical editions of the poets. To accommodate the many different editions readers may use, I have eliminated line references to short poems, cited passages in novels and prose works by their location in the text rather than page references, and letters by dates. The following are some specific primary sources cited throughout the text by abbreviations.

George Gordon, Lord Byron, *Letters and Journals,* ed. Leslie A. Marchand, 12 vols. (1973–82), cited as *L and J.*

William Blake, *The Poetry and Prose,* ed. David Erdman (1965), cited as Erdman.

Samuel Taylor Coleridge, *The Collected Letters,* ed. E. L. Griggs, 6 vols. (1956–71) cited as *CL.*

Thomas Carlyle, *Sartor Resartus: The Life and Opinions of Herr Teufelsdröckh,* ed. Charles Frederick Harrold (1937).

William Hazlitt, *The Completed Works,* ed. P. P. Howe, 21 vols. (1930–34), cited as Howe.

John Keats, *Letters . . . 1814–1821,* ed. Hyder E. Rollins, 2 vols. (1958), cited as *Letters.*

Charles Lamb, *The Letters of . . . to which are added those of his Sister Mary*

Lamb, ed. E. V. Lucas, 3 vols. (1935), cited as Lucas. *The Letters of Charles and Mary Lamb,* ed. Edwin W. Marrs, 3 vols. (1975–), cited as Marrs.

Sir Walter Scott, *The Letters,* ed. Sir Herbert Grierson, 12 vols. (1937), cited as *Letters. The Journal,* ed. W. E. K. Anderson (1972), cited as *Journal.*

Robert Southey, *New Letters,* ed. Kenneth Curry, 2 vols. (1965), cited as *NL. Letters from England,* ed. Jack Simmons (1952).

William Wordsworth, *The Letters. . . . Early Years,* ed. Chester Shaver (1967), cited as *EY; Middle Years,* ed. Mary Moorman (1969), cited as *MY;* and *Later Years,* ed. Alan G. Hill (1978), cited as *LY.*

The following are journals cited in the Notes.

CLB	*Charles Lamb Bulletin*
CL	*Comparative Literature*
HLQ	*Huntington Library Quarterly*
JELH	*Journal of English Literary History*
JHI	*Journal of the History of Ideas*
K-SJ	*Keats-Shelley Journal*
MP	*Modern Philology*
PAPS	*Papers of the American Philosophical Society*
PQ	*Philological Quarterly*
PMLA	*Publication of the Modern Language Association*
RES	*Review of English Studies*
SQ	*Shakespeare Quarterly*
SiR	*Studies in Romanticism*
VS	*Victorian Studies*
TWC	*The Wordsworth Circle*

PREFACE

1. Some histories of the period: M. H. Abrams, "English Romanticism, the Spirit of the Age," *Romanticism Reconsidered,* ed. Northrop Frye (1963), pp. 26–72, emphasizes the impact of the Revolution; Ian Jack, *English Literature: 1815–1832* (1963, 1976); Marilyn Butler, *Romantics, Rebels, and Reactionaries: English Literature and Its Background, 1760–1830* (1982); Asa Briggs, *The Making of Modern England, 1783–1867: The Age of Improvement* (1960); Elie Halévy, *A History of the English People in the Nineteenth Century: England in 1815,* Vol. I (1961); Ronald W. Harris, *Romanticism and the Social Order, 1780–1830* (1969); E. J. Hobsbawm, *The Age of Revolution, 1789–1848* (1962); G. M. Trevelyan, *British History of the Nineteenth Century* (1937), *English Social History* (1942); J. Steven Watson, *The Reign of George III, 1760–1815* (1960); R. J. White, *The Age of George III* (1969), *From Waterloo to Peterloo* (1957), and *From Peterloo to the Crystal Palace* (1972); Donald A. Low, *The Sunny Dome: A Portrait of Regency England* (1977); and Jerome

McGann, *The Romantic Ideology* (1983), a theoretical justification for considering historical context.

The most comprehensive bibliographic tool for the period is *The English Romantic Poets: A Review of Research and Criticism,* ed. Frank Jordan, 3rd ed. (1972) and 4th ed. (1985). Since 1972, reviews of most books relevant to Romanticism have appeared in *The Wordsworth Circle* annual review issue edited by Paul Magnuson.

2. For history of usage see Lillian R. Furst, *Romanticism* (1969) and the four essays by Morse Peckham collected in *The Triumph of Romanticism* (1970); see especially René Wellek, "The Term and Concept of Classicism in History," *Discriminations: Further Concepts of Criticism* (1970), pp. 55–89, who points out that the term "classicism" was a nineteenth-century invention originating in Italy in 1818, moving through Germany, France, Russia, and appearing in England only in 1831 in Carlyle's essay on Schiller.

CHAPTER I
People during the Romantic Age

1. To convert English pounds from the early decades of the nineteenth century to dollars, multiply by five and again by forty to compensate for inflation. Ten pounds, then, was worth $50 times 40, or $2,000. Until the passage of the Reform Bill, only two percent of the population (27,000 aristocratic families) could vote, but these families owned two-thirds of the land in England. The upper classes consisted of 300–400 families in the peerage, 3,000 families of landed gentry, and the rest families of gentlemen. A minimum annual income for the lowest of this upper class was £30,000 or $6,000,000, which was the fortune Emma Woodhouse had in *Emma.* The middle classes earned from £150 to £1,000 a year. And the lower classes earned under £100, but they comprised two-thirds of the population. This and similarly useful information is to be found in Julia Prewitt Brown, *A Reader's Guide to the Nineteenth-Century English Novel* (1985).

2. Gertrude Himmelfarb, *The Idea of Poverty: England in the Early Industrial Age* (1983); T. S. Ashton, *The Industrial Revolution* (1948); John W. Osborne, *The Silent Revolution: The Industrial Revolution in England as a Source of Cultural Change* (1970); E. P. Thompson, *The Making of the English Working Class* (1963), to which I am especially indebted.

3. Maurice Quinlan, *Victorian Prelude: A History of English Manners, 1700–1830* (1941); Gordon Rattray Taylor, *The Angel-Makers: A Study in the Psychological Origins of Historical Change, 1750–1850* (1958).

4. David Roberts, *Paternalism in Early Victorian England* (1979).

5. Sir Arthur Bryant, *The Age of Elegance, 1812–1822* (1950); Donald Pilcher, *The Regency Style: 1800–1830* (1947).

6. John Cornforth, *English Interiors, 1790–1848: The Quest for Comfort* (1978); Clifford Musgrave, *Regency Furniture, 1800–1830* (1961); H. Perkins, *The Origins of Modern English Society, 1780–1880* (1969); M. Girouard, *Life in the English Country House* (1978); and the indispensible Edward Bulwer-Lytton, *England and the English,* ed. Standish Meacham (1970).

7. Gordon Rattray Taylor, *The Angel-Makers* and *Sex in History* (1954; 1970); Eric Trudgill, *Madonnas and Magdalens: The Origins and Developments of Victorian Sexual Attitudes* (1976).

8. White, *From Waterloo to Peterloo*, p. 48.

CHAPTER II
The Literary Marketplace

1. Raymond Williams, *The Long Revolution* (1961); Richard Altick, *The English Common Reader* (1957); John Cross, *The Rise and Fall of the Man of Letters* (1969); James Hepburn, *The Author's Empty Purse and the Rise of the Literary Agent* (1968); Arthur S. Collins, *The Profession of Letters, 1780–1832* (1928); J. W. Saunders, *The Profession of Letters* (1964); Butler, "The Rise of the Man of Letters: Coleridge," Chapter III, *Romantics, Rebels, and Reactionaries;* Levin Schücking, *The Sociology of Literary Taste* (1966); Julia Prewitt Brown, p. 108.

2. Walter Besant, *The Society of Authors* (1893).

3. Jack, Chapter I; Gerald P. Tyson, *Joseph Johnson: A Liberal Publisher* (1979); see also such classic studies of individual authors as F. A. Mumby, *Publishing and Bookselling: A History from the Earliest Times to the Present Day*, 4th ed. (1956) and Samuel Smiles, *A Publisher and His Friends: Memoirs and Correspondence of the Late John Murray with an Account of the Origin and Progress of the House, 1768–1843*, 2 vols. (1891); Edmund Blunden, *Keats's Publishers: A Memoir of John Taylor* (1936); F. D. Tedrey, *The House of Blackwood, 1804–1954* (1954).

4. John O. Hayden, *The Romantics Reviewed, 1802–1824* (1968); Derek Roper, *Reviewing Before "The Edinburgh," 1788–1802* (1968); Donald Reiman, *The Romantics Reviewed: Contemporary Reviews of British Romantic Writers*, 9 vols. (1972); W. S. Ward, *Index and Finding List of Serials Published in the British Isles, 1789–1832* (1953).

5. John Clive, *Scotch Reviewers: "The Edinburgh Review," 1802–1815* (1957).

6. David Craig, *Scottish Literature and the Scottish People, 1680–1830* (1961).

7. Philip Flynn, *Frances Jeffrey* (1978).

8. Hill Shine and Helen Chadwick Shine, *"The Quarterly Review" under Gifford* (1949).

9. Herschel Baker, *William Hazlitt* (1962); Ralph Wardle, *William Hazlitt* (1971); Virginia Woolf, "Hazlitt," *The Second Common Reader* (1932). For surveys of his ideas, W. P. Albrecht, *Hazlitt and the Creative Imagination* (1965); John Kinnaird, *William Hazlitt: Critic of Power* (1978); Roy Park, *Hazlitt and the Spirit of the Age* (1971); Elisabeth Schneider, *The Aesthetics of William Hazlitt* (1933); James A. Houck, "Hazlitt on the Obligations of the Critic," *TWC*, 4 (1973), 250–58, also *William Hazlitt: A Reference Guide* (1977).

10. Jack, *English Literature*, p. 270.

11. *The Letters of William Hazlitt*, ed. Herschel M. Sikes, assisted by William H. Bonner and Gerald Leahy (1978), p. 221.

12. James A. Houck, "Hazlitt's Divorce: The Court Records," *TWC*, 6 (1975), 115–20.

13. Patrick Story, "Hazlitt's Definition of the Spirit of the Age," *TWC*, 6 (1975), 97–108.

14. Ronald Paulson, *Representations of Revolution (1789–1820)* (1983).

15. Edmund Blunden, *Leigh Hunt* (1930) and *Leigh Hunt's "Examiner" Examined* (1928); William Marshall, *Shelley, Byron, Hunt and the "Liberal"* (1960).

16. Josephine Bauer, *The London Magazine, 1820–29* (1953); Peter F. Morgan, "Taylor and Hessey: Aspects of Their Conduct of the London Magazine," *K-SJ*, VII (1958), 61–68; David Erdman, "Coleridge and the 'Review Business'," *TWC*, 6 (1975), 3–50.

17. John E. Jordan, ed., *A Flame in Sunlight: The Life and Work of Thomas De Quincey* by Edward Sackville-West (1974); Grevel Lindop, *The Opium-Eater: A Life of Thomas De Quincey* (1981); Judson S. Lyon, *Thomas De Quincey* (1969).

18. Lindop, p. 262.

19. John E. Jordan, *De Quincey to Wordsworth: A Biography of a Relationship* (1962); D. D. Devlin, *De Quincey, Wordsworth and the Art of Prose* (1983); John Beer, "De Quincey and the Dark Sublime: The Wordsworth-Coleridge Ethos," in *Thomas De Quincey Bicentenary Studies* (1985), pp. 164–98.

20. Lindop, p. 244.

21. John O. Hayden, "De Quincey's *Confessions* and the Reviewers," *TWC*, 6 (1975), 273. De Quincey's style, its virtues, continuity, failures are still of much concern. Because it explores the connection between the private and aesthetic values of literature and the public and functional values of journalism, I am especially indebted to Robert M. Maniquis, "Lonely Empires: Personal and Public Visions of Thomas De Quincey," *Literary Monographs*, vol. 8, ed. Eric Rothstein and Joseph Anthony Wittreich, Jr. (1976).

22. Mario Praz, *The Romantic Agony* (1951) and *The Hero in Eclipse in Victorian Fiction* (1969), depicts De Quincey as someone torn between middle-class values and a deep neurotic need for persecution, exposure, and humiliation, which accounts for the ambiguity in his narrative voice.

23. Stephen Prickett, "Dreams and Nightmares," *Victorian Fantasy* (1979).

24. Audry Peterson, *Victorian Masters of Mystery* (1984); A. S. Plumtree, "The Artist as Murderer," *Thomas De Quincey: Bicentenary Studies*, ed. Robert Lance Snyder (1985), pp. 140–61.

25. After nursing him through an illness, Mrs. Carlyle wrote, "What would one give to have him in a box and take him out to talk!" as quoted in Lindop, p. 288.

26. John E. Jordan, *Thomas De Quincey, Literary Critic* (1952); and René Wellek, "De Quincey's Status in the History of Ideas," *Confrontations* (1965), pp. 114–52.

27. Arden Reed, " 'Booked for Utter Perplexity' on De Quincey's *English Mail-Coach"* in *Thomas De Quincey: Bicentenary Studies,* ed. Robert Lance Snyder (1985), pp. 279–307.

28. This quotation was brought to my attention by Charles Proudfit who used it as the epigraph in his stimulating, "Thomas De Quincey and Sigmund Freud: Sons, Fathers, Dreamers—Precursors of Psychoanalytic Developmental Psychology," *Thomas De Quincey: Bicentenary Studies,* ed. Robert Lance Snyder (1985), pp. 88–108.

29. Arthur Aspinall, "The Social Status of Journalists at the Beginning of the 19th Century," *RES,* 21 (1945), 216–32, "The Circulation of Newspapers in the Early Nineteenth Century," *RES,* 22 (1946), 29–43, and *Politics and the Press: 1780–1850* (1949); Stanley Morison, *The English Newspaper: Some Account of the Physical Development of Journals Printed in London Between 1622 and the Present Day* (1932); Felix Sper, *The Periodic Press of London, 1800–1830* (1937); Williams, "The Growth of the Popular Press," *The Long Revolution.*

30. E. P. Thompson, *The Making of the English Working Class* (1963), pp. 718–33.

31. G. D. H. and M. Cole, *The Opinions of Cobbett* (1944); Raymond Williams, "Edmund Burke and William Cobbett," *Culture and Society, 1780–1950,* Ch. I (1961), pp. 23–38.

32. Thompson, pp. 746–62.

33. *The Autobiography,* ed. William Reitzel (1947), p. 186.

34. Maurice Quinlan, *Victorian Prelude;* Samuel Pickering, Jr., *The Moral Tradition in English Fiction, 1785–1850* (1976), especially, "The Sunday School Movement: New Readers and the Novel," pp. 11–64; Albert M. Lyles, *Methodism Mocked: The Satiric Reaction to Methodism in the Eighteenth Century* (1960).

35. Wordsworth's letter to Charles Fox, MP, January, 1801, accompanying a presentation copy of *The Lyrical Ballads.* For suggesting this similarity between Mrs. More and Wordsworth, I am indebted to Paul M. Zall, "The Cool World . . . More for the Millions," *TWC,* 4 (1973), 152–57.

CHAPTER III
Children's Literature and Education

1. Gillian Avery, *Childhood's Pattern: A Study of the Heroes and Heroines of Children's Fiction, 1770–1950* (1975); Harvey Darton, *Children's Books in England: Five Centuries of Social Life* (1932); Cornelia Meigs, ed., *A Critical History of Children's Literature* (1953); Percy Muir, *English Children's Books, 1600–1900* (1954); Samuel Pickering, Jr., *John Locke and Children's Books in Eighteenth-Century England* (1981); M. F. Thwaite, *From Primer to Pleasure: An Introduction to the History of Children's Books in England, from the Invention of Printing to 1914* (1963). Also, Bruno Bettleheim, *The Uses of Enchantment* (1977); and Paul Hazard, *Books, Children, and Men,* trans. Marguerita Mitchell, 4th ed. (1963); Geoffrey Summerfield, *Fantasy and Reason: Children's Literature in the Eighteenth Century* (1984).

2. The term "fairy tale" originated in the *Contes de feés* by Countess D'Aulnoy (1698) translated in 1699 as *Tales of the Fairies.*

3. Paul M. Zall, "The Cool World of Samuel Taylor Coleridge: Mrs. Barbauld's Crew and the Building of a Mass Reading Class," *TWC*, 2 (1971), 74–79.

4. Altick, *English Common Reader,* pp. 360–64, for the development of domestic periodical literature. On the 1804 edition of *Cinderella, Blue Beard, and Little Red Riding Hood,* Mrs. Trimmer commented that the language was vulgar, the stories absurd, and the illustrations too explicit, inspiring, she feared, juvenile readers to imitate the action.

5. Desmod Clarke, *The Ingenious Mr. Edgeworth* (1965); Marilyn Butler, *Maria Edgeworth: A Literary Biography* (1972).

6. Quoted in Harry Stone, *Dickens and the Invisible World: Fairy Tales, Fantasy, and Novel-Making* (1979), p. 19; Summerfield, ch. 5, pp. 144–73.

7. Butler; James Newcomer, *Maria Edgeworth* (1973).

8. W. H. G. Armytage, *Four Hundred Years of English Education* (1970); John Lawson and Harold Silver, *A Social History of Education in England* (1973); Stanley Curtis and M. E. A. Boultwood, *An Introductory History of English Education Since 1800,* 3rd ed. (1964); Stanley James Curtis, *A History of Education in Britain,* 6th ed. (1965); G. F. A. Best, "National Education in England, 1800–1870," *Cambridge Historical Journal,* 12 (1956), 155–73.

9. "If it seems grotesquely paradoxical today that Wordsworth, Coleridge, and Southey, along with most educators of their time and place should have thought of this steam-intellect system as a way of defeating the mechanization of the human spirit, it is equally painful to acknowledge that the tens on tens of thousands . . . had been so far debased that the monitorial system could seem to make souls blossom within them," Carl Woodring, *Politics in English Romantic Poetry* (1970), pp. 136–37.

10. Altick, "The Mechanics Institutes and After," *English Common Reader,* pp. 169, 188–212.

11. Don Locke, *A Fantasy of Reason: The Life and Thought of William Godwin* (1980); Peter H. Marshall, *William Godwin* (1984).

12. Locke, pp. 212–14.

13. George L. Barnett, *Charles Lamb* (1976) and "Charles Lamb and Children's Literature," *CLB,* n.s. 25 (1979), 1–17; Winifred Courtney, *Young Charles Lamb, 1775–1802* (1983).

14. "Witches and Other Night Fears." Modern psychology and anthropology have vindicated Lamb's theory. See Carl Sagan, *The Dragons of Eden* (1977), proposing that in the collective unconscious of the race is a memory of a time when man shared the earth with dragons. Similarly, in the conclusion to "Old Benchers of the Inner Temple," Lamb writes, "Let the dreams of classic idolatry perish,—extinct be the fairies and fairy trumpery of legendary fabling,—in the heart of childhood, there will, forever spring up a well of innocent or wholesome superstition—the seeds of exaggeration will be busy there, and vital—from every-day forms educing the unknown and the uncommon." See also Joseph Riehl, "Charles Lamb's *Mrs. Leicester's School* and *Elia:* The Fearful Imagination," *CLB,* n.s. 39 (July, 1982), 138–41.

15. According to Summerfield, Mrs. Barbauld wrote *Hymns in Prose*

because she felt children were too limited to appreciate the same hymns written in verse. She provoked Blake into writing *Songs of Innocence* in which he depicted her and Mary Wollstonecraft, whose *Original Stories* he had engraved, as the repressive nurse figures who lack sympathy with the pleasures of childhood (p. 220). It is difficult to share Summerfield's belief that Blake's *Songs* are a major contribution to the verse written for children since they weren't published or even widely circulated and had no influence on the verse that was published or on the evidence.

16. In 1842, in *Nursery Rhymes of England* collected for the Percy Society, James Orchard-Halliwell dismissed "Humpty-Dumpty" as a riddle about an egg. Social anthropologists, however, have attributed a nefarious past to it as ridiculing the institutional failure of the Church in England. See, for example, Katherine Thomas, *The Real Personages of Mother Goose* (1930) and Lidia Eckstein, *Comparative Studies in Nursery Rhymes* (1906).

17. The Henry E. Huntington Library and Art Gallery, San Marino, Calif., issued an inexpensive facsimile in 1962, with an introduction by Carey S. Bliss, to whom I am indebted for the factual background. For nursery rhymes, W. and C. Baring-Gould, *The Annotated Mother Goose* (1962); and Iona and Peter Opie, *Oxford Dictionary of Nursery Rhymes* (1952).

18. Paul M. Zall, "The Gothic Voice of Father Bear," *TWC*, 5 (1974), 124–28; *The Story of the Three Bears: The Evolution of an International Classic, Photoreproductions of Fifteen Versions of the Tale,* ed. Warren U. Ober (1981).

19. Edward Dowden, *Southey* (1879); Kenneth Curry, *Southey* (1975), *Robert Southey: A Reference Guide* (1977); Jack Simmons, *Southey* (1945); Ernest Bernhardt-Kabisch, *Robert Southey* (1977).

20. *The Life and Correspondence,* ed. Rev. Charles C. Southey, 6 vols. (1849), I, 34–35.

21. Thomas De Quincey, *Recollections of the Lakes and Lake Poets* (1970), p. 230.

22. Dowden, pp. 198–99; Curry demonstrated the resemblance between Lamb's essays and *The Doctor* in "Lamb, Southey, and *The Doctor*," *CLB,* n.s. 10 (1975), 36–38.

23. Harry Stone, *Dickens and the Invisible World: Fairy Tales, Fantasy and Novel-Making* (1979); Michael C. Kotzin, *Dickens and the Fairy Tale* (1972).

24. Jack Zipes in *Breaking the Magic Spell: Radical Theories of Folk and Fairy Tales* (1979) identifies two ways of getting rid of fairy tales: banishing them, as in the century we have been describing, or assimilating them, as we do in the twentieth century, making them ubiquitous by adapting characters and themes to amusement parks, restaurants, movies, television, breakfast cereals, even pornographic movies (p. 1). Also, for the function and transformation of certain kinds of fantasy in the Romantic period, Prickett, *Victorian Fantasy.*

CHAPTER IV
The Theater

1. Some general histories of theater, drama, and the stage used in this chapter: Richard Altick, *The Shows of London* (1978); Michael R. Booth,

Richard Southern, Frederick and Lise-Lone Marker, and Robertson Davies, *The Revels History of Drama in English,* Vol. VI, *1750–1880* (1975); Joseph W. Donohue, Jr., *Dramatic Character in the English Romantic Movement* (1970), *Theatre in the Age of Kean* (1975); Richard Fletcher, *English Romantic Drama 1795–1843: A Critical History* (1966); Rev. John Genest, *Some Account of the English Stage,* 10 vols. (1832); Victor Glasstone, *Victorian and Edwardian Theatres: An Architectural and Social History* (1975); Phyllis Hartnoll, ed., *Oxford Companion to the Theatre,* 2nd ed. (1957); Charles Beecher Hogan, *The London Stage 1776–1800,* part 5 of *The London Stage, 1660–1880* (1968); Thomas Holcroft, *The Theatrical Recorder,* 2 vols. (1805; rpt. 1968); Leo Hughes, *The Drama's Patrons: A Study of the Eighteenth-Century London Audience* (1971); R. Leacroft, *The Development of the English Playhouse* (1973); Allardyce Nicoll, *A History of the English Drama, 1660–1900,* 6 vols., Vol. IV, *Early Nineteenth-Century Drama, 1800–1850,* 2nd ed. (1963); Harry W. Pedicord, *The Theatrical Public in the Time of Garrick* (1954); James Roose-Evans, *London Theatre: From the Globe to the National* (1977). A version of this chapter was presented at the annual Wordsworth Summer Conference, Grasmere, England, 1983, and was subsequently published in *TWC,* 14 (1983).

2. Donohue, *Theatre,* pp. 143–44; Carl Stratham, *Britain's Theatrical Periodicals, 1720–1967* (1972).

3. Brian Dobbs, *Drury Lane: Three Centuries of the Theatre Royal, 1663–1971* (1972); Frederick Penzel, *Theatre Lighting Before Electricity* (1978).

4. Leonard W. Conolly, *The Censorship of English Drama, 1737–1824* (1976); Dewey Ganzel, "Patent Wrongs and Patent Theatres: Drama and the Law in the Early Nineteenth Century," *PMLA,* 76 (1961); Watson Nicholson, *The Struggle for a Free Stage in London* (1906).

5. Edward Bulwer-Lytton, *England and the English,* ed. Standish Meacham (1970), p. 306.

6. Sybil Rosenfield, *A Short History of Scenic Design in Great Britain* (1973); Richard Southern, *Changeable Scenery: Its Origin and Development in the British Theatre* (1952); Donohue, *Dramatic Character,* pp. 66–68, 71–73; Davies, *Revels History,* p. 187; for background and illustrations, William Feaver, *The Art of John Martin,* (1975); and for the best survey of the entire movement in visual exhibitions, Altick, *Shows,* pp. 141–62.

7. Frank D. McConnell, *The Spoken Seen: Film and the Romantic Imagination* (1975), p. 189; C. W. Ceram (Kurt W. Marek), *Archaeology of the Cinema.*

8. Dennis Arundell, *The Story of Sadler's Wells 1683–1964* (1965); A. H. Saxon, *Enter Foot and Horse: A History of Hippodrama in England and France* (1968); Charles Dibdin, *Professional and Literary Memoirs. . . . ,* ed. George Speaight (1956); Altick, *Shows;* and Cross.

9. Molly Lefebure, *Samuel Taylor Coleridge: A Bondage of Opium* (1975), Appendix 2, pp. 496–99.

10. Arundell, pp. 35–45; 72–74; Dibdin, p. 99.

11. Christopher Murray, "Elliston's Coronation Spectacle, 1821," *Theatre Notebook* (1971), pp. 57–64.

12. Gilbert Cross, *Next Week—"East Lynne": Domestic Drama in Performance, 1820–74* (1977), pp. 227–39; James Grant, *Penny Theatres* (1838), The Society of Theatre Research, no. 1 (1950–51).

13. George Speaight, *The History of the English Toy Theater* (1969); A. E. Wilson, *Penny Plain, Two-Pence Coloured: A History of the Juvenile Drama* (1932).

14. Donohue, *Theatre,* suggests that the theater may have been an agent for change (p. 142).

15. The pantomime does not appear in most histories of the drama. Nicoll claimed that along with extravaganzas and burlesques "they helped to retard the development of more serious drama" (IV, 153). For all the information on the pantomime, I am indebted to David Mayer, III, *Harlequin in His Element: The English Pantomime 1806–1836* (1969), an engaging book I would recommend to all students of the period. For point of view, drama as ritual, I am indebted to C. L. Barber, *Shakespeare's Festive Comedy* (1959; 1963), and Northrop Frye, *Anatomy of Criticism* (1968). For a comparative approach, R. Storey, *Pierrot: A Critical History of the Mask* (1978).

16. *Memoirs of Joseph Grimaldi* (1838), written by himself, were completed and edited by Charles Dickens and illustrated by Cruikshank, then edited for a modern audience by Richard Findlater (1968). Quoted on page 290. Richard Findlater also wrote his own independent biography under several titles, the most recent being *Joe Grimaldi, His Life and Theatre,* 2nd ed. (1978). Also, Maurice W. Disher, *Clowns and Pantomimes* (1925; 1968).

17. Michael R. Booth, *English Melodrama* (1965), p. 44. Also, for melodrama, see Maurice Disher, *Blood and Thunder: Mid-Victorian Melodrama and Its Origins* (1949); Cross, *Next Week* (1977); Frank Rahill, *The World of Melodrama* (1967); Bertrand Evans, *Gothic Drama from Walpole to Shelley* (1947).

18. Mayer identifies a number of analogies between the plot of gothic drama and pantomime: a girl compelled to marry by her father, supernatural intervention, transformation, flight, a dark scene, and the temporary loss of the hero's power through captivity or the theft of his bat / sword (pp. 90–91).

19. Booth, pp. 15–39. Booth offers a colorful and informative description of melodramatic characters to which I am clearly indebted. For a more subtle, philosophical, and literary approach, Donohue, *Dramatic Character.*

20. Hartnoll, *Oxford Companion,* p. 540.

21. Murray Roston, *Biblical Drama in England: From the Middle Ages to the Present Day* (1968), p. 198.

22. Davies, *Revels,* pp. 265–66. Davies quotes from C. G. Jung, *Memoirs, Dreams, Reflections,* trans. Richard and Clara Winston (1963), pp. 177–78.

23. There are a number of illustrated handbooks on acting that are illuminating both to the historical study of literature and personality. For a survey, see Alan S. Downer, "Players and the Painted Stage: Nineteenth-Century Acting," *PMLA,* 61 (1964), 522–76. Recently reprinted, Henry Siddons, *Practical Illustrations of Rhetorical Gesture and Action: Adapted to the English Drama* (1822, 1968) offers sixty-nine passions while *The Actor; or, Guide to the Stage* (1821), offers only a dozen.

24. Giles Playfair, *The Prodigy: A Study of the Strange Life of Master Betty* (1967); Roose-Evans, pp. 70–72.

25. Hartnoll, p. 741; Thomas Campbell, *Life of Mrs. Siddons,* 2 vols. (1834, 1969); Roger Manvell, *Sarah Siddons: Portrait of an Actress* (1971); Herschel Baker, *John Philip Kemble: The Actor in His Theatre* (1942).

26. *A Regency Visitor: The English Tour of Prince Pückler-Muskau Described in His Letters, 1826–28,* ed. E. M. Butler (1957).

27. Manvell, p. 186.

28. Brian Fothergill, *Mrs. Jordan: Portrait of an Actress* (1965).

29. H. N. Hillebrand, *Edmund Kean* (1933); Raymond Fitzsimons, *Edmund Kean: Fire from Heaven* (1976).

30. Hampstead Edition, V, 227–28.

31. Robert Lougy, *Charles Robert Maturin* (1975); Dale Kramer, *Charles Robert Maturin* (1973).

32. *The Letters, 1817–1819,* ed. H. J. C. Grierson (1933), V, 96–97; Althea Hayter, "Coleridge, Maturin's *Bertram* and Drury Lane," *New Approaches to Coleridge: Biographical and Critical Essays,* ed. Donald Sultana (1981).

33. Donohue, *Dramatic Character,* is absolutely essential for understanding this kind of drama. Also, Patricia Ball, *The Central Self: A Study in Romantic and Victorian Imagination* (1968), Ch. II.

34. Margaret Carhart, *The Life and Work of Joanna Baillie,* Yale Studies in English, no. 64 (1923); *The Dramatic and Poetical Works* (1851; 1976); Paul M. Zall, "The Question of Joanna Baillie," *TWC,* 13 (1982), 17–20.

35. In defense of her originality the following appeared in the *Quarterly Review,* reprinted by Carhart, who seems to have missed the point: "few writers could be proved out of their own works to have read so little" (p. 69); M. Norton, "The Plays of Joanna Baillie," *RES* (1947), 131–43.

36. Kenneth Neill Cameron, Ch. 11, "Shelley as Dramatist," *Shelley: The Golden Years* (1974); Stuart Curran, *Shelley's Cenci: Scorpions Ringed with Fire* (1970); Donohue, *Dramatic Character,* pp. 162–86; Erika Gottlieb, *Lost Angels of a Ruined Paradise: Themes of Cosmic Strife in Romantic Tragedy* (1981). For exchange of letters: to Peacock, July 1819; to Amelia Curran, August 5, 1819; to Leigh Hunt, April 5, 1820; to Thomas Medwin, May 1, 1820 and July 20, 1820. Handy study materials can be found in the edition of *The Cenci,* ed. Roland Duerksen (Library of Liberal Arts, 1970).

37. For stage history, Boleslaw Taborski, *Byron and the Theatre* (1922), pp. 152–326; S. C. Chew, *The Dramas of Lord Byron* (1915; 1964).

38. Donohue, *Theatre,* pp. 161–75, comes to a negative conclusion; Lucas, I, 97–111; Joan Coldwell, "The Playgoer as Critic: Charles Lamb on Shakespeare's Characters," *SQ,* 26 (1975), 184; Wayne McKenna, *Charles Lamb and the Theatre* (1978); René Wellek, *Dramatic Character in the English Romantic Age* (1970).

39. Royal H. Snow, *Thomas Lovell Beddoes: Eccentric and Poet* (1928, 1970), p. 10; *The Works of Thomas Lovell Beddoes,* ed. H. W. Donner (1935, 1978); *The Letters of Thomas Lovell Beddoes,* ed. Edmund Gosse (1894, 1971).

40. Samuel Chew, *A Literary History of England,* ed. Albert Baugh (1948), p. 1257; Lytton Strachey, "The Last Elizabethan," *Books and Characters* (1922), pp. 235–65; Northrop Frye, *A Study of English Romanticism* (1968), pp. 52–85.

41. *Letters,* p. 50.

Chapter V
Poets and a Gallery of
"Sophisters, Economists, and Calculators"

1. I am focusing on poetry because it is such a revealing index to the many political problems of the age, their impact on literature and the arts. The novel tended to reflect middle-class attitudes uncritically. The drama, as we have seen, functioned under strict censorship, and represented or ridiculed the status quo. Like the Greek drama that it closely resembles, it was a communal expression of public values.

2. M. H. Abrams, *Natural Supernaturalism,* "The Politics of Vision: Mastery, Servitude, and Freedom," pp. 356–72. See also Thomas R. Edwards, *Imagination and Power: A Study of Poetry on Public Issues* (1971).

3. For background, Asa Briggs, *The Making of Modern England, 1783–1867: The Age of Improvement* (1965); Crane Brinton, *The Political Ideas of the English Romantics* (1926); Ronald Paulson, *Representations of Revolution, 1789–1830* (1983); Marilyn Butler, *Burke, Paine, Godwin and the Revolutionary Controversy* (1984); as well as White, Watson, Hobsbawm, Halévy, Trevelyan, and other listed in Ch. I.

4. *Autobiography,* ed. J. H. Morpurgo (1948), p. 20.

5. The appropriation of religious concepts to secular purposes was evident in such radical reformers as Paine or Owen, and in such politically awakened poets as Blake, Coleridge, and Shelley, as M. H. Abrams claims in *Natural Supernaturalism.* But even rigorously secular and worldly philosophers such as Adam Smith and anticlerical ones such as Godwin, Owen, and Bentham, however unconsciously, adapted the syntax of religious experience, religion providing, among other things, a universal language.

6. A good introduction for the general reader to Adam Smith, as well as to Malthus, is Robert L. Heilbroner, *The Worldly Philosophers: The Lives, Times, and Ideas of the Great Economic Thinkers* (1961).

7. Adam Smith, *The Wealth of Nations,* ed. Andrew Skinner (1970).

8. E. P. Thompson, *The Making of the English Working Class* (1963), to which I am profoundly indebted. And, of equal importance, Gertrude Himmelfarb, *The Idea of Poverty: England in the Early Industrial Age* (1983).

9. Thompson; Halévy; White; J. L. and B. Hammond, *The Village Labourer* (1912) and *The Town Labourer* (1917).

10. Halévy, pp. 572–73.

11. Introduction to the Penguin edition, *An Essay on the Principle of Population,* ed. Philip Appleman (1976), for useful background information.

In an engaging essay on Malthus, the economist John Maynard Keynes notes that Malthus, during his fellowship years at Jesus College, was partly responsible for the punishment assigned to Coleridge for having abandoned his studies to enlist in the 15th Dragoons under the alias "Silas Tomkyns Comberbache." In his official report Malthus wrote: "Agreed, that if Coleridge, who has left College without leave, should not return within a month from this day, and pay his debts to his tutor, or give reasonable security that they should be paid, his name be taken off the Boards." When four months later, April, 1974, following the intervention of family and friends, Coleridge was discharged, and returned to the College, he was confined for another month during which time he was required to translate Demetrius Phalerus into English. Keynes suggests that the bitterness of Coleridge's attack on Malthus reflects his continued resentment over the entire affair. (*Essays in Biography,* Vol. X, *The Collected Writings of John Maynard Keynes* [Royal Economic Society, 1972], pp. 79–80.)

12. Byron, *Letters and Journals,* II, 35–36.

13. James Steintrager, *Bentham* (1977).

14. John Stuart Mill, *Mills' Essays on Literature and Society,* ed. Schneewind (1965), p. 249. The sources and dissemination of Bentham's ideas are complex. Some meticulous and useful surveys, Elie Halévy, *The Growth of Philosophic Radicalism,* trans. Mary Morris (1955) and J. P. Plamenatz, *The English Utilitarians* (1949).

15. Gertrude Himmelfarb, "The Haunted House of Jeremy Bentham," *Victorian Minds: A Study of Intellectuals in Crisis and of Ideologies in Transition* (1968), p. 35.

16. According to Plamenetz, it was a theologian, William Paley, who described "the one true utilitarian in the universe," a God who so desired man's happiness that he designed a world toward that end" (p. 52).

17. Mill, *Essays* (ed. Schneewind), p. 259.

18. For an extended comparison between Burke and Bentham, see Halévy, *Philosophic Radicalism,* pp. 155–64. For a range of approaches to Burke, see Alfred Cobban, *Edmund Burke and the Revolt against the Eighteenth Century* (1929); Gertrude Himmelfarb, *Victorian Minds* (1970), pp. 3–31; Basil Willey, *The English Moralists* (1967), pp. 271–83; Thomas Copeland, *Our Eminent Friend Edmund Burke* (1949); Gerald W. Chapman, *Edmund Burke: The Practical Imagination* (1967); Ronald Paulson, "Burke, Paine, and Mary Wollstonecraft: The Sublime and the Beautiful," *Representation of Revolution, 1789–1820* (1983).

19. *The Inquiring Spirit,* ed. Coburn, p. 268.

20. Tom Paine, *The Rights of Man,* ed. Henry Collins (1969); A. O. Aldridge, *Man of Reason: The Life of Thomas Paine* (1960).

21. Ralph Wardle, *Mary Wollstonecraft: A Critical Biography* (1951; rpt. 1966); Eleanor Flaxman, *Mary Wollstonecraft: A Biography* (1972); Emily Sunstein, *A Different Face: The Life of Mary Wollstonecraft* (1975); Claire Tomalin, *The Life and Death of Mary Wollstonecraft* (1974); Moira Ferguson and Janet Todd, *Mary Wollstonecraft* (TEA, 1984).

22. Wardle, p. 136.

23. Don Locke, *A Fantasy of Reason: The Life and Thought of William Godwin* (1980); R. G. Grylls, *William Godwin and His World* (1953); J. B. Boulton, *The Language of Politics* (1965).

24. Robert Owen, *A New View of Society,* ed. V. A. C. Gotrell (1970); J. F. C. Harrison, *Robert Owen and the Owenites in Britain and America* (1968); G. D. H. Cole, *Robert Owen* (1965); Raymond Williams, *Culture and Society* (1963), Ch. I; Thompson, "Owenism," pp. 779–806 especially.

25. R. J. White, *The Political Thought of Samuel Taylor Coleridge* (1938); Carl Woodring, *Politics in the Poetry of Coleridge* (1961); John Colmer, *Coleridge: Critic of Society* (Oxford, 1959) and "Coleridge and Politics," *S. T. Coleridge,* ed. R. L. Brett (1972), 244–70; John Cornwell, *Coleridge: Poet*

and Revolutionary, 1772–1804 (1973); Laurence Lockridge, *Coleridge the Moralist* (1977); David Calleo, *Coleridge and the Idea of the Modern State* (1966).

26. Mill, *Essays* (ed. Schneewind), p. 273.

27. *The Inquiring Spirit,* ed. Coburn, p. 367.

28. Woodring, *Politics in English Romantic Poetry* (1970) is especially useful here.

CHAPTER VI
Heroes and Heroism

1. Explorations of literary and artistic heroic figures are Morse Peekham, *Beyond the Tragic Vision: The Quest for Identity in the Nineteenth Century* (1962); Peter Thorslev, *The Byronic Hero: Types and Prototypes* (1962); and H. M. Jones, *Revolution and Romanticism* (1974); Donald A. Low, *The Sunny Dome: A Portrait of Regency Britain* (1977), especially "Brummell or Byron—the Search for a Hero," pp. 76–96.

2. R. J. White, *The Age of George III* (1969); Stephen Watson, *The Reign of George III* (1960).

3. J. B. Priestley, *The Prince of Pleasure and His Regency* (1969), pp. 15–18; Roger Fulford, *Royal Dukes: The Father and Uncles of Queen Victoria* (1973).

4. John Ashton, *When William IV Was King* (1896, 1968).

5. Priestley; Christopher Hibbert, *George IV: Regent and King, 1811–1830;* R. J. White, *Life in Regency England* (1963); Sir Arthur Bryant, *The Age of Elegance, 1812–1822* (1950).

6. John Ashton, *Florizel's Folly: George IV and Brighton* (1899); Clifford Musgrave, *The Royal Pavilion: An Episode in the Romantic* (1964); John Summerson, *The Life and Works of John Nashe, Architect* (1980).

7. Priestley, p. 144.

8. Hibbert, p. 208.

9. Roger Fulford, *The Trial of Queen Caroline* (1967); Carl Woodring, *Politics in English Romantic Poetry* (1970), pp. 269–72, for Shelley's satire *Oedipus Tyrannis: or Swellfoot the Tyrant.*

10. Hibbert, p. 279.

11. Lewis Melville, *The Beaux of the Regency* (1909); Samuel Tanenbaum, *The Incredible Beau Brummell* (1967); Ellen Moers, *The Dandy, Brummell to Beergohm* (1960).

12. Moers, p. 21.

13. As quoted in Moers, p. 54.

14. Bulwer-Lytton, *On England and the English,* p. 188.

15. *England in 1815* (1961), pp. 395–99. See also Stephen Prickett, *Romanticism and Religion* (1976), and "The Religious Context," Ch. III, *The Context of English Literature,* ed. Stephen Prickett (1981).

16. *Recollections of the Lake Poets,* ed. David Wright (1970), pp. 85–87.

17. Ashton, *When William IV Was King,* pp. 90–91.

18. My interpretation of the social significance of the Methodist movement in the eighteenth century is indebted to E. P. Thompson, *The Making of the English Working Class* (1963), especially pages 350–400, "The

Transforming Power of the Cross," and Quinlan, *Victorian Prelude*. See also Richard Brantley, *Locke, Wesley and the Method of English Romanticism* (1984).

19. Thompson, pp. 368–74.

20. As quoted in Thompson, pp. 370–71.

21. Charles A. Whitney, *The Discovery of Our Galaxy* (1971), p. 71.

22. While he had reservations about the monogomous nature of Swedenborg's angels and about his having dated the new age in the past, even if that past did fall on his birthday, Blake clearly rejected Swedenborg's unaccountable belief in original sin and satirized him in *The Marriage of Heaven and Hell*, the title itself derived from Swedenborg's *Heaven and Hell*. Mark Schorer, *William Blake: The Politics of Vision* (1959), pp. 93–106; David Erdman, *Blake: Prophet Against Empire* (1969), pp. 141–46.

23. R. J. White, *The Age of George III*, p. 52; Clarke Garrett, *Respectable Folly: Millenarians and the French Revolution in France and England* (1975); J. F. C. Harrison, *The Second Coming: Popular Millenarianism, 1780–1850* (1979).

24. Southey, *Letters from England*, pp. 427–32; Thompson, *English Working Class*, pp. 116–18; Garrett, pp. 178–207.

25. Southey, *Letters from England*, pp. 433–46; Thompson, pp. 382–87; Garrett, pp. 207–23.

26. Letter to Anna Seward, 1803.

27. For the way Byron used the epic form to deride the pointless "glory" of modern warfare, see Brian Wilkie, *Romantic Poets and the Epic Tradition* (1965), pp. 202–11.

28. Robert Southey, *Life of Nelson*, ed. Kenneth Fenwick (Folio Society, 1956), p. 282.

29. "Essays on His Own Times," from a letter to the *Courier*, December 20, 1799, as quoted in K. Coburn, ed., *Inquiring Spirit: A Coleridge Reader* (1968), p. 324.

30. Among many readable sources, I have used Elizabeth Longford, *Wellington: The Years of the Sword* (1971), pp. 141, 155.

31. Longford, p. 474.

32. Longford, p. 592.

33. Geraldine Pelles, *Art, Artists and Society: Origins of a Modern Dilemma: Painting in England and France, 1750–1850* (1963), p. 110. A satirical tribute to Waterloo, suggesting the antiheroic response of writers, was proposed in the *Literary Gazette*, I (April 26, 1817), 210–11: "a congress of poets," each to contribute something characteristic to a collective epic: Byron would describe the "feelings" of each army; Scott, the "names of the leaders, their dreams, their genealogy, and the foaming bits of their steeds"; Campbell would offer a "pathetic tale" of a girl who was shot with a bullet intended for her sweetheart as she arrived on the battlefield; Rogers would write three lines on a tear; and Wordsworth and Coleridge would describe "the unsophisticated death of an aid-de-camp's horse."

34. E. J. Hobsbawm, *The Age of Revolution: 1789–1848* (1962), p. 98.

35. Hobsbawm, pp. 99–100.

36. J. M. S. Tompkins, *The Popular Novel in England, 1770–1800* (1961), p. 88. For the political myth, see E. Tangye Lean, *The Napoleonists: A*

Study in Political Disaffection, 1760–1960 (1970). For the image of Napoleon in the poetry of Blake, Byron, and Shelley, see Harold Bloom, "Napoleon and Prometheus: The Romantic Myth of Organic Energy," *Ringers in the Tower: Studies in Romantic Tradition* (1972), pp. 81–84.

37. Herbert Muller, *Freedom in the Modern World: The 19th and 20th Centuries* (1966), pp. 41, 51. Muller describes the paradox of how freedom as a democratic ideal justifies "new forms of compulsion, massive tendencies to regimentation and dehumanization, a pervasive kind of psychological unfreedom, and in the individual a feeling of impotence intensified by the immense collective power."

38. Donald Gray's comments on the hero in Victorian poetry are particularly illuminating here: "A great man can remake the world. . . . But he must remake it, and in that necessity lies his vulnerability. For by clear implication an age in need of heroes is an unheroic age. The hero will therefore enter alien to its character and values. He will come to destroy the old order whose errors have required his coming. . . . Destroyer and rebuilder; a man different from other men who must remake them in his alien image. . . ." ("Arthur, Roland, Empedocles, Sigurd, and the Despair of Heroes in Victorian Poetry," *Boston University Studies in English*, 5 [1961], 2).

39. Leslie A. Marchand, *Byron: A Biography,* 3 vols. (1957). In the early works, the hero was not all that original, as Peter Thorslev has demonstrated in *The Byronic Hero: Types and Prototypes* (1962). Indeed, much of his popularity can be attributed to the familiarity of character types on which he was based and which Byron's audience recognized. The eighteenth-century Child of Nature, the Man of Feeling, and the Gothic Villain, as well as other more ancient but contemporary types such as the Wandering Jew, Satan-Prometheus, and the Noble Outlaw, familiar to readers of Scott. For relevant readings of Byron's poetry, Leslie A. Marchand, *Byron's Poetry: A Critical Introduction* (1965); Andrew Rutherford, *Byron: A Critical Study* (1961); Michael G. Cooke, *The Blind Man Traces the Circle* (1969).

CHAPTER VII
Inventing the Past

1. Loren Eiseley, *Darwin's Century: Evolution and the Men who Discovered It* (1961), pp. 27–28. These same illusions became *The Burden of the Past,* as Walter Jackson Bate described it in his book of that title (1970), a weight of precedence that inhibited creativity in English writers; Harold Bloom, on the other hand, in *The Anxiety of Influence* and subsequent volumes, believes that the tradition stimulated certain authors to originality through what he calls "creative misreading." For our purposes, it is important to remember that the history that either stimulated or inhibited them was of their own invention. See also, James Heffernan, "The Displacement of History," Ch. VII in *The Recreation of Landscape,* pp. 54–101, on the decline of public history; and, for another perspective, Herbert Lindenberger, *Historical Drama* (1975).

2. This illusion that the time humans measure with clocks and calendars was part of the immutable divine order survived even the 1751 Act of Parliament which demonstrated the arbitrary nature of dates by moving the new year from March 25 to January 1. For an introduction to the invention of time, Daniel J. Boorstin, *The Discoverers: A History of Man's Search to Know His World and Himself* (1983), especially Part II, "From Sun Time to Clock Time."

3. Murray Roston, *Prophet and Poet: The Bible and the Growth of Romanticism* (1965); James G. Benziger, *Images of Eternity: Studies in the Poetry of Religious Vision* (1962); Northrop Frye, *The Great Code: The Bible and Literature* (1981); E. S. Shaffer, *"Kubla Khan" and the Fall of Jerusalem: The Mythological School in Biblical Criticism and Secular Literature, 1770–1880* (1975); Leslie Tannenbaum, *Biblical Tradition in Blake's Early Prophecies* (1982); and Abrams, *Natural Supernaturalism.*

4. Altick, *English Common Reader,* p. 101.

5. Ronald Paulson, *Book and Painting: Shakespeare, Milton, and the Bible: Literary Texts and the Emergence of English Painting* (1982).

6. E. P. Thompson, *The Making of the English Working Class* (1963) and Carl Woodring, *Politics in English Romantic Poetry* (1970).

7. Anthony J. Harding, *The Inspired Word* (1985); Stephen Prickett, *Romanticism and Religion* (1976); J. Robert Barth, S. J., *Coleridge and Christian Doctrine* (1969).

8. To Wordsworth's claim that the language of the Lake District shepherd-farmers was purer and more philosophical because of their occupation and environment, and, therefore, was suited to poetry, Coleridge commented in the *Biographia Literaria,* Ch. XVI, that its strengths actually came from their education based on the Bible.

9. Edward Hungerford, *Shores of Darkness: A Study of the Influence of Mythology on the Romantic Movement in Poetry* (1941); Burton Feldman and Robert Richardson, *The Rise of Modern Mythology, 1680–1860* (1972); Albert J. Kuhn, "English Deism and the Development of Mythological Syncretism," *PMLA* (1956); Alex Zwerdling, "The Mythographers and the Romantic Revival of Greek Myth," *PMLA* (1964), 447–56; Paul Korshin, *Typologies in England, 1650–1820* (1982), a learned account of the way Christians viewed Greek myth.

10. Stephen Piggott, *The Druids* (1975); Leon Stever and Bruce Kraig, *Stone-henge: The Indo-European Heritage* (1978); Ruthven Todd, *Tracks in the Snow* (1947).

11. Hungerford, pp. 29–30; Davies is summarized in Bernard Blackstone, *The Consecrated Urn: An Interpretation of Keats in Terms of Growth and Form* (1959), pp. 386–403. Blake claimed that his "All Religions are One" was influenced by Davies, but Frye believes he hadn't read it (*Fearful Symmetry* [1967], p. 173). See Todd, p. 37.

12. Dina Taylor, "A Note on Blake and the Druids of Primrose Hill," *Blake: An Illustrated Quarterly,* XVII (1983–84), 104–5; Todd, pp. 29–60; Peter Fischer, *The Valley of Vision: Blake as Prophet and Revolutionary* (1961); A. L. Owens, *The Famous Druids* (1962).

13. Anya Taylor, *Magic and English Romanticism* (1979); see also special issue of *TWC* on the Occult, Vol. XIII (1977).

14. To place the Greek revival in perspective, Herbert J. Muller, *The Uses of the Past: Profiles of Former Societies* (1952), especially Ch. 5, "The Romantic Glory of Classical Greece," and standard interpretations of Greek antiquity such as C. M. Bowra, *The Greek Experience* (1957) and H. D. F. Kitto, *The Greeks* (1951).

15. C. W. Ceram, *Gods, Graves and Scholars: The Story of Archaeology* (1972); Bernard Stern, *The Rise of Romantic Hellenism in English Literature, 1732–86* (1940); Timothy Webb, *English Romantic Hellenism (1700–1824)* (1982); Douglas Bush, *Mythology and the Romantic Tradition* (1937) and *Pagan Myth and the Christian Tradition in English Poetry* (1968); Lois Whitney, *Primitivism and the Idea of Progress in English Popular Literature of the Eighteenth Century* (1934); John Buxton, *The Grecian Taste, 1740–1820* (1978); M. L. Clark, *Greek Studies in England, 1700–1830* (1945); J. M. Crook, *The Greek Revival* (1972).

16. Webb, *Hellenism*, p. 111.

17. H. M. Jones, *Revolution and Romanticism*, pp. 144 ff.

18. Frank E. Manuel, *The Eighteenth Century Confronts the Gods* (1959), pp. 259–80.

19. Frank J. Messman, *Richard Payne Knight: The Twilight of Virtuosity* (1974), one of the few studies of this remarkable and respectable Member of Parliament and aesthetician. Jean Hagstrum, *The Romantic Body: Love and Sexuality in Keats, Wordsworth, and Blake* (1985), pp. 15–16.

20. The mystery cults: Gordon Rattray Taylor, "Sex as Sacrament," *Sex in History* (1959); W. K. C. Guthrie, *Orpheus and Greek Religion: A Study of the Orphic Movement* (1952); George Mylonas, *Eleusis and the Eleusinian Mysteries* (1961).

21. Donald Hassler, *Erasmus Darwin* (1973); James V. Logan, *The Poetry and Aesthetics of Erasmus Darwin* (1936); Desmond King-Hele, *Doctor of Revolution: The Life and Genius of Erasmus Darwin* (1977).

22. Blake also claimed that the myths grew out of natural forces in *The Marriage of Heaven and Hell,* as did Godwin in *The Pantheon,* and Wordsworth in *The Excursion,* IV, 620–860. See also Theresa M. Kelley, "Proteus, Nature, and Romantic Mythography," *TWC* (1980), 78–79, for another point of view.

23. Irvin Primer, "Erasmus Darwin's *Temple of Nature:* Progress, Evolution, and Eleusinian Mysteries," *JHI,* XXV (1964), 58–76. See also references to Darwin in Elizabeth Sewell, *The Orphic Voice* (1960) and Bernard Blackstone, *The Consecrated Urn* (1959).

24. Zwerdling, p. 452; R. M. Ogilvie, *Latin and Greek: A History of the Influence of the Classics on English Life from 1600–1918* (1964), p. 80; Locke, *A Fantasy of Reason,* p. 214.

25. Early essays on Homer used the poetry to reconstruct the author and his times: Robert Wood, *Essay on the Original Genius and Writings of Homer* (1775), assisted by Jacob Bryant. In 1795, F. A. Wolf, a German scholar, in his *Prolegomena to Homer* carried this method to its ultimate extreme, claiming that Homer did not write either the *Odyssey* or the *Iliad,* that it could not have been the work of a single person.

26. Jean Clay, *Romanticism* (1981), p. 256; H. J. Muller, *The Uses of the Past* (1954), pp. 104–5.

27. Frank B. Evans, "Thomas Taylor, Platonist of the Romantic Period," *PMLA,* LV (1940), 1060–79; G. M. Harper, *The Neo-Platonism of Willian Blake* (1961); David Newsome, *Two Classes of Men: Platonism and English Romantic Thought* (1972).

28. Hagstrum, p. 19. Taylor read mythology as if sexuality were responsible for everything evil in human life.

29. Blackstone, *The Well-Consecrated Urn, passim* for influence on Keats and Wordsworth.

30. Webb, p. 182.

31. Richard Jenkyns, *The Victorians and Ancient Greece* (1980), pp. 227–63, shows reasons why Plato was unfashionable. Julia Prewitt-Brown, *A Reader's Guide,* p. 123 n., offers the following conversion: English pound times five times forty to account for inflation, making each volume cost $2,000 in contemporary dollars.

32. Robert Rosenblum, *The International Style of 1800: A Study in Linear Abstraction* and Clay, *Romanticism,* p. 25.

33. William St. Clair, *Lord Elgin and the Marbles* (1967); Stephen Larabee, *English Bards and Grecian Marbles* (1943).

34. Benjamin Robert Haydon, *Autobiography,* ed. Tom Taylor (1926), pp. 67–68.

35. Hungerford, p. 137; Ian Jack, *Keats and The Mirror of Art* (1967), pp. 161–76.

36. Gods' names often are associated with scientific acitivity that is mysterious or frightening: geological schools in the eighteenth century and rockets such as the Apollo space mission in the twentieth.

37. Stuart Curran, *Shelley's Annus Mirabilis* (1975), p. xvi; James Reiger, *The Mutiny Within: The Heresies of Percy Bysshe Shelley* (1967): "Shelley was the first poet in English who kept one eye on the learned journals" (p. 17).

38. Newman Ivey White, *Shelley* (rev. 1947); Kenneth Neil Cameron, *The Young Shelley: Genesis of a Radical* (1950) and *Shelley, The Golden Years* (1974).

39. J. A. Notopoulos, *The Platonism of Shelley* (1949); see also C. E. Pulos, *The Deep Truth: A Study of Shelley's Scepticism* (1962).

40. Cameron, *Genesis,* p. 243.

41. Curran, *Mirabilis,* pp. 87–88.

42. Godwin to John Taylor of Norwich, Aug. 27, 1814, as quoted in Cameron, *The Golden Years,* p. 7.

43. Brown, p. 123 n.

44. Cameron, *The Golden Years,* pp. 52–53.

45. Benjamin Robert Haydon, *Autobiography,* ed. Edmund Blunden (1927), p. 338.

46. Nathaniel Brown, *Sexuality and Feminism in Shelley* (1979), an insightful explication of the *Discourse on the Manners.*

47. M. H. Abrams in *Natural Supernaturalism* describes the shape of history common to Romantic philosophers and poets as a spiral based on Biblical design.

48. Timothy Webb, *The Violet and the Crucible: Shelley and Translation* (1976).

49. Joseph Raben, "Shelley and Dionysius," *Shelley Revalued: Essays from the Greggnog Conference,* ed. Kevin Everest (1983), pp. 21–36; and, in the same collection, Marilyn Butler, "Myth and Mythmaking in the Shelley Circle," pp. 1–19.

50. Butler, p. 17, suggests Knight as the source of cave imagery, fountains, hermaphrodites, and heraldic animals.

51. Orphic tradition, Rieger, pp. 163–82.

52. William St. Clair, *That Greece Might Still be Free* (1972); Carl Woodring, *Politics in English Romantic Poetry* (1970).

53. Timothy Webb, *Shelley: A Voice Not Understood* (1977), p. 203.

54. Jenkyns, *The Victorians and Ancient Greece;* Frank Turner, *The Greek Heritage in Victorian Britain* (1981).

55. According to Curran in *Shelley's Annus Mirabilis,* it is "the fundamental truth of Romantic philosophical idealism," p. 104.

56. René Wellek, "The Term and Concept of Classicism in Literary History," *Discriminations* (1970), pp. 55–89.

57. Harry Levin, "Some Meanings of Myth," *Refractions* (1966).

CHAPTER VIII
Natural History and Its Illusion

1. For the history of science, David E. Allen, *The Naturalist in Britain* (1976); D. S. L. Cardwell, *The Organization of Science in England* (1957); J. Bernal, *Science in History* (1969); Thomas Kuhn, *The Structure of Scientific Revolutions* (1970); Stephen Mason, *A History of the Sciences* (1962); Basil Willey, *The Seventeenth Century Background* (1934), and *The Eighteenth Century Background* (1940); Francis C. Haber, *The Age of the World: Moses to Darwin* (1959).

2. Abrams, *Natural Supernaturalism,* pp. 97–101; Willey, *The Eighteenth-Century Background* (1940; 1961), pp. 27–42. Coleridge considered the *Sacred Theory* "a grand Miltonic Romance," proof "that poetry of the highest kind may exist without meter" (*Biographia Literaria,* p. 173). For discussion of Burnet and Coleridge, and a great footnote, John Livingston Lowes, *The Road to Xanadu: A Study in the Ways of Imagination* (1927, 1955), pp. 16, 458–59.

3. Roy Porter, *The Making of Geology: Earth Science in Britain, 1660–1815* (1977) and "Philosophy and Politics of a Geologist, 1754–1817," *JHI,* 39 (1978), 435–50; Charles C. Gillispie, *Genesis and Geology: A Study in the Relations of Scientific Thought, Natural Theology, and Social Opinion in Great Britain, 1790–1850* (1951; 1959); Eiseley, *Darwin's Century* (1958); Marilyn Gaull, "From Wordsworth to Darwin: 'On to the Fields of Praise'," *TWC,* 10 (1979), 33–48; Rhoda Rappaport, "Geology and Orthodoxy," *British Journal of the History of Science,* 11 (1978), 1–18; Martin J. S. Rudwick, *The Great Devonian Controversy; The Shaping of Scientific Knowledge Among Gentlemanly Specialists* (1986), rev. Stephen J. Gould, *NYR* (2 / 27 / 86), 9–15. Stephen J. Gould's *Time's Arrow, Time's Cycle* (1987) appeared after I completed this manuscript. The book is a re-interpretation of this entire

period in geology tempering our impression of Burnet's naive faith, of Hutton's and Lyell's secularity.

4. R. H. Dott, "James Hutton and the Concept of a Dynamic Earth," *Toward a History of Geology,* ed. Cecil J. Schneer (1969), pp. 122–41; Dennis R. Dean, "James Hutton on Religion and Geology: the Unpublished Preface to His *Theory of the Earth* (1788)," *Annals of Science,* 32 (1975), 187–93; Edward Battersby Bailey, *James Hutton: The Founder of Modern Geology* (1967). In his biography of Hutton, John Playfair conveys the genial atmosphere of the Philosophical Society of Edinburgh, of which Hutton was a popular member "in the most enviable situation in which a man of science can be placed. He was in the midst of a literary society of men of the first abilities [including Adam Smith, Joseph Black, and David Hume], to all of whom he was peculiarly acceptable, as bringing along with him a vast fund of information and originality, combined with that gayety and animation which so rarely accompany the profounder attainments of science," as quoted in Lewis S. Feuer, *The Scientific Intellectual: The Psychological and Sociological Origins of Modern Science* (1963), p. 213. Feuer claims that the society encouraged a philosophical hedonism basic to creative thought: a belief in the goodness of man, the cheerfulness of life, and the right to pursue all the comfort and pleasure knowledge could provide. I think it is an important context for viewing Hutton's theory of the earth.

5. Actually, few geologists were educated in the profession. When Adam Sedgwick was elected to the chair of geology at Cambridge, he claimed that his victory was attributable to his knowing absolutely nothing about geology while his rival, who lost, "knew a great deal—but it was all wrong." T. M. Hughes, ed., *The Life and Letters of Adam Sedgwick,* 2 vols. (1890), I, 160–61; T. W. Heyck, *The Transformation of Intellectual Life in Victorian England* (1982).

6. Eisley, p. 84.

7. Porter, p. 141.

8. Carl Grabo, *A Newton Among Poets,* pp. 175–80; Kenneth Neill Cameron, *The Young Shelley,* p. 427, n. 54 and *The Golden Years,* pp. 656–57, n. 47. Shelley read Parkinson, whose *Organic Remains of a Former World* (1811) proposed that the world had been created in stages and repeatedly destroyed by floods entombing the giant animals that naturalists were now discovering as fossils.

9. William Feaver, *The Art of John Martin* (1975).

10. Ruthven Todd, "The Imagination of John Martin," *Tracks in the Snow: Studies in English Science and Art* (1947), pp. 94–122.

11. Martin's documentary quality led Lamb in his essay the "Barrenness of the Imaginative Faculty in the Productions of Modern Art," to compare *Belshazzar's Feast* with a practical joke after a dinner party at the Brighton Pavilion, to dismiss Martin's epic riot as a "huddle of vulgar consternation," the "sort we have seen among a flock of disquieted wild geese."

12. Bulwer-Lytton, *England and the English,* pp. 333–34.

13. As quoted in Feaver, p. 113, who comments on the irony of Martin's civic dedication since as a painter he had represented "almost every conceivable ordeal a city could suffer."

14. Bulwer-Lytton, *England and the English,* p. 333; Feaver, p. 103.

15. This coincidence of imagery from science, scripture, and fantasy has been identified and illustrated by Stephen Prickett, *Victorian Fantasy* (1979). For another context, see Carl Sagan, *The Dragons of Eden* (1977).

16. H. M. Jones, "Sensibility," *Revolution and Romanticism* (1974), pp. 81–175; M. S. Tomkins, *The Popular Novel in England* (1932), pp. 70–111; Louis I. Bredvold, *The Natural History of Sensibility* (1962); George Dekker, *Coleridge and the Literature of Sensibility* (1978); Northrop Frye, "Toward Defining an Age of Sensibility," *Fables of Identity* (1963), pp. 130–37; W. P. Albrecht, *The Sublime Pleasures of Tragedy* (1975); James H. Averill, "The Sentimental Background," *Wordsworth and the Poetry of Human Suffering* (1980), pp. 21–54.

17. R. L. Brett, *The Earl of Shaftesbury* (1951); Basil Willey, *The English Moralists* (1967), pp. 204–22.

18. Jones, *Revolution and Romanticism,* pp. 92–97; Laurence Goldstein, *Ruins and Empire,* especially "Graveyard Literature: the Politics of Melancholy."

19. Dr. George Cheyne, *The English Malady* (1733), as quoted in Cecil Moore, *Backgrounds of English Literature, 1700–1760* (1953).

20. For Wordsworth, Ernest Bernhardt-Kabisch, "Wordsworth: The Monumental Poet," *PQ* (1945) and "The Epitaph and the Romantic Poets: A Survey," *HLQ* (1967); Frances Ferguson, *Wordsworth: Language as Counter-Spirit* (1977); D. D. Devlin, *Wordsworth and the Poetry of Epitaphs* (1981); and Averill.

21. Walter Jackson Bate, *John Keats* (1963); Aileen Ward, *John Keats: The Making of a Poet* (1963).

22. Stuart Sperry, "Keats and the Chemistry of Poetic Process," *PMLA,* 85 (1970), 268–77, and *Keats the Poet* (1973), pp. 30–71; Donald C. Goellnicht, *The Poet-Physician: Keats and Medical Science* (1984).

23. As quoted in John O. Hayden, *The Romantic Reviewers, 1802–24* (1969), p. 195: "Keats, in fact, had little to complain of; he enjoyed the best critical reception accorded any poet of the period, a much better reception than was given to Wordsworth. . . ."

24. Raymond Williams, "The Romantic Artist," *Culture and Society, 1780–1950* (1961), pp. 48–64.

25. The classic discussion is in Bate, pp. 233–63. For critical perspective, Sperry, *Keats;* David Perkins, *The Quest for Permanence: The Symbolism of Wordsworth, Shelley, and Keats* (1959); Jack Stillinger, *The Hoodwinking of Madeline and Other Essays on Keat's Poems* (1971); Morris Dickstein, *Keats and His Poetry: A Study in Development* (1971); Walter Evart, *Aesthetic and Myth in the Poetry of Keats* (1964). The sympathetic imagination originates in the eighteenth century, Adam Smith proposing it as the basis for moral action (1759) and Hazlitt as a capacity to anticipate consequences in the *Essay on the Principles of Human Action* (1805).

CHAPTER IX
The Gothic

1. Laurence Goldstein, *Ruins and Empire* (1977); Geoffrey Scott, in *The Architecture of Humanism: A Study in the History of Taste* (1956), calls gothic

"a catastrophe for style . . . a catastrophe for thought" (p. 49); Kenneth Clark, *The Gothic Revival, An Essay in the History of Taste* (1928).

2. Austin Dobson, *Eighteenth-Century Vignettes,* "A Day at Strawberry Hill," pp. 206–17.

3. Montague Summers, *The Gothic Quest* (1938) and *A Gothic Bibliography* (1941); Devendra P. Varma, *The Gothic Flame* (1956); Edith Birkhead, *The Tale of Terror* (1921); Peter Renzoldt, *The Supernatural in Fiction* (1965); Eino Railo, *The Haunted Castle: A Study of the Elements of English Romanticism* (1964); Ann Tracy, *The Gothic Novel (1790–1830)* (1981); Karl Kroeber, *Romantic Narrative Art* (1960).

4. Robert Kiely, *The Romantic Novel in England* (1972), p. 4: "one of the pervading characteristics of all Gothic fiction—and initially one of its failings—that individual personality is subordinated to physical setting."

5. Railo, pp. 71–72; K. K. Mehrota, *Horace Walpole and the English Novel . . . The Influence of "The Castle of Otranto," 1764–1820* (1934).

6. C. F. McIntyre, *Ann Radcliffe in Relation to Her Time* (1920); A. A. S. Wietens, *Mrs. Radcliffe—Her Relations Towards Romanticism* (1926); Kiely, pp. 65–80.

7. Peter Thorslev, *The Byronic Hero: Types and Prototypes* (1962).

8. Walter Jackson Bate, *From Classic to Romantic* (1946); Samuel H. Monk, *The Sublime: A Study of Critical Theories in XVIII-Century England, 1674–1800* (1935; 1960); W. J. Hipple, Jr., *The Beautiful, the Sublime, and the Picturesque in Eighteenth-Century British Poetic Theory* (1957); Thomas Weiskel, *The Romantic Sublime: Studies in the Structure and Psychology of the Sublime* (1977); W. P. Albrecht, *The Sublime Pleasures of Tragedy: A Study of Critical Theory from Dennis to Keats* (1975).

9. I, 7; as quoted in Monk, p. 91.

10. Monk, p. 93.

11. M. R. Ridley, *Keats's Craftsmanship: A Study in Development* (1933).

12. I have used Frye's categories from *Anatomy of Criticism* (1965), pp. 186–206, because I believe that such analyses can explain the appeal and importance of what seem to be trivial writings. The prevalence of the gothic style is of considerable interest since there was never a gothic period in English literature, but, Frye notes, "the list of Gothic revivalists stretches completely across its entire history, from the *Beowulf* poets to writers of our own day" (p. 186).

13. Boyd Alexander, ed., *Life at Fonthill, 1807–1822: From the Correspondence of William Beckford* (1957), p. 143.

14. Boyd Alexander, *England's Wealthiest Son* (1962); Peter Quennell, *Romantic England* (1970), pp. 23–35; Howard Gotlieb, *William Beckford of Fonthill* (1960).

15. Mario Praz, *The Romantic Agony* (1956); Railo, pp. 81–83, 88.

16. Kiely, *Romantic Novel,* pp. 118–20.

17. Ronald Paulson, *Representations of Revolution 1789–1820* (1983), especially Ch. 6, "The Grotesque, Gillray, and Political Caricature" and Ch. 7, "The Gothic: Ambrosio to Frankenstein," pp. 168–247; Arthur Clayborough, *The Grotesque in English Literature* (1967); Wolfgang Kayser, *The Grotestque in Art and Literature* (1966); Frances K. Barasch, *The Grotesque: A Study in Meanings* (1971); and Prickett, *Victorian Fantasy* (1979).

18. Ruthven Todd, *Tracks in the Snow, Studies in English Science and*

Art (1947), pp. 61–93; Eudo C. Mason, ed., *The Mind of Henry Fuseli* (1951); Nicolas Powell, *The Drawings of Henry Fuseli* (1951).

19. Mason, p. 70.

20. *The Autobiography and Journals of Benjamin Robert Haydon* (1786–1846), ed. Malcolm Elwin (1950), p. 25.

21. Ralph Wardle, *Mary Wollstonecraft* (1951), p. 171.

22. Mason, pp. 326–27.

23. That it could be part of the revival of interest in the vampire is suggested in James B. Twitchell, *The Living Dead: A Study of the Vampire in Romantic Literature* (1981).

24. Varma, *The Gothic Flame,* pp. 175–203. Altick, *The English Common Reader,* pp. 288, 291, 292, 321.

25. In 1813, Eaton Stanley Barret published *The Heroine, or the Adventures of Cherubina,* a novel about a country girl who believes she is really an heiress and goes in search of her true parents, changing her name along the way and displaying as much sensibility as her pedestrian environment will allow. "Tears," she claims, "are my sole consolation. Oft times I sit and weep, I know not why; and then I weep to find myself weeping. Then, when I can't weep, I weep at having nothing to weep at; and then when I have something to weep at, I weep that I cannot weep." In 1964, Railo commented on it as still "enjoyable" and "apt": "Its author deserves to be rescued from oblivion" (p. 29); Varma, p. 183.

26. Julia Prewitt-Brown, *Jane Austen's Novels: Social Change and Literary Form* (1979); Marilyn Butler, *Jane Austen and the War of Ideas* (1975); Warren Roberts, *Jane Austen and the French Revolution* (1979); Susan Morgan, *In the Meantime: Character and Perception in Jane Austen's Fiction* (1980); Stuart Tave, *Some Words of Jane Austen* (1973); Anne Henry Ehrenpreis, ed., Introduction, *Northanger Abbey* (1972).

27. By 1798, the taste for the artificial gothic had waned, as Jane Austen in *Mansfield Park,* Ch. IX, demonstrates, a criticism shared by Coleridge, Byron, Wordsworth, even Cobbett.

28. Carl Dawson, *His Fine Wit: A Study of Thomas Love Peacock* (1970); Lionel Madden, *Thomas Love Peacock* (1967); Howard Mills, *Peacock, His Circle and His Age* (1968); Marilyn Butler, *Peacock Displayed: A Satirist in His Context* (1979); Kiely, pp. 174–88.

29. As Mary Shelley explained in the Preface to the third edition (1831), which appears in James Reiger's 1974 edition, *Frankenstein: or the Modern Prometheus (1818),* pp. 222–29, and defended by John Clubbe, "Mary Shelley as Autobiographer: The Evidence of the 1831 Introduction to *Frankenstein," TWC,* 12 (1981), 102–6.

30. Ernest Bernhardt-Kabisch, *Robert Southey* (1977), as quoted on pp. 58–60.

31. Harold Bloom, "Frankenstein, or the Modern Prometheus," *Ringers in the Tower: Studies in Romantic Tradition* (1971), pp. 119–30; Burton R. Pollin, "Philosophical and Literary Sources of *Frankenstein," CL,* 17 (1965), 97–108; George Levine and U. K. Knoepflmacher, eds., *The Endurance of Frankenstein: Essays on Mary Shelley's Novel* (1979)—I am especially indebted to essays by Levine, Ellen Moers, Knoepflmacher, and Stevick.

32. Kiely, p. 156.

33. Twitchell, *The Living Dead*.

34. Twitchell, pp. 40–48; Werner Beyer, *The Enchanted Forest* (1963); Arthur Nethercott, *The Road to Tryermaine* (1939).

35. Text in Reiger, ed., *Frankenstein*, pp. 266–87.

36. Kiely, pp. 189–207; Railo, pp. 192–214; Mario Praz, *The Romantic Agony*, pp. 116–20. Text is *Melmouth the Wanderer*, ed. Douglas Grant (1968).

37. James Hogg, *The Private Memoirs and Confessions of a Justified Sinner* with an introduction by Robert M. Adams and an afterward by André Gide (1970); Coleman O. Parsons, *Witchcraft and Demonology in Scott's Fiction* (1964); Elizabeth W. Harries, "Duplication and Duplicity: James Hogg's *Private Memoirs and Confessions of a Justified Sinner*," *TWC*, 10 (1979), 187–96.

38. Edith Batho, *The Ettrick Shepherd* (1927); Louis Simpson, *James Hogg: A Critical Study* (1962); Nelson C. Smith, *James Hogg* (1980).

CHAPTER X
Bards and Minstrelsy

1. Alice Chandler, *The Medieval Ideal in Nineteenth-Century English Literature* (1970); David Roberts, *Paternalism in Early Victorian England* (1979).

2. Albert B. Friedman, *The Ballad Revival: Studies in the Influence of Popular on Sophisticated Poetry* (1961); Francis B. Gunmere, *The Popular Ballad* (1907; 1959); David C. Fowler, *The Literary History of the Popular Ballad* (1968); Leslie Shepard, *The History of Street Literature* (1973); G. Malcolm Laws, *The British Literary Ballad* (1972).

3. Howard Mumford Jones, *Revolution and Romanticism* (1974), pp. 98–102.

4. Lois Whitney, *Primitivism and the Idea of Progress in English Popular Literature of the Eighteenth Century* (1934); M. H. Abrams, "Primitive Language and Primitive Poetry," *The Mirror and the Lamp*, pp. 78–84; Gladys Bryson, *Man and Society: The Scottish Inquiry of the Eighteenth Century* (1945).

5. "Essay Supplementary to the Preface," *Prose*, III, 781; Albert B. Friedman, *The Ballad Revival*, pp. 185–232; Karl Kroeber, *Romantic Narrative Art*.

6. Friedman, p. 222; Leslie Shepard, *The Broadside Ballad: A Study in Origins and Meaning* (1962).

7. Friedman, pp. 205–12.

8. William Howard, *John Clare* (1981), p. 125; *The Letters*, ed., J. W. and Anne Tibble (rpt. 1970), p. 57; *The Prose*, ed. J. W. and Anne Tibble (rpt. 1970), p. 120.

9. Shepherd, pp. 99–106.

10. Letter, January, 1808, to Wrangham Patrick Cruttwell, "Wordsworth, the Public and the People," *Sawanee Review*, LXIV (1956), 72–80; Robert Mayo, "The Contemporaneity of the *Lyrical Ballads*," *PMLA*, 69 (1954), 486–522; Stephen M. Parrish, *The Art of the "Lyrical Ballads"* (1973); John E. Jordan, *Why the "Lyrical Ballads"?: The Background, Writing, and Character of Wordsworth's 1798 "Lyrical Ballads"* (1976).

11. Everard H. King, *James Beattie* (1977).

12. King, p. 91.

13. Donald I. Taylor, *Thomas Chatterton's Experiments in Imagined History* (1978).

14. Robert Fitzhugh, *Robert Burns: The Man and the Poet* (1970); Thomas Crawford, *Burns: A Study of the Poems and Songs* (1960); David Daiches, *Robert Burns* (1966); Donald Low, *Robert Burns: The Critical Heritage* (1974); John Butt; "The Revival of Vernacular Scottish Poetry in the Eighteenth Century," pp. 219–37; Raymond Bentman, "Robert Burns's Use of Scottish Diction," *From Sensibility to Romanticism,* ed. Frederick W. Hilles and Harold Bloom (1970), pp. 239–58.

15. Fitzhugh, p. 8.

16. *Ibid.,* p. 17.

17. *Ibid.,* p. 279.

18. *Ibid.,* p. 334.

19. *Ibid.,* p. 431.

20. *Ibid.,* p. 435.

21. Raymond Bentman, "Robert Burns's Declining Fame," *SiR,* 11 (1972), 207–24; Russell Noyes, "Wordsworth and Burns," *PMLA,* 59 (1944), 813–32.

22. Daiches, p. 113.

23. For Burns's reputation, Low, *Robert Burns* (1974); see Wordsworth, *Letters, EY,* I, 256, and the *Journals of Dorothy Wordsworth,* ed. E. De Slincourt (1941), I, 202.

24. B. H. Bronson, *Joseph Ritson, Scholar-at-Arms* (1939).

25. *The Popular Ballad* (1907, rpt. 1959), p. 314.

26. Friedman, pp. 249–56.

27. Arthur Lovejoy, "Monboddo and Rousseau," *Essays in the History of Ideas* (1948; 1960), 38–61.

28. Patricia Meyer Spacks, *The Insistance of Horror: Aspects of the Supernatural in Eighteenth-Century Poetry* (1962); Mary Jacobus, *Tradition and Experiment in Wordsworth's Lyrical Ballads (1798)* (1976).

29. Edgar Johnson, *Sir Walter Scott: The Great Unknown,* 2 vols. (1970), I, 113.

30. Johnson, II, 704. The Prince Regent gave him his title and later claimed, Scott was "the first creation of my reign."

31. For reputation, see Jill Rubenstein, *Sir Walter Scott: A Reference Guide* (1978); John O. Hayden, *The Romantic Reviewers (1802–1824)* (1968), pp. 125–34.

32. Along with Johnson, Avrom Fleishman, *The English Historical Novels* (1971); Francis Hart, *Scott's Novel: The Plottings of Historical Survival* (1966); Alexander Welsh, *The Hero of the Waverley Novels* (1969); George Levine, "Sir Walter Scott: The End of Romance," *TWC,* 10 (1979), 147–60 and *The Realistic Imagination: English Fiction from "Frankenstein" to "Lady Chatterly"* (1981); Gerald McMaster, *Scott and Society* (1982); Karl Kroeber, *Romantic Narrative Art* (1960).

33. Jane Austen, "Walter Scott has no business to write novels, especially good ones—It is not fair. He has fame and profit enough as a poet and should not be taking the bread out of other people's mouths." *Jane Austen's Letters,* ed. Chapman (1952), p. 404.

34. Johnson, II, 1260–62; G. M. Young, "Scott and the Historians," *Last Essays* (1950), pp. 17–40.

35. Kenneth Curry, *Sir Walter Scott's "Edinburgh Annual Register"* (1977).

36. George Levine, *The Boundaries of Fiction: Carlyle, Macaulay, Newman* (1968); Hill Shine, *Carlyle's Fusion of Poetry, History, and Religion by 1834* (1938); Louise M. Young, *Thomas Carlyle and the Art of History* (1939); Raymond Williams, *Culture and Society, 1780–1950* (1958), pp. 85–98; John Clubbe, ed., *Carlyle and His Contemporaries* (1976); Basil Willey, *Nineteenth-Century Studies: Coleridge to Matthew Arnold* (1966); Herbert J. Muller, *Freedom in the Modern World: The 19th and 20th Centuries* (1966), pp. 224–36; Morse Pechham, *Beyond the Tragic Vision: The Quest for Identity in the Nineteenth Century* (1962), pp. 177–89.

37. Emery Neff, *Carlyle* (1932; 1968).

38. At the time, John Playfair was living in a house purchased from Sir Walter Scott's brother. Sometime before, Jane Kerr, Sir Walter's high-spirited widowed cousin, had rejected him in marriage because he was too old. Instead she married Humphry Davy, who gained her "handsome fortune" while she acquired a "distinguished place in the literary society" of London, although, according to Scott's journal, they quarreled bitterly in public (p. 79).

39. Charles Frederick Harrold, ed., *Carlyle: Sartor Resartus: The Life and Opinions of Herr Teufelsdröckh* (1937); G. B. Tennyson, *Sartor Called Resartus: The Genesis, Structure, and Style of Thomas Carlyle's First Major Work* (1965).

40. For an important reading of this experience, M. H. Abrams, "The Crisis Autobiography," "The New Mythos: Wordsworth, Keats, and Carlyle," and "Carlyle and His Contemporaries," *Natural Supernaturalism* (1971), pp. 122–33, 307–12, and *passim*.

41. Schneewind, p. 184.

42. Among many good histories of the period, Asa Briggs, *The Making of Modern England, 1783–1867: The Age of Improvement* (1959).

43. Richard Altick, "Past and Present: Topicality as Technique," *Carlyle and His Contemporaries*, ed. John Clubbe (1976), pp. 112–28; David Roberts, *Paternalism in Early Victorian England* (1979).

44. For an introduction to these thinkers emphasizing their literary qualities, Stanley Edgar Hyman, *The Tangled Bank: Darwin, Marx, Frazer, and Freud* (1962).

45. "English Romanticism: The Spirit of the Age," *Romanticism Reconsidered*, ed. Northrop Frye (1963), pp. 26–72.

46. For an illuminating comparison, Karl Kroeber, "Romantic Historicism: The Temporal Sublime," *Images of Romanticism: Verbal and Visual Affinities*, eds. Karl Kroeber and William Walling (1978), pp. 149–65; Heyck, *The Transformation of Intellectual Life*, Ch. IV; G. P. Gooch, *History and Historians in the Nineteenth Century* (1953); Butterfield, *Man on His Past: The Study of the History of Historical Scholarship* (1955); Felix Gilbert, "The Professionalization of History in the Nineteenth Century," *History*, eds. Higham, Krieger, and Gilbert (1965), pp. 320–39.

Chapter XI
The Poetry of Life: The Philosophical Background

1. A. D. Nuttal, *A Common Sky: Philosophy and the Literary Imagination* (1974); Basil Willey, *The Seventeenth-Century Background* (1934) and *The Eighteenth-Century Background* (1940); Earl Wasserman, "The English Romantics: The Grounds of Knowledge," *SiR* (1964); Ernest Lee Tuveson, *The Imagination as a Means of Grace: Locke and the Aesthetics of Romanticism* (1960); Martin Kallich, *The Association of Ideas and Critical Theory in Eighteenth-Century England* (1970).

2. Richard Haven, "Coleridge, Hartley and the Mystics," *JHI*, XX (1959), 477–94; R. B. Hatch, "David Hartley, Free Will and Mystical Associations," *Mosaic*, 7 (1974), 29–39; Arthur Beatty, *William Wordsworth: His Doctrine and Art in Their Historical Relations* (1966); Alan Grob, *The Philosophic Mind: A Study of Wordsworth's Poetry and Thought, 1797–1805* (1973); Newton Stallknecht, *Strange Seas of Thought* (1958); Stephen Prickett, *Coleridge and Wordsworth: The Poetry of Growth* (1970).

3. C. E. Pulos, *The Deep Truth: A Study of Shelley's Scepticism* (1954); Timothy Webb, *Shelley: A Voice Not Understood* (1977).

4. Walter Jackson Bate, *From Classic to Romantic*, p. 102.

5. Grave, *The Scottish Philosophy of Common Sense* (1960); Louis Schneider, *The Scottish Moralists* (1967); R. G. Collingwood, *The Principles of Art* (1958), Book II, "The Theory of Imagination," pp. 157–221, an analysis of Berkeley and Hume.

6. H. R. Hays, *Birds, Beasts, and Man: A Humanist History of Zoology* (1973), p. 244; John Graham, "Character, Description, and Meaning in the Romantic Novel," *SiR*, 5 (1965), 208–18; Robert Darnton, *Mesmerism and the End of the Enlightenment in France* (1968).

7. Jason Y. Hall, "Gall's Phrenology: A Romantic Psychology (1758–1828)," *SiR*, 16 (1977), 305–17; G. N. Cantor and Steven Shapin, "Phrenology in Early Nineteenth-Century Edinburgh: An Historiographical Discussion," *Annals of Science*, 32 (1975), 195–256.

8. *Aids to Reflection*, VI, 100, as quoted in John Harris, "Coleridge's Readings in Medicine," *TWC*, 3 (1972), 85–95.

9. Haydon, *Autobiography*, pp. 231–33.

10. Willey, *The English Moralists*, p. 192.

11. Willey, "Wordsworth and the Locke Tradition," *Seventeenth-Century Background*, p. 294.

12. The concept of imagination differs considerably from poet to poet and changes radically during the period. While much is to be learned from the primary sources and from studies of individual authors, the following ranging studies are especially useful: M. H. Abrams, *The Mirror and The Lamp* (1958), and *Natural Supernaturalism* (1970); John O. Hayden, *Polestar of the Ancients* (1979); Earl Wasserman, *The Subtler Language* (1959); R. A. Foakes, *The Romantic Assertion* (1958); Edward Bostetter, *The Romantic Ventriloquists* (1963); Morse Peckham, *Beyond the Tragic Vision* (1962); C. M. Bowra, *The Romantic Imagination* (1961); Patricia M. Ball, *The Central Self: A Study in Romantic and Victorian Imagination* (1968); Robert Langbaum, *The Poetry of Experience* (1957); Harold Bloom, *The Visionary Com-*

pany (1961); James Engell, *The Creative Imagination: Enlightenment to Romanticism* (1981).

13. Abrams, *Natural Supernaturalism*, p. 65.

14. M. H. Abrams, "Structure and Style in the Greater Romantic Lyric," in *Romanticism and Consciousness*, ed. Harold Bloom (1970), p. 202: "Romantic writers, though nature poets, were humanists above all, for they dealt with the non-human only insofar as it is the occasion for the activity which defines man: thought, the process of intellection."

15. Parrish, *The Art of the Lyrical Ballads*, especially Chapters 3 and 4, "The Ballad as Drama"; Jordan, *Why the "Lyrical Ballads"?*, especially Chapter VII, "Wordsworth's Purpose in the 1798 *Lyrical Ballads*," pp. 155–71.

16. E. D. Hirsch, for example, *Innocence and Experience: An Introduction to Blake* (1964), and Stillinger, *The Hood-winking of Madeline;* Wayne Booth, *The Rhetoric of Fiction* (1961) for analyses of narrative voices.

17. Parrish, *Ballads*, pp. 97–119.

18. M. H. Abrams, "The Correspondent Breeze: A Romantic Metaphor," *English Romantic Poets: Modern Essays in Criticism* (1960), pp. 31–54.

19. Mary Moorman, *William Wordsworth: A Biography*, 2 vols. (1957; 1965); T. W. Thompson, *Wordsworth's Hawkshead*, ed. Robert Woof (1970); Ben Ross Schneider, *Wordsworth's Cambridge Education* (1957); F. W. Meyer, *Wordsworth's Formative Years* (1943); Russell Noyes, *William Wordsworth* (1971); F. M. Todd, *Politics and the Poet: A Study of Wordsworth* (1957); Michael Friedman, *The Making of a Tory Humanist* (1979).

20. Geoffrey Hartman, *Wordsworth's Poetry, 1787–1814* (1964, 1972); James Hefferman, *Wordsworth's Theory of Poetry* (1969); W. J. B. Owen, *Wordsworth as Critic* (1969); Carl Woodring, *Wordsworth* (1965); Jonathan Wordsworth, *The Borders of Vision* (1982); Paul Sheats, *The Making of Wordsworth's Poetry, 1785–1798* (1973); Jared Curtis, *Wordsworth's Experiments with Tradition: The Lyric Poems of 1802* (1971); John Jones, *The Egotistical Sublime* (1954); Kenneth Johnston, *Wordsworth and "The Recluse"* (1984).

21. Parrish; Jordan, *Why the "Lyrical Ballads"?* and "The Novelty of the *Lyrical Ballads*," *Bicentenary Wordsworth Studies in Memory of John Alban Finch,* ed. Jonathan Wordsworth (1970), pp. 340–50; Mary Jacobus, *Tradition and Experiment in Wordsworth's Lyrical Ballads (1798)* (1976); Russell Noyes, "Wordsworth and Burns," *PMLA*, 59 (1944), 813–21; John O. Hayden, "The Road to Tintern Abbey," *TWC*, 12 (1981), 211–16; *Wordsworth and Coleridge: Lyrical Ballads (1798)*, ed. W. J. B. Owen (1967); William Heath, *Wordsworth and Coleridge* (1970); John R. Nabholtz, *"My Reader, My Fellow-Labourer": A Study of English Romantic Prose* (1986), pp. 67–96.

22. *William Wordsworth: The Prelude, 1799, 1805, 1850*, eds. Jonathan Wordsworth, M. H. Abrams, Stephen Gill (1979); Kenneth R. Johnston, *Wordsworth and "The Recluse"* (1984); Lindenberger, *On Wordsworth's Prelude;* Frank McConnell, *The Confessional Imagination: A Reading of Wordsworth's Prelude* (1974); Richard Onarato, *The Character of the Poet: Wordsworth in "The Prelude"* (1971); Karl Kroeber, "Wordsworth: The Personal Epic," *Romantic Narrative Art* (1960).

23. Jonathan Wordsworth, *The Music of Humanity* (1969); Karl Kroeber, " 'Home at Grasmere': Ecological Holiness," *PMLA,* 89 (1974), 132–41.

24. For a fresh insight into that relationship, *My Dearest Love: Letters of William and Mary Wordsworth (1810),* ed. Beth Darlington (1981).

25. Adam Sedgwick, *The Life and Letters . . .* (1890), I, 248–49.

26. Russell Noyes, *Wordsworth and the Art of Landscape* (1968).

27. Richard Altick, *The English Common Reader* (1957; 1963), Appendices B and C, pp. 381–96.

28. Frank Prentice Rand, *Wordsworth's Mariner Brother* (1966).

29. Averill, *Wordsworth and the Poetry of Human Suffering;* J. Wordsworth, *The Music of Humanity;* and Stallknecht, *Strange Seas of Thought.*

30. Lionel Trilling, "The Fate of Pleasure: Wordsworth to Dostoevsky," *Romanticism Reconsidered,* ed. Northrop Frye (1963), pp. 73–106.

31. Patrick Cruttwell, "Wordsworth, the Public, and the People," *Sewanee Review,* LXIV (1956), 71–80.

32. For critical reception, Judson Stanely Lyon, *The Excursion: A Study* (1950), pp. 1–6; Enid Welsford, *Salisbury Plain: A Study in the Development of Wordsworth's Mind and Art* (1966); N. Stephen Bauer, *William Wordsworth: A Reference Guide.*

33. One of the most interesting and significant responses to *The Excursion* came from Charles Darwin who, from 1837 to 1839, while searching for a synthesis that would explain the observations he gathered on the voyage of the *Beagle,* read it twice, with "delight." In the majestic concluding passage of *The Origin of Species* (1859), the Wanderer's voice is clear: "Thus, from the war of nature, from famine and death, the most exalted object which we are capable of conceiving, namely the production of the higher animals, directly follows. There is grandeur in this view of life, with its several powers, having been originally breathed by the Creator into a few forms, or into one; and that, whilst this planet has gone cycling on according to the fixed law of gravity, from so simple a beginning endless forms most beautiful and most wonderful have been, and are being evolved." *Darwin,* ed. Philip Appleman (1970), pp. 107–12. Charles Darwin, *Autobiography,* ed. Sir Francis Darwin (1950), p. 43; Edward Manier, *The Young Darwin and His Cultural Circle . . . Studies in the History of Modern Science,* Volume II (1978); Marilyn Gaull, "From Wordsworth to Darwin," *TWC,* 10 (1979), 33–48. For criticism of *The Excursion* see Kenneth R. Johnston, "The Reckless Recluse: The Solitary," Ch. VIII, *Wordsworth and "The Recluse"; TWC,* 9 (1978) is devoted to *The Excursion.*

34. Frances Ferguson, *Wordsworth: Language as Counter-Spirit* (1977); Gene W. Ruoff, "Critical Implications of Wordsworth's 1815 Categories," *TWC,* 8 (1978), 75–81; James Hefferman, "Mutilated Autobiography: Wordsworth's Poems of 1815," *TWC,* 10 (1979), 107–12; Donald Ross, "Poems 'Bound Each to Each' in the 1815 Edition of Wordsworth," *TWC,* 12 (1981), 133–40.

35. For the best text, Prose, II, 123, and notes. The introduction to De Selincourt, ed., *Wordsworth's Guide to the Lakes* (1906; rpt. 1970) for background; Russell Noyes, "Wordsworth and the Art of Scenic Travel," *Wordsworth and the Art of Landscape* (1968), 143 ff.; Martin Price, "The Pic-

turesque Moment," *From Sensibility to Romanticism,* eds. Federick Hilles and Harold Bloom (1965), pp. 259–89; Charles Coe, *Wordsworth and the Literature of Travel* (1953).

36. Thirty such books appeared in 1804 alone, all reviewed in the *Monthly Magazine.* They offer a splendid introduction into the character of middle class provincial, the background as well as the audiences for Wordsworth, Scott, and Jane Austen. A survey of this literature suggests that more people were walking around peering at this or that historical curiosity or horticultural specimen, and exchanging information about the easiest or fastest route to here and there than were standing on hilltops, absorbed in the aesthetics of landscapes, a distorted reflection in a Claude glass.

37. John R. Nabholtz, "Wordsworth's *Guide to the Lakes* and the Picturesque Tradition," *MP,* 61 (1964), 288–97.

CHAPTER XII
Painting and the Other Visual Arts

1. Some general histories of English art to which this chapter is indebted: T. S. R. Boase, *English Art, 1800–1870* (1959); Joseph Burke, *English Art, 1714–1800* (1976); Michel Le Bris, *Romantics and Romanticism* (1981); Francis Klingender, *Art and the Industrial Revolution* (1972); Karl Kroeber and William Walling, eds., *Images of Romanticism: Verbal and Visual Affinities* (1978); Frederick Cummings and Allen Staley, *Romantic Art in Britain: Paintings and Drawings, 1760–1860* (1968); Peter Quennell, *Romantic England: Writing and Painting, 1717–1851* (1970); Richard and Samuel Redgrave, *A Century of British Painters,* ed. Ruthven Todd (1947); R. H. Wilenski, *English Painting,* (1964); Robert Rosenblum, *Transformations in Late Eighteenth-Century Art* (1967) and *Modern Painting and the Northern Romantic Tradition* (1975); Geraldine Pelles, *Art, Artists and Society: Origins of a Modern Dilemma: Painting in England and France, 1750–1850* (1963); Ronald Paulson, *Emblem and Expression: Meaning in English Art of the Eighteenth Century* (1975) and *Representations of Revolution (1789–1820);* Jean Clay, *Romanticism* (1981); James Twitchell, *Aspects of the Sublime in English Poetry and Painting, 1770–1850* (1983).

2. Morse Peckham, *Man's Rage for Chaos: Biology, Behavior, and the Arts* (1965), pp. 305–7, cites the Romantic technique of isolating a "type" from its "traditional situation," giving both the type and the new context a different value. For example, Beethoven's using the ecclesiastic fugue in his secular 3rd symphony, Wordsworth's adapting the epic for his biography, churches designed after pagan classical temples, and banks imitating gothic castles. This appropriation of otherwise inappropriate forms, according to Peckham, helps differentiate the self from the role, the form from the function. "The role of the artist," he concludes, "demands that he create external discontinuity" (p. 306).

3. The relations between writing and painting, especially parallel subjects, are explored in such general studies as Jean Hagstrum, *The Sister Arts* (1958); Mario Praz, *Mnemosyne: The Parallel Between Literature and the Visual*

Arts (1970); Morse Peckham, *Beyond the Tragic Vision* (1962); Abrams, *The Mirror and the Lamp, passim;* R. G. Collingwood, *The Principles of Art* (1958); E. H. Gomberich, *Art and Illusion* (1968); and such specific studies as E. Malins, *English Landscaping and Literature* (1966); John Barrell, *The Idea of Landscape and the Sense of Place, 1730–1840* (1972); Alec King, *Wordsworth and the Artist's Vision* (1966); Russell Noyes, *Wordsworth and the Art of Landscape* (1968); Karl Kroeber, *Romantic Landscape Vision* (1975); Roy Park, *Hazlitt and the Spirit of the Age: Abstraction and Critical Theory* (1971), especially Chapters IV to VI; James Heffernan, *The Re-creation of Landscape* (1984); Ronald Paulson, *Literary Landscape: Turner and Constable* (1981); J. R. Watson, *Picturesque Landscape and English Romantic Poetry* (1970).

4. Biographies include Alexander Gilchrist, *The Life of William Blake* (1880) and Jack Lindsay, *William Blake: His Life and Work* (1978). Blake has inspired an exceptional array of exciting studies and publishing ventures to which I am indebted, works such as David Bindman, *Blake as an Artist* (1977); Harold Bloom, *Blake's Apocalypse* (1963); David Erdman, *Blake: Prophet Against Empire* (1954); Northrop Frye, *Fearful Symmetry* (1947); Jean H. Hagstrum, *William Blake: Poet and Painter* (1964); Mark Schorer, *William Blake: The Politics of Vision* (1946); Kathleen Raine, *William Blake* (1970); Ruthven Todd; *William Blake: The Artist* (1971); Robert N. Essick, *William Blake: Printmaker* (1980); and for all sorts of indispensable things, *Blake: An Illustrated Quarterly* (1967—). While I have used the Erdman edition of *The Poetry and Prose of William Blake* (1965; 1982) throughout my text, the Norton Critical Edition, *Blake's Poetry and Designs* (1979), edited by Mary Lynn Johnson and John E. Grant, with its notes, bibliography, and critical essays is especially useful and illuminating. And a ranging essay that stimulated much of my thinking on Blake is Morris Eaves, "Romantic Expressive Theory and Blake's Idea of the Audience," *PMLA*, 95 (1980), 784–801.

5. Todd, *Tracks in the Snow* (1947).

6. Raine, pp. 29–39.

7. Morton D. Paley, " 'A New Heaven is Begun': William Blake and Swedenborgianism," *Blake: An Ilustrated Quarterly,* 13 (1979), 64–87.

8. Malcolm C. Salamon, *The Old Engravers of England in their Relation to Contemporary Life and Art, 1540–1800* (1966); Sacheverell Sitwell, *Narrative Pictures: A Survey of English Genre and its Painters* (1936; 1969); Benedict Nicolson, *Joseph Wright of Derby* (1968).

9. Kenneth Clark, *Landscape into Art* (1961).

10. Raymond Williams, *Culture and Society, 1780–1850* (1958), pp. 60–61 especially. Williams demonstrates how the word "art" came to be associated with painting in general during the eighteenth century and the differentiation during the same period of the artist as painter from the artisan, any skilled worker. See also R. G. Collingwood, *The Principles of Art* (1958), Book I, "Art and not Art," pp. 15–151. For an introduction to the popular or applied arts see Edward Craft-Murray, *Decorative Painting in England, 1537–1837*, 2 vols. (1962–1970).

11. W. R. M. Lamb, *The Royal Academy* (1951).

12. John Gage, *Color in Turner: Poetry and Truth* (1969), Ch. IX, p. 151 for quote.

13. For a survey, see Frank Hermann, *The English as Collectors: A Documentary Chrestomathy* (1972).

14. *The Diary of Benjamin Robert Hayden,* ed. Willard Bissell Pope, 5 vols. (1963), III, 16–18. This work, the *Journals,* and *The Autobiography and Memoirs, 1786–1846,* ed. Tom Taylor, 2 vols. (1926) offer insight into the community of Regency artists, the writers with whom they associated, and the experiences they shared.

15. Richard Godfrey, *Printmaking in Britain: A General History from Its Beginning to the Present Day* (1978). Contains an especially valuable bibliography.

16. David Piper, *The English Face* (1957), p. 221; John Murdock, Jim Murrell, Patrick Noon, Ray Strong, *The English Miniature* (1981).

17. Piper, pp. 216–218.

18. Gilchrist, p. 80; Ann Mellor, "Physiognomy, Phrenology, and Blake's Visionary Heads," *Blake In His Time,* ed. Robert N. Essick and Donald Pierce (1978); Tyler Graeme, *Physiognomy in the European Novel: Faces and Fortunes* (1982).

19. Thomas Wright, *A History of Caricature and Grotesque in Literature and Art,* int. Frances K. Barasch (1865; 1968); Wolfgang Kayser, *The Grotesque in Art and Literature* (1966); Paulson, *Representations of Revolution,* Chapters V and VI.

20. Erdman, *Prophet Against Empire,* pp. 100–101; Carmen Reiter, "Evolution and William Blake," *SiR,* 4 (1965), 110–18; Philip Ritterbush, *Overtures to Biology: The Speculations of Eighteenth-Century Naturalists* (1964), pp. 186–97; H. R. Hayes, "Giraffe in the Hallway," *Birds, Beasts, and Men: A Humanist History of Zoology* (1972), Ch. 12, pp. 146–53; and Ernest A. Gray, *Portrait of a Surgeon* (1952). John Hunter was a self-taught Scottish peasant who was unable to attend a university because he couldn't learn Latin and Greek. He acquired his training in an apprenticeship to his older brother and, ultimately, after election to the Royal Society, served as surgeon to George III. His wife, Ann Hone, was a poet. At his death, his famous anatomical collection, housed in a museum called the Hunterian, passed to his nephew, Matthew Baillie, who in 1799 wrote the first treatise on morbid anatomy, describing with engraved illustrations the physiological changes caused by disease. His sister Joanna came to London to help care for him and in her *Plays on the Passions* performed her own form of anatomy on the criminal mind.

21. Suggesting the importance of horses, John Laurence, *History and Delineation of the Horse* (1809); Basil Taylor, *Animal Painting in England* (1955); Ronald Paulson, *Emblem and Expression* (1975).

22. Basil Taylor, *Stubbs* (1971); Constance Anne Parker, *Mr. Stubbs the Horse Painter* (1971); and Paulson, pp. 181–83.

23. Frederick Cummings, *Romantic Art in Britain,* pp. 48–54.

24. Many intelligent people with similar scientific resources shared Stubbs's interest in the sentimental capabilities of animals. Erasmus Darwin in fact, had extended feelings, desires, passions, to plants; and his grandson, Charles, in spite of having a mind that could synthesize a hundred years of complex scientific speculation, attempted to vindicate this anthro-

pomorphism in *The Expression of Emotion in Man and Animals* (1872), a bizarre study of sufficient interest to anthropologists to justify a modern edition in 1955, with an introduction by Margaret Mead.

25. For information on natural histories, I am indebted to Roy Goodman, Librarian at the American Philosophical Society, and Jacob Gruber, Professor Emeritus of Anthropology at Temple University. Reference works of particular interest and to which I am especially indebted: Blanche Henrey, *British Botanical and Horticultural Literature Before 1800,* 3 vols. (1975); R. B. Freeman, *British Natural History Books: 1495–1900, A Handlist* (1980); and "Children's Natural History Books before Queen Victoria," *Bulletin of the History of Education Society* (1976), No. 17, pp. 17–21; No. 18, pp. 6–34; and the monumental Claus Nissen, *Die Zoologische Buchillustration: Ihre Bibliographie und Geschiechte,* 2 vols. (1969).

26. Fuseli, as Keeper at the Royal Academy, an ardent entymologist and illustrator for Erasmus Darwin, influenced many students in depicting insects. For the other view of nature, more European, it is useful to review the picturesque tradition in England in, for example, J. R. Watson's *Picturesque Landscape and English Romantic Poetry* (1970) and Christopher Hussey, *The Picturesque* (1927; 1967).

27. Paul Laurence Farber, *The Emergence of Ornithology as a Scientific Discipline, 1760–1850* (1982).

28. C. R. Leslie, *Memoirs of the Life of John Constable,* ed. Jonathan Mayne (1951); Graham Reynolds, *Constable the Natural Painter* (1965); Basil Taylor, *Constable* (1973); Reg. Gadney, *Constable and His World* (1976); R. B. Beckett, *John Constable's Correspondence,* 6 vols. (1962–1968), and *John Constable's Discourses* (1970); Ronald Paulson, *Literary Landscape: Turner and Constable* (1982).

29. Among the many provocative studies of Wordsworth and Constable: Russell Noyes, *Wordsworth and the Art of Landscape* (1968); Morse Peckham, "Wordsworth and Constable," Ch. VI in *The Triumph of Romanticism* (1970); Karl Kroeber, *Romantic Landscape Vision: Constable and Wordsworth* (1975); Heffernan, *The Recreation of Landscape;* Paulson, *Literacy Landscape.*

30. Kurt Badt in *John Constable's Clouds* (1950) points out the influence of contemporary meteorology on, among others, Constable.

31. He did transcribe "My Heart Leaps Up" and, in 1835, reflecting the political conservatism they shared, a sonnet to Wordsworth, "Thou second Milton," appealing to him to "maintain our cause." Noyes, pp. 81–82; and J. R. Watson, "Wordsworth and Constable," *RES,* 13 (1962), 361–67.

32. Kroeber calls it a poignant comment: "the man who said he never saw an ugly thing in his life seldom knew the refuge of inspiration. He was bound to the rigorous task of representing correctly a world outside him" p. 108; Leslie, p. 280.

33. As quoted in Noyes, *Wordsworth,* p. 81.

34. As quoted in Gadney, p. 104.

35. As quoted in Gadney, p. 110. Charles Darwin's mental development offers some interesting parallels; see Donald Fleming, "Charles Darwin, the Anaesthetic Man," *Victorian Studies* (1961), 219–36.

36. As quoted in Gadney, p. 93.

37. Andrew Wilson, *J. M. W. Turner: His Art and Life* (1979); Jack Lindsay, *J. M. W. Turner: His Life and Work, A Critical Biography* (1966); A. J. Finberg, *The Life of J. M. W. Turner, R.A.*, 2nd rev. ed. by Hilda Finberg (1961); W. Thornbury, *Life and Correspondence of J. M. W. Turner*, 2nd ed. (1904); and Paulson, *Literary Landscape: Turner and Constable* (1982). Many of Turner's eccentricities have been given plausible and intelligent explanation by John Gage, *Color in Turner: Poetry and Truth* (1969), a useful reminder of the importance of background information.

38. Michel Le Bris claims that Turner's problems with portraits are the price of "modernity," and arise from a "conceptual incapacity": "because the human face is the very place where the symbolic is revealed, it is the place of Presence. Long before the Futurist Marinetti came forward to announce the substitution of man by the lyrical obsession with matter, long before all those avant-gards whose connections with the Mussolinian, Hitlerian and Marxist totalitarianism will one day need to be clarified, long before them Turner, in the sweep of his colours towards the 'Nowhere' of a radical disorientation announced, quite simply, the death of Man." He concludes, "Turner, then, stands for an absolute anti-romanticism," *Romantics and Romanticism* (1981).

39. Lindsay, p. 70.

40. Jerrold Ziff, "J. M. W. Turner on Poetry and Painting," *SiR*, 3 (1964), 193–215.

41. For an interesting insight into contemporary understanding of photography, see Robert Hunt, *A Popular Treatise on the Art of Photography . . . and all new methods of producing pictures by the chemical agency of light* (1841).

42. Gage, pp. 122–26.

43. John Gage, *Turner: Rain, Steam and Speed* (1972).

44. Gage, *Color*, p. 162.

Chapter XIII
Science

1. David M. Knight, "The Scientist as Sage," *SiR*, 6 (1967), 65–68. Relevant histories of science and scientific thought: Stephen F. Mason, *A History of the Sciences* (rev. 1962); Philip C. Ritterbush, *Overtures To Biology* (1964); William Coleman, *Biology in the Nineteenth Century: Problems of Form, Function and Transformation* (1971); P. M. Harman, *Energy, Force, and Matter: The Conceptual Development of Nineteenth-Century Physics* (1982); James R. Partington, *History of Chemistry* (1962); Lester S. King, *The Medical World of the Eighteenth Century* (1958) and *The Growth of Medical Thought* (1963); Lewis S. Feuer, *The Scientific Intellectual: The Psychological and Sociological Origins of Modern Science* (1963); Paul L. Farber, "The Transformation of Natural History in the Nineteenth Century," *Journal of the History of Biology*, 15 (1982), 145–52; Everett Mendelsohn, "The Emergence of Science as a Profession in Nineteenth-Century Europe," *The Management of Scientists*, ed. K. Hill (1964); Charles C. Gillispie, *Genesis and Geology: A*

Study in the Relations of Scientific Thought, Natural Theology, and Social Opinion in Great Britain, 1790–1850 (1951); Howard Becker and Harry E. Barnes, *Social Thought from Lore to Science* (1952); George A. Foote, "Science and Its Function in Early Nineteenth-Century England," *Osiris*, 11 (1954), 438–54; Susan Faye Cannon, *Science in Culture: The Early Victorian Period* (1978); David M. Knight, "The Physical Sciences and the Romantic Movement," *History of Science*, 9 (1970), 54–75; Robert E. Schofield, *Mechanism and Materialism: British Natural Philosophy in An Age of Reason* (1970). Several studies on the history and philosophy of science: Jacob Bronowski, *The Common Sense of Science* (1967); Alfred North Whitehead, *Science and the Modern World* (1925; 1967); Thomas S. Kuhn, *The Structure of Scientific Revolutions* 2nd ed. (1970); Edward Proffit, "Science and Romanticism," *The Georgia Review*, 34 (1980), 55–104; Charles Coulston Gillispie, *The Edge of Objectivity: An Essay in the History of Scientific Ideas* (1960); Hans Eichner, "The Rise of Modern Science and the Genesis of Romanticism," *PMLA*, 97 (1982), 18–30. Many of the above contain useful bibliographic essays.

2. Arthur O. Lovejoy, *The Great Chain of Being: A Study of the History of an Idea* (1936; 1960); Basil Willey, *The Seventeenth-Century Background: The Thought of the Age in Relation to Religion and Poetry* (1934); *The Eighteenth-Century Background: Studies on the Idea of Nature in the Thought of the Period* (1940); and in relation to later science, Loren Eiseley, *Darwin's Century: Evolution and the Men who Discovered It* (1958). For literature, Douglas Bush, *Science and English Poetry: A Historical Sketch 1590–1950* (1950); Earl R. Wasserman, *The Subtler Language: Critical Readings of Neo-Classical and Romantic Poems* (1959); Marjorie Hope Nicolson, *Newton Demands the Muse* (1946).

3. F. W. Gibbs, *Joseph Priestley, Revolutions of the Eighteenth Century* (1967); Robert E. Schofield, ed., *A Scientific Autobiography of Joseph Priestley 1733–1804* (1966). Everett Mendelsohn, *Heat and Life: The Development of the Theory of Animal Heat* (1964); Trevor H. Levere, *Poetry Realized in Nature: Samuel Taylor Coleridge and Early Nineteenth-Century Science* (1981), pp. 195–196; Ritterbush.

4. Levere, pp. 194–98; Desmond King-Hele, *Doctor of Revolution: The Life and Genius of Erasmus Darwin* (1977), pp. 275–82. The complete exposition waited for the German Justus Liebig, whose *Agricultural Chemistry* (1840) and *Animal Chemistry* (1842) reconciled chemistry with phsiology. Everett Mendelsohn, *Heat and Life: The Development of the Theory of Animal Heat* (1964).

5. Levere; Thomas McFarland, *Coleridge and the Pantheist Tradition* (1969); Jonathan Wordsworth, *The Music of Humanity* (1969), 184–232; H. W. Piper, *The Active Universe* (1962); Stephen Prickett, *Coleridge and Wordsworth: The Poetry of Growth* (1970).

6. Coleridge was especially enthusiastic about it. M. H. Abrams, "Coleridge and the Romantic Vision of the World," *Coleridge's Variety: Bicentenary Studies,* ed. John Beer (1974); also Levere. Quotation from K. Coburn, *The Inquiring Spirit* (1951), #223.

7. David Knight, "The Scientist as Sage," p. 75.

8. Northrop Frye, *A Study of English Romanticism* (1968), p. 47.

9. For the entire issue of analogues, I am indebted to Ritterbush, "The Triumph of Botanical Analogy," pp. 109–57.

10. Pierce C. Mullen, "The Romantic as Scientist: Laurenz Oken," *SiR*, 16 (1977), 381–99; Abrams, *Natural Supernaturalism*, "Divided and Reunited Man: The Esoteric Tradition," pp. 154–63.

11. Ritterbush, pp. 152–54, who believes that it was this attribution of feelings to plants that aroused an interest in gardening.

12. Ritterbush, p. 203. Paul Sheats, *The Making of Wordsworth's Poetry, 1785–1798* (1975) describes Wordsworth's use of analogy, perhaps his "favorite" figure, to embody subjective states. Reference to *The Prelude*, III, 122 *ff*:

> From deep analogies by thought supplied
> Or consciousnesses not to be subdued,
> To every natural form, rock, fruit or flower,
> Even the loose stones that cover the highway,
> I gave a moral life—I saw them feel,
> Or lined them to some feeling. The great mass
> Lay bedded in a quickening soul, and all
> That I beheld respired with inward meaning.

See also, Earl R. Wasserman, "Nature Moralized: The Divine Analogy in the 18th Century," *JELH*, 20 (1953), and *The Subtler Language* (1959). Of great interest, Robert Maniquis, "The Puzzling *Mimosa*: Sensitivity and Plant Symbols in Romanticism," *SiR*, 8 (1969), 129–55.

13. Schofield, *Mechanism and Materialism*, Ch. VIII. For electricity, I. Bernard Cohen, *Franklin and Newton* (1956); Geoffrey Sutton, "Electricity, Medicine and Mesmerism," *Isis*, 72 (1981); 375–92; J. L. Heilbron, *Electricity in the 17th and 18th Centuries: A Study of Early Modern Physics* (1979). Also Terry M. Parssinen, "Mesmeric Performers," *VS*, 21 (1977), 87–104, and "Professional Deviants and the History of Medicine," *Sociological Review Monograph*, 27 (1979), 103–20.

14. "Man is a myth-making as well as a tool-using animal, but constant vigilance is needed to make sure that he keeps control of what he makes. For it is with myths as it is with technology: just as man invents the wheel and then talks about a wheel of fate or fortune overriding everything he does, so he creates gods and then announces that the gods have created him" (Northrop Frye, *A Study of English Romanticism*, p. 88).

15. Ritterbush, pp. 24–25, 208.

16. Thomas McFarland, *Coleridge and the Pantheist Tradition* (1969); Levere, pp. 64–69. To the accusation that he had plagiarized from his German mentors, he replied in *Biographia*: "I regard truth as a divine ventriloquist: I care not from whose mouth the sounds are supposed to proceed, if only the words are audible and intelligible," an idea especially suited to the life force implicit in German *naturphilosophie*.

17. Levere, pp. 45–52; Oswei Temkin, "Basic Science, Medicine, and the Romantic Era," *Bulletin of the History of Medicine*, 37 (1963), 97–129. Edward Manier, *The Young Darwin and His Cultural Circle* (1978), pp. 64–66.

18. *Lectures on Physiology* (1819), p. 38; Ritterbush, p. 190; G. J. Good-field, *The Growth of Scientific Physiology* (1960).

19. Bush, *Science and English Poetry;* Nicolson, *Newton;* Whitehead, *Science;* for Keats, Stuart Sperry, "Keats and the Chemistry of Poetic Creation," *PMLA,* 85 (1970), 268–77, reprinted in *Keats the Poet* (1974); for Coleridge, see Levere; M. H. Abrams, "Coleridge's 'A Light in Sound': Science, Metascience, and Poetic Imagination," *PAPS,* 116 (1972), 458–72; Kathleen Coburn, "Coleridge, a Bridge between Science and Poetry: Reflections on the Bicentenary of his Birth," *Coleridge's Variety,* ed. John Beer (1974); Timothy Corrigan, *"Biographia Literaria* and the Language of Science," *JHI,* 41 (1980), 399–420, and *Coleridge, Language, and Criticism* (1982).

20. Whitehead, p. 84. Unfortunately, his comments on Wordsworth and Keats are short-sighted. See Timothy Webb, *Shelley: A Voice Not Understood* (1977).

21. As quoted in Levere, pp. 185, 177; *Table Talk* (1832); *The Friend* (1818); for Davy, see Sir Humphry Davy, *The Collected Works,* ed. John Davy (1839–40); Sir Harold Hartley, *Humphry Davy* (1966, 1972); Trevor H. Levere, *Affinity and Matter: Elements of Chemical Philosophy, 1800–1865* (1971); J. G. Crowther, *British Scientists of the Nineteenth Century* (1962), pp. 3–66; Dorothy A. Stansfield, *Thomas Beddoes M.D., 1760–1808* (1984); Joyce Z. Fullmer, "The Poetry of Sir Humphry Davy," *Chymia,* 6 (1960), 102–26; Sophie Forjan, "Humphry Davy, 'The Sons of Genius,' and the Idea of Glory," *Science and the Sons of Genius: Studies on Sir Humphry Davy* (1980), pp. 33–58.

22. The book itself is fascinating and immensely readable. For a sensitive reading, see Knight, "The Scientist as Sage."

23. *Consolations,* pp. 245, 259.

24. Owen, Commentary, I, 181: "The distinction . . . represents Wordsworth's reaction to the claims of Humphry Davy on behalf of science, and in particular to Davy's introductory lecture given at the Royal Institution on 21 January 1802"; Roger Sharrock, "The Chemist and the Poet: Sir Humphry Davy and the Preface to *Lyrical Ballads,"* *Notes and Records of the Royal Society of London,* 17 (1962), 57–76.

25. Arthur Hughes, "Science in English Encyclopedias, 1704–1875," *Annals of Science,* 7 (1951), 340–70, and 8 (1952), 323–67; S. Padraig Walsh, *Anglo-American General Encyclopedias, 1703–1967: A Historical Bibliography* (1968). For a survey of the state of knowledge or at least what readers were interested in knowing during that period, the best encyclopedias are *Britannica* (1771); the *New Royal Cyclopaedia* (1788); *A Dictionary of Arts and Sciences* (1806); *British Encyclopedia* (1809).

26. J. W. Clark and T. M. Hughes, *The Life and Letters of Adam Sedgwick,* 2 vols. (1890), I, 160–61; Marilyn Gaull, "From Wordsworth to Darwin," *TWC,* 10 (1979), 33–48.

27. Morris Berman, *Social Change and Scientific Organization: The Royal Institution, 1799–1844* (1978); D. S. L. Cardwell, *The Organization of Science in England* (1957); R. S. Schofield, "Histories of Scientific Societies: Needs and Opportunities for Research," *History of Science,* 2 (1963), 76–83; also Mason, *A History of the Sciences.* The best contemporary source,

Rev. A. Hume, *The Learned Societies and Printing Clubs of the United Kingdom* . . . (1847), a rare and valuable work, for which I am especially grateful to Roy Goodman, Librarian, American Philosophical Society. Gerald Lemain, Ray MacLeod, Michael Mulkay, and Peter Weingart, eds. *Perspectives on the Emergence of Scientific Disciplines* (1976).

28. R. E. Schofield, *The Lunar Society of Birmingham* (1963); F. D. Klingender, *Art and the Industrial Revolution,* 2nd ed. (1968), p. 35, called them the "scientific general staff for the industrial revolution."

29. Hume, p. 21.

30. Mason, p. 441.

31. Gillispie, *Genesis and Geology,* p. 115; David Allen, *The Naturalist in Britain* (1976).

32. Paul Laurence Farber, *The Emergence of Ornithology as a Scientific Discipline, 1760–1850* (1982).

33. As quoted in Francis C. Haber, *The Age of the World: Moses to Darwin* (1959), p. 228.

34. Benedict Nicolson, *Joseph Wright of Derby,* 2 vols. (1968); Norman Paulson, *Emblem and Expression,* pp. 184–213.

35. J. L. Crammer-Byng and Trevor J. Levere, "A Case Study in Cultural Collision: Scientific Apparatus in the Macartney Embassy to China, 1793," *Annals of Science,* 38 (1981), 503–25, for a description of the array of machinery sent to express national pride in instrumentation. Best introduction and illustration, A. Wolf, *A History of Science, Technology and Philosophy in the Eighteenth Century* (1952).

36. Mason, pp. 269–78.

37. Paul Mantoux, *The Industrial Revolution in the Eighteenth Century: An Outline of the Beginnings of the Modern Factory System in England* (1928, 1961).

38. Milton K. Munitz, ed. *Theories of the Universe from Babylonian Myth to Modern Science* (1957).

39. David M. Knight, "The Atomic Theory and the Elements," *SiR,* 5 (1966), 185–207. Dalton's sensitivity to the invisible may have been in part developed in his youth by John Gough, the blind Kendal Quaker who taught him Latin, Greek, and French, and served as a model for the Pedlar in Wordsworth's *Excursion* (Arnold Thackray, *John Dalton: Critical Assessments: His Life and Science* [1972]).

40. For comment, see Ritterbush, p. 190.

41. "Modern science is distinguished by the calm acceptance of empty spaces, the calm awareness of the meaningless question. . . . This attitude results in part from the assumption that process and energy, not matter is the fundamental fact; if one thinks of existence as activity rather than being, he is less likely to ask how the universe 'came into being' " (Herbert J. Muller, *Science and Criticism: The Humanistic Tradition in Contemporary Thought* [1943], pp. 78, 82).

42. Werner Heisenberg, "The Teaching of Goethe and Newton on Colour in the Light of Modern Physics," in *Philosophic Problems of Nuclear Science* (1952), pp. 81–82 and *The Physicist's Conception of Nature* (1958) (I am especially indebted to my colleague, James Mall, for directing me to this source); Muller, pp. 81–82; C. A. Coulson, *Science and Christian Belief*

(1955); and J. Bronowski, for discussion of Heisenberg's Principle of Uncertainty, as it is variously called, to which the discussion in the text is related.

43. The concept of creativity in science that I have accepted assumes a relationship between science and the scientist, the relevance of biography, first acknowledged by Robert Hunt, whose nineteenth-century study was designed to illustrate the "influence of human thought on the physical forces which regulate the great phenomena of the universe,—the operation of the powers of mind, on the material constituents of the planet," *Memoirs of the Distinguished Men of Science of Great Britain Living in the Year, 1807–8,* pp. vi–vii. More recent studies include I. Bernard Cohen, *Franklin and Newton* (1956), especially Ch. III, "The Scientific Personality of Franklin and of Newton," in which Cohen distinguishes between the inevitability of discoveries and the form they take, their expression being unique to the investigator. Ritterbush, to whom I am deeply indebted for biological history, also claims, "The growth of scientific ideas is influenced not only by observation and experiment, but also by the emotional endowment of the investigator and the temper of the age" (p. vii). Ian Mitroff shows how a collective psychology can influence contemporary scientific interpretations in *The Subjective Side of Science: A Philosophical Inquiry into the Psychology of the Apollo Moon Scientists* (1974). Other useful inquiries into scientific creativity to which I am indebted include Henri Bergson, *Creative Evolution* (1944); Myron A. Coler, ed., *Essays on Creativity in the Sciences* (1963); Loren Eiseley, *The Mind as Nature* (1962); R. W. Gerard, "The Biological Basis of Imagination," *The Creative Process,* ed. Brewster Ghiselin (1952); Arthur Koestler, *The Act of Creation: A Study of the Conscious and Unconscious in Science and Art* (1964); Jacques Hadamard, *An Essay on the Psychology of Invention in the Mathematic Fields* (1964); two primarily biographical studies, Stanley Edgar Hyman *The Tangled Bank: Darwin, Marx, Frazer and Freud as Imaginative Writers* (1962), and Howard E. Gruber, *Darwin on Man: A Psychological Study of Scientific Creativity,* trans. Paul H. Barrett (1974).

Index